Making
Sense of the
Molly Maguires

Making Sense of the Molly Maguires

KEVIN KENNY

New York Oxford

Oxford University Press

1998

Oxford University Press

Oxford New York
Athens Auckland Bangkok Bogota Bombay Buenos Aires
Calcutta Cape Town Dar es Salaam Delhi Florence Hong Kong
Istanbul Karachi Kuala Lumpur Madras Madrid Melbourne
Mexico City Nairobi Paris Singapore Taipei Tokyo Toronto Warsaw

and associated companies in
Berlin Ibadan

Published by Oxford University Press, Inc.
198 Madison Avenue, New York, New York 10016

Part of chapter 3 was published as "Nativism, Labor, and Slavery:
The Political Odyssey of Benjamin Bannan, 1850–1860,"
Pennsylvania Magazine of History and Biography, 118 (October
1994): 325–61. Some of the material on Catholicism in chapters 3,
6, 7, 8, and 9 was published as "The Molly Maguires and the
Catholic Church," *Labor History*, 36 (Summer 1995): 345–76.

Library of Congress Cataloging-in-Publication Data

Kenny, Kevin, 1960–
Making Sense of the Molly Maguires / Kevin Kenny.
p. cm.
Includes bibliographical references and index.
ISBN 0-19-510664-4; 0-19-511631-3 (pbk.)
1. Molly Maguires. 2. Coal miners—Pennsylvania—History.
3. Irish Americans—Pennsylvania—History. 4. Irish Americans—
Pennsylvania—Social conditions. I. Title.
HV6452.P4M64 1998
364.1'06'09748—dc21 96-53599

1 2 3 4 5 6 7 8 9
Printed in the United States of America
on acid free paper

Per Rosanna, senz'altro . . .

Acknowledgments

In the eight years it took to complete this project, I was fortunate to receive advice, encouragement, and assistance from many friends and colleagues, from the staff at numerous libraries and institutions, and from the universities with which I have been affiliated. Without this support, the project could not have been started, let alone completed.

Let me begin by thanking Jim Shenton, Eric Foner, David Cannadine, and Anders Stephanson of Columbia University, to whom I owe my principal intellectual debts. The two anonymous readers for Oxford University Press also offered suggestions and criticisms that greatly enriched my argument. Josh Brown and Jim Sidbury deserve special thanks for their many helpful comments on the manuscript. I would like to thank the following friends, colleagues, and teachers who read all or part of the manuscript: Betsy Blackmar, Steve Brier, Patrick Campbell, Nancy Cohen, Leon Fink, Tom Fredell, Joshua Freeman, Walter Friedman, Dirk Hoerder, Anne Kane, Joanna Swanger, and Emilio Zamora. Michael Denning and Luke Dodd offered generous assistance in locating some important primary sources. And helpful comments and criticisms were offered by the members of the U.S. History Dissertation Seminar at Columbia University; the Columbia University Seminar on Irish Studies; and the Atlantic History Seminar at the University of Texas at Austin. Finally I would like to thank Owen Dudley Edwards and Alan Day, who introduced me to American history as an undergraduate at the University of Edinburgh.

I owe a second major debt to the librarians and archivists in various parts of the United States and Ireland who helped me in so many ways. In particular, I want to thank the staff at the Butler Library, Columbia University; the New York Public Library; the New York Historical Society; the Historical Society of Pennsylvania; the Schuylkill County Historical Society; the Philadelphia Free Library; the Pottsville Public Library; the Hagley Museum and Library; the Library of Congress; the Beinecke Rare Book and Manuscript Library, Yale University; the American Antiquarian Society; the Pattee Library, Penn State University; Pinkerton Investigations and Security Services; St. Charles of Borromeo Seminary; the Gilbert Library; the National Library of Ireland; and the Perry-Castañeda Library at the University of Texas at Austin.

Without financial support, in the form of fellowships and grants, I could never have completed this book. I gratefully acknowledge the funding provided by the Graduate School of Arts and Sciences at Columbia University; the American Historical Association; the New York Irish History Roundtable; the Center for Labor-Management Policy Studies at the City University of New York; the Whiting Foundation; the Irish American Cultural Institute; the University Research Institute and the British Studies Seminar at the University of Texas at Austin; and the Bancroft Dissertation Award, 1994.

At Oxford University Press, I would like to thank Thomas LeBien and Lisa Stallings for guiding me through the intricacies of the publishing process. I would also like to acknowledge the contribution of Brandon Trissler and Jeffrey Soloway. Special thanks are due to Sheldon Meyer, who accepted the initial manuscript.

Finally, I would like to thank Michael and Bernadette Kenny, my brothers and sisters, the Crocitto family, and in a class of his own, Michael Crocitto Kenny, *il nostro Michelino*. Rosanna Crocitto helped me in more ways than she will ever know, and to her I dedicate this book.

Austin, Texas
April 1997

K. K.

Contents

Abbreviations Used in Footnotes

A	Accession
AP	Allan Pinkerton
B	Box
BF	Benjamin Franklin
F	File or Folder
FBG	Franklin B. Gowen
FBG 1875	*Argument of Franklin B. Gowen Before the Joint Committee of the Legislature of Pennsylvania, Appointed to Inquire into the Affairs of the Philadelphia and Reading Coal and Iron Company, and the Reading Railroad, July 29th and 30th, 1875*
HML	Hagley Museum and Library, Wilmington, Delaware
HSC	Historical Society of Schuylkill County, Pottsville, Pennsylvania
HSP	Historical Society of Pennsylvania
JMCP	James McParlan
LC	Library of Congress
MJ	*Miners' Journal*
MS	Manuscript
NYPL	New York Public Library
NYT	*New York Times*
OR	*War of the Rebellion: A Compilation of the Official Records of the Union and Confederate Armies*

PBIS 1	*Pennsylvania Bureau of Industrial Statistics. Annual Reports, Number 1* (1872–73)
PBIS 2	*Pennsylvania Bureau of Industrial Statistics. Annual Reports, Number 2* (1873–74)
PCA	Pinkerton Corporate Archives, Van Nuys, California
PGA	*Report of the Committee on the Judiciary, General, of the Senate of Pennsylvania, in Relation to the Anthracite Coal Difficulties* (1871)
PH	*Pennsylvania History*
PMHB	*Pennsylvania Magazine of History and Biography*
PNDA	Pinkerton's National Detective Agency
RCK	*Report of the Case of the Commonwealth v. Kehoe et al. . . . for Aggravated Assault and Battery with intent to kill William M. Thomas*
RSCD	*Report from the Select Committee on Destitution (Gweedore and Cloughaneely)*. House of Commons, 1858
SC	Society Collection
SCBS	St. Charles of Borromeo Seminary, Overbrook, Pennsylvania
SH	*Shenandoah Herald*
V	Volume

Making
Sense of the
Molly Maguires

Introduction

In the 1860s and 1870s, the anthracite coal fields of Pennsylvania drew national attention for their violence. After a series of assaults and killings, deep-rooted fears of a secret Irish terrorist organization hardened into certainty. Sixteen men were assassinated, most of them mine officials, and there were numerous beatings and acts of industrial sabotage. The culprits, it was believed, were members of the Molly Maguires, an oath-bound secret society imported from Ireland. Pinkerton detectives were sent into the anthracite district under cover and the hunt for the Molly Maguires culminated in a series of showcase trials. Twenty Irishmen were convicted of a range of heinous crimes and sentenced to be hanged. Their trials and executions were the spectacular climax to a singular episode in American history, one that remains shrouded in ambiguity.

Because of the uncertainties built into the subject, the Molly Maguires have been depicted in every imaginable way, from sociopaths and terrorists at one end of the spectrum to innocent victims and proletarian revolutionaries at the other. But ever since the 1870s one specific narrative has been dominant: the Molly Maguires as inherently evil Irishmen who terrorized the anthracite region for two decades before being brought to justice by the heroic exploits of James McParlan, a Pinkerton detective. This interpretation dominated the newspapers, pamphlets, and local histories of the time, as well as the first full-length books devoted to the subject, Allan Pinkerton's semifictional work, *The Molly Maguires and the Detectives,* and Francis P. Dewees's ostensibly factual history, *The Molly Maguires,* both of which were based on McParlan's testimony and published in 1877.[1] The same viewpoint was repeated, in its essentials, by the journalist Cleveland Moffett in 1894; by the historian James Ford Rhodes in 1909; and as literary fiction, by Sir Arthur Conan Doyle in 1915.[2]

As late as the 1930s, the Molly Maguires were still generally seen as evil terrorists, but the historiographical tide was fast beginning to turn.[3] The old interpretation was denounced as a myth and effectively undermined by a new generation of left-leaning historians, who placed the violence of the 1870s firmly in the context of a general conflict between labor and capital. The landmarks in this revisionism were Anthony Bimba's *The Molly Maguires,* published in 1932; and J. Walter Coleman's *The Molly Maguire Riots,* which appeared four years later. Of the two, Coleman's was the most convincing and subtle, by virtue of its skeptical critique of the evidence and its close attention to ethnicity as well as class. In several respects it remains the best book published on the subject to date.[4] The Molly Maguires, Coleman argued, were a type of secret labor union, representing a natural response to the exploitation of miners, but differing in ideology, strategy, and ethnic affiliation from the trade union organized by the mine workers in 1868. Coleman was the first historian to treat McParlan's activities, and the tactics of the prosecuting attorneys, with the skepticism they deserved. He was the first to point out what now seems obvious: that the historian "must admit of serious doubts before exonerating the detective of injustice. His entire career was based upon tactics so questionable that he can no longer be dismissed with merely a prayer of thanks for ridding the country of a gang of cutthroats."[5] In this way, Coleman threw down a gauntlet that subsequent historians have yet to take up.

That a book published as long ago as 1936 should be the best account of the subject available today indicates a significant hiatus in the historiography of the Molly Maguires. Perhaps the most striking aspect of that historiography, indeed, is that it has yet to undergo the comprehensive revision so characteristic of American historical writing since the 1960s. This was in part an oversight, but it was also in part a deliberate choice. As Herbert Gutman put it in 1963: "Excessive interest in the Haymarket Riot, the 'Molly Maguires,' the great strikes of

1. Allan Pinkerton, *The Molly Maguires and the Detectives* (1877; New York, 1905); Francis P. Dewees, *The Molly Maguires: The Origin, Growth, and Character of the Organization* (Philadelphia, 1877).

2. Cleveland Moffett, "The Overthrow of the Molly Maguires," *McClure's Magazine,* 4 (December 1894 to May 1895): 90–100; James Ford Rhodes, "The Molly Maguires in the Anthracite Region of Pennsylvania," *American Historical Review,* 15 (April 1910): 547–61, and *History of the United States, 1850–1896,* vol. 8, 1919 (New York, 1928), 1–87; Sir Arthur Conan Doyle, *The Valley of Fear* (1915; Oxford, 1994).

3. On popular conceptions of the Molly Maguires as gangsters, and Detective James McParlan as a forerunner of the "G-Men," see *Detroit Times,* June 22, 1936; *Chicago American,* June 23, 1936.

4. Anthony Bimba, *The Molly Maguires* (1932; New York, 1950); J. Walter Coleman, *The Molly Maguire Riots: Industrial Conflict in the Pennsylvania Coal Region* (Richmond, 1936).

5. Coleman, *The Molly Maguire Riots,* 171. For the impact of Coleman's work on popular conceptions of the Molly Maguires, see *New York Daily News,* December 8, 1940; *NYT,* November 1, 1936, review by Henry Steele Commager.

1877, the Homestead Lockout, and the Pullman strike has obscured the more important currents of which these things were only symptoms."[6] Gutman and his followers inaugurated a rich new field of labor history, which focused on work, culture, and everyday life, rather than spectacular confrontations between capital and labor. New accounts of Haymarket and Homestead were eventually written; but the Molly Maguires, largely because of the problems of evidence and interpretation they present, were ignored.[7] The irony is that any attempt to rewrite the history of the subject today involves an extension of the themes pioneered by Herbert Gutman, not a departure from them—especially his emphasis on the need to understand American labor history in transatlantic perspective and to examine the impact of repeated waves of immigration on American class formation.

In light of all this, the standard work on the subject for the last generation, Wayne G. Broehl, Jr.'s, *The Molly Maguires* (1964), is clearly in need of revision.[8] Conceived and researched in the late 1950s, and very much bearing the stamp of that decade, Broehl's work predated the extensive revision in Irish and American social history that has occurred since 1960. Moreover, it constituted a regression from the type of skeptical interpretation called for by J. Walter Coleman a generation earlier, relying on the biased accounts of James McParlan and Allan Pinkerton as the basis for an ostensibly factual account of the Molly Maguires. Historians can never know for certain who and what the Molly Maguires were, and to accept the hostile accounts of contemporary observers at face value is at best rather naive. But this epistemological naivete, of course, is admirably suited to portraying the Molly Maguires as terrorists and the Pinkertons as heroes. Broehl's is a finely crafted piece of historical writing, but its guiding assumptions have not withstood the passage of time. A fresh look at the Molly Maguires is long overdue.

The starting point in any attempt to rewrite the history of the Molly Maguires today is to treat the surviving evidence with the skepticism it deserves. The Molly Maguires themselves left virtually no evidence of their existence, let alone their aims and motivation. Almost everything that is known about them was written by hostile contemporary observers. Given the nature of the evidence, recent historians have conceded that the subject is peculiarly prone to bias and distortion. As Harold D. Aurand and William A. Gudelunas, Jr., put it in 1982: "The vagueness of many 'facts' surrounding the Molly Maguire period will forever permit the era great 'historical elasticity.' Many schools of thought can use 'Molly Maguire' to justify their ideological positions or validify a particular belief."[9] But this formulation, while it offers a useful

6. Herbert G. Gutman, "The Workers' Search for Power in the Gilded Age," in Gutman, *Power and Culture: Essays on the American Working Class,* ed. Ira Berlin (New York, 1987), 70.

7. Paul Avrich, *The Haymarket Tragedy* (Princeton, N.J., 1984); Paul Krause, *The Battle for Homestead, 1880–1892: Politics, Culture, Steel* (Pittsburgh, 1992).

8. Wayne G. Broehl, Jr., *The Molly Maguires* (1964; New York, 1983).

9. Harold D. Aurand and William A. Gudelunas, Jr., "The Mythical Quality of Molly Maguire," *PH,* 49 (April 1982): 103.

corrective to much of the old history of the subject, does not go nearly far enough. What is needed is a formulation that extends beyond the rather obvious question of the biases historians bring to their evidence and moves to the deeper question of the biases and distortions inherent in the evidence itself.[10]

If writings about the past are often ideological, this is all the more true of what contemporaries said and wrote about the events they lived through. Twentieth-century historians have disagreed to a remarkable extent about the meaning and nature of the Molly Maguires; but the uncertainty and controversy were much greater in the mid nineteenth century, when Molly Maguireism was a live and highly contentious issue. Quite simply, none of the surviving evidence is neutral, nor was it ever so; it demands an ideological reading, which not only searches for the outlines of a credible factual narrative about the Molly Maguires, but also inquires into the social origins and the ideological impact of descriptions written about them by their enemies and detractors.

The Molly Maguires always existed on two related levels: as a sporadic pattern of violence engaged in by a specific type of Irishman, and as a ubiquitous concept in a system of ideological representation that sought to explain the variety of social problems besetting the anthracite region in the mid nineteenth century. In other words, the violence in which the Molly Maguires undoubtedly engaged was put to all sorts of uses by contemporaries, most effectively by those who were opposed to Irish immigrants and organized labor. Any reinterpretation of the Molly Maguires today needs to inquire simultaneously into how the Molly Maguires were represented and what they may have been in fact. In this respect, the subject presents an exaggerated version of a dilemma inherent in most forms of historical interpretation.[11]

This book takes the form of an overlapping social and cultural history, and it sets out to answer three related questions: How were the Molly Maguires described by contemporaries? Why were they described in that way? And who were the Molly Maguires, what did they do, and why? The first of these questions is easy enough to answer, as plenty of evidence has survived on the subject. The second is more difficult to answer, but the gap between past reality and past representation was filled by ideology, in the form of narratives constructed by contemporary observers. People's statements about the Molly Maguires can tell historians a great deal about the type of society these people lived in, even when they provide little reliable evidence on the nature of the Molly Maguires themselves. By examining these statements as instances of ideology instead of

10. For one such formulation, see Barbara Jeanne Fields, "The Nineteenth-Century American South: History and Theory," *Plantation Society*, 2 (April 1983): 26–27.

11. Cf. Lynn Hunt, ed., *The New Cultural History* (Berkeley, 1989); Joyce Appleby, Lynn Hunt, and Margaret Jacobs, *Telling the Truth About History* (New York, 1994); Bryan D. Palmer, *Descent Into Discourse: The Reification of Language and the Writing of Social History* (Philadelphia, 1990); Fredric Jameson, *The Political Unconscious: Narrative as a Socially Symbolic Act* (Ithaca, N.Y., 1981); Lenard Berlanstein, ed., *Rethinking Labor History: Essays on Discourse and Class Analysis* (Urbana, Ill., 1993); ILWCH Roundtable, "What Next for Labor and Working-Class History?" *International Labor and Working Class History*, 46 (Fall 1994): 7–92.

straightforward representations of fact, one can begin to understand why the rather implausible description of the Molly Maguires as nothing more than a group of depraved Irish terrorists made sense to so many people at the time. Among these people were the opponents of organized labor; anti-Catholic nativists; and conversely, Catholic clergymen whose definition of Irish-American ethnicity excluded the version of Irishness embodied by the Molly Maguires.[12]

Much of the present work, therefore, is necessarily devoted to an ideological reading of what people said about the Molly Maguires. By the late 1850s, the term *Molly Maguires* was being used in the anthracite region as a synonym for Irish social depravity. It was introduced into the political language of the region in 1857 by the nativist editor Benjamin Bannan as a shorthand term for the various aspects of "the Irish character" he found most objectionable and threatening, including poverty, drunkenness, criminality, insanity, laziness, idolatry, and political corruption.

When a marked propensity for violence was added to the list of Irish characteristics in the 1860s, the term assumed its full meaning of an evil terrorist conspiracy. During the Civil War, this notion of a terrorist conspiracy was applied to a pattern of violence that often had as much to do with sporadic and rudimentary labor activism as with resistance to the military draft. By the time the mine workers formed their first durable trade union (the Workingmen's Benevolent Association) in 1868, it was all but inevitable that it too would be identified with the Molly Maguires. The hostility of the Catholic church to secrecy, labor activism, and violence, and to the cultural practices of immigrants from the more remote parts of Ireland, added yet another powerful condemnatory voice. The result was a power struggle within the Irish-American community over the meaning and limits of ethnicity, even as that community was seeking to accommodate itself to the larger American society that surrounded it.[13]

None of this is meant to suggest that the violence attributed to the Molly Maguires was a figment of the nativist, capitalist, or clerical imagination. Hostile contemporaries undoubtedly put the Molly Maguire violence to all sorts of ideological uses that transcended the immediate question of who the perpetrators were and what they stood for. But despite this disparity between social facts and their ideological representation, there was a very real pattern of Irish violence in the anthracite region. The Molly Maguires may not have existed in terms of the gigantic conspiracy depicted by contemporaries; but as a pattern of violence engaged in by a certain type of Irishman under specific historical conditions, they emphatically did exist. The task of historians is to try to explain why this violence occurred (see Table 1).

This raises the third and most difficult question: Who were the Molly

12. On the relation between narrative and ideology, see Jameson, *The Political Unconscious,* especially chapter 1. In the present work, the term *ideology* is used to mean the series of narratives through which people attempt to make sense of their social worlds. Cf. Terry Eagleton, *Ideology: An Introduction* (New York, 1991), chapter 1, especially 6–16.

13. Cf. Kevin Kenny, "The Molly Maguires and the Catholic Church," *Labor History,* 36 (Summer 1995): 345–76.

TABLE 1. Killings Attributed to the Molly Maguires, 1862–75

Name	Occupation	Location and Date
F.W. Langdon	Foreman	Audenried, Carbon Co., June 14, 1862
George K. Smith	Mine Owner	Audenried, Carbon Co., Nov. 5, 1863
David Muir	Superintendent	Foster Township, Aug. 25, 1865
Henry H. Dunne	Superintendent	Heckscherville, Jan. 10, 1866
Wm. Littlehales	Foreman	Cass Township, Mar. 15, 1867
Alexander Rea	Superintendent	Centralia, Columbia Co., Oct. 17, 1868
Patrick Burns	Foreman	Tuscarora, Apr. 15, 1870
Morgan Powell	Superintendent	Summit Hill, Carbon Co., Dec. 2, 1871
George Major	Chief Burgess	Mahanoy City, Oct. 31, 1874
Frederick Hesser	Mine Watchman	Shamokin, Northumb'd Co., Dec. 18, 1874
Benjamin Yost	Policeman	Tamaqua, July 5, 1875
Thomas Gwyther	Justice of Peace	Girardville, Aug. 14, 1875
Gomer James	Miner	Shenandoah, Aug. 14, 1875
Thomas Sanger	Foreman	Raven Run, Sept. 1, 1875
William Uren	Foreman	Raven Run, Sept. 1, 1875
John P. Jones	Superintendent	Lansford, Carbon Co., Sept. 3, 1875

These are the killings in which the Molly Maguires were implicated during the trials of the1870s. Unless otherwise stated, they took place in Schuylkill County.

Maguires, what did they do, and why? Because of the scarcity and nature of the evidence, the question can never be answered definitively. But it can be addressed, and quite profitably, by locating the Molly Maguires in a particular historical context, namely the abrupt removal of large numbers of people from a specific part of Ireland and their resettlement in a part of the United States that was undergoing the transition known as the industrial revolution. The Molly Maguires embodied a rare, transatlantic strand of a pattern of violent protest characteristic of different parts of the Irish countryside at different times between 1760 and 1850. This pattern of protest was adapted in Pennsylvania to the conditions of industrial exploitation faced by the immigrant workers in their new homes. Accustomed to oppression, but not to its industrial form, the immigrants responded with a type of violence that had its roots in the Irish countryside. The type of violence in question has been aptly described as a form of "retributive justice."[14]

The term *retributive justice* is used in this book to describe a form of collective violence designed to redress violations against a particular understanding of what was socially right and wrong. To capture the spirit of this violence, the term *assassination* has been employed in preference to the more pejorative word *murder;* the term *killing* is also used where evidence is lacking, or simply

14. Anthony F. C. Wallace, *St. Clair: A Nineteenth-Century Coal Town's Experience With a Disaster-Prone Industry* (New York, 1987), chapter 6, "Justice and Violence."

for purposes of variation. In Ireland, the tradition of violence in question was directed against landlords and their agents, policemen and magistrates, small farmers, and tenants. In Pennsylvania, it was directed against mine owners and superintendents, policemen and municipal officials, and skilled British miners. Collective violence of this sort typically arose in nonindustrial European societies threatened by external economic and political change. Molly Maguireism first emerged in the disintegrating peasant societies of north-central Ireland in the 1840s. But a form of Molly Maguireism also took root in the United States in the 1860s and 1870s, where it was bound up in the distinctively modern struggles of the industrial revolution. The American Molly Maguires make little sense unless the specifically Irish origins of their strategy of violence are understood, along with the manner in which that strategy was deployed and transformed in the context of American industrial society. What is needed is an account that is at once transatlantic and regional, explaining broad patterns of continuity and change in national and international history, while at the same time looking in detail at specific geographical and temporal contexts in Ireland and Pennsylvania.

In this respect, the prevailing interpretation of the Molly Maguires is once again in need of major revision. Not only does it emphasize personal grievances over collective violence, its treatment of Irish history is dated and one-dimensional. "On both sides of the Atlantic," Broehl concluded, "the antagonists of the Irish were the same—the English. In Ireland they were landlords and agents; in Pennsylvania they were mine owners and mine bosses."[15] This is really the crux of the currently accepted interpretation of the Molly Maguires. The conflict is explained in terms of deep-rooted primordial identities based on religion and national origin, which found expression in Pennsylvania as a series of bitter personal disputes between individual Irishmen and their British enemies. As a theory of ethnicity, an explanation of social violence, and an account of Irish history, this thesis is no longer adequate.

Irish historiography has changed greatly in the last thirty years. A series of myths has been demolished by recent Irish historians, in particular the myth of a homogeneous, Catholic nationalist peasantry doing valiant battle against an alien, landlord class. The old linear narrative of nationalist consciousness and struggle has been called into question in Ireland, and a similar move in Irish-American historiography is long overdue. Drawing on the writings of recent Irish historians, the present work attempts to historicize the category of "Irishness" employed in most previous interpretations of the Molly Maguires. In the case of the Molly Maguires at least, territorial and regional affiliations were of greater importance than abstract (and often anachronistic) notions of nationalist consciousness and conflict. By the same token, Irish-American ethnic identity needs to be understood as historical, contingent, and contested, rather than essential, fixed, and agreed upon. In the nineteenth-

15. Broehl, *The Molly Maguires,* 1.

century anthracite region, it was the subject of bitter and protracted dispute, with labor activists, politicians, and Catholic clergymen as the major players in the drama. Definitions of Irish-American ethnicity, moreover, were caught up in a larger social conflict whose outlines are best described in terms of social class.[16]

If the Molly Maguires did not exist as the ominous and highly organized conspiracy that contemporaries and historians have described, two other organizations that certainly did exist in the immigrant working-class community of the mining region were a fraternal organization called the Ancient Order of Hibernians (AOH) and a trade union called the Workingmen's Benevolent Association (WBA). The convicted men were all members of the AOH, which many contemporaries claimed was merely the Molly Maguires under another name. But the Molly Maguires were also identified, particularly between 1870 and 1875, with the miners' trade union, the WBA. The identification of the Molly Maguires with the fraternal society and the labor union provided the alleged terrorist conspiracy with an institutional structure it otherwise lacked, transforming it in the first case into part of a national and international network, and in the second into the well-organized, militant arm of the labor movement. This strategy was central to the construction of knowledge about the Molly Maguires, and it provided an important rationale for their eventual destruction. One of the primary goals of the present work is to disentangle these separate modes of organization and protest, and to demonstrate how their deliberate confusion contributed to the ideological definition and eventual eradication not only of Molly Maguireism but also of trade unionism.

While the trade union, the fraternal society, and "Molly Maguireism" did certainly overlap to an extent, they must be kept distinct, both analytically and institutionally, if the Molly Maguires are to make any sense. The trade union undoubtedly included some "Molly Maguires" among its members; but the union leaders always opposed violence. Some local lodges of the AOH were clearly used for violent as well as fraternal purposes, though most AOH members had nothing to do with the Molly Maguires. And, far from belonging to a well-organized conspiracy, the Molly Maguires engaged in a sporadic pattern of violence that focused on individual and local concerns and lacked a coherent strategy or stable institutional base. Their only significant predecessors in industrial America were the Irish canal laborers of the early nineteenth century, whose response to oppression was occasionally channelled through secret societies but more often dissipated through faction fighting and heavy drinking.

16. On Irish-American ethnicity in the anthracite region, see Kenny, "The Molly Maguires and the Catholic Church"; on Irish-American ethnicity in the United States in general, see Kerby A. Miller, "Class, Culture, and Immigrant Group Identity in the United States: The Case of Irish-American Ethnicity," in Virginia Yans-McLaughlin, ed., *Immigration Reconsidered: History, Sociology, and Politics* (New York, 1990), 96–129. Ira Katznelson, "Working-Class Formation: Constructing Cases and Comparisons," in Ira Katzneslon and Aristide Zolberg, eds., *Working-Class Formation: Nineteenth-Century Patterns in Western Europe and the United States* (Princeton, 1986), proposes a typology of class involving four interrelated levels: structure, ways of life, dispositions, and collective action. All four levels inform the conception of class in the present work.

Clearly, the Molly Maguires were better organized and more powerful than their unfortunate predecessors on the canals, even if they never assumed the proportions attributed to them by their conspiracy-minded contemporaries. But, like the canal workers, they belonged to a largely forgotten narrative of nineteenth-century American labor history, that of the unskilled immigrant worker.[17]

The canal workers and the Molly Maguires brought to industrial America a tradition of violent protest rooted in the Irish countryside. In the case of the Molly Maguires, that tradition involved a form of gender inversion that would take on new meanings in the United States. In Ireland, the Molly Maguires disguised themselves in women's clothing and pledged their allegiance to a mythical woman who symbolized their struggle against injustice. Dressed in long white smocks, with their faces blackened (or sometimes whitened), they roamed the countryside, calling themselves the "sons" or "daughters" of "Mistress Molly Maguire," and enforcing "midnight legislation" against those who had offended them. Cross-dressing was not reported in the anthracite region of Pennsylvania, though blackened faces were. And the idea of fighting on behalf of a mythical woman took on a new significance in mining communities, where abnormally high numbers of women were widowed by industrial accidents.[18]

The starting point for understanding the Molly Maguires in Pennsylvania is the history of Irish landholding, agrarian violence, and emigration, along with the economic and social development of the Pennsylvania anthracite region in the nineteenth century. These are the subjects of the first two chapters of this book, which set the scene for the story that unfolded in Pennsylvania between 1850 and 1880. Out of the meeting of two very different worlds, rural Ireland and industrializing Pennsylvania, emerged the American Molly Maguires. The remaining chapters offer an intertwined social and cultural history of the Molly Maguires in Pennsylania, proceeding chronologically from the political crisis of the 1850s through the trials and executions of the late 1870s. The Mollys first came to prominence during the social turmoil of the Civil War. In conscious opposition to their strategy of violence, a powerful new trade union movement was organized in the late 1860s, transcending barriers of craft and ethnicity among the mine workers. The rise of corporate economic power in the lower anthracite region was the final act in the drama, leading

17. Peter Way, *Common Labour: Workers and the Digging of North American Canals, 1780–1860* (New York, 1993), chapters 6 and 7; Way, "Evil Humors and Ardent Spirits: The Rough Culture of Canal Construction Laborers," *Journal of American History,* 79 (March 1993): 1,397–1,428; Way, "Shovel and Shamrock: Irish Workers and Labor Violence in the Digging of the Chesapeake and Ohio Canal," *Labor History,* 30 (Fall 1989): 489–517. See, also, W. David Baird, "Violence Along the Chesapeake Canal: 1839," *Maryland Historical Magazine,* 66 (Summer 1971): 121–34; Richard D. Borgeson, "Irish Canal Laborers in America: 1817–1846" (M.A. thesis, Pennsylvania State University, 1964), 48, 62–70; George W. Potter, *To the Golden Door: The Story of the Irish in Ireland and America* (Boston, 1960), 327–36.

18. These themes and others are developed in chapters 1 and 2. The connection with widowhood was suggested to me by Kerby Miller.

as it did to the eventual downfall of both the trade union and the Molly Maguires. At the heart of this story was violence, employed not only by Irish immigrant workers but by Pinkerton detectives, private policemen, vigilantes, and the state authorities.

But the battle against the Molly Maguires was as much ideological and cultural as social and political. Hand-in-hand with the complicated social processes at work in the nineteenth-century anthracite region went equally complicated patterns of ideological and cultural representation. These included the emergence of a "free labor" view of society; the related nativist indictment of Irish immigrants; the condemnation of Molly Maguireism by the Catholic church; the discursive equation of violence and disorder with the feminine and the irrational; and the construction of a powerful and enduring myth that denied Irish perpetrators of violence all rationality and motivation, explaining their actions instead as a matter of inherent depravity. By examining these various social and ideological processes as parts of a single history, it becomes possible to make sense of the Molly Maguires.

1

Whiteboys, Ribbonmen, and Molly Maguires

Contrary to the nineteenth-century conspiracy theorists, it is highly unlikely that an organization called the "Molly Maguires" was imported directly from Ireland to the United States. Nonetheless, the social structure and cultural practices in the parts of Ireland where the American Mollys originated offer some important clues about the nature of Molly Maguireism in Pennsylvania. In the first half of the nineteenth century, the Irish countryside was infamous for its violence. At the heart of the violence was a mysterious, secret-society tradition that had emerged with the Whiteboy movement of the 1760s. In time, the term *Whiteboyism* came to be used generically, describing agrarian violence as a whole. So, too, did the term *Ribbonism,* though there was also a distinct Society of Ribbonmen active in the 1820s and 1830s. The Molly Maguires, who emerged in Ireland in the 1840s, were the last of the long line of rural secret societies that began with the Whiteboys. The American Molly Maguires were a rare transatlantic example of this Irish rural tradition. Without an understanding of Irish rural history, the eventual outbreak of Molly Maguire violence in Pennsylvania makes little sense. A detailed examination is needed, first, of the general pattern of protest and violence in the Irish countryside; and second, of the highly distinctive history and culture of north-central and northwestern Ireland. For it was in this part of Ireland, and the single county of Donegal in particular, that most of the American Molly Maguires originated.

Where in Ireland were the Molly Maguires active? What institutional form did they take? And what were their motivation and strategy? The first of these questions can be answered with some accuracy. The second and third are more difficult to answer, as the Molly Maguires left virtually no evidence for the historian to use. But partial answers can be extracted from the elite sources, specifically the reports and observations of Detective James McParlan, the land agent W. Steuart Trench, the English journalist Thomas Campbell Foster, and the contemporary press.[1]

When James McParlan was assigned by Allan Pinkerton to investigate the Molly Maguires in Pennsylvania in October 1873, his first task was to draw up a preliminary report on the origins of the society in Ireland. The result was a seven-page memorandum giving details of various Irish secret societies. McParlan was an Ulster Catholic, born and raised in County Armagh, and his report concentrated on the societies in his part of the country, with an emphasis on their sectarian nature. He began by tracing the history of secret societies like "the Society of Molly McGuire" back to organizations in eighteenth-century Ulster. At first, he claimed, these societies accepted members "irrespective of religious opinions." Then, following the bloody insurrection of 1798, the societies took on a rigidly sectarian form, with Protestants banding together in the Orange Order, and Catholics, despite the strong opposition of their clergymen, forming rival groups such as the "Threshers" and the "Ribbonmen." These were the predecessors of the Molly Maguires, who first emerged in south Ulster and east Connacht during the Great Famine of the late 1840s.[2]

Proceeding clockwise from County Monaghan, the area in question includes counties Cavan, Longford, Roscommon, Leitrim, and Fermanagh. (See map 1.) W. Steuart Trench, the author of the best-selling *Realities of Irish Life,* which would be frequently cited at the trials in Pennsylvania in the 1870s, claimed that he first came across a tenant organization called the Molly Maguires in County Monaghan (south Ulster) in 1843. Trench claimed to have encountered the secret society for a second time in 1851, when he was appointed land agent on the Bath estate, also in County Monaghan. This time he learned that he had been sentenced to death by "the leaders of the Ribbon Association." "In accordance with this specimen of Ribbonite 'fair play,'" Trench recalled, "a document was drawn up, and the next Sunday the police found a notice, formally posted on every Roman Catholic chapel in the district, of which the following is an exact copy:"

1. HML, A 1520, B 979, F, "Memoranda and Papers," report of JMCP to AP, October 10, 1873; W. Steuart Trench, *Realities of Irish Life* (1868; London, 1966); Thomas Campbell Foster, *Letters on the Condition of the People in Ireland* (London, 1846).

2. HML, A 1520, B 979, F, "Memoranda and Papers," report of JMCP to AP, October 10, 1873.

> To Landlords, Agents, Bailiffs, Grippers, process-servers, and usurpers or underminers who wish to step into the evicted tenants' property, and to all others concerned in Tyranny and Oppression of the poor on the Bath Estate.
>
> TAKE NOTICE
>
> That you are hereby (under the pain of a certain punishment which will inevitably occur) prohibited from evicting tenants, executing decrees, serving process, distraining for rent, or going into another's land, or to assist any tyrant, Landlord, Agent in his insatiable desire for depopulation. Recollect the fate of Mauleverer, on this his anniversary. Dated May 23, 1851.[3]

After two men were convicted and hanged for conspiring to murder a bailiff on the Bath estate, the local Ribbonmen were not heard from again.

While Trench concentrated on the single county of Monaghan, Thomas Campbell Foster extended the geographical net to include the neighboring counties of Cavan (in south Ulster) and Leitrim (in east Connacht).[4] In 1845 and 1846, Campbell traveled throughout Ireland, sending back a series of letters to the *Times* of London describing Irish rural life and, in particular, agrarian violence. He began his journey in the area then most disturbed by violence, south Ulster. "It is a matter of notoriety that the county of Cavan has for some time been in an excited and disturbed state, and that several very shocking outrages have been perpetrated in it," Foster reported from Cavan Town on August 15. "Armed police and soldiers are everywhere seen about the town." Notices were posted offering rewards and seeking information on "the secret society commonly called 'Ribandmen' or 'Molly Maguires.'" A local magistrate, Mr. Bell, had recently been assassinated; and there were numerous reports of threats, assaults, armed robberies, and murders elsewhere in south Ulster and east Connacht, especially county Leitrim.[5]

The question of geography aside, the most important matter on which McParlan, Trench, and Foster agreed was the identification of the Molly Maguires, the Ribbonmen, and the Ancient Order of Hibernians as different names for the same organization. "Now, what is the 'Molly Maguireism' which has disturbed this county?" Foster inquired from Cavan on August 21, 1845. "'It is the same as 'Ribandism,' say the magistrates, in their placards offering rewards for the apprehension of 'Molly Maguires.'"[6] "Molly Maguireism," Foster

3. Quotes from Trench, *Realities of Irish Life,* 117, 126. Mauleverer was a magistrate and land agent killed at Crossmaglen on May 23, 1850, by two assassins who allegedly belonged to the Ribbonmen. It is unlikely that the notice reproduced by Trench is an "exact copy" as its orthography is suspiciously flawless. For citations of Trench in the Pennsylvania trials see, for example, the arguments of Franklin B. Gowen and George Kaercher in RCK, 20, 220; and [G.V. Town], *Commonwealth v. Patrick Hester, Patrick Tully, and Peter McHugh, 1877. Argument of Hon. F. W. Hughes, for Commonwealth* (Philadelphia, 1877), 18–21.

4. Foster traced the origin of the name "Molly Maguires" to the aftermath of a particularly brutal eviction in County Longford (just south of Cavan, in north Leinster) a decade earlier. But Longford does not appear to have been a center of Molly Maguire activity thereafter. Cf. Broehl, *The Molly Maguires,* 27.

5. Quote from Foster, *Letters on the Condition of the People,* 5; on Leitrim, see page 27. The assassination of Bell is commemorated in the ballads reproduced in appendix 5 of the present work.

6. Foster, *Letters on the Condition of the People,* 20.

concluded, was a local generic term for agrarian unrest: "it is, in fact, but the *embodyment of the spirit of discontent;* it is an old-existing malady with a new name."[7]

This "malady" had first manifested itself in the Whiteboy movement of the 1760s. There had been a specific society of Whiteboys in the eighteenth century, but the term *Whiteboyism* was used generically thereafter to describe agrarian violence in general. The term *Ribbonism* was also used as a catchall for rural violence in the early nineteenth century, but there was also a distinct organization called the Society of Ribbonmen, which needs to be distinguished from the generic usage. The society was an outgrowth of the Defenders, a Catholic sectarian organization active in south Ulster, east Connacht, and north Leinster in the late eighteenth century. The Defenders appear to have been absorbed into the United Irish network prior to the insurrection of 1798. The Ribbonmen emerged from the debacle of the uprising, inheriting from the Defenders a sense of the republican radicalism of the French Revolution and casting off sectarianism in favor of an often pronounced anticlericalism. The Irish Molly Maguires of the 1840s and 1850s were active in the parts of the country that had been the centers of Defenderism and Ribbonism, and there appears to have been some institutional continuity from the Defenders through the Ribbonmen to the Molly Maguires.[8]

Between 1822 and 1840 there were two main Ribbon networks in Ireland, one based in Dublin and the other in the old Defender territory in the north-central region. Branches of Ribbonism were also organized in England and Scotland, just as McParlan reported, under the name Hibernian Funeral Society. In 1825 the Ribbonmen adopted the name St. Patrick's Fraternal Society, in order to placate the Catholic church.[9] According to an American history of the AOH published in 1898, "there was a large number of members who rebelled against those changes and withdrew from the order and continued under the name Molly Maguires and Ribbonmen," especially in south Ulster.[10] In that part of the country the terms *Ribbonmen* and *Molly Maguires* were used interchangeably in the 1840s. But they were typically used in a loose, generic sense, and the Molly Maguires seem to have been an agrarian secret society of the "Whiteboy" variety rather than an alternative Society of Ribbonmen, even if the generic term *Ribbonism* was used to describe them. The rural, local, and often Gaelic flavor of agrarian agitators like the Molly Maguires, Threshers, and

7. Ibid., 21; italics in original. In evidence taken before a committee of the House of Lords in 1839, Foster noted, "Ribandism" or "Ribbonism" was identified with "Whitefootism," "Blackfootism," "Terryaltism," "Rockiteism," and even trade unionism.

8. Tom Garvin, "Defenders, Ribbonmen, and Others: Underground Political Networks in Pre-famine Ireland," in C. H. E. Philpin, ed., *Nationalism and Popular Protest in Ireland* (Cambridge and New York, 1987), 226–27.

9. James J. Bergin, *History of the Ancient Order of Hibernians* (Dublin, 1910), 29.

10. T. F. McGrath, *History of the Ancient Order of Hibernians from the Earliest Period to the Joint National Convention at Trenton, New Jersey, June 27, 1898* (Cleveland, 1898), 52.

Lady Clares, marked them off as very different from the secular, cosmopolitan, and protonationalist Society of Ribbonmen.[11]

The name Ancient Order of Hibernians was first adopted in the United States in 1838. "It was the Ribbonmen who carried the Order across the Atlantic," according to the official history of the American AOH.[12] Members of St. Patrick's Fraternal Society in New York City, "together with some others who had been Ribbonmen in Ireland," met with some Ribbonmen from Schuylkill County, Pennsylvania, to organize a new society in 1836.[13] Divisions of the society were organized in Schuylkill County and in New York City, and two years later the title Ancient Order of Hibernians was adopted. "The Order thrived among the coal miners in Pennsylvania," the official history of the AOH noted, "and the headquarters remained in that State until shortly before the first American charter was granted to the New York body in 1853."[14] Branches of the AOH were also organized in Scotland, England, and Ireland.

In his initial memorandum to Allan Pinkerton, James McParlan claimed that the Molly Maguires, as a well-organized conspiratorial organization, had been imported from Ireland to the United States by way of England. In the 1850s, according to McParlan, the Molly Maguires and the Ribbonmen were one and the same organization. Although the society was soon crushed by the Irish authorities, many of its members emigrated to England and Scotland, where they operated under the name Ancient Order of Hibernians (AOH). The detective reported that he had first come across the Order in 1856 while working in the manufacturing and mining district along the river Tyne in northeast England. Most AOH members from this area had since moved to the United States, McParlan claimed, and "being that their training in the Mines & Manufacturys of England had them somewhat skilled in that business the[y] early found employment in the Eastern states," where they reestablished their secret society. In the anthracite region of Pennsylvania, McParlan claimed, the Molly Maguires operated under the name Ancient Order of Hibernians. His memorandum concluded with an account of the inner workings of this society in the United States.[15]

In retrospect, McParlan's claim of direct continuity from Ireland to Pennsylvania via precisely the part of Britain where he had lived in the 1850s is rather too neat to be convincing. While branches of the Ribbonmen and the Ancient Order of Hibernians certainly existed in Britain, there is no evidence that any such organization was exported directly to the United States. If the AOH was a

11. Cf. Garvin, "Defenders, Ribbonmen, and Others," and Michael R. Beames, "The Ribbon Societies: Lower-Class Nationalism in Pre-famine Ireland," in Philpin, ed., *Nationalism and Popular Protest in Ireland.*

12. John O'Dea, *History of the Ancient Order of Hibernians and Ladies' Auxiliary,* 3 vols. (Philadelphia, 1923), vol. 1, 14.

13. Ibid., vol. 2, 884.

14. Ibid., vol. 2, 14.

15. HML, A 1520, B 979, F, "Memoranda and Papers," report of JMCP to AP, October 10, 1873.

transatlantic outgrowth of Ribbonism, it was clearly a peaceful fraternal society rather than a violent conspiratorial one. The order had lodges throughout the northeastern United States, but it was only in the lower anthracite region that these lodges became associated with violence. The violence in Pennsylvania was clearly inspired by its Irish prototype, but it was also rooted in local industrial conditions. And most of it occurred in the 1860s and 1870s, almost a generation after the violence in Ireland had ended.

The third and most difficult question about the Molly Maguires in Ireland concerns their motivation and strategy. Until quite recently, Irish agrarian violence in general tended to be explained in terms of a nationalist, Catholic populace struggling to cast off the yoke of the British, Protestant oppressor. But, in what has amounted to a sea-change in Irish historical writing since the 1960s, one myth in particular has been overturned: that of a homogeneous, nationalist peasantry doing valiant battle against an alien, landlord class. This effort to liberate Irish historiography from what one historian has called "the paralyzing straight-jacket of nationalist orthodoxy" has been the defining characteristic of recent Irish historical writing.[16]

As part of this move away from the old nationalist synthesis, historians of the Irish countryside have tried to devise an alternative explanation for the rural violence endemic in Ireland between 1760 and 1850.[17] The most convincing school of interpretation concedes a point that was anathema to the old orthodoxy: The oppressors of the Irish were as often Irishmen as Englishmen, and the victims of agrarian violence were much more commonly Irish land agents, middlemen, and tenants than English usurpers. Abstract concepts of "Irishness" and nationalist struggle have been replaced by an analysis emphasizing socioeconomic relations and local concerns and grievances. Above all, the violence is understood in terms of the disruption of traditional

16. Cf. R. F. Foster, "History and the Irish Question," *Royal Historical Society Transactions,* 5th ser., 32 (1983): 169–92; Brendan Bradshaw, "Nationalism and Historical Scholarship in Modern Ireland," *Irish Historical Studies,* 26 (November 1989): 329–51. Quote from Joseph Lee, "The Ribbonmen," in T. Desmond Williams, ed., *Secret Societies in Ireland* (Dublin, 1973), 26.

17. On Irish agrarian violence, see Joseph Lee, "The Ribbonmen," and Maureen Wall, "The Whiteboys," in Williams, ed., *Secret Societies in Ireland*; Michael R. Beames, *Peasants and Power: The Whiteboy Movements and Their Control in Pre-famine Ireland* (New York, 1983); Beames, "The Ribbon Societies"; Beames, "Rural Conflict in Pre-famine Ireland"; Garvin, "Defenders, Ribbonmen, and Others"; Paul Bew, *Land and the National Question in Ireland, 1858–82* (Atlantic Highlands, N.J.: 1979); Philpin, ed., *Nationalism and Popular Protest in Ireland*; Samuel J. Clark and James S. Donnelly, Jr., eds., *Irish Peasants: Violence and Political Unrest, 1780–1914* (Madison, 1983); S. J. Connolly, *Priests and People in Pre-famine Ireland, 1780–1845* (New York, 1982), chapter 6; John William Knott, "Land, Kinship and Identity: The Cultural Roots of Agrarian Agitation in Eighteenth- and Nineteenth-Century Ireland," *Journal of Peasant Studies,* 12 (October 1984): 93–108; Kerby A. Miller, *Emigrants and Exiles: Ireland and the Irish Exodus to North America* (New York, 1985), 61–69; and the articles by James S. Donnelly, Jr., listed in notes 29 and 61 below.

practices of landholding and land use, which violated the "moral economy" of the rural poor.[18]

The response to such violations was direct, violent action. Fences were torn down, and animals grazing on newly enclosed land were driven off, mutilated, or killed. Landlords' agents were threatened, beaten, and assassinated, as were tenants who settled on land from which others had been evicted. Merchants and millers who charged prices deemed unjust were threatened and attacked. Land converted to pasture was dug up at night to make it arable once again, in an effort to expand the availability of land for small-scale potato cultivation. Far from being irrational or bloodthirsty, the violence had a specific purpose and "legitimizing notion," namely the attempt to restore traditional conceptions of a just society and economy in the face of innovations and intrusions.[19] The type of violence in question may be described as a form of retributive justice enforced to correct transgressions against traditional moral and social codes.[20]

With the exception of the frankly sectarian organizations in Ulster, the presence of agrarian societies in a given part of Ireland can be seen as a measure of the extent to which that region had undergone the process of agrarian transformation that typically provoked rural popular protest. In general, the agitation was a protest not against the existing land system but against attempts to change it. A particular type of enterprising landlord, or more often his agents, usually initiated the violence by seeking to alter traditional patterns of estate management. Landlords' agents were the principal victims, but peasant farmers were also attacked for taking land from which other tenants had been ejected. A great deal of the agitation had to do with access to arable land, particularly in the form of conacre (tiny patches of land rented for the time necessary to plant and sow a crop of potatoes). The occupation and control of land, not some general notion of Irish nationhood, was the chief source of conflict. Above all, the struggle needs to be conceived of in regional rather than nationwide terms. It occurred at different times in different places, and local agrarian societies

18. The concept of a moral economy has been borrowed by Irish historians from E. P. Thompson, "The Moral Economy of the English Crowd in the Eighteenth Century," *Past and Present*, 50 (February 1971): 76–136.

19. The study of similar movements in Britain produced some of the classic writings in English social history. See Raymond Williams, *The Country and the City* (New York, 1973); E. P. Thompson, "The Crime of Anonymity," in Douglas Hay, ed., *Albion's Fatal Tree: Crime and Society in Eighteenth-Century England* (New York, 1975); Thompson, "The Moral Economy of the English Crowd" (on the notion of a "legitimizing right," p. 78); Eric Hobsbawm, *Primitive Rebels: Studies in Archaic Forms of Social Movement in the Nineteenth and Twentieth Centuries* (New York, 1965); Eric Hobsbawm and George Rudé, *Captain Swing* (New York, 1968).

20. On analogous movements in nineteenth-century India, see Ranajit Guha, *Elementary Aspects of Peasant Insurgency* (Delhi, 1983), and Ranajit Guha and Gayatri Spivak, eds., *Selected Subaltern Studies* (New York, 1988). On twentieth-century Southeast Asia, see James C. Scott, *The Moral Economy of the Peasant: Rebellion and Subsistence in Southeast Asia* (New Haven, 1976); Scott, "Protest and Profanation: Agrarian Revolt and the Little Tradition," *Theory and Society*, 4 (Spring and Summer 1977): 1–38, 211–46; and Scott, "Hegemony and the Peasantry," *Politics and Society*, 7 (1977): 267–96.

were rarely concerned with, or even aware of, developments in other parts of the country.[21]

The object of the Irish Molly Maguires in the 1840s, James McParlan reported, was "to take from those who had abundance and give it to the poor."[22] The strategies he outlined, such as the intimidation of shopkeepers in an attempt to enforce just prices, resemble the behavior historians of the eighteenth and nineteenth centuries have described in their work on the "moral economy" of popular protesters and demonstrators.[23] "Their mode of operation," McParlan reported, "was to have there [sic] leader dressed up in a suit of womens clothing to represent the Irish mother begging bread for her children under the disguise." The leader, or "Molly," approached a storekeeper "and demanded the Amount Levyed on him in the shape of meal flour and general Groceries." If the storekeeper refused to comply, the "Molly" instructed his followers to enter the store and help themselves, and warned the owner of dire consequences should he report the incident to the authorities.[24]

Agrarian violence in Ireland coincided closely with seasonal and festive rituals, particularly the conjunction of half-yearly rents with the Celtic festivals of Halloween and May Eve. There were "clear linkages between Whiteboyism, the cycle of peasant economy, and rural custom," as one historian has observed.[25] The agrarian agitators displayed a conviction that they were enforcing a just law of their own in opposition to the inequities of landlord law, the police and court system, and the transgressions of land-grabbers. In Ireland, as in Pennsylvania, many of the Irish clearly had little stake in the official legal system, which they experienced as an instrument of injustice and oppression. Significantly, the Whiteboys and Ribbonmen were referred to by their detractors as "midnight legislators" who enforced a secret law by violence. In the revealing words of Sir Thomas Larcom: "There are in fact two codes of law in force and in antagonism—one the statute law enforced by judges and jurors, in which the people do not yet trust—the other a secret law, enforced by themselves—its agents the Ribbonmen and the bullet." The Molly Maguires, on both sides of the Atlantic, embodied an alternative, informal system of law, which could not permanently be tolerated by the authorities.[26]

Having briefly portrayed the Irish Molly Maguires as crusaders for social justice, James McParlan was quick to point out that they rapidly outgrew their modest and justifiable beginnings, becoming instead a bloodthirsty terrorist organization. "Instead of performing the simple Acts of taking from the rich and

21. Cf. Lee, "The Ribbonmen," 28.

22. HML, A 1520, B 979, F, "Memoranda and Papers," report of JMCP to AP, October 10, 1873.

23. The definitive thesis is Thompson, "The Moral Economy of the English Crowd in the Eighteenth Century."

24. HML, A 1520, B 979, F, "Memoranda and Papers," report of JMCP to AP, October 10, 1873.

25. Michael R. Beames, "Rural Conflict in Pre-famine Ireland," in Philpin, ed., *Nationalism and Popular Protest in Ireland,* 276.

26. Potter, *To the Golden Door,* 54–57 (quote by Larcom, 54). For the term *midnight legislators,* see, for example, *Ballyshannon Herald,* July 24, 1857.

giving to the poor," he wrote, "the[y] commenced hostilities something after the fashion of the KuKluxKlahn [sic] of the Southern States of the Country but as the[y] had no negros [sic] to kill the[y] commenced shooting down Landlords Agents Bailiffs or any unoffending neighbour who might not coincide with their views." He went on to give vivid details of the torture, intimidation, and killings supposedly perpetrated by this nefarious society, "one of the most formidable organizations for Rapine & Murder [that] ever existed in Ireland."[27] Yet, despite this condemnation, the image that sticks in one's mind is the earlier one of the "Molly" demanding food for "her" starving children.

Trench and Foster also emphasized the economic dimension of the Molly Maguire conflict in Ireland, even in border counties like Monaghan, next to McParlan's native Armagh. Given that most landlords and their agents were Protestants, the conflict often assumed the form of religious hatred. But this should not obscure the fundamental issues of land and property at the heart of the matter. The struggle over these issues was most pronounced in the eastern portion of the province of Connacht, where Molly Maguire activities reached their peak of intensity. Thomas Campbell Foster had no hesitation in declaring that the root cause of the conflict, both here and in Cavan, was a struggle over access to the land.[28]

Unlike the rest of northern Connacht, the land of Roscommon was particularly well suited to conversion from small-scale tillage to large-scale pasture and cattle farming. In this respect, Roscommon was undergoing changes similar to those that much of the provinces of Leinster and Munster had already experienced. As a result, the problems faced by Roscommon smallholders and the tactics they employed in response, duplicated developments seen in other parts of Ireland since the 1760s. A central issue among the Molly Maguires in Roscommon was the desire to retain the tiny patches of land held under the conacre system, on which a family could raise sufficient potatoes to live. These holdings were threatened by an enclosure movement, and the Molly Maguires responded by digging up newly enclosed pasture land to render it fit only for conacre. This tactic had also been employed by the Whiteboys in the 1760s and a group called the Terry Alts in the late 1820s and early 1830s, to name but two examples.[29]

Another tactic in Roscommon was to attack and maim animals grazing on pasture. The Molly Maguires allegedly concealed needles in the grass, which were then swallowed by cattle, with fatal consequences. In one reported incident, they killed a hunting dog and left a notice to its owner expressing their wish that they had killed him instead.[30] In other parts of the county, herdsmen were intimidated and attacked, and countless animals were killed or

27. HML, A 1520, B 979, F, "Memoranda and Papers," report of JMCP to AP, October 10, 1873.

28. Foster, *Letters on the Condition of the People,* 20.

29. Beames, *Peasants and Power,* 79; James S. Donnelly, Jr, "The Whiteboy Movement, 1761–65," *Irish Historical Studies,* 21 (March 1978): 33–44; Donnelly, "The Terry Alt Movement," *History Ireland,* 2 (Winter 1994): 34.

30. *Roscommon and Leitrim Gazette,* March 8, 1845, cited by Beames, *Peasants and Power,* 79.

mutilated.[31] Here, too, the Molly Maguires were duplicating tactics inaugurated by the Whiteboys eighty years earlier. In one such incident, "a bay gelding, as if a substitute for its hated owner, was tried, found guilty, tortured and shot."[32]

One final, intriguing question about the Irish Molly Maguires of the 1840s is the origin of their name. A number of stories were told about the name in the nineteenth century. One version held that an old widow called Molly Maguire had been evicted from her house and local peasants had banded together to avenge her. Another version held that Molly Maguire was the owner of the "shebeen" (illicit tavern) where the secret society met to plan its activities. According to a third version, Molly Maguire was a fierce young woman, pistols strapped to each thigh, who led bands of men through the countryside on their nocturnal raids. Though conveniently simple, these stories were doubtless apocryphal; they cropped up in various unconnected parts of Ireland, from Antrim to Roscommon, and they are best seen as elements of folklore rather than accurate sociological descriptions.[33]

The most plausible explanation of the name "Molly Maguires" is that the men who engaged in the violence disguised themselves as women. "These 'Molly Maguires,'" as W. Steuart Trench observed, "were generally stout active young men, dressed up in women's clothes, with faces blackened or otherwise disguised; sometimes they wore crape over their countenances, sometimes they smeared themselves in the most fantastic manner with burnt cork about their eyes, mouths and cheeks."[34] Similar practices were common to nearly all Irish agrarian societies in the period 1760 to 1850. The Whiteboys (*na Buachaillí Bána*), for example, were so named because they wore white linen frocks over their clothes and white bands or handkerchiefs around their hats. At the same time, they apparently pledged allegiance to a mythical woman, Sieve Oultagh (from the Irish *Sadhbh Amhaltach,* or Ghostly Sally), whom they designated as their queen. The Molly Maguires appear to have done much the same thing. Disguised as women when they went out at night, they dedicated themselves to a mythical woman who symbolized their struggle against injustice, whether sectarian, nationalist, or economic. The clothing was not just a means of disguise; it also served to endow the agrarian agitator with legitimacy, investing him with "the character of the disinterested agent of a higher authority," the "son" or "daughter" of Molly Maguire.[35]

One possible cultural source for the costumes of the Molly Maguires is the practice of mummery imported to Ireland by English and Scottish settlers in the seventeenth century. Mummery was strongest in the North, and in the predominantly Catholic borderlands of Ulster and Leinster it was soon

31. Beames, *Peasants and Power,* 79.

32. Donnelly, "The Whiteboy Movement," 24.

33. Cf. Sidney Lens, *The Labor Wars: From the Molly Maguires to the Sitdowns* (Garden City, N.Y., 1973), 12; Broehl, *The Molly Maguires,* 25; *New York Weekly Story Teller,* March 13, April 3, 1876.

34. Trench, *Realities of Irish Life,* 30.

35. Donnelly, "The Whiteboy Movement, 1761–65," 26–29. Quote from Knott, "Land, Kinship, and Identity," 107.

assimilated into the indigenous culture. On festive days, like midsummer's or New Year's, the mummers travelled from door to door demanding food, money, or drink in exchange for a performance. There was often a somewhat ominous undertone to their festivities; they threatened retribution if they were spurned, and the threat was not always made in jest. They dressed in straw costumes, white shirts, or brightly colored women's clothing, and their faces were usually blackened. The Molly Maguires dressed in very similar costumes, perhaps to signal that they too were acting on behalf of their community, upholding an alternative social order against external authorities. Rather than being an aberration, the Mollys were very much an outgrowth of the cultural world that surrounded them. Moving quickly from taunts and threats to outright violence, they presented themselves as the custodians of their community.[36]

In Ireland, as one of the leading historians of early modern Europe has observed, "we have the most extensive example of disturbances led by men disguised as women."[37] The "Threshers," for example, dressed in white sheets before going out at night to enforce "Captain Thresher's Laws." The "Peep o'Day Boys," the "Lady Rocks," and the "Lady Clares" all disguised themselves, often quite elaborately, in women's clothing.[38] How is this pattern of gender inversion to be explained? Given the preliterate character of Gaelic culture, no written evidence on this point has survived. But it is clear that allegiance to a mythical woman was a common theme in nineteenth-century Irish culture, not just among agrarian rebels. In parishes and villages the residents were "children of the one mother"; in the nation at large, to the extent that a concept of it existed, they were "children of the Gael." Ireland was typically symbolized by a beautiful woman in the *aisling* poetry of the eighteenth century. And the members of agrarian secret societies were "children" of "Sieve," or "Molly Maguire," or "Terry's Mother." In McParlan's initial report to Allan Pinkerton, the leader of the Molly Maguires wore "a suit of womens clothing to represent the Irish mother begging bread for her children."[39]

As for the motif of cross-dressing, it was characteristic of most communal societies in the Irish countryside, not just those that had recourse to violence. Indeed, the violent societies appear to have been an outgrowth of nonviolent ones, representing the transformation of cultural play into social protest. "Contemporary accounts," as one historian has observed, ". . . suggest that the organisation of the Whiteboys may have owed something to the traditional

36. Cf. Mark Bulik, "Mummers and Mollies: The Political Semantic of Irish Folk Drama and its Uses in Rebel Symbolism," unpublished conference paper (courtesy of author). I am grateful to Mr. Bulik for sharing his ideas on this point.

37. Natalie Zemon Davis, *Society and Culture in Early Modern France* (Stanford, 1975), 149.

38. On the clothing of members of Irish secret societies, see Beames, *Peasants and Power,* passim.

39. Miller, *Emigrants and Exiles*; HML, A 1520, B 979, F, "Memoranda and Papers," report of JMcP to AP, October 10, 1873. The word *aisling* means dream; the Irish-language *aisling* poems combined the themes of love and politics, the narrator being awakened to a sense of national identity by a woman who came to him in a dream or vision.

pattern of rural life, with its Mayboys, Wrenboys, Strawboys and their captains."[40] Disguise, transvestism, and overt sexual games also characterized one of the most distinctively Irish cultural forms of the time, boisterous and often sacrilegious wakes for the dead.[41]

This propensity to dress in women's clothing was not just a cultural peculiarity of the Irish. It was a common motif in the festive rituals of early modern Europe, for example, in France on St. Stephen's Day and New Year's Day, and in northern England and the Scottish lowlands during the twelve days of Christmas. The more remote a region was from developed agricultural areas and metropolitan and industrial centers, the longer these cultural traditions survived. They were still thriving in rural Wales (the "Rebeccas"), in parts of France (*les demoiselles d'Ariège*), and in many parts of Ireland as late as the mid-nineteenth century. Indeed, the "Wren Boys" who continue to cavort through parts of rural Ireland on St. Stephen's Day are an eerie residue of this bygone culture.[42]

The impulse behind disguise and cross-dressing was not, of course, some collective confusion over sexual identity. But if sex was not being questioned, gender and other forms of social hierarchy were. In societies where the word "woman" often signified the passionate, the disorderly, the violent and chaotic side of human nature, temporary assumption of women's identity by men was fraught with significance. Recent historians have detected in the practice of carnival, for example, not just a social safety valve but real alternatives to the prevailing social order, particularly in terms of gender.[43] The world of Mediterranean festival, social mockery, and cultural play may seem a long way from the rainswept boglands of north-central and northwest Ireland. But the social and cultural roots of the Molly Maguires apparently lay in this obscure world of ritual and protest, common to different parts of early modern Europe at different times. In general, the patterns of protest and violence in question survived longer in Ireland than elsewhere in Western Europe. And the Molly Maguires were the last of the long line of violent secret societies to emerge in the Irish countryside in the century after 1760.

These, then, were the types of social practices and traditions that certain Irish immigrants brought with them to the anthracite region of Pennsylvania. Threatening notices signed "Mollie's Children" were being posted in the region as

40. Wall, "The Whiteboys," 16.

41. Connolly, *Priests and People in Pre-famine Ireland,* 148–58.

42. John M. Merriman, "The *Demoiselles* of the Ariège," in Merriman, ed., *1830 in France* (New York, 1975), 97; George Rudé, *The Crowd in the French Revolution* (New York, 1972), 236, n.3; David Williams, *The Rebecca Riots: A Study in Agrarian Discontent* (Cardiff, 1955); David J.V. Jones, *Rebecca's Children: A Study of Rural Society, Crime and Protest* (New York, 1989).

43. Davis, *Society and Culture in Early Modern France,* 123; cf. Joan Wallach Scott, *Gender and the Politics of History* (New York, 1988), chapters 1, 2, on gender as a category of analysis.

early as 1848. The term *Molly Maguires* first came into circulation there in the late 1850s, as the culmination of nativist attacks on Irish immigrants. There is no way of knowing for certain the extent to which the immigrants themselves used the term. Nonetheless, their cultural background is crucial to explaining the Molly Maguire story in Pennsylvania. And any proper understanding of that background requires close attention to the particular parts of Ireland from which they emigrated.[44]

It is not easy to find precise information on the geographical origins of the immigrants. The federal census recorded only countries of birth, and no state census was taken in Pennsylvania. Schuylkill County started keeping death records only in 1893, too late for the purposes of this study. At least fifty-one people were implicated in the Molly Maguire conspiracy in Pennsylvania. Documented evidence has survived on the origins of fourteen of them, and all but one of these documented cases came from north-central and northwest Ireland. A similar figure emerges from an analysis of the surnames of the thirty-seven undocumented cases in terms of their regional frequency in Ireland. Three-quarters of the undocumented Molly Maguires bore names most commonly found in this same part of Ireland. Combining both sets of figures, it appears that four of every five American Molly Maguires were either born in, or bore a surname most common in, north-central and northwestern Ireland.[45]

The region in question extends due west from counties Monaghan and Cavan through Leitrim, Sligo, and upper Roscommon and Mayo; and northwest through Fermanagh and parts of Tyrone to Donegal. It includes the areas where the Molly Maguires were active in the 1840s and 1850s; but it also includes more remote regions, like Mayo to the west and Donegal to the northwest, where the Molly Maguires were only sporadically active and there was no sustained tradition of agrarian agitation. Fully one third of the American Molly Maguires (fifteen of the forty-five names analyzed) were born in, or bore a surname most commonly found in, the single county of Donegal.[46]

The crucial importance of immigrants from Donegal in the Molly Maguire story is borne out by patterns of ethnic settlement in the anthracite region. A list of members of the Ancient Order of Hibernians drawn up by Pinkerton's Detective Agency in the 1870s reveals significant clusters of immigrants from Donegal in precisely the areas most involved in the Molly Maguire violence. All four members of the Coal Dale lodge of the AOH, for example, fit into this category; nine of eleven at Hazleton; five of six at Junction, Northumberland

44. On the use of the term *Mollie's Children* in the anthracite region as early as 1848, see [W.W. Munsell & Co.], *History of Schuylkill County* (New York, 1881), 99. On the use of the term *Molly Maguires* in the anthracite region in the 1850s, see *MJ*, October 3, 1857, and chapter 3 of the present work.

45. See appendix 2. Naturalization records are available from 1811 onward, but they do not include counties of birth until 1907, except inadvertently in a handful of cases. Death certificates and naturalization records can be found in the Archives Center of the Schuylkill County Courthouse in Pottsville, Pennsylvania.

46. See appendixes 1 and 2 and map 1.

County; all three members at Mauch Chunk; twelve of thirteen at Storm Hill; all thirteen members at Summit Hill; and five of six at Wiggans Patch. Immigrants from north-central and northwest Ireland also dominated the lodges at Shenandoah and Mahanoy City, the two principal centers of Molly Maguire activities in the 1870s.[47]

All of these lodges of the Ancient Order of Hibernians were located in the turbulent, semirural part of the anthracite region where the bulk of the Molly Maguire activities took place. The coal-mining area of western Carbon County that included Mauch Chunk, Storm Hill, and Summit Hill contained the highest concentration of immigrants from Donegal. Along with settlers from north-central and northwestern Ireland in general, these immigrants appear to have used their local lodges for "Ribbonite" or "Whiteboy" purposes. In this way, they adapted to the distinctive way of life in the anthracite region a strategy for winning social justice that had originated in Ireland. Given that the AOH and the Ribbonmen were known as "Molly Maguires" in the part of Ireland many of them had lived in, they presumably adopted this regional nomenclature as well. Direct violent action in pursuit of justice was the hallmark of their activity on both sides of the Atlantic.[48]

As well as confirming the preponderance of Donegal men in the most turbulent part of the anthracite region, this pattern of settlement is highly suggestive of the nature of Irish national and ethnic identity in the nineteenth century. In both Ireland and the United States, the Irish tended to affiliate along parish, local, and regional lines, rather than adhering to some abstract identity of Irishness. In the anthracite region, immigrants from Donegal or Mayo were evidently more likely to seek out and identify themselves with people from their own region, and preferably their own county or parish, than to find automatic kinship with emigrants from Kilkenny or Wexford, whom they might find just as strange and almost as alien as the Welsh or the English. This was particularly true when regional differences corresponded to differences of religion and labor skills.[49]

This pattern of regional affiliation is strikingly borne out by the list of AOH members compiled by the Pinkertons. People from Donegal congregated with others from their county, and indeed with others from the same part of their county. Places like Storm Hill and Summit Hill in Carbon County, and Wiggans Patch in Schuylkill County, for example, were dominated by immigrants from west Donegal. Isolated settlements like these were the enclaves of a transplanted Irish regional identity with its own specific forms of language and culture. The people who settled in these areas soon found themselves in conflict not only with their employers, British miners, and the authorities; they clashed also with the Catholic church and with immigrants from other parts of Ireland, who had different ideas on what it meant to be Irish in America. In Ireland, the

47. See appendix 3 and map 3.

48. See chapter 2 for the geographical location of Molly Maguireism in the anthracite region.

49. On Protestant miners from Kilkenny in the anthracite region, see chapter 2.

people of West Donegal typically had a strong sense of territoriality; in the mining region of Pennsylvania, some of them tried to recover this lost sense of rootedness, and the forms of social justice that went with it, by turning to Molly Maguireism. On both sides of the Atlantic, an understanding of local and territorial identity is essential to making sense of the Molly Maguires.[50]

The starting point for any such analysis is a close examination of the economic, social, and cultural history of the parts of Ireland from which the American Molly Maguires emigrated. Ulster in general was the most prosperous province in Ireland. But, whereas Antrim and parts of Down and Armagh enjoyed the highest standard of living in Ireland, the more remote regions of the province were among the poorest places in the country. "Along the Donegal coast and in the uplands of central and southern Ulster," as one historian puts it, "most rural dwellers fared little better than the peasants of Mayo and Kerry."[51] Together with the adjacent areas of north Leinster and east Connacht, these were the parts of Ireland from which the Molly Maguires of Pennsylvania emigrated in the mid nineteenth century.

Precisely because it was so undeveloped, this region lacked the deep-rooted tradition of agrarian violence characteristic of places like Tipperary and Kilkenny in the fertile, commercially developed south midlands. There had been sporadic agitation in places like Sligo, Leitrim, and Roscommon in the first decades of the nineteenth century, and a shadowy secret society labeled the "Molly Maguires" had emerged in north-central Ireland in the 1840s. But in Mayo and Donegal there was no significant rural violence until the late 1850s and 1860s, and it never assumed the intensity that prefamine agrarian violence had achieved elsewhere in Ireland. The Land War that commenced in Mayo in 1879 was national rather than local; it was a form of mass agitation of a different order from the clandestine activities of the old agrarian societies; and it began just as the last of the Molly Maguires were being hanged in Pottsville, too late to have any impact on the story in Pennsylvania.[52]

North Leinster, south and west Ulster, and north and east Connacht, where most of the American Molly Maguires came from, embraced some of the most impoverished parts of Ireland.[53] For the Catholic majority, life in this region in the mid nineteenth century was characterized by the related themes of poverty, emigration, famine, and religious sectarianism. In economic terms, the central

50. See appendix 3 on the Donegal Irish in the anthracite region, and chapters 7 and 8 on the involvement of people from Storm Hill, Summit Hill, and Wiggans Patch in Molly Maguire activities. For an application of the concept of territoriality to Indian peasant violence, see Guha, *Elementary Aspects of Peasant Insurgency*. Guha defines territoriality as "a sense of belonging to a common lineage as well as a common habitat—an intersection of two primordial referents" (p.279).

51. Miller, *Emigrants and Exiles*, 351.

52. On the chronology and geography of Irish agrarian violence, see Beames, *Peasants and Power*, 25, 43.

53. There were some partial exceptions to this rule, notably the sections of Roscommon and Mayo in which there was good grazing land, the fertile lands of Tyrone, and the eastern half of County Donegal.

development in the history of the region was the expansion and subsequent contraction of the linen industry. Counties like Cavan and Monaghan had participated in a thriving linen trade in the late eighteenth and early nineteenth centuries, growing flax, spinning it into yarn, weaving it into linen, and marketing the final product. Weaving, and particularly spinning, had also spread to west Donegal, and the industry brought prosperity to many parts of southern Ireland as well. But the mechanization of spinning after 1828 and of weaving after 1845 led to the contraction of the linen industry in and around Belfast, causing severe economic dislocation in north Leinster and south and west Ulster, large stretches of which were transformed into "rural slums."[54]

For many smallholders in these latter areas, the only solution was emigration, which grew steadily from the 1820s onward. The areas in question were among the hardest hit during the Great Famine, with population losses (through mortality and emigration) of almost 30 percent in Longford, Cavan, Monaghan, Leitrim, and Sligo between 1841 and 1851. County Donegal, too, suffered from the mechanization and contraction of the linen industry, but fared relatively better during the famine, losing 14 percent of its population in the decade after 1840.[55]

North-central and northwest Ireland also shared a distinctive religious history that shaped every aspect of social life. While east Ulster was overwhelmingly Protestant and southern Ireland overwhelmingly Catholic, the borderlands and County Donegal had significant numbers of each religious group living side by side. In 1861, for example, County Cavan was 80.5 percent Catholic and 19.4 percent Protestant, Monaghan 73.4 percent Catholic and 26.3 percent Protestant, and Donegal 75.1 percent Catholic and 24.6 percent Protestant. The other counties from which significant numbers of Molly Maguires emigrated were much more heavily Catholic, with figures as high as 96 percent in Mayo and Roscommon and 90 percent in Leitrim and Longford. The uneasy coexistence of relatively large numbers of each group in Cavan, Monaghan, and Donegal heightened, rather than diminished, religious hatreds, lending a significant sectarian twist to Molly Maguireism. This is all the more clear given the

54. Brenda Collins, "Proto-industrialization and Pre-famine Emigration," *Social History,* 7 (1982): 127–46; W. H. Crawford, *The Handloom Weavers and the Ulster Linen Industry* (1972; Belfast, 1994), "The Rise of the Linen Industry," in L.M. Cullen, ed., *The Formation of the Irish Economy* (1968; Cork, 1976), and "The Evolution of the Linen Trade of Ulster before Industrialization," *Irish Economic and Social History,* 15 (1988): 32–53; L. M. Cullen, *An Economic History of Ireland Since 1660* (London, 1972), 60–66, 80–81, 86, 97, 117; Conrad Gill, *The Rise of the Irish Linen Industry* (Oxford, 1925); Miller, *Emigrants and Exiles,* 34, 208, 372 (quote, 208); W. J. Smyth, "Locational Patterns and Trends Within the Pre-famine Linen Industry," *Irish Geography,* 8 (1975): 97–110; Peter M. Solar, "The Irish Linen Trade, 1820–1852," *Textile History,* 21 (Spring 1990): 57–85.

55. Population figures from W. E. Vaughan and A. J. Fitzpatrick, eds., *Irish Historical Statistics: Population, 1821–1971* (Dublin, 1978), 6, 11–15. In west Donegal, assistance from landlords and Quakers helped keep emigration down; in prosperous (and Protestant) east Donegal, people generally had more resources and were less likely to starve to death or be forced to emigrate. Cf. S. H. Cousens, "The Regional Pattern of Emigration During the Great Irish Famine, 1846–51," *Transactions of the Institute of British Geographers,* 28 (1960): 126–27.

preponderance of Protestants among the ranks of landlords, agents, and authority figures in Ireland, and among mine superintendents and skilled miners in Pennsylvania. The latter group was dominated by the Welsh, who were notorious for their contempt for Irish Catholics on both sides of the Atlantic. In Pennsylvania that contempt was expressed by the Welsh and reciprocated by the Molly Maguires in the form of violence.[56]

This sectarian element is particularly important in understanding the disproportionately large number of Molly Maguires who came from County Donegal. In no other county in Ireland did an impoverished, Irish-speaking peasantry live in such close proximity to large numbers of Protestants, many of whom were organized in Orange Lodges.[57] The prevalence of seasonal migration from the county meant that many of its men had experience working for Protestant employers in Ulster's Lagan Valley (east Donegal), in east Ulster, and especially, in Scotland. All three places were marked by a particularly virulent form of anti-Catholicism in the mid nineteenth century, and it is likely that many emigrants from Donegal carried with them to the United States bitter memories of religious discrimination in Ulster and Britain. As a result, they were peculiarly predisposed to interpret economic exploitation in sectarian terms. This predisposition hardened in Pennsylvania, when they found themselves laboring for skilled Welsh miners and native-born, Protestant mine owners, and were the targets of venomous attack by the fiercely anti-Catholic nativist press.[58]

Elements of sectarianism were clearly evident in Molly Maguireism in Ireland. On August 9, 1845, for example, a newspaper in County Roscommon printed a copy of the following threatening letter:

> Turk Dickson—we the undersigned as head and representatives of the society called the Molly's men, having heard so many valid witnesses against you, as a damned Orange rascal, and underminding [sic] rogue, a two-faced false villain, a back biting infernal black guard, not content with stealing your neighbour's

56. Figures from Vaughan and Fitzpatrick, eds., *Irish Historical Statistics,* 51–53. On Welsh attitudes to the Irish in the nineteenth century, see Alan Conway, ed., *The Welsh in America: Letters from the Immigrants* (Minneapolis, 1961), 16, 21, 24, 30, 38–39, 43, 45, 48–49. On the rivalry between the Welsh and the Irish in the anthracite region, see chapters 6 and 7 of the present work.

57. The religious demography was roughly similar in Cavan and Monaghan, but in these counties less than a quarter of the population spoke Irish, whereas in west Donegal more than 80 percent used it as a first or sole language. Cf. R. F. Foster, *Modern Ireland, 1600–1972* (London, 1988), 517.

58. On anti-Irish, anti-Catholic nativism in the anthracite region, see chapter 3. On seasonal migration, see Cormac Ó Gráda, "Seasonal Migration and Post-famine Adjustment in the West of Ireland," *Studia Hibernica,* 13 (1973): 48–76; J. H. Johnson, "Harvest Migration from Nineteenth-Century Ireland," *Transactions of the Institute of British Geographers,* 20 (1965): 97–112; James E. Handley, *The Irish in Scotland* (Cork, 1945), chapter 2; J. N. H. Douglas, "Emigration and Irish Peasant Life," *Ulster Folklife,* 9 (1963): 9–19, especially 12–13. On the Ribbonmen, the AOH, and the Orange Order in Britain, see Handley, *The Irish in Scotland,* 161, 306–12; John Archer Jackson, *The Irish in Britain* (London, 1983), 155.

> goods, you then proceed to undermind them, and get their land. We give you this as the first and last notice, to give up this farm, to its proper owner.[59]

Here, sectarian animosity is inseparable from economic grievances; both are necessarily intertwined in a single struggle for social justice.

Nonetheless, economic issues clearly predominated over religious ones in Molly Maguireism as a whole in the 1840s and 1850s. It would be quite misleading to cast the Molly Maguires solely, or even primarily, as Catholic nationalists engaged in sectarian conflict with their Protestant oppressors. The most celebrated case of Molly Maguire activity in Roscommon, the assassination of Major Denis Mahon on November 2, 1847, did feature accusations that the local clergyman, Fr. Michael McDermott, had taken the side of the tenantry and provoked them to kill their landlord.[60] But, more often, the targets of the Molly Maguires included the Roman Catholic church itself. The *Athlone Sentinel* of January 23, 1846, for example, reported that the Molly Maguires had "wholly demolished" the pews in a Catholic church in Roscommon. Similar attacks and threats on the clergy by secret societies had taken place all over Ireland during the previous half century, in an attempt to regulate the fees charged by the clergy or in response to clerical denunciations of secrecy and violence.[61]

On neither side of the Atlantic can the activities of the Molly Maguires be explained in one-dimensional sectarian terms. In Pennsylvania, the Catholic church waged a concerted campaign against the Mollys. And, while Irish Catholics did fight Welsh Protestants in Pennsylvania, they did so as part of a larger struggle involving issues of status and control in the mines. In Ireland, the Church and the Molly Maguires were frequently at loggerheads; and formal Roman Catholicism had only a very tenuous hold over the peasantry in Irish-speaking counties like Donegal and Mayo, where so many of the American Molly Maguires originated. These were precisely the types of place targeted by the Irish Catholic hierarchy in the "devotional revolution" of the mid nineteenth century, which enforced a new doctrinal discipline in the remoter, least anglicized, and least commercially developed areas of western Ireland.[62]

59. *Roscommon and Leitrim Gazette,* August 9, 1845, quoted in Beames, *Peasants and Power,* 92.

60. On the Mahon episode, and the related case of the Reverend John Lloyd, see Dublin *Freeman's Journal,* November 4, December 9, 1847; April 29, 1848; July 15, 18, 1848; August 10, 1848; Stephen J. Campbell, *The Great Irish Famine: Words and Images from the Famine Museum, Strokestown Park, County Roscommon* (Strokestown, 1994), 46–50; Robert James Scally, *The End of Hidden Ireland: Rebellion, Famine, and Emigration* (New York, 1995), Part 1. See, also, letters by and about the Molly Maguires in the archive of the Famine Museum at Strokestown House.

61. *Athlone Sentinel,* January 23, 1846, quoted in Beames, *Peasants and Power,* 78. Cf. James Warren Doyle, *The Pastoral Address of the Right Rev. Dr. Doyle, R.C. Bishop of Kildare and Leighlin, Against the Illegal Associations of Ribbonmen* (Dublin, 1822); Connolly, *Priests and People,* 116–17, 128–29, 229–30, 239–50, 308–9; James S. Donnelly, Jr., "Irish Agrarian Rebellion: The Whiteboys of 1769–76," *Proceedings of the Royal Irish Academy,* C, 83 (1983): 322, and "The Rightboy Movement, 1785–88," *Studia Hibernica,* 17 & 18 (1977–78): 163–71.

62. Emmet Larkin, "The Devotional Revolution in Ireland, 1850–75," *American Historical Review,* 77 (June 1972): 625–52; David W. Miller, "Irish Catholicism and the Great Famine," *Journal of Social History,* 9 (Fall 1975): 81–98.

This Romanization of Irish Catholicism involved the introduction of regular devotional practices and the eradication of residual cultural forms, including holy wells, fairies, curses, cures, and above all, wakes. In few places did these forms survive so robustly as in west Donegal, where as few as 20 percent of the population attended Sunday mass on a weekly basis, compared to figures as high as 80 percent and more in the anglicized east of Ireland. Religious practice in remote areas like west Donegal tended to syncretize formal Catholic beliefs with folk custom and popular magic. This is not to say that the Donegal Irish were in any way pre-Catholic or non-Catholic; they doubtless regarded themselves as devoutly Catholic, even if their version of the religion differed markedly from that of the metropolitan hierarchy. But even without the violence, there would surely have been a profound cultural conflict between the Molly Maguires and the Catholic hierarchy on both sides of the Atlantic.[63]

County Donegal, and especially its western portion, was of central importance in the Molly Maguire story. A detailed examination of its distinctive economic, social, and cultural history is therefore in order. The second largest county in Ireland, Donegal was composed of three separate regions, only one of which made a significant contribution to the Molly Maguire story. East Donegal, where the land was fertile, shared in the general prosperity of Ulster. The southern section of the county, around Ballyshannon and Donegal Town, was also quite prosperous. But more than half the county's land was uncultivated, and most of this waste and bog land lay in its western section, one of the poorest and most isolated places in Ireland and the birthplace of many of the American Molly Maguires. "The wastelands of this county are more extensive than any other in Ireland, with the exception of Mayo," as one British government report noted, "and owing to the wetness of the climate and nature of the subsoil, they are probably the least improvable."[64] Contemporary British observers described west Donegal in the bleakest terms, the following account being typical:

> The coast, over the greater part of the distance, is singularly broken and intersected . . . the sea-board is almost a chaos,—a dismal wilderness of bog and pool, of barren sand and naked rock,—a tract of desolation in which moors, ponds, shivering torrents, drifting sands, and denuded granite, are mingled in utter melée, and severally striving for the mastery.

63. Figures from Miller, "Irish Catholicism and the Great Famine," 89–94; cf. Kenny, "The Molly Maguires and the Catholic Church."

64. *Evidence Taken Before Her Majesty's Commissioners of Inquiry into the State of the Law and Practice in Respect to Occupation of the Land,* 2 vols.(Dublin, 1845), vol. 1, 49. Hereafter referred to as Report of the Devon Commission. According to the *Parliamentary Gazetteer of Ireland, 1844–45* (Dublin, London, and Edinburgh, 1845), Donegal consisted of 1,193,443 acres, of which 393,191 were arable and 759,587 uncultivated, the remainder being composed of lakes, towns, and "continuous plantations" (p.33).

Descriptions of this sort certainly captured the isolated character of the region, though they in no way did justice to its unique, rugged beauty.[65]

Between the towns of Dungloe and Gweedore lay the Irish-speaking area known as the Rosses, sixty thousand rock-strewn acres situated in the upper section of the Barony of Boylagh. The term *na rossa* means "headlands" in Donegal Irish, and the area in question is composed of a series of islands and inlets, along with a bleak and rugged interior. "Even amidst the wilds of Boylagh and Bannagh are cultivated and well-peopled valleys, but the district of the Rosses presents mostly a desolate waste," one contemporary reported. North of the Rosses lay an equally impoverished Irish-speaking region, Cloughaneely, "entirely composed of disjointed rocks and dark heath, except where, at a lesser elevation near the sea, a stunted swarth appears." The most common names in the Rosses and Cloughaneely were O'Donnell, Gallagher, Sweeney, Boyle, Duffy, McGehan (or McGeehan), and Mulhearn, names that occurred with remarkable frequency among the American Molly Maguires.[66]

The land in the Rosses, and indeed almost the entire Barony of Boylagh, belonged to a single absentee landlord, the Marquis of Conyngham. When they were resident in Ireland, the Conynghams lived in Slane Castle, County Meath. The marquis in the mid nineteenth century visited his Donegal estate only once in his lifetime, staying for a couple of days. The tenants held their land at the will of their absentee landlord; there were no leases, and hence no security of tenure. But there were very few evictions on the estate; arrears of rents stretched back for years, and the Conyngham estate was, to say the least, not a profitable enterprise. To the north of the Conyngham estate lay the estate of Lord George Hill, which included most of Gweedore parish; and the biggest landowner north of Gweedore was Lord Leitrim. Unlike Conyngham, both Hill and Leitrim were resident on their estates. There were also several smaller estates in the region.[67]

Both Conyngham and Hill tried to introduce a new form of landholding on their estates in the 1830s and 1840s. Their aim was to abolish the system of communal landholding known as rundale, which stretched back to the Middle Ages and had long since died out in other parts of Ireland. Instead of holding their land in single plots, the tenants held it in small, geographically scattered pieces, graded according to the quality of land available. With constant subdivision of holdings among the children of each family, the number of holdings increased and their size diminished, so that tenants often held their land in a

65. *The Parliamentary Gazetteer of Ireland,* 34. The six baronies of Donegal were Innishowen, to the north; Raphoe to the east; Tyrhugh to the south; Bannagh to the southwest; Boylagh to the west; and Kilmacrenan to the northwest. See map 2.

66. Quotes from Samuel Lewis, *A Topographical Dictionary of Ireland,* 2 vols. (London, 1837), vol. 1, 473. See map 2.

67. The Conyngham estate is described by Foster, *Letters on the Condition of the People,* 98–111. The prevalence of tenantry-at-will was noted in the Report of the Devon Commission, vol. 1, 148, 151, 164. See, also, Proinnsias Ó Gallchobhair, *The History of Landlordism in Donegal* (Ballyshannon, 1975), chapters 2, 3.

dozen or more places. One tenant in Donegal in the 1840s reportedly held his land in forty-two different places, and a half acre of land on the estate of Lord George Hill was held by twenty-six men. The practice of rundale even extended to the ownership of animals. Rundale had been abolished on the Conyngham estate (except on the remote island of Arranmore) by the mid-1840s, but on the Hill estate the campaign against it was more protracted.[68]

Hill set about abolishing the system as soon as he acquired his estate in 1837. The tenants held strips of rundale land, graded according to quality, in an "infield" where they grew crops. Between the infield and the mountainous areas was an "outfield," also held in common. Rights of outfield cultivation, mountain grazing, and seaweed cultivation were allotted in proportion to holdings in the infield. The people of this community lived together in "clachans," clusters of buildings erected by the shore, adjacent to the infield. These were not "villages" in any real sense, as they lacked stores, churches, public houses, and other amenities. Many of the tenants practiced a form of transhumance, grazing their livestock on the mountain in the summer, when the infield was under crops, and taking them to the islands for the winter. The livestock were typically moved on May 1 and November 1, the same dates when seasonal migrants left and returned, when half-yearly rents were due, and when agrarian violence elsewhere in Ireland often coincided with the religious holidays inaugurating the summer and winter seasons.[69]

Determined to abolish this ancient system of land use, Hill set about dividing the land into square farms of six to ten acres. The only incident of violent resistance occurred when he tried to create new farms out of the outfield, thereby depriving the tenants of their rights to common cultivation and, more importantly, cutting off access to the mountain. In response, bands of men tore down the fencing in the outfield. This resistance was short-lived, however, and Hill pressed ahead with his "improvements."He had already substantially reduced access to the mountain by reserving twelve thousand acres (more than half the estate) to graze his own livestock, impounding any of his tenants' cattle that happened to stray onto his part of the mountain.[70]

Even in the face of these reforms, the remarkable fact about the history of west Donegal in the 1840s was how little violence there was, especially by comparison with north-central Ireland, where the Molly Maguire agitation was at its peak. A survey of the reports of the annual assizes in the local newspapers reveals no pattern of organized resistance. And the investigation of the Devon Commission into the causes of agrarian "outrages" found no history of such

68. Report of the Devon Commission, vol. 1, 147, 152, 164, 429; Lord George Hill, *Facts from Gweedore* (5th ed., London, 1887), 23, 26. On rundale in Arranmore, see Foster, *Letters on the Condition of the People,* 110. On rundale elsewhere in Ireland, see Kevin Whelan, "Pre- and Post-famine Landscape Change," in Cathal Póirtéir, ed., *The Great Irish Famine* (Cork, 1995), 23–24; Campbell, *The Great Irish Famine,* 14–16; Scally, *The End of Hidden Ireland,* Part 1, especially 13, 29–30, 76.

69. Hill, *Facts From Gweedore,* viii–ix, 15–25; Douglas, "Emigration and Irish Peasant Life," 9–11.

70. Foster, *Letters on the Condition of the People,* 121–22; Hill, *Facts from Gweedore,* xiv–xv, 40–42; Ó Gallchobhair, *History of Landlordism in Donegal,* 23.

violence in Donegal. As one witness from the Conyngham estate testified: "Yet, with all this suffering, no disturbance or act of violence has occurred in Donegal during the severe privations of the last summer, when numbers were actually in need of sustenance. There was no dishonesty, no plundering. The people starved, but they would not steal."[71]

If violent resistance to the power of Lord George Hill was futile in the 1830s and 1840s, the tenantry did find more devious and effective ways to resist their landlord's plans. Tenant committees appointed by Hill to expedite his reforms routinely recommended the retention of long, strip farms. As a result, the new "squared" farms were often only a few feet wide but hundreds of yards long. One four-acre farm was reported as being a mile long. In this way, each individual farm consisted of bad as well as good land, retaining the communal emphasis of the old system; at the same time, each tenant retained access to the common lands, in particular the mountain and the seashore. Moreover, parts of the estate reverted to rundale after the early 1840s, and it was clearly being practiced there in the 1850s, when a new round of reforms inaugurated the "sheep wars" of that decade.[72]

The rundale system suggests a fundamentally different conception of property from the rationalized compartmentalization typical of agrarian capitalism, and there is strong evidence that this conception survived even when the land had been "squared out." The absence of resistance to the innovations of the 1830s and 1840s suggests that the squaring out of land had not radically altered life for most tenants, perhaps because of the compromise of the long strip farm. Despite the efforts of improving landlords, farming practices in west Donegal seem not to have changed substantially throughout the nineteenth century. Tenants continued to divide land among themselves according to customary usage. The standard measure of land by the tenantry of west Donegal, at least until the 1870s, was by quality rather than quantity. Instead of dividing land into acres priced at a specific rent or quantified by a specific measure, they divided it into a measure of use value called "a cow's grass." This was the amount of mountain land required to graze a cow for a year, along with the amount of arable land required to grow fodder to feed it in the winter. Depending on the quality of the land, the actual size of "a cow's grass" could vary considerably.[73] Nor did the attempt to abolish rundale entail an end to the system of partible inheritance, whereby land was divided among all the children

71. The assizes were reported in the *Ballyshannon Herald* each July. Quote from Report of the Devon Commission, vol. 1, 151.

72. Hill, *Facts from Gweedore,* xiii; Douglas, "Emigration and Irish Peasant Life," 14. On the survival of rundale in parts of the Gweedore area until the 1930s, see E. Estyn Evans, Introduction, *Facts from Gweedore,* v. On the "sheep wars," see below.

73. Foster, *Letters on the Condition of the People,* 104; Hill, *Facts from Gweedore,* 26; cf. Cousens, "The Regional Pattern of Emigration During the Great Irish Famine," 125. A "cow's foot" was half a "cow's grass," a "cow's toe" was a quarter, and a "sheep's foot" a sixteenth. For a strikingly similar measurement of land in terms of subsistence in twentieth-century Vietnam, see Scott, *The Moral Economy of the Peasant,* 47.

rather than bequeathed to the eldest son. The individually rented farms introduced in the 1830s and 1840s were constantly subdivided. Each new farm, which required an additional rent, was called a "new cut." Any improvements on these farms were met with an increase in rent. Elsewhere in Ireland, partible inheritance came to an end after the Great Famine of the 1840s. It survived until the early twentieth century in west Donegal, where the system of landholding retained a structure characteristic of prefamine rather than postfamine Ireland.[74]

The landholding system in question yielded only a very bare subsistence, bordering on destitution. Squalid poverty was the norm in west Donegal in the 1840s and 1850s, as was frequently noted by outside observers. "From one end of his large estate here to the other, nothing is to be found but poverty, misery, wretched cultivation, and infinite subdivision of land," Thomas Campbell Foster wrote from the estate of Marquis of Conyngham in 1845. "There are no gentry, no middle class,—all are poor—wretchedly poor. Every shilling the tenants can raise from their half-cultivated land is paid in rent, whilst the people subsist for the most part on potatoes and water."[75] Pigs, ducks, and even cattle were often housed on one side of the thatched cottages; the family slept together on loose hay on the other side of the dwelling.[76]

Most of the farms were ten acres or less, just sufficient for a family to raise enough crops to live on and to graze an animal or two in order to pay the rent. The bulk of the population of west Donegal were precarious tenant farmers, typically without leases or security of tenure, who drew what living they could from the stony, unproductive soil. Holding land as a tenant was by no means a sign of prosperity. Whereas tenant farmers in rural England and parts of southern Ireland were generally better off than laborers, distinctions between these two classes were negligible in the west of Ireland, where landholdings were precariously small. Indeed, one witness at the Devon Commission testified that the small farmers of Donegal were worse off than the minority of locals who worked as wage laborers and at least had regular employment.[77]

The economy of the peasantry in west Donegal remained largely self-sufficient and isolated from the dictates of the market. Tenants grew their own oats and potatoes and supplemented this diet with seaweed, peppered water, and occasionally, salt fish. Clothing was homemade and, in the case of women and children, rudimentary to the point of scandalizing visitors from abroad. Few men worked for wages, except on a temporary basis. "There are very few of them indeed who depend on being hired as laborers," a witness from Dungloe testified before the Devon Commission. "Almost every one has a lot of ground with his house, which occupies a large portion of his time in the cultivation of

74. RSCD, x; Miller, *Emigrants and Exiles,* 434.

75. Foster, *Letters on the Condition of the People,* 103.

76. Ibid., 106; RSCD, x.

77. Report of the Devon Commission, vol. 1, 161; cf. Scott, *The Moral Economy of the Peasant,* passim, on the maintenance of subsistence as the moral basis of peasant revolt.

it."[78] Women sometimes took in piece work from the clothing manufacturers of Derry, knitting stockings, sewing embroidery, and finishing shirts, typically at "grossly exploitive" wages.[79] Money to pay the rent was raised by selling all the produce except potatoes, or by raising a cow with the sole purpose of selling it for cash to pay the rent. Some families were forced to buy a heifer on credit at an exorbitant price and sell it a considerably lower price, simply to pay the rent and local taxes.[80]

An alternative source for paying annual expenses was seasonal migrant labor. More than a quarter of a family's receipts might come from seasonal labor in the Lagan Valley of east Donegal, in the Foyle Valley around Belfast, or in rural Scotland. Donegal was second only to County Mayo in the number of harvest workers it sent to Scotland each summer, and the great majority of these men (there were no women) came from the western seaboard. While some historians have seen seasonal labor as undermining the peasant economy of west Donegal, it is perhaps better seen as a central component of the subsistence economy. Migrant labor allowed the distinctive way of life in west Donegal to survive longer than it otherwise would have, preserving until the 1880s social practices considered more typical of prefamine than postfamine Ireland.[81]

Seasonal migration did introduce the people of west Donegal to the idea of permanent emigration, which would eventually undermine the old way of life. But the experience of migration to Scotland may well have conditioned the emigrants from west Donegal to the United States to regard their removal as temporary rather than permanent, even if few immigrants from Donegal actually succeeded in returning to Ireland. At the same time, migrant labor for Protestant employers in Ulster and Scotland gave the people of west Donegal at least some exposure to the nature of labor in a capitalist marketplace and a predisposition to understand it in terms of religious bigotry. Together, these developments explain, at least in part, the sense of alienation and rootlessness so evident among the Molly Maguires in Pennsylvania.[82]

This alienation was compounded by a final cultural peculiarity of the people of west Donegal. Unlike the majority of people in nineteenth-century Ireland (and the majority of Irish immigrants to the United States), they were native speakers of the Irish language and remained so in the postfamine period. Irish was most widely spoken at this time in the counties of the far west:

78. Foster, *Letters on the Condition of the People,* 106–7; Report of the Devon Commission, vol. 1, 161; quote, 164; RSCD, 393.

79. Miller, *Emigrants and Exiles,* 372. See, also, Crawford, *The Handloom Weavers,* 72.

80. Foster, *Letters on the Condition of the People,* 104. The county cess was an annual tax paid to the local authorities.

81. Ó Gráda, "Seasonal Migration and Post-famine Adjustment in the West of Ireland"; Johnson, "Harvest Migration from Nineteenth-Century Ireland"; Handley, *The Irish in Scotland,* chapter 2; Douglas, "Emigration and Irish Peasant Life," 12–13. Ó Gráda's interpretation is followed here.

82. Two emigrants from west Donegal who did eventually return were Patrick O'Donnell, a cousin of the suspected Molly Maguires killed by vigilantes at Wiggans Patch (see chapter 7); and James Campbell, a brother of the executed Molly Maguire, Alexander Campbell. See Patrick Campbell, *A Molly Maguire Story* (Jersey City, N.J., 1992), 1.

Donegal, Sligo, Mayo, north Roscommon, Galway, Clare, Limerick, Kerry, and Cork. In Mayo in 1851, for example, between 50 and 80 percent of the population were Irish speakers, and on the county's western seaboard the figure was as high as 80 percent. In Sligo and most of Donegal, the figure was 25 to 50 percent; in western Donegal between 50 and 80 percent of the people spoke Irish, and there were areas within this western section where more than 80 percent spoke Irish as their first or only language.[83] "The people here are for the most part the aboriginal Irish and speak the Erse language," Thomas Campbell Foster reported from west Donegal in 1845. Not until the 1890s did English become widespread in this part of Ireland, and today it is one of the last bastions of Irish-speaking *gaeltacht* culture.[84]

From Detective McParlan's field reports it is clear that many of the alleged Molly Maguires in Pennsylvania could not read or write English. It was because of the illiteracy of his fellow-members of the AOH in Shenandoah, McParlan claimed, that he was appointed to the post of secretary of that lodge after he had infiltrated the organization.[85] In counties Galway, Mayo, and Donegal, 85 percent of Catholics were illiterate as late as the 1840s. Strictly speaking, of course, they "were not illiterate but preliterate: through the oral medium they transmitted a rich robust, traditional culture."[86] Language was a crucial component of the territorial identity that appears to have been at the heart of Molly Maguireism on both sides of the Atlantic. "Irish-speakers," as one historian has observed, "maintained an . . . intimate relationship with the natural features of their environment: the shapes and colors of the landscape—the birds, trees, rivers, rocks, and hills of their native surroundings. They lavished names on the land; every field, cleft, and hollow had a distinctive appellation which recalled some ancient owner or legendary occurrence."[87]

Significant numbers of the Irish immigrants in Pennsylvania came from a preliterate Gaelic culture, marking them off as fundamentally different not only from the Welsh and the English, but also from the people of eastern and southern Ireland, where much of the population had little or no knowledge of the Irish language. It was these Irish-speakers, and not the Irish in general, who became "Molly Maguires" in Pennsylvania. There can be no doubt that substantial numbers of Irish speakers made their way from Donegal to Pennsylvania, where they featured prominently in the Molly Maguire story. For example, in June 1877, a reporter of the *New York Sun* visited Alexander Campbell's hotel at Lansford, Carbon County, where a boisterous wake was being held the day after Campbell's execution. He found that some of the women leading the "keening" (emotional lamentations peculiar to Irish wakes) did so in Irish—in part,

83. Foster, *Modern Ireland,* 517. In the other relevant counties—Cavan, Fermanagh, Monaghan, Tyrone, and Derry—less than 25 percent of the population spoke Irish.

84. Foster, *Letters on the Condition of the People,* 120.

85. Broehl, *The Molly Maguires,* 176.

86. Miller, *Emigrants and Exiles,* 71.

87. Ibid., 92; cf. Guha, *Elementary Aspects of Peasant Insurgency,* 279, on the concept of territoriality.

the reporter thought, so that their curses on the Pennsylvania authorities, the informers, and the Pinkertons, could go undetected by strangers like himself.[88] One of the witnesses at Campbell's trial was a sixty-year-old woman, Mrs. Celia O'Donnell, whose testimony had to be translated to the court by a bilingual interpreter, John McGinley. Like Mrs. O'Donnell, who spoke only Irish, McGinley bore a classic Donegal surname.[89] The informer Daniel Kelly (also known as "Manus Cull" and "Kelly the Bum") was also an Irish speaker, and he told the Pinkertons that the assassins of Alexander Rea were all Irish-speakers as well.[90] Another executed Molly Maguire, James Roarity, was a native Irish speaker; he was apparently bilingual, though his wife could speak only Irish.[91] Campbell, Kelly, and the Roaritys all came from the same region in west Donegal, in and around the Rosses.

This preponderance of native Irish speakers makes the Molly Maguires quite distinctive in terms of the general pattern of Irish settlement in the United States. Though significant numbers of Irish-speakers left western Ireland for America during the Great Famine, the West as a whole and Donegal in particular had much lower rates of emigration than the rest of Ireland in the immediate postfamine era. The Molly Maguires were among the relatively few emigrants who left Donegal in the 1850s, 1860s, and 1870s. They were also among the relatively few emigrants to leave the western, Irish-speaking regions of Ireland as a whole in the same period. It was not until the 1880s that Irish-speakers once again became a significant presence among Irish emigrants to the United States. The Irish-speaking Molly Maguires who made their way to Pennsylvania, therefore, stand out as quite anomalous in the American context. Because of their language, culture, and customs, they were the archetypal "wild Irish," noticeably and ominously different from the mass of Irish immigrants.

As for violence in Donegal, there was no sustained tradition of agrarian agitation there in the first half of the nineteenth century, even as the agrarian tradition reached its peak elsewhere in Ireland. The remote wastelands of west Donegal never experienced the transformation typical of the fertile lands of Leinster and Munster, or even the grazing country of Roscommon and Mayo. The land was simply too poor. There was little profit to be gained from consolidating it into large holdings, and no prospect of converting it from tillage to dairy farming. But there were some signs of trouble on the land in Donegal in the 1850s and 1860s, including reports that the "Molly Maguires" were active.

88. *New York Sun,* June 23, 1877.

89. *sh,* December 29, 1876.

90. HSP, SC, PNDA, "Synopsis for Mr. Gowen, September 1, 1876" includes the statement of Manus Cull, a.k.a. Daniel Kelly, dated August 22, 1876. The following day Linden reported that Cull told him of Rea's assassins that "they all speak Irish."

91. Campbell, *A Molly Maguire Story,* 156.

The trouble had to do with a brief-lived but highly disruptive experiment in intensive sheep farming. While the land of west Donegal was not suitable for cattle farming, a number of local landlords introduced flocks of black-faced sheep from Scotland in the mid-1850s. In some cases, tracts of land were leased to graziers who came over from Scotland with the sheep; in others, such as the Hill estate, the landlord became more directly involved, hiring Scottish shepherds to tend the sheep. But in each case, the impact on the local tenantry was the same: Large amounts of common land, on which the tenants had traditionally grazed their own animals, were reserved for sheep farming. Animals who strayed onto this land were impounded.

The conflict provoked by this experiment in large-scale sheep farming pitted the moral economy of the peasantry against the legalistic market economy of the landlords and the authorities. According to witnesses who testified at an inquiry into the disturbed state of west Donegal in 1857, "the privilege of free commonage had been enjoyed [by the tenants] from 'time immemorial.'"[92] The British government commission that sat to consider these complaints disagreed. "No attempt has been made to drive the tenants from their holdings, or to take from them any land over which they had *real* rights," as the authors of the Majority Report put it.[93] From the tenants' point of view the landlords' intrusion was entirely arbitrary; from the landlords' point of view the tenants' rights were illusory, because they had not been written down. The report of 1857 noted: "It appears to your committee that an erroneous opinion exists in the minds of these people as to their rights over the mountains near which they reside and that their not being well-advised on this point has led to the outrages which have been committed."[94] Here, then, were the classic preconditions for agrarian violence, which generally rested on some legitimizing notion of right. In the preliterate culture in question, the basis of that notion was customary rather than codified law. In defense of this standard of justice, the tenants of west Donegal forcibly resisted the innovations of their landlords.

The violence, which began in 1857 and lasted intermittently until 1863, exhibited some of the classic features of "Whiteboyism." Bands of men dressed in white shirts visited shepherds at night, warning them to leave the country. Several thousand sheep were reported maliciously killed in the Rosses and Kilmacrenan. They were found on the mountainsides, with their ribs beaten in, their testicles tied together to prevent breeding, or their heads cut off. Carcasses and bags of wool were found in bogs and other places of burial. The trouble was blamed on "midnight legislators," "Whiteboys," and "Ribbonmen." The term "Molly Maguires" was also used occasionally. The authorities responded by imposing a sheep tax on all the tenantry to pay for the animals lost, along with a police tax to fund an extra force of constabulary. Several local men

92. RSCD, ix.

93. Ibid., iii; italics added.

94. Ibid., iii.

were sentenced to penal servitude abroad and several more to terms in prison with hard labor.[95]

Yet, there are very good reasons for doubting that all or even most of the sheep were maliciously killed and, by extension, that any well-organized conspiracy was involved. There can be no doubt that some sheep were mutilated and killed for intimidatory reasons. Others may have been stolen for food or wool, particularly after the onerous sheep and police taxes were imposed. But it is likely that large numbers of sheep simply perished in making the transition to the harsh conditions of Donegal, while many more were stolen by the Scottish shepherds and rustlers from outside the county with whom they were in cooperation.[96] Embattled local landlords, along with policemen and government officials, were quick to blame the disappearance of all the animals on an ominous secret society. But there was a remarkable degree of innuendo and exaggeration surrounding the Donegal "sheep wars" of the late 1850s, just as there would be in the case of the Molly Maguires in Pennsylvania over the next two decades.

Nowhere is this world of rumor and half-truth more evident than in the best-known case of alleged agrarian "outrages" in Donegal, the events that occurred on the Derryveagh estate of John George Adair in the early 1860s. Adair was one of a new generation of Irish-born land speculators who emerged in Ireland after the famine of the 1840s. Like several other local landlords, he became involved in the sheep-farming experiment in the late 1850s. His sheep were tended by imported Scottish shepherds, who impounded cows or horses that strayed onto what had until recently been common pasture land. In response, Adair claimed, his shepherds were attacked and his sheep were mutilated and killed.[97] In this context, Adair carried out one of the more notorious mass evictions in Irish history. On April 8, 1861, 47 families were evicted, after the murder of Adair's steward, James Murray; 244 people, most of them native Irish-speakers, were turned out of their homes, 28 houses were leveled or had their roofs removed, and 11,602 acres of virtually barren land was cleared of human habitation.[98] According to Adair, the murder of his steward was the culmination of a long line of activities engaged in by local representatives of "the infernal combination called the Ribbon Society, which has so fatally spread itself over the country."[99]

But did any such conspiracy exist in west Donegal? Adair was the nephew of William Steuart Trench, from whom he had apparently learned more than the

95. *Ballyshannon Herald*, July 24, 1857; February 26, 1858; August 3, 1860; July 17, 24, 1863; RSCD, 237–54, 349, 352–53, 373–74.

96. RSCD, 68–71, 81–82, 115–16, 167.

97. W. E. Vaughan, *Sheep, Sin and Scotsmen: John George Adair and the Derryveagh Evictions, 1861* (Belfast, 1983); Liam Dolan, *Land War and Eviction in Derryveagh, 1840–1865* (Dundalk, 1980); *Ballyshannon Herald, Derry Journal*, and Dublin *Freeman's Journal*, especially April 1861.

98. Vaughan, *Sin, Sheep and Scotsmen*, 11. Most of the evictees emigrated, but alas for historians of the American Molly Maguires, nearly all of them went to Australia rather than America.

99. Dublin *Freeman's Journal*, December 16, 1861.

ethos of agricultural rationalization typified by the "improving" landlords of postfamine Ireland. He may also have learned from him a peculiar capacity to detect Ribbonism in every instance of rural discontent, however slight, that came to his notice. The most recent historian of the affair has concluded that the Ribbon conspiracy was partly a figment of Adair's imagination, partly a convenient rationale for proceeding with a long-term plan to remodel the Derryveagh estate. It is very doubtful if Ribbonism existed in Derryveagh "before, or even after the Derryveagh evictions. . . . It was predictable, however, that the nephew of William Steuart Trench should imagine that any resistance to his will was hatched in the small hours, aided by deep potions of illicitly distilled whiskey."[100] If Ribbonism and Whiteboyism were generic terms for agrarian violence of all sorts, rather than precise designations of individual organizations, the Adair case was an extreme example of the ideological manipulation of these two terms.

Despite the occasionally hysterical way in which the "sheep wars" were reported, Donegal was generally known for its peacefulness rather than its violence in the 1850s and 1860s. The records of the annual county assizes reveal a significant but small number of cases in which sheep were mutilated or killed. But, in general, the presiding magistrate began the sessions of the assizes in these years by congratulating the assembled gentry on "the peaceable" and "eminently satisfactory state" of their county.[101]

Those who left west Donegal for America in this period presumably had some knowledge of the sheep wars and had doubtless heard something of "Ribbonism" or "Whiteboyism." Once settled in Pennsylvania, some of them went on to practice an American variant of Irish agrarian violence. But the origins of this violence lie as much in the conditions of American industrial life as in any sustained tradition imported from the wilds of northwest Ireland.

The final link in the story, one whose details are mostly missing, is the precise manner whereby the people of north-central and northwest Ireland made their way to the Pennsylvania anthracite region. When did the Molly Maguires leave Ireland, why, and how? Did they go directly to Pennsylvania, or did they break their journeys first in Britain and then in the northeastern United States? Reliable evidence has survived in only a small number of cases; for the remainder, absence of evidence means that these questions simply cannot be answered. Nonetheless, when the surviving documented information is viewed in terms of the general profile of emigration from northwest Ireland in the mid nineteenth century, a suggestive pattern emerges.

100. Vaughan, *Sheep, Sin and Scotsmen,* 31–33, 41–42 (quote, 33). The origins of the Murray murder apparently did not lie in issues of land and property at all. Murray was most probably murdered by another Scotsman, the shepherd Dugald Rankin, who appears to have been Mrs. Murray's lover. The Dublin *Freeman's Journal,* April 17, 1861, claimed that Adair had fallen victim to "imaginary terrors." Local Catholic and Protestant clergymen joined forces to defend the tenantry against charges of violence (*Freeman's Journal,* December 16, 1861).

101. See, for example, *Ballyshannon Herald,* July 23, 1858; August 3, 1860; July 17, 1863 (quote); July 22, 1865.

Many of the American Molly Maguires emigrated from north-central and northwestern Ireland in the 1840s and 1850s, when the Irish Mollys were active. Twenty-one-year-old Patrick Hester came to the United States from County Roscommon in 1846, when the Molly Maguire agitation was at its height in that part of Ireland. Patrick Tully, a native of County Cavan, left Ireland for Scotland in 1844 and came to the United States in either 1854 or 1863. Nineteen-year-old Thomas Munley emigrated to America from County Mayo in 1864, and it is possible that he had some experience with the tensions between large farmers and smallholders that marked that county in the 1860s and 1870s. But there is no evidence that these three men, or any of the other Molly Maguires in Pennsylvania, were involved in the Irish phase of activities.[102]

The same is true of west Donegal. The violence there, such as it was, reached its peak just when many of the future American Molly Maguires were leaving west Donegal for the United States. There is no way of knowing whether any of the people who emigrated to Pennsylvania were involved. But the most significant fact about immigration from Donegal is that it differed sharply from the trajectory followed elsewhere in Ireland. Population loss in the county during the decade of the Great Famine was among the lowest in the country, only one-third the rate in north-central Ireland. Nor were the primary causes of emigration in postfamine Ireland (commercialization of agriculture and a shift from partible inheritance to primogeniture) significant in west Donegal. The typical postfamine emigrant was twenty-two years old and single; men and women emigrated in more or less equal numbers. The same is likely to have been true of west Donegal, but younger sons never faced the same pressure to leave the land as they did in other parts of Ireland. And the availability of work in Scotland meant that seasonal migration was a viable alternative to permanent emigration until the 1880s.[103]

West Donegal is a prime example of the pattern whereby the western seaboard of Ireland retained significant features of the prefamine economy and social structure in the postfamine era. As well as speaking Irish and practicing partible inheritance, people married younger and had larger families than elsewhere in Ireland, allowing for continued population increase, and delaying the onset of mass emigration until the 1880s. The Rosses is a case in point. Emigration was still the exception rather than the norm there in the mid nineteenth century. The population of the region was 8,359 in 1841 and 8,360 in 1851, after a decade in which famine had reduced the population elsewhere in Ireland by as much as a third. Thereafter, the population of the Rosses continued to rise,

102. See appendix 1. PCA, Molly Maguire Collection, typed copy of the "Confession of Patrick Tully made to Capt. Aldersen at Bloomsburg on March 18, 1878," states that Tully "came to this country in 1863 and joined the A.O.H. in Centralia[,] Columbia Co., Columbus McGee, Bodymaster." *MJ*, March 28, 1878, contained two more "confessions" by Tully, the first stating that he came to the United States via Scotland in 1854, the second that he arrived in the United States in 1863.

103. Cecil Woodham-Smith, *The Great Hunger* (London, 1962), 153–55, 189, 288, 309–11; Vaughan and Fitzpatrick, *Irish Historical Statistics*, 5–16; Miller, *Emigrants and Exiles*, 345–53.

even as the number of people in the country as a whole fell rapidly. There were 9,048 people in the Rosses in 1861, 9,614 in 1871, and 10,924 in 1881. It was this distinctive part of western Ireland that produced so many of the American Molly Maguires.[104]

Several of the Molly Maguires were born in the United States of parents who had emigrated in the 1850s or earlier; others made their way to Pennsylvania in the 1860s and 1870s. James Boyle, Thomas Duffy, and Hugh McGehan, all of whom were twenty-five years old at the time of their executions, were either born in the anthracite region of parents from Donegal, or emigrated to the region with their parents as children. John Morris was born in the anthracite region in 1855 to a family of immigrants from Mayo. The members of the extended O'Donnell family from Gweedore were present in the anthracite region by the mid-1860s, though no precise information on their date of arrival has survived. Columbus McGee had also arrived in Schuylkill County from Donegal by that time. James Roarity spent five years working as a stonemason's assistant in Scotland before coming to the United States in 1869, at the age of twenty-three. Along with the American-born Michael Doyle and Edward Kelly, Boyle, Duffy, McGehan, Morris, Roarity, and Charles and James O'Donnell belonged to a younger generation of Molly Maguires, all of whom were in their twenties in the mid-1870s.[105]

The alleged ringleaders of the Molly Maguire conspiracy, by contrast, were generally in their thirties and forties in the 1870s. John Kehoe, who married into the O'Donnell family in Schuylkill County in 1866, was born in 1837.[106] James Carroll (born in Wilkes-Barre of Irish parents and married to another member of the O'Donnell family) was forty years old when he was executed. Patrick Hester, who was older than most, was born in 1825 and left his native County Roscommon for the anthracite region in 1846. Thomas Fisher was born in Donegal in 1837 and came to the United States in 1849. Several other Molly Maguires emigrated from Donegal in the late 1860s, after the sheep wars had ended. The informer Daniel Kelly, born in Donegal in 1842, came to the

104. On the population of the Rosses, see Douglas, "Emigration and Irish Peasant Life," 16. On general patterns of demography and emigration, see S. H. Cousens, "The Regional Pattern of Emigration during the Great Irish Famine," 119–33; Cousens, "Emigration and Demographic Change in Ireland, 1851–1861," *The Economic History Review,* 14 (December 1961): 275–288; Cousens, "The Regional Variations in Population Changes in Ireland, 1861–1881," *The Economic History Review,* 17 (December 1964): 301–21; Brendan M. Walsh, "A Perspective on Irish Population Patterns," *Éire-Ireland: A Journal of Irish Studies,* 4 (Autumn 1969): 3–21; Walsh, "Marriage Rates and Population Pressure: Ireland, 1871 and 1911," *The Economic History Review,* 23 (April 1970): 148–62; Robert E. Kennedy, Jr., *The Irish: Emigration, Marriage, and Fertility* (Berkeley, 1973).

105. For biographical details, see appendix 1. On Columbus McGee, see *or,* ser. 3, vol. 3, 332. Patrick O'Donnell, a cousin of the O'Donnells of Wiggans Patch, left Donegal for Schuylkill County in 1857, at the age of seventeen, before returning to Ireland in 1881 (see chapter 7).

106. Charles A. McCarthy, *The Great Molly Maguire Hoax* (Wyoming, Penn., 1969), 101. Kehoe married Mary Ann O'Donnell (born August 21, 1848, daughter of Manus and Margaret O'Donnell) on September 30, 1866, at St. Ignatius Church, Mahanoy City. Columbus McGee, another Molly Maguire from west Donegal, was a witness. McGee and Kehoe were accused, in the late 1870s, of having assassinated Frank W. Langdon in 1862 (see chapter 8).

United States in 1865. And Alexander Campbell, the alleged ringleader of the Molly Maguires in Carbon County, came to the United States in 1868 at the age of thirty-five, accompanied by a brother and two sisters.[107]

"Within the last ten years, great changes took place in Donegal," the *Ballyshannon Herald* observed on April 13, 1861. The violent protest against these changes was similar to the pattern of Molly Maguire activities that was soon to emerge in Pennsylvania. That does not mean, however, that a preexisting institution called the "Molly Maguires" was imported from Donegal to the United States, directly or via Britain, as part of an ominous transatlantic conspiracy. Given the evidence, no such argument is tenable. Nor, despite the opinion of many hostile contemporaries, is any such argument necessary in making sense of the Molly Maguires. Instead, the immigrants arrived in the United States with a distinctive culture that would be painfully and violently adapted to the equally distinctive way of life they encountered in the Pennsylvania anthracite region. Out of the meeting of these two worlds emerged the American Molly Maguires.

107. For biographies, see appendix 1; on Campbell, see Campbell, *A Molly Maguire Story,* 10.

2

The World of Anthracite

The hard coal district of eastern Pennsylvania was an important industrial center in the nineteenth century. But it was far from the urban paradigm often associated with the industrial revolution. Its cities and towns were separated by long stretches of rural and semirural landscape, much of it mountainous and heavily wooded. Molly Maguireism could never have taken hold in cities like New York or Philadelphia; but the unique geography and topography of the anthracite region were ideally suited to the adaptation to American soil of violent practices derived from the Irish countryside.

What was it like to live in the anthracite region in the nineteenth century? What were the patterns of migration, settlement, and economic development? How did the metropolitan centers differ from the wilder, outlying districts? What was the structure of work in the mines, and how important was national origin in determining occupation? What was the position of women and children in a world dominated by the masculine ethos of mine work? And what sort of labor movement did the mine workers develop before the emergence of the Molly Maguires and trade unionism in the 1860s? The answers to these questions point to a specific conjunction of circumstances that, together with the historical background in Ireland, provides the context necessary for understanding why the Molly Maguire violence in Pennsylvania took the peculiar form it did.

The Molly Maguires were active at different times in different places, and the distinctions between these times and places are of considerable importance. Amid the hysteria of the trials in the mid-1870s, all the crimes, regardless of their timing and location, were blamed on a single, evil conspiracy labeled "Molly Maguireism." But the types of Molly Maguire activity reported in Pennsylvania changed substantially over time, in terms of personnel, ideology, and location. The Molly Maguires, in other words, had a history—and a geography. The starting point for explaining the conflict in Pennsylvania in the 1860s and 1870s is a thorough understanding of the distinctive topography, geology, and economy of the lower anthracite region.

Until the mid eighteenth century, the area of northeastern Pennsylvania that later became known as the anthracite region was populated by the Lenape Indians, who were called "Delawares" by the Euro-American settlers. In 1749 the proprietors of Pennsylvania paid the Lenapes five hundred dollars for the title to the lands that embraced most of the counties that would later produce coal. By 1778 the last of the Lenapes had been driven from the area, and settlement by Euro-Americans was well underway. Because of the gloomy and forbidding character of the landscape, the first settlers referred to the area as "St. Anthony's Wilderness." From the 1820s onward, as the extent and the potential of the coal deposits came to be known, it would be called the anthracite region of Pennsylvania.[1] The coal fields extended across seven counties: Schuylkill, Lebanon, Dauphin, Northumberland, Columbia, Luzerne, and Carbon. Covering an area of 484 square miles, the fields contained the largest concentration of high-ash anthracite in the world. Within this area there were two distinct geographical regions, each including two principal coal beds. The upper anthracite region consisted of the Northern Coal Field and most of the Eastern Middle Coal Field. The largest of these two coal beds, the Northern Field, was located in the upper part of Luzerne County. Fifty-five miles long and between two and six miles wide, its economic center was the city of Scranton. The second bed, the Eastern Middle Field, was the smallest of the four, covering an area of thirty-seven square miles. With the town of Hazleton at its center, it lay primarily in the southern end of Luzerne County, though its southwestern tip jutted into northeastern Schuylkill County, the heartland of the lower anthracite region.[2]

The lower region contained the other two coal beds. The Western Middle Field, thirty-six miles long and four to five miles wide, extended from the towns of Treverton and Shamokin in Northumberland County, across the southern tip of Columbia County, and on through northern Schuylkill County. It included the towns of Ashland, Girardville, Shenandoah, and Mahanoy City, the chief centers of Molly Maguire activity in the 1870s. Finally, the largest of the four coal

1. Munsell, *History of Schuylkill County,* 21–32.

2. Perry K. Blatz, "Ever-Shifting Ground: Work and Labor Relations in the Anthracite Coal Industry, 1868–1903" (Ph.D. diss., Princeton University, 1987), 6–15. See map 3.

beds, the Southern Coal Field, extended all the way across central Schuylkill County, westward across the northern tip of Lebanon County and central Dauphin County, and eastward through Carbon County to two other infamous centers of Molly Maguire activity, Lansford and Mauch Chunk. The Southern Field was about fifty miles long and reached eight miles at its widest point. Its geographical, economic, and political center was Pottsville, the seat of Schuylkill County.[3]

There were important geological and economic differences between the upper and lower regions. In the Northern Field, the anthracite lay in horizontal, or only slightly pitched, seams. It could therefore be blasted out of the coal face without much difficulty. In the two middle fields, the coal lay in a wide variety of inclines, from moderate to steep. In the Southern Field, where the seams generally pitched very steeply, the coal strata had been subjected to more powerful lateral forces in the course of mountain formation, so that they lay in undulating seams, sometimes tilting almost to the vertical. This made it much more difficult to extract the coal. Due to erosion, the tops of the coal seams in the south had often been sheared off, so that some of the coal lay on or just beneath the surface, where it was readily accessible to small entrepreneurs. But the bulk of the coal lay far below the ground. The Southern Field was the deepest of the four coal beds, reaching a depth of three thousand feet and more in the area around Pottsville, where the best coal was to be found.[4]

The irony is that the upper region had the type of economic structure the lower region needed in order to overcome the obstacles of geology. Only large-scale corporations had sufficient resources to sink deep shafts, erect massive breakers, and maintain the extensive operations necessary for mining deep-lying coal. But, until the 1870s, the economy of the lower anthracite region was run by small operators rather than large corporations. The coal industry of the upper region was dominated, from the beginning, by a few large companies, most of them railroad corporations who mined coal as well as carried it. The most powerful were the Delaware & Hudson Canal, and the Delaware, Lackawanna & Western Railroad, in the Northern Field; and the Lehigh Coal & Navigation Company, in the Western Middle Field. The first two had outlets in New York City rather than Pennsylvania. As a result, the coal trade of upper Luzerne County was always directed eastward rather than southward. The Lehigh Company had outlets in both Philadelphia and New York, but the coal trade of the Lehigh Region (the Western Middle Field) was generally affiliated with that of the Northern Field. In the lower region, the transportation links, first by river, then by canal and railroad, pointed the trade southeastward, so that Philadelphia was always the principal outlet for Schuylkill coal.[5]

3. Ibid., 6–15.

4. Munsell, *History of Schuylkill County,* 38.

5. Clifton K. Yearley, Jr., *Enterprise and Anthracite: Economics and Democracy in Schuylkill County, 1820–1875* (Baltimore, 1961), passim, especially 44–50; Edward J. Davies, *The Anthracite Aristocracy: Leadership and Social Change in the Hard Coal Regions of Northeastern Pennsylvania, 1800–1930* (DeKalb, Ill., 1985), passim.

The large corporate enterprises that dominated Luzerne County lent an air of stability to its coal industry, and the northern region was always less turbulent than the lower fields. In general, the workers in the northern region worked in large mines controlled by big corporations, allowing for somewhat tighter discipline in the workplace. As late as 1870, there were still 160 operators in the lower region running more than 200 collieries, compared to only 25 coal companies in the north, who ran 90 collieries but produced more than twice as much coal. The 91 collieries in Schuylkill County in that year employed 15,778 men, while the 90 collieries in Luzerne County, where all the northern trade was based, employed 28,016. The large companies in the upper region also tended to pay higher rates; miners on wages in 1870 made $2.65 a day in the north, compared to $2.33 in the south.[6]

In sharp contrast to the upper region, the lower coal fields, and especially Schuylkill County, were characterized by a large number of small, individual operators. Until the mid-1870s, an average of 100 mining operations were active in the county each year. In 1853, for example, 86 different operators ran 115 collieries in Schuylkill County and employed 9,972 miners and laborers.[7] One historian has identified 585 individual mining enterprises active in Schuylkill County between 1820 and 1875, which he estimated as half the total number of operations in the county in that period. Of these, fewer than 50 percent survived the first year of operation, 78 percent failed before the end of the fifth year, 87 percent by the end of the tenth, and 94 percent by the end of the fifteenth.[8]

At no time prior to the early 1870s was the Schuylkill coal trade as tightly concentrated as in the upper region. There were large operations as well as small ones in the lower region, of course; by the late 1850s, for example, 25 percent of the operators were producing 66 percent of the coal in Schuylkill County.[9] But, as one historian has aptly put it, Schuylkill County "was the bastion of comparatively small-scale, unincorporated, individual enterprise: the enterprise of lone proprietors, partners, and to a much lesser extent of unchartered companies." The evolution of the coal industry in the lower anthracite region was a matter of "the rise and fall of a deeply rooted, pervasive nineteenth-century American social ideal, the ideal of individual entrepreneurship."[10]

In the early 1870s, Franklin B. Gowen and the Reading Railroad set out to duplicate the situation in the north, buying up tens of thousands of acres of coal lands in a successful effort to bring the industry of the lower region under the control of a single corporation. By 1875, only thirty-six of the region's

6. PBIS I, 341–43, 365–66; *Ninth Census,* vol. 3 (Washington, 1872), 786–77; Davies, *The Anthracite Aristocracy,* 115.

7. Samuel T. Wiley, *Biographical and Portrait Cyclopedia of Schuylkill County, Pennsylvania* (Philadelphia, 1893), 127.

8. Yearley, *Enterprise and Anthracite,* 58–59. Those operators who failed, of course, often worked more than one mine, or moved to another mine after the failure.

9. Yearley, *Enterprise and Anthracite,* 66.

10. Ibid., 15–16.

collieries would remain in the hands of individual operators. Gowen's campaign to win control of the Schuylkill industry led directly to the second wave of Molly Maguire activities, which peaked in the violent summer of 1875. The economy of the lower region did eventually come to resemble the economy of the upper region, but only at the price of destroying a trade union movement and eradicating the Molly Maguires, the two forms of organized labor that stood in the way of Gowen's grand designs.[11]

The economic differences between the upper and lower mining regions explain in large measure why the latter rather than the former became the center of both trade unionism and Molly Maguireism. The higher wages in the north, together with larger work units and tighter discipline, posed a serious obstacle to the formation of a regionwide labor movement. As the Pennsylvania Bureau of Industrial Statistics reported in 1873:

> The great mining companies, . . . by concert of action that enabled them to control to a greater degree the issue of contracts between employers and employed, did much to prevent the isolated conflicts and strikes that in Schuylkill and the other lower counties were so prolific of dissension, bitterness and disaster.[12]

When the anthracite workers formed a trade union in 1868, the initiative came from the lower region; over the next seven years the men in the north rarely supported their striking brethren in the south. And, if the upper region differed from the lower in terms of trade unionism, it did so even more starkly in terms of Molly Maguire activities. There were sporadic reports of Molly Maguireism in the upper region in the 1870s, but by and large the area remained free of the type of violence that characterized the lower region. The absence of corporate control and the general instability of the economy in the south made for a much more turbulent society. It was here, rather than in the north, that the Molly Maguires were active. And at the center of the violence was Schuylkill County.

An average of thirty miles long and twenty-four miles wide, Schuylkill County consists of a series of hills, valleys, and mountain chains intersected by gaps at irregular intervals. The Southern Field extends westward across the entirety of

11. Ibid., 211. Even before 1875, the bulk of the land in the lower region had fallen into the hands of a small group of powerful landowners, many of them based in Philadelphia and New York. But, in contrast to the situation in the upper region, these landowners did not enter the business of carrying coal, and most of them did not mine coal either. Instead, they leased their holdings out to small operators, making mining rights accessible to thousands of individual entrepreneurs on short-term leases, thereby discouraging long-term investment and encouraging the operators to move from mine to mine in rapid succession as the surface coal in each was exhausted. Yearley, *Enterprise and Anthracite,* 44–50. On the violence of 1875, see chapters 6 and 7 of the present work.

12. PBIS I, 364.

southern Schuylkill County, bounded by Sharp Mountain to the south and Locust and Broad mountains to the north. The northern portion of the county contains a small section of the Eastern Middle Coal Field and about half the Western Middle Coal Field. Located in the latter are the towns of Ashland, Girardville, Shenandoah, and Mahanoy City, the stronghold of the Molly Maguires in the 1870s. The valleys in which Shenandoah and Mahanoy City were situated were separated by Bear Ridge, which rose to a height of five hundred feet between them. The Western Middle Field as a whole lay between Broad and Mahanoy mountains, which enclosed it on the north, south, and east.[13]

These geographical considerations are central to any understanding of the Molly Maguires in Pennsylvania. Despite a distance of less than fifteen miles, the northern part of Schuylkill County was remarkably isolated from the southern part of the county. The Western Middle Field was cut off from the Southern Field by a series of hills and mountains, broken only by a gap at Ashland, through which Mahanoy Creek flowed down to the Susquehanna River. The citizens of Pottsville, the largest and most cosmopolitan urban setting in the lower anthracite region, referred to the wild territory around Shenandoah as "over the mountain," and it was there that most of the violence in the 1870s occurred. Indeed, it is difficult to imagine how Molly Maguireism could have prospered in a more urbanized and better policed environment. There might well have been violence, but it would surely have taken a different form; it could scarcely have come so close to duplicating the pattern of agitation in the Irish countryside.

Though the lower anthracite region was undergoing an industrial revolution in the mid nineteenth century, its landscape and social structure were far removed from the model suggested by the urban, factory town. It was, instead, an area where most of the terrain was mountainous and heavily wooded, and where much of the work was conducted underground. Fifteen of its thirty-six townships were rural in 1870; populated mainly by German-American farmers, they were located for the most part in the lower part of the county, below the Southern Coal Field. The county's twenty-four urban settlements (incorporated from the townships as separate boroughs) were situated mostly in the mining section of the county. But, outside these towns and small cities, the mining section consisted primarily of numerous villages and mine patches, semirural in character. This was particularly true of northern Schuylkill County, much of which was settled only in the late 1860s and 1870s.[14]

The most substantial urban settlements in Schuylkill County were Pottsville, St. Clair, Tamaqua, Shenandoah, and Mahanoy City. The first two were located in the south of the county, the metropolitan heart of the Southern Coal Field. Tamaqua lay in the more rural eastern section of the county; and Shenandoah and Mahanoy City were new towns located "over the mountain" in the wild,

13. Munsell, *History of Schuylkill County,* 32–34. See map 3.
14. Ibid., Table of Contents.

rapidly developing north. Unlike Pottsville and St. Clair, these three latter towns were centers of Molly Maguire activity. The differences between and within these various settlements provide one key to understanding the history of the Molly Maguires. The history of the anthracite region in the mid nineteenth century can be told in terms of a conflict between larger urban settlements and less developed areas of the coal fields, and a related conflict within the urban settlements of these less developed areas.

Pottsville, the county seat of Schuylkill and its largest city, was settled in 1800 and laid out as a town by John Pott in 1816. In 1828 Pottsville was incorporated as a borough; by 1830 it contained more than five hundred houses. As the superiority of anthracite for domestic and industrial use became evident in the 1830s, Schuylkill County was the scene of "a wild spirit of speculation and adventure."[15] The population of Pottsville rose from 2,464 in 1830 to 7,515 in 1850, 9,444 in 1860 and 12,384 in 1870, as it became the economic center of the lower anthracite industry and the site of an important iron and steel industry. Pottsville was also the home of the region's leading newspaper, the *Miners' Journal,* established by George Taylor in 1825.[16]

Two miles north of Pottsville lay St. Clair, a large mining town incorporated as a borough in 1850, at which time it had a population of 2,016. By 1860 the population was 4,901 and by 1870 it had risen to 5,726. A decade later, however, because of the depletion of its readily accessible coal and the migration of some of its population to the northern part of the county, its population had fallen to 4,149.[17] One result of the geological obstacles and lack of large-scale capital in the lower region was a pattern of small-scale surface mining, in which the surface coal of the Southern Field was quickly depleted. In parts of the Southern Field the anthracite industry stagnated in the late 1860s and 1870s, despite the presence of abundant supplies of coal far beneath the surface. Operators then moved to the two Middle Fields, in the northern part of the county, where it was somewhat easier to mine coal. The history of St. Clair offers a fine example of this transformation.[18]

A similar pattern is evident elsewhere in the Southern Field. The populations of several boroughs declined in the 1860s and 1870s, even as the population of Schuylkill County as a whole continued to grow and the northern part of the county underwent explosive growth. The population of Tamaqua, for example, had risen from 3,080 to 4,919 between 1850 and 1860 but declined from 5,960 to 5,751 between 1870 and 1880, after the cessation of mining in Tamaqua in 1874.[19] Similarly, Blythe Township, which bordered St. Clair on the east, lay directly on top of the vast coal deposits of the Mammoth Vein, yet the mining industry was in decline there by the 1870s. The population of the

15. Ibid., 44.
16. *Ninth Census,* vol. 1, 254; Davies, *The Anthracite Aristocracy,* 102.
17. *Ninth Census,* vol. 1, 254; Wallace, *St. Clair,* 436–37.
18. Munsell, *History of Schuylkill County,* 40.
19. Ibid., 328.

township fell from a high of 3,778 in 1850 to 3,421 in 1860, before dropping precipitously to 1,924 in 1870.[20] As one contemporary noted:

> Almost immeasurable deposits of anthracite underlie the surface of the township, but at such a depth it cannot be mined successfully in competition with coal obtained more cheaply near the surface in other sections. When the era of deep mining arrives, Blythe will again be the scene of great activity in coal production.[21]

St. Clair, Tamaqua, and Blythe were among several boroughs and townships in the southern half of Schuylkill County to decline in population in the 1870s. At the same time, the population of the northern part of the county began to grow rapidly, as mine operators and mine workers migrated northward and opened new mines. The principal urban settlements in the northern part of Schuylkill County were Mahanoy City and Shenandoah, both of which were formed much later than their counterparts in the south of the county. Mahanoy City, incorporated as a borough in 1864, had a population of 5,533 by 1870 and 6,892 by 1880.[22] Throughout the late 1860s and the 1870s it was noted for its ethnic tensions, especially between Welsh and Irish gangs and fire companies. It was also the scene of the murder of George Major on October 31, 1874, for which the AOH member and alleged Molly Maguire, Daniel Dougherty, was tried and acquitted the following year.[23]

Shenandoah, though it was incorporated only in 1866, quickly became the second largest city in Schuylkill County, after Pottsville. Located in the center of the Schuylkill County portion of the Western Middle Coal Field, its population rose from 2,951 in 1870 to 10,061 in 1880.[24] Its very rapid economic and demographic growth in the 1870s came at precisely the time when it was also reputed to be the chief stronghold of the Molly Maguires. It was here that the Pinkerton Detective James McParlan infiltrated the AOH, eventually being appointed to the post of secretary of the local lodge. Four of the more infamous Molly Maguire crimes were committed in and around Shenandoah: the assassination of Gomer James, at Glover's Grove, just outside the city, on August 14, 1875; of Thomas Gwyther at Girardville, five miles to the east, on the same day; and of Thomas Sanger and William Uren at Raven Run, three miles north of Shenandoah, on September 1, 1875. Shenandoah was also the home of Thomas J. Foster, the fiery young editor of the *Herald,* who repeatedly denounced the Molly Maguires in print and issued strident calls for the formation of vigilante committees after the assassinations of 1875.[25]

Although the lower anthracite region presented an image of general social turbulence to outside observers, it is clear that the turmoil was in large part a

20. *Ninth Census,* vol. 1, 254.
21. Munsell, *History of Schuylkill County,* 158.
22. Ibid., 229.
23. The events in Mahanoy City are discussed in chapters 6 and 7.
24. Munsell, *History of Schuylkill County,* 377.
25. The role of vigilantes is discussed in chapter 7.

matter of an internal struggle between urban, urbanizing, and semirural areas within the region. No Molly Maguire crimes were ever committed in Pottsville, the self-conscious center of civilization and justice in the lower anthracite region. But northern Schuylkill County, with its class and ethnic tensions and its general social instability, was the antithesis of metropolitan Pottsville. Especially in the 1870s, the Molly Maguire episode involved a concerted effort by the authorities in the metropolis to tame the wilder, less developed regions of northern Schuylkill County, western Carbon County, southern Luzerne County, and eastern Northumberland County.[26]

The area in question was a triangle of land stretching from Shamokin (in Northumberland County) northeastward as far as Hazleton (in lower Luzerne County) and eastward through Ashland, Shenandoah, Mahanoy City, Tuscarora, and Tamaqua (all in Schuylkill County) as far as Mauch Chunk, the seat of Carbon County. The infamous social turmoil of the anthracite region, in short, was to be found primarily in its wilder, less settled areas, and in particular the area under consideration. It was here that immigrants from north-central and northwestern Ireland tended to settle. All but two of the twenty Molly Maguires who were hanged lived in this territory. And thirteen of the sixteen Molly Maguire assassinations, including all the killings after 1868, occurred in the triangle of land in question.[27]

Schuylkill County was the stronghold of the Molly Maguires. The population of the county, which stood at 11,311 in 1820, had risen to 60,713 by 1850 and almost doubled during the next two decades, reaching 116,428 by 1870. In that year, 30,856 residents of the county were foreign-born, 630 of them from Scotland, 6,709 from Germany, 9,333 from England and Wales, and 13,465 from Ireland. The Irish-born made up 43.5 percent of the immigrant population, and 11.5 percent of the population as a whole. Given that the vast majority of them worked in the mines rather than in the outlying agricultural areas, the Irish formed an even higher proportion of the population in the mining districts of the county: at least half in most mining townships, and a clear majority in the northern parts of the county settled in the late 1860s and the 1870s.[28]

26. Cf. Dewees, *The Molly Maguires,* 20–21; Moffett, "The Overthrow of the Molly Maguires," 90.

27. See map 3. The other three assassinations occurred in Cass Township, Schuylkill County, in the immediate aftermath of the Civil War.

28. *Census of the United States: 1850* (Washington, 1853), 157; *Population of the United States in 1860* (Washington, 1864), 412; *Ninth Census,* vol. 1, 58, 320. Aggregate data on the national origins of the immigrant population in counties, states, and the United States as a whole, were published for the first time in 1870, improving on the previous categorization of "foreign" and "native." The unpublished manuscript returns did list nativity by country before 1870. None of the censuses recorded counties of origin in Ireland, which would have been particularly useful for the present study. Nor did the published returns in 1870 provide detailed information on the nativity of immigrants in individual townships within American counties, listing them simply as "native" and "foreign-born." Once again, the individual returns must be consulted for this information.

Within this population structure, as might be expected in a newly settled mining region, men outnumbered women. In Schuylkill County in 1850 there were 31,560 males (52 percent) and 29,153 females (48 percent); in 1870 the figures were 59,555 (51.25 percent) and 56,873 (48.75 percent). In neighboring Carbon County, the disparity between the sexes was even greater, though it decreased over time. In 1850 males outnumbered females by 8,684 (55.25 percent) to 7,002 (44.75 percent), and in 1870 by 14,711 (52.25 percent) to 13,433 (47.75 percent).[29] The demographic pattern in the metropolitan centers of the anthracite region differed significantly from that in the more isolated mining areas where the Molly Maguires were active. In Pottsville, for example, females outnumbered males as early as 1850 by 3,845 (51.25 percent) to 3,670 (48.75 percent). In Blythe Township, by contrast, men outnumbered women by 2,055 (54.5 percent) to 1,723 (45.5 percent). In Cass Township, the disparity was identical: 2,244 males (54.5 percent) to only 1,871 females (45.5 percent).[30]

The sex ratios in Cass and Blythe were beginning to converge by 1870, but an even greater disparity was evident in the newly settled regions of northern Schuylkill County, the centers of Molly Maguire activity thereafter. In Pottsville that year, there were 6,503 females (52.5 percent) compared to only 5,881 males (47.5 percent). But in Mahanoy Township, which contained the Molly Maguire strongholds of Shenandoah and Mahanoy City, males outnumbered females by 5,154 (54.75 percent) to 4,246 (45.25 percent). More significantly, the disparity between the sexes in the township's principal urban center in 1870—Mahanoy City, which was infamous for its interethnic violence—was the same percentage, with males outnumbering females by 3,028 (54.75 percent) to 2,505 (45.25 percent). Figures on the age distribution of the population are lacking before 1870, but in that year 22.25 percent of the population of Mahanoy Township, and 22.75 percent of Mahanoy City, consisted of males between the ages of 18 and 45, compared to only 18.75 percent in Pottsville. These figures, along with the disparities in sex ratios, the conditions of labor, and the structure of households, strongly suggest that the more violent areas of the mining region contained higher numbers of young, single, rootless males.[31]

These young men often lived as boarders in the homes of Irish families. Extended households were not the norm in the anthracite region, but they were very common. In addition to a married couple and their children, households

29. Figures computed from *Census of the United States: 1850,* 157; *Population of the United States in 1860,* 412; *Ninth Census,* vol. 1, 634.

30. Figures computed from *Census of the United States: 1850,* 180.

31. Figures computed from *Population of the United States in 1860,* 432–33; *Ninth Census,* vol. 1, 654. Not only do these figures reveal a significant distinction between the metropolis and the isolated mining areas, they also underestimate the degree of that disparity by including all residents, children as well as adults. Among children, sex ratios were obviously more or less equal; among adults, therefore, the preponderance of males over females would have been correspondingly greater. The published census records before 1870 did not make distinctions of this sort within individual counties. The census of 1870 did make some distinctions between age groups on the local level, but only among males.

often included other relatives, or a number of boarders, or in some cases a second family. These households were almost always ethnically exclusive, Irish living with Irish and Welsh with Welsh. In Blythe Township in 1850, for example, thirty-two-year-old Thomas O'Brien, an Irish-born blacksmith, headed a household that included not only his wife and two young children, but also an apprentice blacksmith, seventeen-year-old Matthew O'Brien, who was presumably related to the family, along with five Irish-born laborers who varied in age from twenty-one to forty-nine. In Cass Township in the same year, forty-one-year-old Michael McAvoy, a laborer born in Ireland, lived with his Irish-born wife, Bridget, aged forty-two, his five children, and four Irishmen who were presumably boarders (one of them a miner and the other three laborers).[32]

A striking number of households were headed by women whose positions in life were evidently precarious. Some of these households contained an elderly male, presumably the woman's father or father-in-law. But all of them lacked males filling the roles of husbands and providers. The most precarious cases were those of single women with numerous young children and no visible means of support. The less vulnerable households included children of working age, and various other young men who, judged by their names, were boarders or relatives, and typically worked as miners or laborers. One can only speculate about the precise status of the women who headed these households; the census listed them as "keeping house" and did not use the classification "widow." But, while a fair number of these women may have been abandoned, permanently or temporarily, it is fair to assume that many of them were widows. Some would have lost their husbands in the process of upheaval and resettlement that brought them to the anthracite region; others, perhaps a majority, would have lost them to accidents in the mines.[33]

In this latter respect, the dry statistics of the census manuscripts are grimly suggestive. In Blythe Township in 1870, for example, the adjacent households numbered 60, 61, 62, and 63 were headed by single women (most of whom had working children), as were households 127, 128, and 129, and 334, 335, and 336. The adult males of these households may have been away in search of work. But an equally plausible explanation is that they had worked together as well as being neighbors, and had perished in the same accidents in the same mines. If nothing else, these figures lend a peculiar poignancy to the Molly Maguires' implicit claim that they were the children of a mythical woman who needed their protection and assistance.[34]

Statistics of this sort become more interesting if one examines the individuals

32. HSP, U.S. Census Office, Seventh Census on Population, 1850, original unpublished returns, Blythe Township, household 1350; Cass Township, household 505.

33. It seems unlikely that the men were simply away at work in some other part of the mining region, as they were not listed as belonging to the household at all. On widowhood and male desertion elsewhere in nineteenth-century Irish America, see Hasia R. Diner, *Erin's Daughters in America: Irish Immigrant Women in the Nineteenth Century* (Baltimore, 1983).

34. HSP, U.S. Census Office, Ninth Census on Population, 1870, original unpublished returns, Blythe Township.

who lie behind them. In Blythe Township in 1850, for example, twenty-four-year-old Ann Ryan, born in Ireland, had no visible means of support for her two small children, Patrick and John. The situation of thirty-five-year-old Mary Freeley, also born in Ireland, was even more precarious, for she had five children aged ten or under, and there were no adult males living in her house. Irish-born Bridget Phalen, on the other hand, was in a stronger position. She had five children under the age of twelve and no husband; but her household included three other members of the Phalen family, who may have been her husband's relatives: Joseph, aged seventy-two and unemployed; Michael, twenty-three, a laborer; and sixteen-year-old Mary, for whom no occupation was listed. Fifty-year-old Catherine Brennan, who lived in Blythe Township in 1860, also had some means of support. Born in Ireland, she lived with her two sons, Richard, sixteen, who worked as a laborer, and Patrick, nine. An Irish-born laborer named Michael Whalen also lived in the household and presumably contributed his share of the rent and other expenses.[35]

The census of 1870 yields a clearer picture of family structure and domestic economy than the previous two censuses. For the first time, the occupations of children (both girls and boys) were listed. In Blythe Township, for example, forty-five-year-old Mary McGowan, a native of Ireland, earned some income from the labor of her fifteen-year-old son, William, a slate picker. In North Cass, the three children of fifty-year-old Ann Purcell, another native of Ireland, worked in the mines: twenty-two-year-old Patrick and eighteen-year-old Martin as laborers and thirteen-year-old John as a slate picker. The household also included three Irish-born miners and a fifteen-year-old slate picker, born, like Mrs. Purcell's sons, in Pennsylvania.[36] One-quarter of the work force in the mines of Schuylkill County in 1870 was composed of boys, and three-quarters of these boys were slate pickers.[37]

Nor was it only the male children who contributed to the finances of the household. Teenage girls worked regularly as milliners, seamstresses, and domestic servants in all households, not just those of widows. For example, the two eldest daughters of Patrick Brennan, an Irish-born laborer who lived in South Cass in 1870, worked as a shirtmaker and a milliner. And all five children of his Irish-born neighbor Elizabeth Whalen, aged fifty-seven, were gainfully employed, compensating for the lack of a husband. Her three sons, James, John, and Martin, worked, in descending order of age, as a miner, a laborer, and a slate picker; her daughter Margaret worked as a dressmaker, and her daughter Kate as

35. HSP, U.S. Census Office, Seventh Census on Population, 1850, original unpublished returns, Blythe Township, households 1279, 1501, and 1543; Eighth Census on Population, 1860, original unpublished returns, Blythe Township, household 235.

36. HSP, U.S. Census Office, Ninth Census on Population, 1870, original unpublished returns, Blythe Township, household 138; North Cass, household 34.

37. Of a total work force of 15,778, 3,980 were boys, of whom 886 worked below ground and 3,094 in the breaker picking slate. PBIS 1, 341.

a domestic servant. In the anthracite region, children were introduced early to the demanding world of work.[38]

The dominant myth of the Molly Maguires, fashioned in the nineteenth century and repeated in many subsequent histories, is that they were gangsters whose criminal activities had little or nothing to do with labor relations. It is quite clear, however, that the Molly Maguires were fighting in their own way for justice, and that their struggle had its ultimate basis in patterns of discrimination at the mines. In the most direct sense, the Mollys punished the mine superintendents who managed the places where they and their countrymen worked; more indirectly, they engaged in a species of gang warfare with Welsh miners that makes sense only in terms of the ethnic discrimination that reserved the best jobs for the British and the worst for the Irish. To understand the context in which the Molly Maguires emerged in Pennsylvania, it will be useful to begin with the nature of work at the mines.

Initially, coal was simply dug or scraped from outcrops. The first, rudimentary mines were pits sunk from elevated positions, from which the coal (and excess water) was hauled by hand with a windlass. At a depth of thirty to forty feet these mines had to be abandoned because of flooding. The openings used thereafter can be classified into four types: drifts, slopes, tunnels, and shafts. The type of opening selected depended on surface conditions and the angle and depth of the coal beds.[39]

Drifts were used when the coal seams sloped upward and lay exposed on a hillside. They were the easiest openings to develop, and the cheapest. The opening was driven directly into the coal at an uphill gradient, often from ravines at the foot of hills, which provided natural drainage. Gangways were then driven at right angles from the drift. Coal was removed at first by wheelbarrows, then rails were laid in the gangways, and coal was hauled out by mule or horse. Initially, there were no coal breakers, machinery, or steam engines. Picks, shovels, hammers, and riddles were the only implements in use. Drifts were almost the sole means of extracting coal in the southern region before the mid-1840s. They were

38. HSP, U.S Census Office, Ninth Census on Population, 1870, original unpublished returns, South Cass, households 131 and 159.

39. Much of the following discussion is based on the exhibition on the history of anthracite at the Anthracite Museum in Ashland, Schuylkill County. See, also, [Hudson Coal Company], *The Story of Anthracite* (New York, 1932), 114–54; Munsell, *History of Schuylkill County,* 34–41; Andrew Roy, *The Coal Mines* (Cleveland, 1876), chapter 18; Peter Roberts, *The Anthracite Coal Industry* (New York, 1901), chapter 1; G.O. Virtue, "The Anthracite Mine Laborers," *Bulletin of the Department of Labor,* 13 (November 1897): 728–74; Hugh Archbald, *The Four Hour Day in Coal* (New York, 1922); Wallace, *St. Clair;* Yearley, *Enterprise and Anthracite;* Alfred D. Chandler, Jr., "Anthracite Coal and the Beginnings of the Industrial Revolution in the United States," *Business History Review,* 46 (Summer 1972): 141–81; Priscilla Long, *Where the Sun Never Shines: A History of America's Bloody Coal Industry* (New York, 1989), chapters 1, 2, and 3.

well adapted to a region where the outcrops had been exposed at many places by the erosive effects of streams and weather. But their use also reflected the prevailing belief, until the late 1830s, that coal lay only above the water level. In 1839 there were 120 collieries above water level in Schuylkill County, and only 10 below; and as late as 1850 there were still 122 above and only 44 below.[40] The problem with drift mines was that the surface deposits quickly became exhausted, in many areas as early as the mid-1850s. But drift mining was particularly well-suited to the individual enterprise that characterized the lower region, as it required no great outlay of capital. When surface deposits were exhausted, a new mine could be opened and the old one abandoned. As a result, drifts remained very common until the takeover of the lower anthracite industry by the Reading Railroad in the 1870s. In many ways, they symbolized the frenetic, get-rich-quick mentality of the operators in the lower region.[41]

To get access to coal lying below the water level, operators introduced two other types of mines: slopes and tunnels. While drifts were driven upward, slopes followed the downward course of a seam, or cut through slate and rock to reach the coal. As in drift mines, gangways were driven at right angles from the slope. The gangways were ten to fifteen feet wide, and usually a few hundred yards long. The coal had to be hauled considerable distances to the surface. Slopes could be driven either from the surface to the coal, or entirely within a mine, along a coal seam. Though they required greater outlay than drift mines, slopes were generally constructed in the hope of extracting a quick profit from a single vein of coal. Of the 66 slope mines in operation in Schuylkill County in 1854, only 4 were more than 400 yards deep, 11 were over 200 yards deep, and the remaining 51 reached depths of 100 yards or less.[42] Another way of extracting coal from below the water level was to construct a tunnel mine. Tunnels were similar to drifts in that they were driven horizontally into the hillside. But, instead of following the thrust of the coal vein, they were driven into it at right angles through solid rock, and gangways were then driven through the coal in both directions. Tunnels could penetrate several coal seams and provide passageways from one coal seam to another.[43]

With greater knowledge, patience, and above all, capital, the operators could have gained greater command over several veins of coal at once by sinking a shaft from directly above the coal deposits. Shafts were vertical openings from the surface which penetrated one or more levels of rock and coal. Miners and material were hoisted in and out of the mine through the shaft. Mine water was drained into a reservoir at the bottom of the shaft, and then either hoisted or pumped to the surface. Deep-shaft mining did not become common until the

40. Yearley, *Enterprise and Anthracite,* 111.

41. Ibid., 111. In 1860 there were 134 drift mines in Schuylkill County, and as late as 1874 there were still 102.

42. Ibid., 118.

43. A fine example of a tunnel mine can be found at Ashland, Schuylkill County, the site of the Anthracite Museum.

takeover by the Reading Railroad, through its subsidiary, the Philadelphia & Reading Coal & Iron Company. There were, of course, several shafts and several large mines in Schuylkill County before that, the best-known of which was the shaft sunk by Enoch McGinness to reach the Mammoth Vein in 1853.[44]

Once a mine had been opened, the method used to extract the anthracite depended on several considerations, including the pitch and thickness of the seam, the texture of the coal, and the pressure and composition of the roof, walls, and floor. There were two principal systems of extracting coal (other than scraping or digging it from the surface): room and pillar mining, and pitch mining. The first of these methods was most common in the upper anthracite region and the bituminous coal fields of western Pennsylvania, where the coal was more readily accessible. The second was the favored method of extracting coal in the sharply pitched seams of the lower anthracite region.

Room and pillar mining, also known as "breast and pillar" and "port and stall" mining, was used where the seams were relatively flat, as they were in most of the upper anthracite region and parts of the lower region. The working was divided into blocks by main entries, which might be vertical or horizontal, and gangways intercepted these entries at right angles. Chambers ("rooms" or "breasts") were then driven into these gangways at regular intervals and the coal was extracted from the chambers. Solid pillars of coal were left between the chambers to support the roof. But these pillars contained up to 50 percent of the minable coal, and they were generally removed on a second run. This dangerous operation was known as "robbing the pillars": As each pillar was removed a section of the mine would collapse. In 1871 Governor Geary of Pennsylvania described it as a "reprehensible practice," and called for a law making it illegal "to remove the coal supports without supplying their places with others of substantial masonry of something equivalent."[45]

Room and pillar mining could be used in the Schuylkill region only where the coal was relatively easy to extract. But most coal in the lower region, with its steeply inclined seams, required one form or other of pitch mining. The most popular of these was chute mining. In this method, a gangway was driven near the bottom of the seam, and from the gangway a timbered chute was driven upward into the coal at an angle. A narrow passageway or manway, or more often two (one upcast and own downcast), allowed the miner to ascend to and descend from the coal face. These manways also allowed air to circulate, and ventilation was further improved by crosscuts from one manway to the other. If the angle of the chute was less than thirty degrees the coal slid steadily down to the gangway by gravity. Where the inclines were steeper, the chutes contained batteries (or "bulkheads") constructed of heavy timber and used to support and control the loose coal released by the miner from the coal face above. A laborer

44. On deep shaft mining by the PRCI in the mid-1870s, see Roy, *The Coal Mines,* 244–46; on McGinness and the Mammoth Vein, see *MJ,* December 17, 1853; Wallace, *St. Clair,* 98–101; Yearley, *Enterprise and Anthracite,* 128–31.

45. Tamaqua *Anthracite Monitor,* January 6, 1871.

opened the batteries periodically, and the coal fell through it, down through a chute and into a mine car waiting in the gangway below. Because so much coal dust was released into the air during this process, the loader could see only a couple of feet ahead of him at most. To check if the car was full, he had to dangle his feet down from the chute and touch the car with his feet.

In the work year June 1869 to June 1870, there were 91 collieries active in Schuylkill County. They employed a total of 15,778 persons. The employees fell into the following categories: 6,180 skilled workers (5,056 contract miners and 1,124 miners by wage), 2,249 first-class laborers (below ground), 2,550 second-class laborers (above ground), 3,980 boys, and 819 "full-time hands." The term "full-time hands" referred to salaried employees of the operators who supervised the mines. They consisted of 91 mine bosses (who were paid $1,200 a year), 91 assistant mining bosses ($800 a year), 91 breaker bosses ($1,000 a year), 273 engineers ($15 a week), and 273 mechanics ($15 a week).[46]

Perhaps the most striking aspect of these figures is how few managers there were compared to workers. In Schuylkill County in 1870 there were only 273 bosses (one mine boss, one assistant mine boss, and one breaker boss at each of the 91 mines) to supervise 14,759 miners, laborers, and boys. Clearly, the men underground worked without much direct supervision. With gangways often extending hundreds of feet, and teams of two or more men working at individual coal faces, the possibilities of supervision by employers were very limited. This was particularly true of the skilled miners. But it would be a mistake to assume that all mine workers were equally independent. Miners accounted for only 39 percent of the work force in 1870; 30 percent were laborers, and 25 percent boys. Fully 40 percent of the work force was employed above ground, including 78 percent of the boys and 47 percent of the laborers.[47]

Within the ranks of the mine workers, then, there were important social distinctions. Women were never employed in the anthracite mines, but the most obvious division was between men and boys. Three thousand nine hundred and eighty boys worked in the mines of Schuylkill County in 1870; 886 (22 percent) of them below ground, in charge of mules and ventilation, and 3,094 (78 percent) above ground, picking slate out of coal in the breaker.[48] A law enacted in 1870 prohibited the employment of boys under twelve years old inside the mines, but made no provision for boys who worked outside the mines, including the unfortunate slate pickers. There was no law on the use of child slate pickers in Pennsylvania until 1885, and it was common for boys as young as eight to work ten-hour shifts in the breakers. The law of 1885 raised the age for inside workers to fourteen and, for the first time, set a limit of twelve years old for employment above ground.[49]

46. PBIS I, 341.

47. Figures computed from PBIS I, 341.

48. Figures compiled from ibid. Twelve thousand boys worked as slate pickers in the anthracite region as a whole in 1880; see Long, *Where the Sun Never Shines,* 75.

49. Alexander Trachtenberg, *A History of Legislation for the Protection of Coal Miners in Pennsylvania, 1824–1915* (New York, 1942), 6–8, 14, 116, 203. Pennsylvania's first child-labor law, passed in 1848, did not apply to the mining industry.

The elite of the workforce were the skilled miners. They were divided into two classes, "miners on contract" (5,056 in Schuylkill County in 1870, or 82 percent of the total number of miners) and "miners on wages" (1,124, 18 percent). The contract miners, in particular, had a great deal of independence and exercised considerable control over the production process. By and large, they determined the length of their working day. The bulk of their work involved setting props, looking after safety, and drilling and blasting anthracite from the coal face. A small number of truly independent miner-contractors took on the tasks of opening and timbering new mines, employing their own crews of men. Miners on daily wages had less independence than the contract workers, but they enjoyed some of the same privileges and were separated by a similar divide from manual laborers.

Most of the contract miners were paid not by daily wages but according to the amount they produced. In the upper anthracite region, production was typically measured by the carload or by weight; in the lower region, miners were paid by the "yard," that is, by their rate of advance into the coal seam. Most contract miners employed their own laborers, paying them one third or so of their income.[50] There was always a strong craft tradition among these highly skilled workmen, emphasizing independence and the dignity of labor. They were independent craftsmen who learned their jobs through an apprenticeship and were proud of their artisan status.[51] Miners would sometimes refuse to work in front of the operator's foreman, ostentatiously downing their tools and instructing their laborers to stop working as well.[52] As the leading historian of the subject has explained, the skilled contract miner

> took a raw material, anthracite, from the coal face and converted it into a product, freed coal. The miner worked for an individually negotiated price rather than a wage. Whether measured by the linear yard, ton, or wagon, the unit of compensation acknowledged that the miner was selling a product, not his labor, to the operator.[53]

The fabled independence of the nineteenth-century miner, in short, had a solid material basis.

So, too, did the dependence of the nineteenth-century mine laborer. Once the miners had done their jobs, they were free to leave the mines. The laborers stayed behind to shovel the coal into cars for transport to the surface and pile the waste to one side. As one Welsh miner put it:

50. Harold D. Aurand, "The Anthracite Miner: An Occupational Analysis," PMHB, 104 (1980): 467; Perry K. Blatz, *Democratic Miners: Work and Labor Relations in the Anthracite Coal Industry, 1875–1925* (Albany, N.Y., 1994), 12.

51. Long, *Where the Sun Never Shines,* 60.

52. Aurand, "The Anthracite Miner," 467.

53. Ibid., 466. This is the ideal case; it appears, however, that many miners worked for wages as well as by contract, turning to the former when the latter was unavailable. Though miners retained more autonomy than most workers, they lost some of their independence over the course of the half-century after 1850. PBIS 1, 345; Long, *Where the Sun Never Shines,* 63–64.

> Look again at the unfairness of the system to the laborer who has to fill from six to seven cars a day with coal and he gets but one third of the wages of the miner. . . . The miner and laborer go to work at seven o'clock in the morning and probably the miner will cut enough coal by ten or twelve o'clock. Then he will go out leaving the poor laborer up to his waist in water and he will have to pile the lumps and fill three or four cars with coal after the gentleman has left. . . . Between five and six, the laborer, poor thing, arrives home wet as a fish.[54]

Thus, the laborers found themselves in a markedly inferior position to the miners. In many cases, they worked directly for the miners rather than the mine operator.[55] Laborers who worked beneath the surface (47 percent of them in Schuylkill County in 1870) were better paid and had a slightly higher status in the work force than those who toiled above ground (53 percent). But the social position of both types of laborer was far removed from that of the skilled miners.

This social division took on considerable importance in the anthracite region because it corresponded directly to a fundamental ethnic division. Most Welsh and English workers were miners, while most of the laborers were Irish. There was a well-established apprenticeship system through which Welsh, British, and American mine workers could rise up to the best, skilled jobs. The problem was that large numbers of the Irish were not considered eligible for such promotion. While one Welsh miner wrote home in a letter that a Welsh immigrant might have to work for only six or nine months before getting "a place of their own" (i.e., his own coal face, where he worked as a skilled miner), this was decidedly not the case for the Irish, many of whom worked as laborers for years with no hope of becoming miners. Unskilled and often despised, immigrant Irish laborers were the most transient of all workers in the mines.[56]

While historians have generally assumed that the lowly status of the Irish mine workers had something to do with the Molly Maguire conflict, little or no empirical work has been done in this respect. The exception is the mining town of St. Clair, where one historian has demonstrated a pervasive pattern of discrimination against the Irish. In 1850 there were 167 Irish laborers in St. Clair and only 24 Irish miners. In sharp contrast, there were 83 British miners and only 16 British laborers. By 1870, the position of the Irish had improved, so that the 78 Irish miners outnumbered the 58 Irish laborers; but there were now 324 British miners and only 42 British laborers.[57]

Though the position of the Irish had improved by 1870, a more striking development was that the proportion of Irish residents in the town had declined

54. Letter by T. Thomas, December 6, 1873, quoted in Conway, ed., *The Welsh in America,* 194.

55. Aurand, "The Anthracite Miner," 467; Blatz, *Democratic Miners,* 12.

56. Aurand, "The Anthracite Miner," 462–73; Conway, ed., *The Welsh in America,* 185; Blatz, *Democratic Miners,* 19.

57. Wallace, *St. Clair,* 134, 374.

dramatically. There were almost as many Irish residents in St. Clair in 1850 as the English and Welsh populations combined; but by 1870 the English alone outnumbered the Irish, and there were twice as many British residents as Irish residents.[58] The most likely explanation is that the Irish of St. Clair had moved up to the developing mining areas around Mahanoy City and Shenandoah, in northern Schuylkill County. Only in 1880 did the Irish for the first time fill a majority of the miners' as well as laborers' jobs in St. Clair, but by that time the other national groups were moving out of mining altogether into other occupations, such as shopkeeping.[59]

A complementary study of Blythe Township carried out for the present work produced broadly similar results, though the social processes involved were somewhat different.[60] Analysis of the unpublished census returns revealed a social hierarchy extending from the native-born, through the British and German immigrants, down to the Irish. In 1850 the British-born accounted for 23.25 percent of the township's population and the Irish-born for 52.25 percent. One hundred and twenty-two of the 129 British-born men who worked in the mines (94.5 percent) did so as miners rather than laborers. Of the 328 Irish who were employed in the mines, 146 (44.5 percent) worked as miners and 182 (55.5 percent) as laborers; 61.25 percent of the total work force in the mines was Irish, and 24 percent British. The British accounted for 39.5 percent of the miners in the township, but only 3 percent of the laborers; the Irish supplied 47.5 percent of the miners but 80 percent of the laborers. None of this is particularly surprising; it confirms the pattern observed in nineteenth-century Pennsylvania and England by previous historians.[61]

By 1870 the situation had changed in some respects, but what is most interesting is how little it had changed, not how much. The population of Blythe Township declined between 1860 and 1870, from 3,421 to 1,924, as the local coal trade fell into difficulties in the latter part of the decade. The 698 occupied households in Blythe in 1850 had been reduced to 627 in 1860, and 539 in 1870. There were 151 British-born heads of household in Blythe in 1850, 107 in 1860, but only 61 in 1870; there were 340 Irish-born heads of household in 1850, 291 in 1860, and 233 in 1870. A little over 4 percent (4.25 percent) of the population was British-born (compared to 19 percent in 1860 and 23.25 percent in 1850); 54.5 percent was Irish-born (compared to 52 percent in 1860 and

58. Ibid., 130, 372.

59. Ibid., 437.

60. Data on the nativity and occupations of heads of household in Blythe Township were compiled from HSP, U.S. Census Office, Seventh, Eighth, and Ninth Censuses on Population, 1850, 1860, and 1870, for Schuylkill County, Pennsylvania, original unpublished returns. For full details and methodology, see Kevin Kenny, "Making Sense of the Molly Maguires" (Ph.D. diss., Columbia University, 1994), chapter 2 and appendix 4. Most of the townships in northern Schuylkill County were settled only in the 1870s, so it is not possible to do a temporal analysis of occupation and nativity for that part of the county of the type attempted here for Blythe.

61. HSP, U.S. Census Office, Seventh Census on Population, 1850, original unpublished returns, Blythe Township; Wallace, *St. Clair,* loc. cit.; E.P. Thompson, *The Making of the English Working Class* (1963; Harmondsworth, England, 1968), 473–75.

52.25 percent in 1850). Both the British and the Irish populations declined in absolute numbers between 1860 and 1870, in line with the general decrease of population. But, in contrast to St. Clair, the British percentage of the population of Blythe also declined proportionately, whereas the Irish proportion of the population rose between 1860 and 1870 from 52 percent to 54.5 percent.[62]

In 1870, as in previous years, there was a sharp contrast between the Irish and British residents of Blythe Township. The British-born population in the sample had dropped to only sixty-one, but those who remained in the township retained their privileged social position. Though the proportion of the British working in the mines remained fairly constant (75.25 percent in 1870 compared to 76.5 percent in 1860), the British population had declined substantially by 1870, so that the 46 British mine workers represented only 14.75 percent of the total work force in the mines. But 91.25 percent of them were employed as miners, rather than laborers.[63]

Unlike the British, the Irish stayed in Blythe Township and continued to work in the mines, where they accounted for 67.25 percent of the workforce in the sample considered. Fully 89.75 percent of the Irish were still working in the mines in 1870, only a slight decrease from 1860 (93.5 percent). And the ratio between Irish miners and laborers had actually grown slightly worse over the course of the decade: Of the 272 Irish mine workers in Blythe in 1860, exactly half had been miners and half laborers; of the 209 Irish mine workers in 1870, 102 (48.75 percent) were miners but 107 (51.25 percent) were laborers.[64] These totals were even higher than the corresponding national averages in 1870, when 39 percent of Irish-born Americans worked as unskilled laborers or domestic servants, compared to only 16 percent of the labor force as a whole.[65]

The preponderance of the Irish in the population of Blythe Township in 1870 (54.5 percent) meant that they now accounted for a clear majority of the miners (61 percent, compared to 53.5 percent in 1860 and only 47.5 percent in 1850), which might at first sight suggest that the Irish were substantially better off than they had been a decade earlier.[66] But the exodus of the British out of mining, and even out of the township (accompanied by similar upwardly mobile trends in the German population) strongly suggests that the social triumph of the Irish did not really amount to all that much.[67] Sixty-seven and a quarter percent of all mine workers in the sample were Irish in 1870, compared to only 61.25 percent in 1860. And 75 percent of all the laborers were Irish, compared

62. Figures computed from HSP, United States Census Office, Censuses on Population, 1850, 1860, and 1870, original unpublished returns, Blythe Township.

63. Figures computed from ibid.

64. Figures computed from ibid.

65. David Montgomery, "The Irish and the American Labor Movement," in David Noel Doyle and Owen Dudley Edwards, eds., *America and Ireland, 1776–1976: The American Identity and the Irish Connection* (Westport, Conn., 1980), 208.

66. Figures computed from HSP, United States Census Office, Censuses on Population, 1850, 1860, and 1870, original unpublished returns, Blythe Township.

67. For a similar pattern in the 1880 census, see Wallace, *St. Clair,* 437–38.

to only 69.5 percent in 1860, even though the Irish accounted for only slightly more than half the total population. Thus, in 1870, nine of every ten Irishmen in Blythe Township still worked in the mines, five of every ten worked as laborers, and seven of every ten laborers were Irish-born. These figures are substantially the same as those for 1850 and 1860, confirming one historian's judgment that, while some of the Irish were becoming skilled miners by the 1860s, "their chief marketable commodity was not skill but brawn."[68]

Overall, these findings support the argument that only a certain type of Irish immigrant became a Molly Maguire in Pennsylvania. It is important to remember that most Irish immigrants did not become Molly Maguires. Instead, the majority of Irish mine workers joined the trade union movement that emerged in the 1840s and culminated in the Workingmen's Benevolent Association in the period 1868–75. The fact that about half the Irish residents of the anthracite region appear to have worked as miners is quite consistent with this development. Many of them would have had prior experience as miners in Britain, especially in Lancashire and the Newcastle area.[69] The trade union movement was founded by skilled British and Irish-born miners with whom these Irish miners would have had a considerable amount in common. Many Irish laborers also made common cause with skilled miners of whatever nationality. But a large number of Irishmen (a significantly higher proportion than any other ethnic group) were certainly consigned to a lifetime of menial labor. And the most unskilled of all Irish immigrants were those from the north-central and northwestern regions of Ireland, most typically Irish speakers from places like Mayo and west Donegal. Their cultural and historical background already marked them off as substantially different not only from the skilled miners of Wales and Lancashire but from workers originating elsewhere in Ireland; on arrival in Pennsylvania, these differences were reinforced by distinctions of status within the mines. It was these people who were most likely to become Molly Maguires in Pennsylvania.[70]

Several of the Molly Maguire assassinations involved antipathies to mine bosses who were accused of favoring the Welsh over the Irish. The Welsh mine superintendents Morgan Powell and John P. Jones, for example, were assassinated under these circumstances in a section of western Carbon County that had a high concentration of immigrants from Donegal, who dominated the local lodges of the AOH.[71] And in heavily Irish regions like northern Schuylkill County, where an atypically high proportion of the immigrants came from north-central and northwestern Ireland, there was considerable tension between the Welsh and the Irish in the 1870s, corresponding in large part to a divide between miners and laborers. This tension took the form of street warfare

68. Yearley, *Enterprise and Anthracite*, 166.

69. Cf. Coleman, *The Molly Maguire Riots*, 19.

70. Cf. Miller, *Emigrants and Exiles*, 353, on unskilled immigrants from the west of Ireland.

71. The Pinkerton list of AOH members discussed in chapter 1 indicates that the lodges in Summit Hill and Storm Hill, whose members were accused of organizing these two assassinations, came exclusively from Donegal.

between rival Welsh and Irish gangs, and included a series of beatings, assaults, faction fights, and killings that were blamed on the Molly Maguires.[72] There is, therefore, a reasonable basis for concluding that divisions between miners and laborers were one of the primary preconditions of the Molly Maguire conflict in Pennsylvania.

The distinctions between miners and laborers, and the attempt to overcome them, are central to any understanding of the labor movement that emerged in the anthracite region in the 1860s and 1870s. A clear sense of how that labor movement emerged and what it stood for is, in turn, an essential ingredient of any attempt to comprehend the Molly Maguires. To make sense of the Molly Maguires in Pennsylvania, two forms of labor organization and protest need to be kept analytically and ideologically distinct: the trade union movement and the pattern of violence that developed alongside it. In terms of personnel there was undoubtedly a degree of overlap, but the trade union and the Molly Maguires represented fundamentally different answers to the same question: How to improve conditions of life and labor in the anthracite region? The interaction between trade unionism and Molly Maguireism after the emergence of a cohesive labor movement in the 1860s and 1870s will be a principal theme of subsequent chapters. By way of a preliminary analysis, it will be useful to sketch here the history of earlier attempts by the mine workers to organize, and to examine the intersection between violence, crowd activity, and nascent trade unionism in the period before the Civil War.

The first important labor dispute in the anthracite region came at the end of the economic depression of 1837–42. The years 1829–30 had seen a boom in the coal industry, but hard times set in following the financial panic and collapse of 1837, reaching a peak in 1842. There was heavy unemployment in the anthracite region, and those who were still employed received their wages not in money but in orders for goods. To pay their men, the operators bargained with store owners for an advance in credit, against which they wrote orders for merchandise. The employees received these orders instead of cash wages, and the operators redeemed the paper after they received cash for their coal. Since the merchants were taking a considerable risk, they protected themselves by charging high prices for their goods. Sometimes the operators themselves owned the stores and exacted exorbitant profits from their employees, but this practice was rare in the lower anthracite region, with its proliferation of small, independent operators.[73] In this context of low wages and high prices, there were reports in

72. These events are discussed in chapters 6 and 7.

73. *MJ*, July 30, 1842; *Philadelphia Public Ledger*, July 30, 1842; William Itter, "Early Labor Troubles in the Schuylkill Anthracite District," *PH*, 1 (January 1934): 28–37. Stores run by the operators themselves ("company stores") were always more common in the upper anthracite region and the bituminous coal fields of western Pennsylvania than in the Schuylkill region.

1842 that "ferocious threats towards individuals have been for some time past affixed to stores and trees in public places."[74] One of the earliest recorded acts of industrial sabotage in the anthracite region dates from this year, when incendiaries were accused of burning the barn of one of the operators.[75]

Resentment at low wages and the store-order system reached a peak on July 7, 1842, when the men at Minersville (four miles northwest of Pottsville, on the border of Cass Township) met to protest falling wages and payment in store orders rather than cash. On Saturday, July 9, a crowd of mine workers marched from Minersville to Pottsville, reportedly armed with clubs and other weapons. The protestors took out the men at most of the mines they passed, and drove away the laborers loading coal at the canal landings. Two companies of Pottsville volunteers were ordered to Minersville the same evening, amid rumors that the town was to be burned. By Monday, all work in the region had been suspended, and a crowd estimated at fifteen hundred marched on Pottsville for a second time. District Attorney Francis W. Hughes addressed the crowd, advising them what steps they could take within the law. A committee was appointed and a list of grievances drawn up, but the operators refused to recognize this organization. The men soon returned to work and the results of this first strike in the anthracite region were inconclusive.[76]

Seven years later a brief-lived labor union, the first in the anthracite region, was founded in Schuylkill County by John Bates, an English Chartist.[77] The Bates Union, which enrolled as many as five thousand members, seems to have originated in a movement for a lien law protecting miners' wages in cases where their employers went bankrupt. The first time miners were mentioned in a legislative enactment in Pennsylvania was in a law passed in 1849 "for the protection of miners, mechanics, and laborers in certain cases." This act provided that, in cases of assignments of property because of inability to pay debts, the wages of miners and other workers should be paid before the debts of other creditors, provided the claim did not exceed fifty dollars. The law, which applied to Schuylkill, Berks, Washington, Center, Somerset, Westmoreland, and Carbon counties, was enacted as a result of direct pressure exerted by the Bates Union in Schuylkill County. In a resolution adopted at a meeting in Pottsville on January 13, 1849, the mine workers had called upon the workers of Pennsylvania to support a petition to the legislature for a lien law to protect wages. "We ask no favors from nabobs, lordlings or capitalists," the miners declared. "Our rights are our own; we are determined to have them."[78]

By the spring of 1849 the mine workers of Schuylkill County had turned

74. *Philadelphia Public Ledger,* July 19, 1842.

75. *Philadelphia Public Ledger,* May 18, 1842; *MJ,* May 22, 1842; Itter, "Early Labor Troubles," 34.

76. *MJ,* July 9, 16, 23, 30, 1842; *Philadelphia Public Ledger,* July 14, 15, 19, 1842; Munsell, *History of Schuylkill County,* 53; Itter, "Early Labor Troubles," 35.

77. For the connection with Chartism, see Charles Edward Killeen, "John Siney: The Pioneer in American Industrial Unionism and Industrial Government" (Ph.D. diss., University of Wisconsin, 1942), 95.

78. Trachtenberg, *A History of Legislation,* 15; *MJ,* January 27, 1849.

their attention to wages, and it was during the agitation over this question that the Bates Union was formed. Like most subsequent labor leaders in the region, Bates believed that the best way to keep wages high was to raise the price of coal by controlling the amount supplied to market, if necessary by suspending operations.[79] Such suspensions were also in the interest of many operators, of course, and the operators suspended coal shipments for seven consecutive weeks in 1842, from March 19 to May 2. On May 2, the day appointed for a resumption of work at the mines, more than two thousand mine workers met at Minersville. They passed a resolution setting forth their grievances, impressing "upon the miners and laborers of Schuylkill County the importance of unanimous, firm, determined, but at the same time mild and respectful action," and recommending "the appointment of a committee of two from each colliery to form a central committee to make the necessary arrangements for the formation of a miners' union, if they shall deem it necessary, and also to negotiate with employers."[80]

On July 4 several thousand mine workers congregated at St. Clair and a strike was organized. The miners passed several resolutions, one of which introduced a theme that would be central to subsequent labor organizing in the region, the idea that "our interests and the interests of our employers are so connected and identified that it would be impossible to separate them."[81] Despite the leaders' assertion of a harmony of interests between labor and capital, bands of workers reportedly went from colliery to colliery over the coming weeks, armed with cudgels and other weapons, and persuaded nonstriking miners to join their ranks.[82] But the union soon collapsed, amid rumors that Bates had absconded with the treasury.[83]

The third important example of labor activism in the pre-Civil War years occurred in Schuylkill County in 1858, setting the precedent of the use of troops to put down a labor dispute in the anthracite region. When mine workers at Ashland, in northern Schuylkill County, went on strike for higher wages in late May 1858, they called on men from the other collieries to join them, and they were successful in bringing out most of the men in St. Clair. The leaders of the 1858 strike publicly urged the strikers "to keep within the bounds of the fair laws of our country,—not to get drunk, bellow, make threats, give insults, stop those who wish to work from doing so, annoy persons, or other things unlawful."[84] Nonetheless, anonymous warning notices were soon being posted outside collieries manned by blacklegs, complete with figures of coffins and pistols, warning them of dire consequences if they did not stop working.[85] On

79. Harold D. Aurand, "The Anthracite Mine Workers, 1869–1897: A Functional Approach to Labor History" (Ph.D. diss., Pennsylvania State University, 1969), 132.

80. *MJ*, May 5, 1849.

81. *MJ*, July 7, 1849.

82. Roberts, *The Anthracite Coal Industry*, 172–73.

83. Aurand, "The Anthracite Mine Workers, 1869–97," 133; Munsell, *History of Schuylkill County*, 53–57; Killeen, "John Siney," 94–98.

84. *MJ*, May 29, 1858.

85. *MJ*, June 26, 1858; Wallace, *St. Clair*, 285.

May 21 striking mine workers marched through St. Clair, shutting down its collieries. That evening, the operator of Hickory Slope mine, William Milnes, called on the county sheriff to disperse a crowd of demonstrators assembled on the hill above his mine. The sheriff mobilized an entire militia regiment, consisting of two companies of infantry and one each of artillery and cavalry, which marched to St. Clair and arrested five of the mine workers' leaders for riot. Four of these men were convicted, and three were sentenced to sixty days in prison. The combination of military and judicial repression had set an important precedent, as had the pattern of intimidation manifest in the strike, including the use of "coffin notices."[86]

Although contemporary observers undoubtedly exaggerated the extent of the violence and social disorder, there can be no doubt that the sporadic labor organizing of the 1840s and 1850s did involve a high level of crowd activity. This mode of organization was derived in part from the experience of Chartism in England, which was fused in the anthracite region with other forms of popular protest. The events at Ashland, in particular, suggest the fusion of Chartist mass protest, British trade unionism, and modes of direct, intimidatory action derived from the Irish countryside. Signs of that Irish heritage, including threatening notices posted by "Mollie's Children," were reported in the anthracite region from the late 1840s onward.[87]

While the trade union movement of the pre-Civil War decades was primarily British in inspiration, it included large numbers of Irish mine workers. Indeed, there is reason to believe that a specific type of Irish immigrant played a prominent role in the antebellum movement, perhaps lending it some of its distinctively turbulent quality. The part of Schuylkill County where labor organizing was most evident was settled by large numbers of miners from the Castlecomer region of Kilkenny, one of the few places in Ireland to contain workable deposits of coal. The Kilkenny miners arrived in the anthracite region in a position more like that of their British fellow-miners than that of the Irish from the western seaboard. Already experienced in mining, they were able to bypass manual labor and go straight into the skilled jobs.[88]

Among the more striking aspects of the Kilkenny connection is the fact that the coal mines of Castlecomer had a tradition of violent secret societies in the 1830s.[89] As the Molly Maguire violence did not begin in Pennsylvania for another generation, and was dominated by immigrants from another part of Ireland, direct continuities or causal connections can be discounted. But hundreds (perhaps even a few thousand) of the miners who emigrated from

86. *MJ*, May 29, June 19, 1858.

87. Munsell, *History of Schuylkill County*, 99.

88. On the Kilkenny mines, see William Nolan, *Fassadinin: Land, Settlement and Society in Southeast Ireland, 1600–1850* (Dublin, 1979); on the settlement of miners from Kilkenny in Schuylkill County, see Nolan, 207–9, and Thomas Sheehan, *All Those Folks from St. Patrick's* (limited private edition, 1994). I am grateful to Mr. Sheehan for sharing the results of his research with me, especially on the emigration of miners from Castlecomer to Minersville.

89. Nolan, *Fassadinin*, especially 142–48.

Kilkenny in the 1840s and 1850s made their way to the coal fields of Pennsylvania. Large numbers of them settled in Minersville, a borough situated on the border of Cass and Branch Townships, four miles northwest of Pottsville.[90] Minersville and its hinterland were a major location of the pre-Civil War labor movement. The short-lived, rudimentary labor unions formed there before and during the Civil War bore a strong resemblance to the "combinations" organized in the Castlecomer mines in the 1830s and 1840s, as did the strategy of sending threatening notices.[91]

But the Kilkenny miners never became Molly Maguires in Pennsylvania. In fact, by the 1870s, the term "Kilkennyman" had come to signify something quite different in the anthracite region. The area around Shenandoah and Mahanoy City in particular was noted for its ethnic gang warfare at this time, as rival groups like the Welsh "Modocs," the Irish "Sheet Iron Gang," and the "Molly Maguires" engaged in late-night brawling and a species of faction fighting. The remarkable thing about the Sheet Iron Gang is that, despite their Irish membership, they were resolutely opposed to the Molly Maguires, to the extent of allying themselves with the Modocs. This fact becomes less remarkable when it is realized that the Sheet Iron Gang was composed largely of skilled Irish miners from Kilkenny.[92]

Rather than joining the AOH or the Molly Maguires in the 1870s, the Kilkennymen formed a rival gang, variously known as the "Chain Gang," the "Sheet Iron Gang," and the "Iron Clads." Other Irishmen in the anthracite region called the Kilkennymen "soupers," a derisive term for Protestant converts. "They are called 'soup drinkers,'" Detective James McParlan reported on March 27, 1874, "and the Molly Maguires do not associate with them."[93] Many of them would indeed have been Protestants, if not necessarily converts, descendants of British miners who had settled in the Castlecomer region.[94] While this religious division was of considerable cultural resonance, more striking is how closely the conflict between the Molly Maguires and their opponents mirrored the division between skilled and menial labor. This conflict clearly took place among the Irish, not just between the Irish and the British. There were many different sorts of Irish immigrant workers in the anthracite region, and skilled miners from the anglicized southeast evidently had little in common with unskilled laborers from the remote northwest.

One final distinction needs to be made before proceeding to tell the story of the Molly Maguires in Pennsylvania. In addition to its geographical specificity, there was an important temporal dimension to the Molly Maguire violence. Most contemporaries ignored this temporal pattern, lumping all the violence into a single, timeless category of evil. Historians, too, have failed to distinguish

90. Ibid., 207–9; Sheehan, *All Those Folks from St. Patrick's.*

91. See chapter 3.

92. HSP, SC, PNDA, reports of JMCP for February 2, 4, 7, 1874; March 14, 22, 27, 30, 1874; *New York Herald,* September 23, 1876; Broehl, *The Molly Maguires,* 165.

93. HSP, SC, PNDA, report of JMCP, March 27, 1874, in reports of BF to FBG.

94. Nolan, *Fassadinin,* 94, 223.

between the two distinct waves of Molly Maguire violence that occurred in the anthracite region. Between 1862 and 1868 there was a first wave of six assassinations. From 1869 to 1873 there was a transition period, in which two more men were killed in unrelated incidents blamed on the Molly Maguires only subsequently. Then, in 1874–75, there was a second wave of activity, which included eight more assassinations. Cass Township, the center of alleged Molly Maguire activities in the 1860s, was not involved in the second wave of activities in the 1870s.

There were important differences of strategy and ideology between the two outbreaks of violence. The first wave of activities involved the intersection of draft resistance with labor organizing, and it occurred under conditions unique to the Civil War. All of the men assassinated in the first wave were mine owners or superintendents, whereas the victims in the second wave included miners, a justice of the peace, and a policeman. The first wave involved an attempt to set up a rudimentary labor union, known variously as the "Committee," the "Buckshots," and the "Molly Maguires." It represented, to some extent, a continuation of the organizing effort of the 1840s and 1850s, even if the strategy was now considerably more violent. In sharp contrast, the second wave of assassinations took place in opposition to a well-organized labor union, the Workingmen's Benevolent Association. The Molly Maguires of the 1870s were clearly a distinct organization from the "Committeemen" of the 1860s. Indeed, much of the alleged identity between these two separate phases of activity was posited only retrospectively, during the trials of the 1870s.

The differences between the two phases of Molly Maguireism can be explained partly in terms of patterns of immigration from Ireland and settlement within Schuylkill County. The second wave of activities occurred in parts of northern Schuylkill County that had not yet been settled when the first wave of activities took place. It began a decade after the first wave had subsided, and it involved immigrants from north-central and northwestern Ireland, some of whom had not yet arrived in the anthracite region when the first wave of activities commenced. But the main thing that distinguishes the first wave of activities from the second is that it occurred during a momentous period in the history of the anthracite region and the United States as a whole, the American Civil War.

3

Enter the Molly Maguires

The first wave of Molly Maguire activities occurred during the American Civil War. Making sense of this violence requires an understanding of the political crisis of the 1850s and 1860s, along with the economic, social, and cultural context in which the violence took place. The Molly Maguires existed on two related but distinct levels: as a shadowy pattern of actual violence and as an ambiguous concept in a system of ideological representation. The disparity between fact and representation was often quite considerable, but it was mediated by the ideology of the contemporary observers on whom historians have relied for their evidence—journalists, politicians, clergymen, mine operators, and military officials. These people had good reasons for saying what they said about the alleged secret society, and their ideology offers one key to interpreting the Molly Maguires. As for the violence itself, the men who were involved in the pattern of activities labeled "Molly Maguireism" left little direct evidence for historians to examine. But their actions begin to make sense when viewed in terms of the emergence and transformation, in industrializing Pennsylvania, of an ethic of retributive justice with its roots in the Irish countryside.

A great deal of what is known about the Molly Maguires in Pennsylvania is derived from the voluminous writings of a single resident of Pottsville, the newspaper editor Benjamin Bannan. Born in Berks County in 1807 into a Welsh farming family of moderate means, Bannan was apprenticed to the printers' trade when his father died in 1815. In 1829 he moved to Pottsville, Schuylkill County, in the heart of the lower anthracite region. There he purchased the *Miners' Journal,* a newspaper he edited for the next forty-four years. A devout Presbyterian, he was deeply committed to the great politico-religious crusades of his time. His hero was Henry Clay, the perennial Whig candidate for president. Like Clay, he supported a protective tariff, economic expansionism, a national paper currency, and an active role by government to foster economic opportunity. Apart from serving as draft commissioner for Schuylkill County during the Civil War, and as schools commissioner for Pottsville thereafter, Bannan never held political office; his influence was as a journalist and political spokesman rather than a politician.[1]

The *Miners' Journal* was, in turn, the leading Whig, nativist, and Republican newspaper in the lower anthracite region, a position made all the more distinctive by the fact that Schuylkill County was predominantly Democratic in politics. The Democrats, for example, won seven of the ten fall elections held in Schuylkill County between 1844 and 1853. In these years, the Whigs won more than 50 percent of the vote only in 1846, 1847, and 1848.[2] In 1852 Schuylkill County gave 4,758 votes to the victorious Democratic candidate for president, Franklin Pierce, compared to 4,128 for his Whig opponent, General Winfield Scott.[3] Bannan was the leading spokesman of the Whigs in Schuylkill County until the party's collapse in the early 1850s. He then followed a tortuous route through the politics of nativism, finally taking a decisive step toward the Republican camp in 1856.[4]

Despite the instability of party politics in the 1850s, Bannan's political ideology remained remarkably consistent. While this ideology involved an antipathy to Catholic immigrants, it involved an equally strong antipathy to slavery, particularly from 1856 onward. Rather than antislavery being a substitute for anti-Catholicism, the two can be seen as complementary elements in a single, coherent vision of republican society. That vision was based on the concept of honest, productive work and its social rewards; and a strong conviction that a

1. The *Miners' Journal* was founded in 1825 by George Taylor, a Pottsville lawyer. Under Bannan's editorship, it had about four thousand subscribers. Bannan served as editor until 1873, when he sold his remaining half share in the newspaper to the new editor, Robert Ramsey, to whom he had first sold a half share in 1866. See Munsell, *History of Schuylkill County,* 293–94; William A. Gudelunas, Jr., and William G. Shade, *Before the Molly Maguires: The Emergence of the Ethno-Religious Factor in the Politics of the Lower Anthracite Region, 1844–1872* (New York, 1976), 97. For a more elaborate version of the argument presented in this section, see Kevin Kenny, "Nativism, Labor, and Slavery: The Political Odyssey of Benjamin Bannan, 1850–1860," *PMHB,* 118 (October 1994): 325–61. The standard history of political nativism in the 1850s is Tyler Anbinder, *Nativism and Slavery: The Northern Know Nothings and the Politics of the 1850s* (New York, 1992).

2. Gudelunas and Shade, *Before the Molly Maguires,* 33.

3. *MJ,* November 13, 1852.

4. *MJ,* October 11, 1856, editorial supporting the "Union Ticket," an alliance (though not yet a fusion) between the American party and the Republican party in Schuylkill County.

virtuous citizenry was impossible without social mobility and potential economic independence for all.[5]

Benjamin Bannan, in short, was a classic proponent of the "free labor" ideology analyzed by historians of the nineteenth-century United States. This ideology emphasized social mobility as an inherent element of economic expansion, and it employed a category of "labor" that embraced all producers of wealth, not just the minority who worked for wages. Labor was free in the sense that it was dignified and independent. In an economy that centered on the independent, business-oriented farm and the small shop, rather than the factory system, the social paradigm was the small, prosperous, self-employed entrepreneur, and the goal of labor was to achieve economic and political independence. This point was nicely captured in the title of Bannan's newspaper, the *Miners' Journal;* it was always the journal of the small operating class and never the journal of the mine workers, let alone the trade union movement. The focus of Bannan's political doctrines was the general question of labor and social mobility. The vital issue was whether free, independent laborers could attain what Bannan regarded as their just desserts and rise to the position of free, independent entrepreneurs.[6]

At the heart of this vision of society lay the theory of a harmony of interests between honest, productive labor on the one hand, and honest, productive capital on the other.[7] This theory received one of its more cogent expressions in the writings of the Pennsylvania mine owner and economist Henry C. Carey, particularly in his *Principles of Political Economy.* "The interests of the capitalist and the laborer," as Carey put it, "are . . . in perfect harmony with each other, as each derives advantage from every measure that tends to facilitate the growth of capital."[8] In other words, as society prospered, laborers would fulfill their goal of becoming capitalists, and all would live in harmony. Carey's ideas had a powerful influence on Benjamin Bannan, one of his early partners in the mining business of the lower anthracite region.[9]

The bulwark of Bannan's ideal society was a large, independent middle class of prosperous, small-scale entrepreneurs. In the lower anthracite region the entrepreneurs he had in mind took the form of hundreds of small, independent coal operators, as distinct from a small number of powerful corporations. Bannan's ideology was very much determined by the distinctive character of the region where he lived. The basic idea was that a man who started work as a laborer could quickly graduate to the position of miner, and could in turn go on to become a small operator in business for himself.[10]

5. Cf. Kenny, "Nativism, Labor, and Slavery."

6. The classic analysis of the free labor ideology is Eric Foner, *Free Soil, Free Labor, Free Men: The Ideology of the Republican Party Before the Civil War* (New York, 1970). Cf. Kenny, "Nativism, Labor, and Slavery."

7. Cf. Foner, *Free Soil, Free Labor, Free Men,* especially chapter 1.

8. Henry C. Carey, *Principles of Political Economy,* 3 vols. (Philadelphia, 1837), vol. 1, 339.

9. Wallace, *St. Clair,* 55–60, 64–70.

10. On the small operators of the lower anthracite region, see Yearley, *Enterprise and Anthracite,* especially 57–92.

But how could all laborers become independent entrepreneurs, given that the existence of the latter was predicated, to a large extent, on the existence of the former? The answer was that laboring was seen as a temporary rather than a permanent position. There would always be workers; but no individual would be consigned to a lifetime spent working for others. Given the social opportunity thought to be inherent in northern society, free labor spokesmen like Carey and Bannan assumed that most mine laborers would eventually become miners, and most miners would achieve the ownership of capital if they wanted to and were prepared to work hard enough. The most obvious way that this vision of society departed from reality was that the majority of mine workers, no matter their ethnicity, never completed the second stage of the process, while many of the Irish could not even hope to complete the first.[11]

Increasingly aware of this fact, Bannan lashed out at the Irish, complaining about their religion, their culture, their ways of working, and their drinking practices. The Irish habit of voting for proslavery Democrats, moreover, contributed to Bannan's growing awareness of the threat posed to his society by slavery. As unruly immigrant laborers and supporters of the slave power, the Irish were doubly objectionable. Hostility toward them was a consistent feature of Bannan's ideology in both its nativist and its antislavery forms.[12]

While it would be simplistic to dismiss Bannan's anti-Catholicism as nothing other than a front for economic concerns, there can be no doubt that the targets he chose—drunkenness, ignorance, laziness, moral laxity, idolatry, political indoctrination—were relevant not only to the production of a responsible citizenry but also to the production of a responsible, self-sufficient work force. The Protestant notions of a "calling," of "worldly asceticism," and of the modest accumulation of wealth as a sign of grace, were powerful moral sanctions in producing qualities opposite to those Bannan found most reprehensible in Irish Catholics. Self-discipline, sobriety, and punctuality were not only religious obligations but social norms in an expanding capitalist society. This emphasis on economic self-sufficiency helps to explain why Bannan attacked only Irish Catholic immigrants, and not immigrants and Catholics in general. Germans, whether they were Catholic or Protestant, were attacked only on the issue of liquor, and even then only very rarely.[13]

Catholicism, in its Irish variety, was the primary target of Bannan's nativism. But the ultimate source of his hostility to the Irish was the stubborn fact that so many of them worked as laborers rather than miners when they arrived in the anthracite region, and continued to do so for the rest of their working lives. The ethnic and religious divisions between the British and Irish residents of the anthracite region corresponded to rigid social divisions in the mines and mining towns. The variety of cultural attributes that Bannan lamented in the

11. Wallace, *St. Clair,* 133–41, 367–80; cf. chapter 2 of the present work.

12. On Irish voting habits, see Gudelunas and Shade, *Before the Molly Maguires,* passim.

13. Cf. Max Weber, *The Protestant Ethic and the Spirit of Capitalism* (1904–05; New York, 1958), passim, especially 193–94 on "worldly asceticism," and chapter 3 on the "calling."

Irish masked a very real fear that a class of immigrants had arrived who were unwilling or unable to move upward through the social scale. It was this material threat to Bannan's cherished polity of small, upwardly mobile producers that underlay the objections he raised against the Irish throughout the 1850s: their drunkenness and general waywardness, their poverty and laziness, their criminality and insanity, their undemocratic religion and their perverse insistence on taking the wrong side in the great moral crusades of the day, including sabbatarianism, temperance, educational reform, and antislavery.[14]

In the 1850s Bannan's political cause suffered a series of defeats. The Democrats, with their Irish Catholic support, reigned victorious on both the local and the national level. The Whig party collapsed in 1853–54, and the variety of prohibitionist and nativist parties that Bannan supported over the next two years failed to create a new coalition in the resulting political vacuum. But, from the mid-1850s onward, it looked as though the cause of antislavery was capable of uniting a viable political coalition against the triumphant Democrats. Bannan saw the expansion of slavery into the territories as the triumph of a way of life that was the antithesis of his own ideal: a repressive, aristocratic, rigidly hierarchical society where labor did not get its just rewards and where there was no real prospect of social advancement for the majority. As the ideal opposite of slavery, free labor provides the key to deciphering Bannan's ideology throughout the 1850s, whether that ideology took the form of anti-Catholicism or antislavery.[15]

Benjamin Bannan's outright conversion to the cause of antislavery is evident in the presidential election of 1856, a three-way race involving James Buchanan (Democrat), Millard Fillmore (Know Nothing Party), and for the first time, a Republican candidate, John C. Frémont.[16] Though Buchanan carried his own state by only 705 votes, he won the presidential election quite handily. Worse still, from Bannan's point of view, he won 7,035 votes in Schuylkill County compared to only 4,870 for the combined opposition (2,188 for Frémont and 2,682 for Fillmore).[17] In Buchanan's election, Bannan foresaw a dual threat to freedom, on the one hand from Catholicism and on the other from slavery. Both "the slave power" and "the Catholic threat" could be portrayed in much the same terms—a conspiracy by the few to subvert the liberties of the many.[18]

14. On these themes see, for example, *MJ*, November 6, 1852; June 25, 1853; July 2, 1853; August 6, 15, 1853; October 1, 15, 1853; November 5, 12, 1853; April 22, 29, 1854; May 6, 1854; June 10, 17, 24, 1854; July 1, 8, 1854; September 30, 1854; September 29, 1855; October 13, 1855. On the question of slavery see, in particular, October 4, 25, 1856; November 1, 8, 1856; September 26, 1857; October 10, 25, 1857. Cf. Kenny, "Nativism, Labor, and Slavery."

15. Cf. Kenny, "Nativism, Labor, and Slavery."

16. See, for example, *MJ*, June 28, July 26, October 11, 1856.

17. For the local and state results, see *MJ*, November 8, 1856, and October 3, 1857; for the national results, see William E. Gienapp, *The Origins of the Republican Party, 1852–56* (New York, 1987), 414. The 2,682 votes for Fillmore in Schuylkill County were composed of 2,315 votes for the Union ticket and 367 "straight Fillmore" votes.

18. *MJ*, October 25, November 1, 1856; cf. David M. Potter, *The Impending Crisis, 1848–1861* (New York, 1976), 251–52; James L. Huston, "The Demise of the Pennsylvania American Party, 1854–58," *PMHB*, 109 (October 1985): 492.

Without the Irish Catholic vote, Bannan believed, Buchanan would never have won in 1856. Bannan's antipathy to the political influence of Irish immigrants reached its height the following year, in the state gubernatorial election of 1857, when he supported the antislavery candidate, David Wilmot (Union ticket), against William Packer (Democrat). "Let Packer be elected," he declared, "and a shout of exultation from little Delaware to Texas, would re-echo through the Slave States. It would be another nail in the coffin of Freedom."[19] Bannan had precisely these concerns in mind on September 26, 1857, when he warned the workingmen of Schuylkill County to come to a sense of their true interests. "Unfortunately in this country there is a class of workmen, who blind to their own interests, will advocate at the polls, slave-labor," Bannan warned. "They cannot or will not see that the introduction of slave labor degrades their occupation and lessens their remuneration."[20]

There is little doubt that the "class of workmen" that Bannan was referring to were the Irish, or at least the more impoverished and unruly elements among them. Irish Catholics voted overwhelmingly Democratic, while other (mainly Protestant) ethnic groups were more likely to vote Whig, nativist, or Republican. Wilmot's opponents, Bannan announced, were "the slaves of party; the slaves of Propaganda": a clear reference to the link between the Democrats and Irish Catholics.[21] Bannan was by no means certain that his free labor ideology was applicable to people of this type. If it was not, he had a serious problem on his hands. Unless the Irish became more disciplined, more independent, and less Democratic, Bannan faced the prospect of rigid social and political divisions in the anthracite region, which would make his dream of a middle-class republic more remote than ever. The defeat of David Wilmot in the election in October therefore came as a particularly heavy blow. Packer won Schuylkill County by 5,950 votes to 3,079, a majority of 2,871. Packer also won the state vote by a handy margin, and Democrats won most of the local offices in Schuylkill County. It was in this context of defeat and disillusionment that Benjamin Bannan first mentioned the Molly Maguires in print. The charge he made against them, however, was political corruption, rather than the type of violence for which they later became infamous.[22]

This charge of corruption against Irish Catholics is best seen not simply as a narrow political issue but as Bannan's shorthand term for what he saw as their deleterious effect on the body politic as a whole. It was, in other words, a compound of all the other elements in his nativism, along with his immediate concerns over the spread of slavery and Irish support for a party that, under President Buchanan, was not just indifferent to slavery but positively in favor of it. Bannan's uneasiness about Irish Catholic bloc voting is evident as early as 1844, and by 1856 these charges had hardened into an accusation of electoral fraud.

19. *MJ*, September 26, 1857.

20. Ibid.; see, also, November 1, 1856.

21. *MJ*, September 26, 1857; Gudelunas and Shade, *Before the Molly Maguires*, passim.

22. *MJ*, October 10, 1857.

The *Miners' Journal* of October 25, 1856, for example, had reported that the number of people who had voted in an election in Philadelphia earlier that month was ten thousand greater than the total possible electorate. Bannan had no doubt about the culprits: Irish Catholic immigrants and their political and religious leaders. "Fraudulent naturalization papers," he alleged, "were given to thousands of immigrants not entitled to them."[23]

By 1857 Bannan was evidently convinced that behind the various forms of un-Americanism he had been attacking for the previous five years, including support for slavery, there lurked a mysterious secret society called the "Molly Maguires." The society was mentioned for the first time in the *Miners' Journal* of October 3, 1857, four days before Wilmot lost the gubernatorial election to Packer. Fifty-five indictments for fraud had been found by the Grand Jury of Philadelphia against inspectors of the 1856 presidential election, the newspaper reported: "Every one of these inspectors were Irishmen, belonging no doubt to the order of 'Molly Maguires,' a secret Roman Catholic association which the Democracy is using for political purposes." Citing other newspapers, the *Miners' Journal* traced the origin of the society to Boston and claimed that it controlled the Democratic party. Moreover, Bannan stated unequivocally that William Packer, the Democratic candidate for governor, was "supported by this Secret Roman Catholic Association."[24] Yet this ostensibly "Roman Catholic" organization, a second article reported, had already been dissolved by its own Church. In Philadelphia the previous Sunday, a priest had announced from the pulpit that "the members of this secret political organization . . . were not fit to belong to this church," and that "if he succeeded in ascertaining their names, he would certainly excommunicate them from membership; for such societies in a country like this, are not only entirely useless, but calculated to bring reproach upon the religion which the members profess, and to array the native-born population in opposition to the church." The "honest thinking citizens of all parties," the *Miners' Journal* concluded, ought to unite in putting down this "secret association."[25]

Before October 1857, the Molly Maguires had never been mentioned in print in the anthracite region. For the next twenty years the term *Molly Maguires* would be a permanent feature of the political and cultural language of the region, sometimes confined to the margins, at other times occupying center stage. But what sort of secret organization, if any, corresponded to this pattern of ideological representation? The society referred to was presumably the Ancient Order of Hibernians, which had been present in Schuylkill County since it was founded in 1836. From 1836 to 1848, the *Miners' Journal* had reported the St. Patrick's Day banquet organized annually by the AOH. In the nativist 1850s,

23. *MJ*, October 25, 1856; see, also, November 1, 1856.

24. *MJ*, October 3, 1857; the newspapers cited were the *Philadelphia Transcript* and the *Berks and Schuylkill Journal*, n.d.

25. Paraphrase of a sermon delivered by Father Cantwell at the Roman Catholic Church of St. Philip di Neri, Philadelphia, quoted in *MJ*, October 3, 1857, with accompanying editorial.

Bannan stopped printing these reports, though it is safe to assume that the AOH remained in existence and continued to organize its annual dinners. At this stage, however, the AOH was clearly a peaceful fraternal organization; collective violence did not enter into the picture. The names of its officers were printed in the *Miners' Journal* in the 1840s, and none of the individuals named was involved in the violence of the 1860s and 1870s. Before the late 1850s, in any case, the AOH was confined to the Pottsville area.[26]

During the massive wave of immigration from Ireland after 1845, the AOH spread throughout the anthracite region. Aside from the church and the tavern, it was the only significant ethnic organization available to the immigrants. Many of them would have been familiar with its Irish equivalents, most of which were secret, and some violent. In the areas where the Molly Maguire violence occurred in the 1860s and 1870s, the AOH lodges were dominated by men from north-central and northwestern Ireland, Donegal in particular. These men, it appears, adapted their AOH lodges to classic "Ribbonite" purposes, which included some degree of collective violence. In the part of Ireland where many of these immigrants came from, the Ribbonmen and the Ancient Order of Hibernians were known as "Molly Maguires." Threatening notices signed "Mollie's Children" were reportedly being posted in the anthracite region as early as 1848. According to oral tradition in the anthracite region, a loosely organized group calling themselves the "Molly Maguires" first emerged in the 1850s in Cass Township, the most heavily Irish part of Schuylkill County, to avenge discrimination and physical attacks by British Protestant miners. No documentary evidence of the existence of any such organization has survived. But the Irish of Cass Township probably did have some rudimentary form of organization corresponding to Benjamin Bannan's description. If this organization was a local lodge of the Ancient Order of Hibernians, or an inner circle within that lodge, its members would in all likelihood have called themselves "Molly Maguires."[27]

In Schuylkill County in 1857, the AOH was accused of political corruption, not murder and conspiracy; and it was rarely accused of violence in other parts of the United States. Benjamin Bannan was much more concerned about drunkenness, lack of discipline, and political corruption in the 1850s. Violence, as yet, did not feature prominently in his indictment of the Irish. Nonetheless, the sporadic labor activism of the 1840s and 1850s had been characterized by occasional outbreaks of collective violence with a distinctively Irish flavor. And at least one Welshman had been murdered in a way that prefigured the retributive violence of the 1860s and 1870s. The incident in question had occurred in the summer of 1846, after a young Welshman, John Reese, shot and killed an

26. For reports of the AOH in the 1840s, see the mid-March issues of *MJ*.

27. On the Irish predominance in Cass Township, see Grace Palladino, *Another Civil War: Labor, Capital, and the State in the Anthracite Regions of Pennsylvania, 1840–68* (Urbana, Ill., 1990); on the term *Molly's Children* in the 1840s, see Munsell, *History of Schuylkill County,* 99; for oral tradition about the Molly Maguires in Cass, see Arthur H. Lewis, *Lament for the Molly Maguires* (1964; New York, 1969), 10–11.

Irishman named Thomas Collahan at Delaware Mines, a mine patch just north of St. Clair. Reese was arrested and held in prison for a few months; when his case came to trial he was acquitted on the grounds that he had acted in self-defense.[28]

On December 30 Reese decided to visit his brother in Wadesville, and for some reason he took a short cut through his old neighborhood, Delaware Mines. As he was walking up the railroad tracks toward Wadesville, a man rushed up to him and felled him with a single blow from a pick axe. According to the eyewitnesses, the killer's face was whitened with powder. Reese was taken, unconscious, to his brother's house in Wadesville, where he died the following morning. Two days later, an Irishman called Martin Shay was arrested for the crime. At the trial, he was positively identified by Reese's family, but a series of witnesses for the defense provided an alibi. Many of the witnesses claimed that a mysterious stranger, who bore a remarkable resemblance to Shay, had been seen hanging around Delaware Mines on the night of the murder. Some even claimed to know his name—Cummings, or Devine—but an investigation by the prosecution could find no trace of any such individual.[29]

In June 1847 Shay was found guilty of first degree murder, and in September he was sentenced to be hanged, only two years after his arrival in the United States from Ireland. His case prefigured much of the violence of the 1860s and 1870s; the importation of a stranger to do the killing, and the readiness of witnesses to provide an alibi, in particular, suggest a type of community solidarity rooted in Irish rural culture. But the authorities saw the murder as an isolated incident, not as part of a general conspiracy. Only when the type of violence Shay had committed assumed a collective character in the 1860s would the explanation of "Molly Maguireism" be invoked.[30]

Was Benjamin Bannan haunted by the specter of such collective violence when he first named the Molly Maguires in October 1857? Even if violence was not among the accusations he leveled against the Irish in the 1850s, fear of potential collective violence would certainly have been part of his general antipathy toward Irish immigrant workers. For the present, however, he concentrated on political corruption rather than violence. As the most heavily Irish township in Schuylkill County until the late 1860s, Cass Township represented a fundamental obstacle to Bannan's hopes of ending Democratic rule in the county. But, in the early 1860s, Cass became notorious for something else: violent resistance against employers and the military draft. During the American Civil War, Irish violence in the anthracite region took on a collective character for the first time, and the term *Molly Maguires* assumed its more familiar meaning of a murderous conspiratorial society. In this respect, the Civil War was a major turning point.

28. *MJ*, January 2, June 12, September 26, 1847.

29. *MJ*, January 2, June 12, September 26, 1847.

30. Shay's sentence was noted in *MJ*, September 26, 1847, but he does not appear to have been hanged, as *MJ*, June 14, 1878, did not include him among those executed in Schuylkill County prior to 1877.

When President Abraham Lincoln issued a proclamation on April 15, 1861, calling for 75,000 troops to defend the Union, the people of the anthracite region were quick to respond. By April 17 two companies were already on their way to Harrisburg from Schuylkill County, and by April 24 twenty-two companies, a total of 1,860 men, had left the county for Washington.[31] Governor Andrew Curtin authorized Colonel James Nagle of Pottsville to raise a regiment of men from Schuylkill County. The result was the Pennsylvania Forty-eighth, which saw action at the second Battle of Bull Run, Fredricksburg, the Wilderness, Cold Harbor, and most notably, the Battle of the Crater in Petersburg, Virginia.[32]

The Battle of the Crater was one of innumerable incidents involving soldiers from the anthracite region. Like most parts of the North, the region made an important military contribution to the Civil War, a contribution that transformed the personal histories of thousands of its residents. Among the many who served in the Union army were three men who would feature prominently in the Molly Maguire story in the 1870s: Lieutenant Colonel Henry Pleasants, who would later head the notorious Coal & Iron Police; General Charles Albright, who would appear for the prosecution in the mid-1870s ostentatiously dressed in full military uniform; and Private James Kerrigan, who would become the most notorious of the Molly Maguire informers.

But the importance of the Civil War went far beyond the personal histories of the men who enlisted in the Union army. The economic and political structures of the anthracite region were transformed. At first, the war crippled the anthracite trade. In 1861 many mines were slowed or halted by the departure of mine workers who enlisted as volunteers in the Union army. A general business recession, especially in the iron trade, also lessened the demand for coal. But the mining industry quickly recovered and, overall, the Civil War turned out to be a boom time for the operators and the workers. The coal trade picked up briskly in 1862, with the ever-increasing consumption of anthracite by the government for war purposes, and by manufacturers of war materials. The prices paid for coal, transportation, and labor all rose accordingly. At one large mine in Schuylkill County, for example, laborers who had been paid $6 a week in November 1862 were making $12 a week a year later. At the same time, the pay of miners working for wages had risen from $7.50 a week to $18, and the pay of contract miners had risen from $12 a week to $30.[33]

31. Munsell, *History of Schuylkill County,* 110; Wiley, *Biographical and Portrait Cyclopedia of Schuylkill County,* 49.

32. *Report of the Joint Committee on the Conduct of the War at the Second Session of the Thirty-Eighth Congress,* vol. 1, *Battle of Petersburg* (Washington, 1865), 1–247; Bruce Catton, *The Civil War* (1971; New York, 1980), 211–16; Richard Wheeler, *On Fields of Fury. From the Wilderness to the Crater: An Eyewitness History* (New York, 1991), 273–85; Munsell, *History of Schuylkill County,* 119.

33. Munsell, *A History of Schuylkill County,* 64.

From 1862 to 1865, the coal trade prospered as never before, with benefits for everybody involved. At least 130 new mining operations opened in Schuylkill County alone between 1861 and 1865.[34] The Civil War was also a period of increasing economic centralization in the lower anthracite region. Larger coal companies, based in New York City and Philadelphia, took control of production in the northern and middle regions; the Reading Railroad bought out the smaller lateral railroads in Schuylkill County and took control of distribution there.[35] This process of corporate consolidation approached completion in the Schuylkill region only in the early 1870s, when the Reading achieved a near-monopoly over both the production and the distribution of Schuylkill coal.

If the war years were a time of prosperity for the operators and their employees, they were also a time of considerable social unrest. This unrest was generally attributed to the influx of large numbers of foreigners, most of them Irish, to fill the jobs created by the greatly increased demand for anthracite and the absence of mine workers who had enlisted in the army. Given the nativist polemics of the 1850s, the continued influx of unruly Irish immigrants was a source of considerable alarm. Most of the unrest was traced to the antiwar sentiment of Democratic politicians and their Irish immigrant constituencies. In the fusion of a long-standing nativist and antislavery critique of the Irish with the political, military, and economic exigencies of war lay a crucial turning point in the history of the Molly Maguires.

A good starting point for understanding that history in the 1860s, as in the previous decade, is local and national politics. As a state that bordered the neutral, slave-holding territory of Delaware and Maryland, and that was itself a prime target for a Confederate invasion, Pennsylvania was in a notably difficult and ambiguous position during the Civil War. With Ohio, Indiana, Illinois, and New York, it constituted the main center of northern opposition to the war, despite the fact that some 320,000 Pennsylvanians fought in the Union army, a figure exceeded only by New York State.[36]

Among the most radical antiwar politicians in Pennsylvania was Francis W. Hughes, the leading Democrat in Schuylkill County and a prominent figure in state politics. As the leader of the Democratic machine in Schuylkill County, Hughes was in a powerful position. The Republicans won the county in 1860, but the anthracite region remained a Democratic stronghold during the Civil War, just as it had in the 1850s. Andrew Curtin, who was narrowly reelected to the governorship of Pennsylvania in 1863, was easily defeated in five of the six counties of the anthracite region that year by the proslavery Democratic challenger, George Woodward. And Abraham Lincoln was

34. Yearley, *Enterprise and Anthracite,* 62.

35. Palladino, *Another Civil War,* 132.

36. Arnold M. Shankman, "Draft Resistance in Civil War Pennsylvania," *PMHB,* 101 (April 1977): 190.

defeated in all six anthracite counties in 1864, even though he won Pennsylvania as a whole.[37]

The resounding defeats of Curtin and Lincoln are best interpreted not so much as a vote for slavery as a vote against the policies of the federal government. Chief among these was the attempt to raise an army, first through the Militia Act of July 17, 1862, which authorized state drafts to supply the necessary manpower, and then through the Conscription Act of March 3, 1863, which set up an elaborate system for conducting the draft, including the appointment of a provost marshal and enrollment officers for each congressional district. Yet, despite their return to power in the anthracite region, the Democrats often found themselves politically impotent, even on the local level. Local politics were never more subordinate to national concerns than in the 1860s. One result of the war was a tremendous increase in federal power, which sharply tilted the balance of power away from the states. This was particularly true in the anthracite region, where the resurgence of the Democrats was very much a Pyrrhic victory. Although Benjamin Bannan once again found himself in a minority after 1863, he and other local Republicans were part of a network of political power that extended through the state and national levels and could be supplemented by military force if necessary.

In terms of the local politics of the anthracite region during the Civil War, this fact was of decisive importance. When violence erupted in Schuylkill County in 1862, 1863, and 1864, it was suppressed by state and national forces, not by the Democratic officials who ostensibly controlled local affairs. Indeed, much of the trouble was blamed on the Democrats, for the center of the agitation was their stronghold in Schuylkill County, Cass Township. Seventy-seven percent of the electorate in Cass voted for the Democratic candidate for president in 1856, and 82 percent in 1864; even in the presidential election of 1860, when Schuylkill County as a whole voted Republican, the majority of voters (56 percent) in Cass voted Democrat. Lincoln won every township in the mining section of Schuylkill County in 1860 with the exception of Cass, where he got only 43 percent of the vote and the Republican candidates as a whole only 39 percent. The most heavily Irish township in Schuylkill County, Cass was the main center of draft resistance, labor activism, and Molly Maguire activity during and immediately after the Civil War.[38]

When Benjamin Bannan had first used the term *Molly Maguires* to describe a mysterious Irish secret society in 1857, there had not yet been any significant violence in the anthracite region. During the Civil War the term was expanded to cover a new form of Irish popular protest, an amalgam of draft resistance, labor activism, and direct, violent action that, from 1862 onward, went under

37. Munsell, *History of Schuylkill County,* 311–12; Gudelunas and Shade, *Before the Molly Maguires,* 81, 85; *MJ,* November 10, 1860, December 10, 1864; Arnold M. Shankman, *The Pennsylvania Antiwar Movement: 1861–65* (Rutherford, N.J., 1980), 134–36, 199–201. Republicans swept most of the local and national races in Schuylkill County in 1860. Lincoln won 57 percent of the vote in the county, including most of the German and British votes.

38. Electoral returns from Gudelunas and Shade, *Before the Molly Maguires,* 81, 85, 133.

the name of *Molly Maguireism.* The first two of the sixteen assassinations attributed to the Molly Maguires occurred during the war, as did a wave of social disorder, labor activism, and organized resistance to conscription. By the end of the war, the term *Molly Maguires* was being used in the lower anthracite region to describe any and all forms of violence and disorder involving Irish mine workers. The trouble in the anthracite region during the Civil War was concentrated in two distinct areas: Cass Township, which lay in the center of Schuylkill County, only five miles north of Pottsville; and the area around the town of Audenried, at the intersection of Schuylkill, Carbon, and Luzerne counties, at the southern tip of the Eastern Middle Coal Field. The events in these two places during the Civil War gave rise to the theory of the Molly Maguires as a powerful, violent, and subversive conspiracy.

The first assassination attributed to the Molly Maguires was that of the mine foreman Frank W. Langdon, at Audenried on June 14, 1862. The incident apparently involved some opposition to the Union war effort, though not to the draft, as there was no conscription law in the North until the following month, when the Militia Act was passed. Moreover, the assassination was not attributed to the Molly Maguires at the time. Only during the trials of the 1870s was this crime blamed on the machinations of an alleged secret society. John Kehoe, the suspected ringleader of the Molly Maguire conspiracy, was convicted of the crime in January 1877 and executed on December 18, 1878.

Langdon was killed shortly after addressing a public meeting in preparation for the imminent Fourth of July celebration. Irish mine workers in the crowd apparently displayed considerable anti-Union sentiment, and one of them allegedly expressed his resentment by spitting on the American flag. He was later identified as John Kehoe, an Irish-born miner from Shenandoah. Langdon denounced the crowd of Irish mine workers, and Kehoe in particular. At his trial in 1878, witnesses for the prosecution alleged that Kehoe had been heard to say the words "You son of a bitch, I'll kill you" in response to Langdon's tirade. In any case, as soon as Langdon left the meeting he was set upon by a crowd of men and severely beaten. He died the following day.[39] But what, if anything, did this incident have to do with the Molly Maguires? The antiwar sentiment of the crowd is suggestive, but it does not entail the existence of an organized conspiratorial society. Langdon was a foreman at the mine where Kehoe worked, and Kehoe had allegedly threatened to kill him a few weeks earlier, after his pay had been docked. Beyond that nothing is known about the circumstances of Langdon's death, and it is difficult to see how it could have been attributed to the Molly Maguires other than retrospectively.[40]

A second alleged Molly Maguire assassination was to occur in Audenried in

39. Coleman, *The Molly Maguire Riots,* 40; Broehl, *The Molly Maguires,* 90–91.

40. Cf. Broehl, *The Molly Maguires,* 335.

November 1863, but in the intervening eighteen months the attention of the authorities was focussed on Cass Township, the most turbulent area in the anthracite region throughout the 1860s. Incorporated as a township in 1848, Cass was dominated by a single family from New York City, the Heckschers. The financier Charles E. Heckscher had organized the Forest Improvement Company in 1837 to open and prepare coal mines, construct lateral railroads, and underwrite major capital expenditures. His nephew Richard Heckscher soon joined the business, and by 1860 Heckscher & Company was the single largest employer in the lower anthracite region. In that year, the Heckscher family operated the five largest and most productive collieries in the lower region, all of them located in Cass Township. The names of the township's two largest settlements, Forestville and Heckscherville, reflected the dominance of a single family corporation. The Heckschers employed 1,200 of the 1,590 mine workers in Cass Township.[41]

The mine workers in Cass were already experiencing conditions that would not become widespread in most of the lower anthracite region until the 1870s. They worked in mines that were bigger than in the rest of Schuylkill County and were controlled by a single operator. Lists of rules and regulations were posted in the area as early as 1865, whereas they became common in most other places only after the takeover by the Reading Railroad in the mid-1870s. The miners of Cass appear to have been a propertyless, wage-earning class as early as 1860, though this was not yet typical of the anthracite region as a whole.[42]

The first significant social disturbance during the Civil War occurred in Cass Township in May 1862, a month before the assassination of Frank W. Langdon and two months before the passage of the Militia Act of July 1862. It involved a labor dispute rather than overt opposition to the policies of the federal government. But throughout the Civil War, political and military officials consistently equated labor activism with draft resistance, so that all forms of social disorder, especially strike activity or the attempt to form labor unions, could be construed as disloyalty to the Union.[43]

The incident at Cass began when miners and laborers went on strike for higher wages at Heckscherville, stopping the pumps at the mines and bringing work to a halt. The *Miners' Journal* conceded that the men had a right to strike for higher wages, but condemned them for stopping the pumps, declaring that "such action places them in the position of violators of the law." The county

41. Munsell, *History of Schuylkill County,* 195–96; Palladino, *Another Civil War,* 30, 171. The population of Cass was 4,112 in 1850 and 6,493 in 1860 but declined in the late 1860s (to 4,621 in 1870) as the center of the coal industry in the lower region moved to northern Schuylkill County. *Ninth Census,* vol. 1, 254.

42. Palladino, *Another Civil War,* passim. Palladino's analysis of the anthracite region rests on the single, atypically Irish township of Cass. Papers of Charles Heckscher, NYPL, Moses Taylor Collection, B 588, Clippings, 1863–66, p. 54, original handbill setting out the "Rules and Regulations Established by the New York and Schuylkill Coal Company" in 1865. Charles Heckscher and Moses Taylor were partners in the company.

43. Palladino, *Another Civil War,* passim.

sheriff evidently agreed; with the mines in danger of being "drowned out," he proceeded to Heckscherville with a small force of militia and set the pumps in motion. According to the *Miners' Journal*, the militia were then "overpowered by the rioters and compelled to return." The sheriff telegraphed Governor Curtin for assistance, and Curtin authorized General Patterson of Philadelphia to send a battalion of two hundred men to Cass Township. Upon their arrival in Heckscherville and Forestville the troops encountered no opposition, and the *Miners' Journal* blamed the sheriff for overreacting. But when the Cass strike of May 1862 turned out to be the first of a long series of violent incidents, the newspaper changed its tone and soon detected in Cass Township the workings of an ominous secret society, the Molly Maguires.[44]

The next major incident in Cass Township came in October 1862, and this time the military draft was the central issue. The Militia Act of July 17, 1862, had authorized state drafts to supply the Union army with manpower. In August, Lincoln had ordered a draft of 300,000 militiamen, leaving the enrollment procedure to each state. Seventeen thousand Pennsylvanians were requested and Colonel Alexander K. McClure, a personal friend of Lincoln, was appointed to oversee the draft in that state. The choice of a draft commissioner for Schuylkill County was highly significant: Benjamin Bannan. Throughout September, Bannan and his assistants encountered sporadic hostility as they tried to take a census of names from which to draft the conscripts. The hostility included incidents where women and boys threw hot water, sticks, stones, and other missiles.[45]

When the list of conscripts was announced on October 16, 1862, accumulated grievances against the draft exploded in violence. A large crowd gathered in Cass Township, traveling through the mine patches and bringing out the men from colliery after colliery. They soon numbered about one thousand. At the town of Tremont, a few miles west of Cass, they stopped a train transporting draftees from Schuylkill County to Harrisburg. Governor Curtin wired Secretary of War Stanton on October 22, requesting troops and informing him that "the draft is being resisted in several counties of the State. In Schuylkill County I am just informed that 1,000 armed men are assembled, and will not suffer the train to move with the drafted men to this place." Stanton authorized Curtin to use the cavalry he had requested, along with "any other military force" in the state. He also instructed Major General Wool, the commanding general of the Middle Department, to support Curtin "with the whole force of the department." Curtin requested "one thousand regulars," informing Stanton that, "notwithstanding the usual exaggerations," there were "several thousands in arms," organized in a conspiracy to resist the draft. Stanton was unable to spare a thousand battle-seasoned troops for Curtin, but he did order the dispatch of cavalry and artillery. The following day, a relieved Governor Curtin was able

44. All quotes from *MJ*, May 10, 1862.

45. Shankman, *The Pennsylvania Antiwar Movement*, 148.

to inform Stanton that "the riots in Schuylkill County have ceased for the present."[46]

But there was more to the suppression of the draft resistance at Cass in October 1862 than a show of military force. One alternative to using troops was the powerful moral sanction of the Catholic church. The lower anthracite region lay in the diocese of Philadelphia, whose bishop, James Frederic Wood, made a special journey to Cass Township in October 1862 to see if he could pacify the area. "I am happy to say that for the present the necessity for use of force in Schuylkill County is over," Curtin wrote Stanton on October 27. "The decision and promptness, but more the presence of Bishop Wood, who kindly went up when requested, has relieved us all."[47] The *Miners' Journal* was equally complimentary. "The Catholic Bishop of Philadelphia visited this region last week and administered some wholesome advice to men recently engaged in the disturbance here," Benjamin Bannan noted on November 1. "He taught them their duty under the law as good citizens. On Sunday last the priests in this Borough, and County, preached strong sermons on the subject, which had their effect."[48] No further evidence on this matter has survived, but Wood's visit presumably exercised a persuasive influence on the residents of the anthracite region and was doubtless a decisive precedent for his well-publicized opposition to the Molly Maguires thereafter.

Although a combination of military and moral force temporarily pacified Cass Township, it seems that more devious methods were also used to ensure social stability. In his memoirs, Colonel Alexander K. McClure, the official in charge of the draft in Pennsylvania as a whole, had a peculiar story to tell about the events in Cass Township in October 1862.[49] "In several of the mining districts there were positive indications of revolutionary disloyalty," McClure recalled, "and it was especially manifested in Schuylkill, where the Molly Maguires were then in the zenith of their power. The center of their power was in Cass Township, where thirteen murders had been committed within two or three years, and not a single murderer brought to punishment." As Cass township provided so few volunteers, McClure continued, it had an unusually large quota of conscripts. When the draft was made on October 16, it therefore included a disproportionately large number of mine workers, "all of whom were under the absolute influence of the Molly Maguires."[50]

McClure was apparently afraid that the stationing of troops in the region might exacerbate rather than resolve the conflict. As he recalled years later: "It was an imperious necessity to prevent an open, desperate and bloody conflict in the heart of our great Commonwealth, that would have greatly strengthened

46. *OR*, ser. 1, vol. 19, part 2, 468–69, 473, 474, 479, 489–90; Shankman, *The Pennsylvania Antiwar Movement*, 148.

47. *OR*, ser. 1, vol 19, part 2, 500.

48. *MJ*, November 1, 1862.

49. Alexander K. McClure, *Old Time Notes of Pennsylvania*, 2 vols. (Philadelphia, 1905), vol. 1, chapter 49; McClure, *Lincoln and Men of War Times* (1892; Philadelphia, 1961), 429–40.

50. McClure, *Old Time Notes of Pennsylvania*, vol. 1, 545–46.

rebellion in the South and weakened the loyal cause in the North."[51] He communicated these fears to President Lincoln, and according to McClure's memoirs, Lincoln had him understand that he would be satisfied if the draft appeared to have been executed in Cass, even if it were not executed in fact. The following evening, Benjamin Bannan arrived in Harrisburg with the required number of forged affidavits. McClure then issued an order "releasing the conscripts of Cass Township from reporting for duty because the quota had been filled with volunteers."[52]

This attempt to defuse the tension in Cass Township by faking the draft returns did not pacify the region for long. Trouble broke out again in December 1862, which confirms the thesis that the chief source of conflict went far beyond the issue of draft resistance. On December 18, a crowd of two hundred armed men raided the Phoenix Colliery, operated by William Goyne at Forestville, Cass Township. According to the *Miners' Journal*, "The men were armed with shotguns, rifles, muskets, revolvers, etc., and were strangers to the persons at the works," and they "attacked and beat in the most outrageous manner some fifteen persons connected with the works, and in one instance beat a stranger who had no connection whatsoever with the Colliery."[53]

The events at Forestville were strikingly reminiscent of the pattern of activity engaged in by crowds and secret societies in the Irish countryside. Though the *Miners' Journal* portrayed the crowd as an unruly mob, emphasizing the beatings and intimidation, it is evident from the newspaper's own reports that the crowd had mobilized for a specific purpose and chose its targets carefully. The intruders forced the mining engineers to extinguish the furnaces and shut down the mine; they then took control of the colliery store, and before they left, they warned that if the store were reopened or the furnaces at the mine relit, "they would make a volcano of the entire works, and kill every man about the place."[54]

As for the perpetrators of the attack, Benjamin Bannan did not know the names of the individuals concerned, but he had no doubts about the organization that lay behind it: the lawless Molly Maguires of Cass Township. "They claim that at short notice they can rally three thousand men to engage in their unlawful work of stopping operations at collieries; dictating what other men, who are satisfied with their wages, shall work at; and in beating unarmed men." Here was the culmination of Bannan's worst fears: the specter of anarchy and class warfare in Schuylkill County. "If these high-handed outrages are permitted to go unchecked," he concluded, "property in the County will depreciate in value, and life will be more unsafe than it is among the savage guerrillas of the South."[55]

51. Ibid., vol. 2, 431.
52. Ibid., vol. 1, 548–49; McClure, *Lincoln and Men of War Times,* 91.
53. *MJ,* December 20, 1862.
54. Ibid.
55. All quotes from *MJ,* December 20, 1862.

The violence in Schuylkill County, and in particular Cass Township and the area surrounding Audenried, continued unabated in 1863. On January 11 a crowd of about forty Irish mine workers attacked the home of John McDonald in Cass Township. The motive was unclear and McDonald, luckily for him, happened to be absent.[56] On February 24 a mine operator named Thomas Verner was attacked by a crowd of his employees in Heckscherville; again the motive was unclear, but Verner had somehow antagonized his workers and their response was direct, violent action.[57] As in the previous year, the tension in Cass peaked during the summer and the issue, once again, was the military draft.

The Militia Act of July 1862 proved inadequate to the growing military requirements of the Union, and by early 1863 the need for a more comprehensive draft law was evident. The Conscription Act of March 3, 1863, was designed to avoid the inefficiency of the previous system and to guard against popular resistance. An elaborate system for conducting the draft was introduced, including a provost marshal and enrollment officers for each congressional district. The regional provost marshals reported to federal draft officials appointed for each state, and the whole system was supervised by the provost marshal general in Washington. Draftees were given ten days notification, and draft resisters were subject to two years' imprisonment and a five-hundred-dollar fine.[58] This new conscription system, which bypassed state and local authority in order to enforce the draft and root out disloyalty, was an important move in tipping the balance of power away from local to federal authorities. When the Pennsylvania Supreme Court declared the new conscription law unconstitutional, federal officials simply ignored the ruling and ordered that the draft be continued.[59]

Along with precedents like the suspension of habeas corpus for persons resisting the draft or engaging in other disloyal practices, the concentration of power evident in the Conscription Act alarmed not only Democrats but also many Republicans. But the chief source of hostility to the law was the provision that allowed the well-to-do to provide a substitute, or pay a commutation fee of three hundred dollars, in order to avoid serving in the army themselves. In 1863, three hundred dollars was considerably more than a year's wages for most mine workers in Pennsylvania. By contrast, the second best-paid lawyer in Schuylkill County at that time was earning around eight thousand dollars a year. His name was Franklin B. Gowen, and he was one of many wealthy residents who paid the three-hundred-dollar fee in order to avoid serving in the army.[60] Throughout the Northeast and Midwest, the commutation fee was

56. *MJ*, January 17, 1863.

57. *MJ*, February 28, 1863.

58. Shankman, *The Pennsylvania Antiwar Movement*, 142; Long, *Where the Sun Never Shines*, 93.

59. Shankman, "Draft Resistance in Civil War Pennsylvania," 199–20, *The Pennsylvania Antiwar Movement*, 142–53. In January 1864 the court reversed its decision.

60. Marvin W. Schlegel, *Ruler of the Reading: The Life of Franklin B. Gowen* (Harrisburg, 1947), 10; Long, *Where the Sun Never Shines*, 93.

interpreted by many working people and many Democrats as the final proof that this was "a rich man's war and a poor man's fight." Combined with the Emancipation Proclamation of January 1, 1863, the new conscription law provoked civil disorder throughout the North, most notably in New York City, where at least 119 people, and probably hundreds more, died in a week of rioting in July 1863.[61]

In Pennsylvania, the most serious disturbances in 1863 took place in the central, southeastern, and southern parts of the state. Much of the resistance to the draft came in the area between Schuylkill County and Philadelphia. There was also trouble in the anthracite county of Columbia, directly to the north of Schuylkill County. The draft was halted there in August 1863 after someone stole the records, and conflict arose again a year later when Lieutenant J. Stewart Robinson, the assistant provost marshal for the district, was murdered while searching for draft dodgers. The extreme southern tip of Columbia County lay in the Western Middle Coal Field, between Schuylkill and Northumberland County, but the rest of the county was rural, and it was in the agricultural rather than the mining lands that the trouble occurred. Indeed, much of the draft resistance in the counties of the anthracite region in 1863 came from Democratic German farmers, not from Irish miners and laborers.[62]

Just as in 1862, the draft officials in Schuylkill County experienced considerable hostility in their attempt to compile a list of residents as a basis for the draft. Provost Marshal Charlemagne Tower reported that local citizens fired shots at a number of his enrollers and threatened many others. But the draft officials now had troops to back up their activities, and they seized the payroll books of mine operators to help in compiling the lists.[63] On June 10 Tower wrote to the provost marshal general in Washington, reporting "two instances of assault upon the enrolling officers within this district—one in sub-district Number 7 consisting of Schuylkill Township, and the other in sub-district Number 23, consisting of Hegins and Hubley Townships, both within Schuylkill County." The assault in Schuylkill Township occurred in the mining village of Newkirk, fourteen miles east of Pottsville, while the other incident occurred in the German-populated farmlands of Hegins Township, twenty-two miles northwest of Pottsville.[64]

The enrolling officer for Schuylkill Township, Jeremiah F. Werner, wrote to

61. Iver Bernstein, *The New York City Draft Riots: Their Significance for American Society and Politics in the Age of the Civil War* (New York, 1990); Adrian Cook, *The Armies of the Streets: The New York City Draft Riots of 1863* (Lexington, 1974), 193–95. Estimates of the number of killed vary from the 1,500 or so reported by contemporaries to the figure of 119 reported in police records. The first figure is probably too high and the second is probably too low.

62. Shankman, *The Pennsylvania Antiwar Movement,* 145–49, 201; Shankman, "Draft Resistance in Civil War Pennsylvania," 195–96. There was also some opposition to the draft in the bituminous coal regions of western Pennsylvania, but Union sentiment was much stronger there than in the eastern and southern portions of the state.

63. Shankman, "Draft Resistance in Civil War Pennsylvania," 197.

64. *OR,* ser. 3, vol. 3, 330–32.

Tower describing the incident at Newkirk, as did one William K. Jones, who was with Werner at the time. "I was this day in the town of Newkirk to enroll the men of said place, but was driven away by them," Werner wrote on June 4.

> I then took another man along to assist me, but found them determined to resist, and they did so by firing four shots at us with a revolving pistol. I think that it is useless to try to enroll them without having a strong force, for they swore that they would resist any man.

Werner's companion, W. K. Jones, wrote to Tower the same day, informing him that it was "useless for J. F. Werner to undertake the finishing of the enrollment for the village of Newkirk, in Schuylkill Township . . . the Irish are so leagued as to make it necessary to coerce them." Jones then added an intriguing postscript: "If you desire to make examples of any who choose to have resisted the enrollment, I give you the following names, and am willing at any time to appear against them: Columbus McGee, Luke Scanlin, John Kelley, and Manus Burns, Newkirk, Schuylkill Township." Columbus McGee, a native of west Donegal, was one of several men tried in late 1876 for the first of the Molly Maguire killings, that of the mine foreman Frank W. Langdon.[65]

In June and July 1863, Tower's communications with Harrisburg and Washington took on an increasingly frantic tone. From "reliable sources" Tower had learned "that in some of these four [sub-districts] meetings are held twice a week in opposition to the enrollment, and that the feeling against the enrollment is violent in them all." Those offered the job of administering the draft had "declined on the ground that their property would be destroyed and their lives be unsafe if they were to undertake it." The mine operators would voluntarily furnish lists of their employees to the draft authorities if they could, Tower reported, but they were "in danger of having their breakers burned and machinery destroyed and being themselves killed." As a solution to this problem, Tower recommended a powerful show of military force, which would not only enforce the draft but encourage the operators to identify the troublemakers.[66]

The most detailed account of the alleged quasi-military resistance to the draft in Schuylkill County came in a letter from Brigadier General William D. Whipple to the provost marshal general in Washington on July 23, 1863, a week after the great riots in New York City. Whipple was then overseeing the draft in Philadelphia, a process that was eventually completed peacefully, no doubt because of the impressive show of military force. He sent Fry a list of facts that had been reported to him "as being the true state of things in Schuylkill County, Pa." In view of these facts he recommended that the draft "be postponed in that district for the present, and, when it is undertaken, that the whole district be drawn at Pottsville, and in the presence of at least a regiment of

65. All quotes from ibid., 332. Manus Burns may also have been from west Donegal. The name "Manus" is very popular there, as seen in the cases of two other immigrants from Donegal implicated in the Molly Maguire story, Manus O'Donnell and Manus Cull (or Coll), a.k.a. Daniel Kelly.

66. Ibid., 332, 382.

infantry and a battery of artillery." Whipple's six-point report to Fry read as follows:

> First. The miners of Cass Township, near Pottsville, have organized to resist the draft, to the number of 2,500 or 3,000 armed men.
>
> Second. They drill every evening, and are commanded by returned nine months' men and discharged three years' men.
>
> Third. It is positively known that they have two pieces of light artillery, and it is rumored that they have seven.
>
> Fourth. They threatened to burn down the houses and coal breakers owned by Republicans. They have served cautionary notices upon three citizens, Messrs. Bannon, Robert Morris, and another.
>
> Fifth. The U.S. force, commanded by Major Dayton, is stationed at Pottsville, and consists of two companies of the Invalid Corps. Three days ago this force had only twenty rounds of ammunition.
>
> Sixth. Fifteen hundred men and two sections of artillery would enforce the draft in Schuylkill County, probably without using physical force.[67]

Colonel Fry replied on July 27, 1863, approving the course of action Whipple recommended.[68]

Two days later, the assistant provost marshal of Pennsylvania wrote to Washington suggesting that, as the draft had been taken peacefully in Philadelphia, troops should be withdrawn from that city and put in position "at Pottsville or vicinity for operations in the mining districts." He estimated that a force of about two thousand men would be required, along with additional troops to guard the bridges and railroads. This request was met, and by early August Brigadier General Whipple had taken over the command in Pottsville. On August 3 the provost marshal general wrote to Whipple from Washington, advising him that "I have ordered Captain Tower to push his work to completion under the protection of your forces. If the miners resist the law forcibly, I hope you will make a severe example among them." Whipple had no doubt about the need to take stern measures, concluding that if the draft were "enforced here firmly but judiciously, it will go far toward correcting a state of lawlessness which has existed here for the past few years and which has made the name of miner a terror to all law-abiding citizens."[69]

The previous day Whipple had ridden through Heckscherville, "the worst place in the county," with a force of forty dragoons, and it was there that he intended to commence the draft. Two more regiments were needed to secure the county, he believed. On the same day, he reported, "a scheme was put on foot among the miners yesterday to attack the Forty-seventh Pennsylvania Militia encamped at Minersville. The attacking force was about 3,000 strong."[70] Only the arrival of new troops, Whipple reported, forestalled the attack. Just as he had

67. Ibid., 562.
68. Ibid., 579.
69. Ibid., 590, 620, 674–75.
70. Ibid., 674–75.

done in Philadelphia, Whipple used an intimidating display of military power to enforce the draft in Schuylkill County. In fact, there was much less resistance to the draft in the county than there had been in 1862, precisely because of the precautions taken by the authorities.

It is impossible to know the extent to which the military reports overestimated the threat posed by the mine workers of Cass Township. But, given the atmosphere of near-hysteria that accompanied the draft in the summer of 1863, especially after the carnage in New York City, it is safe to assume that there was considerable exaggeration. For example, one officer reported from Schuylkill County that the estimate of four thousand to five thousand men "assembled to resist the draft" was a gross underestimate. He claimed to have "learned from reliable information that there are at least 10,000 men that can assemble within twenty-four hours time."[71] If the figure of five thousand is highly unlikely, that of ten thousand is simply outlandish.

The following year, the neighboring county of Columbia was the scene of one of the most bizarre of all wartime conspiracy theories. In the summer of 1864 wild rumors circulated about an armed band of several hundred disloyal farmers and army deserters who were supposedly camped out in a remote spot in the Fishingcreek Valley, where they had constructed a fort and armed it with artillery smuggled in from Canada. Not only did they intend to organize resistance against the draft, they were also believed to be plotting a Confederate invasion of Pennsylvania.[72] Troops were dispatched to Bloomsburg, the county seat, and during the last two weeks of August hundreds of soldiers, led by Generals Darius N. Couch and George Cadwallader, searched the countryside for the nonexistent fort. The great "Fishingcreek Confederacy" turned out to be a figment of the overtaxed military imagination.[73]

As for the anthracite region, these rumors of organized conspiracy, along with the presence of troops, provided a convenient precedent for mine operators who were concerned about the impact of labor activism and social disorder on business. At Charlemagne Tower's suggestion, a number of operators in Schuylkill County requested military assistance to retain control of their collieries after the draft had been completed. Troops remained in various parts of the anthracite region for the remainder of the Civil War, and though the draft was completed in October 1863, Charlemagne Tower continued to serve as provost marshal until April 1864, employing his repressive tactics against the mine workers. Once the draft had been taken, Tower's activities were increasingly directed against labor activism, which was attacked as a form of disloyalty to the state.

The nexus of political, military, and economic power in the anthracite region during the war was epitomized by Tower's ambiguous status as a servant of the state and an entrepreneur with sizeable investments in coal lands.[74] As

71. Ibid., 543–44.

72. OR, ser. 3, vol. 4, 607.

73. Shankman, *The Pennsylvania Antiwar Movement,* 155–56; OR, ser. 3, vol. 4, 607.

74. Wallace, *St. Clair,* 326.

provost marshal, he was vested with extensive and arbitrary powers. He could draft any eligible man he pleased and arrest those who failed to appear when called. "The provost marshal's power extended far beyond the draft," as one historian has observed. "Tower used the conscription law to fight the union activism of the Irish mine workers, activism having nothing to do with the war."[75] As a result, existing hostility to the war among militant miners increased, even if the extent of actual resistance to the draft was greatly exaggerated. The wartime emergency offered local business and political leaders a fine opportunity to quash a nascent labor movement by equating its activities with treason.[76]

One local mine owner who had no hesitation in equating labor activism with treason in this way was Charles Albright, who attained the rank of general in the Union army during the war and went on to lead the prosecution in several of the Molly Maguire trials in the mid-1870s. In November 1863, Albright wrote to Abraham Lincoln from Mauch Chunk, informing him that "since the commencement of the draft a large majority of the coal operatives have been law-defying, opposing the National Government in every possible way, and making unsafe the lives and property of Union men." The rebels, Albright continued, were

> so numerous that they have the whole community in terror of them. They dictate the prices for their work, and if their employers don't accede they destroy and burn coal breakers, houses, and prevent those disposed from working. They resist the draft, and are organized into societies for this purpose.

They intended to sabotage the Union war effort by cutting off the supply of coal, Albright continued, thereby crippling industry and "setting off riots in the large cities." Rarely had the conjunction between labor organizing and disloyalty been stated so succinctly. And who were the men behind this conspiracy? They were "mostly" Irish, Albright reported, and they called themselves "Buckshots," a term that was used interchangeably with "Molly Maguires" during the Civil War.[77]

Given the prevailing pattern of nativism, there can be no doubt that protest by the Irish was much more likely to be equated with treason than protest by other ethnic groups. The hostility of the Irish in Cass Township toward the authorities was exacerbated by the heavy-handed tactics of Charlemagne Tower, who freely drafted alien residents even though they were exempt if they had not declared their intention of becoming citizens. Moreover, because Tower was not authorized to arrest men for anything other than draft resistance, many workers arrested for activities that had to do with labor organizing were charged with violating the conscription law.[78] Indeed, such was Tower's capacity for detecting

75. Long, *Where the Sun Never Shines,* 94–95; cf. Palladino, *Another Civil War,* 212.

76. See, for example, Bannan's editorial on this matter in MJ, August 22, 1863; cf. Palladino, *Another Civil War,* 135–36.

77. OR, ser. 3, vol. 3, 1,008–9.

78. Cf. Palladino, *Another Civil War,* 222–30.

conspiracies and his zeal in uprooting them, that the provost marshal general in Washington was quite skeptical about some of his claims. On June 27, 1863, for example, he urged Tower to continue taking vigorous measures but warned him not to be overzealous:

> Vigorous measures are what I urge upon you, and for this purpose have sent you a military force that seems adequate to all the wants that have yet shown themselves. I want you to use it vigorously, but use it to put down opposition and not create it, and to be sure that all against whom you adopt vigorous measures are clearly in the wrong.[79]

With Cass Township temporarily pacified by the military, the attention of the authorities shifted once more to the town of Audenried, in Carbon County, where the first Molly Maguire assassination had taken place in June 1862. While the assassination of Frank W. Langdon was added to the roster of Molly Maguire crimes only in the late 1870s, the second assassination at Audenried during the Civil War was explicitly blamed on the secret society at the time and exhibited several of the hallmarks of retributive justice characteristic of violent agrarian societies in Ireland. Audenried lay at the intersection of Schuylkill, Luzerne, and Carbon counties, in the part of the anthracite region most heavily settled by immigrants from Donegal.[80]

The victim was George K. Smith, the only mine owner among the sixteen assassinations blamed on the Molly Maguires. He was shot on the night of November 5, 1863, when a band of disguised men broke into his home. Perhaps because of his social standing, Smith's assassination was the best-publicized of the wartime disturbances in the anthracite region, receiving extensive coverage not only in the local press but also in the newspapers of Philadelphia and New York City, and in the official military dispatches sent from the mining district to Washington.[81] The date of his assassination may also have been of some significance, as it was "Guy Fawkes's Night," the occasion for ritualistic displays of nationalist anti-Catholicism in Britain and America for more than two centuries. Three other men were killed in the mining section of Carbon County, in and around the town of Mauch Chunk, on the same night, in what the *New York Times* described as "an Irish, Welsh and German Row at Mauch Chunk." Such was the level of ethnic hostility that an informant of Charlemagne Tower's reported on November 7 that "six English and Welsh miners had to clear away from Honey Brook and Audenried, and more are going away today," driven out by Irish intimidation and violence."[82]

79. *OR*, ser. 3, vol. 3, 421.

80. Cf. chapter 1.

81. *NYT*, November 7, 1863; *Philadelphia Inquirer*, November 6, 1863; *Philadelphia Bulletin*, November 6, 1863; *OR*, ser. 3, vol. 3, 1,004–6.

82. *OR*, ser. 3, vol. 3, 1,004–6.

While ethnic animosities between Irish laborers and British miners clearly entered into the troubles in Carbon County, the immediate preconditions of Smith's assassination had to do with draft resistance, combined with some form of rudimentary labor activism. Smith was killed, the *New York Times* reported, because he had "incurred the hatred of the Irish miners by his opposition to their secret organization, which had for its object the exclusion of all the workmen of other countries."[83] Whether the Irish in Carbon County actually tried to form an ethnically exclusive labor organization is unclear, but the immediate occasion for Smith's assassination was an attempt by local mine workers to halt the production of coal. In the context of a wartime emergency, of course, any such attempt was liable to be labeled treason. Charles Albright, for example, informed Abraham Lincoln that the shutdown was part of a "rebel programme" organized by the "Buckshots" and designed to sabotage the Union war effort. To restore order, he advised the president that "a military force of several thousand men should be sent to the coal regions, martial law declared, and summary justice dealt out to the traitors."[84]

This equation of labor activism with treason also appeared in other contemporary sources. "On the night of the murder," the *New York Times* reported, "every operator in the Region was warned to stop mining, the penalty, death in case of refusal. The ruffians who perpetrated this high-minded outrage, openly declared that their intention was to embarrass the Government, by stopping its supply of coal."[85] Charlemagne Tower's anonymous informant endorsed this allegation in his letter of November 7, telling the provost marshal that "the reign of terror has now commenced in earnest up here. Yesterday a party of men came from Hazleton and notified us to stop work immediately, otherwise the breakers would either be 'pulled or burned down.' They said the war had gone on long enough and that they were determined to put a stop to it." These reports were presumably exaggerated, though it does seem that the mine workers were trying to halt production. Whether they were doing so to sabotage the war effort rather than simply to raise wages is not clear, but the latter is more probable.[86]

George K. Smith had recently discharged a number of Irishmen from his mines, and some of them may have been involved in his assassination.[87] It was within this context of ethnic tension and labor activism that Smith was killed, but the assassination also involved the third element that animated Irish popular protest during the Civil War, resistance to the military draft. According to Charlemagne Tower, Smith was assassinated because he had assisted the authorities in enforcing conscription. Not only had he furnished the draft officials with the information they needed on his work force, he had also entertained a body of forty or fifty cavalry at his house on October 20, after Tower

83. *NYT*, November 7, 1863.
84. *OR*, ser. 3, vol. 3, 1,008–9.
85. *NYT*, November 7, 1863.
86. *OR*, ser. 3, vol. 3, 1,004–6.
87. *MJ*, November 11, 1863.

had sent them to the Audenried region to enforce the draft. Within a week of this incident Smith was receiving threats on his life, and a week after that he was assassinated.[88]

The assassination of George K. Smith conformed to the classic model of Irish agrarian violence in several respects. In cooperating with the military authorities, he had transgressed the moral and social code of local Irish residents who resisted the draft. As a prominent employer, he had also opposed their attempts to organize a local labor union and to halt the production of coal. The result of these transgressions was direct, violent action on the part of those offended by Smith's actions. And the manner in which the offended parties enforced their vision of justice conformed closely to the model rehearsed so frequently in the Irish countryside.

At 8:00 P.M. on November 5, two men knocked on the door of Smith's house in Honey Brook, half a mile outside the town of Audenried. Smith was already upstairs in bed. The door was opened by a young man named Ulrich, who worked in the store at Smith's mine, and had been asked to stay in the house that night by Mrs. Smith, apparently for protection, as several death threats had already been received. The men at the door claimed to be carrying an important letter from Mauch Chunk, but when Mrs. Smith told them that her husband was too ill to come downstairs, one of the men reportedly took out a pistol. Ulrich then fired his own pistol at the intruders, wounding one and apparently killing the other. Attracted by the commotion, Smith left his bedroom, but by that time "a party of men with blackened faces had crowded into the room." Smith was shot dead as soon as he came downstairs.[89]

As in the assassination of Frank W. Langdon the previous year, nobody was convicted of the crime until the late 1870s. As part of the mopping-up operation after the showcase trials of 1876, Charles Sharp (Ó Geáráin) and James McDonnell, both of whose names strongly suggest a Donegal or west Ulster connection, were tried, found guilty, and executed. They were convicted on the evidence of an informer, Charles Mulhearn, who identified the two men who had knocked on Smith's door as "Humpty" Flynn and "Long John" Donohue (who was killed in another alleged Molly Maguire incident in 1867), and claimed that John Kehoe had also been present. A "List of Fugitive Mollie Maguires" circulated by the Pinkertons in 1879 also named Patrick B. (alias "Pug Nose Pat") Gallagher as one of the killers, adding another classic Donegal name to the roster of Smith's alleged assassins.[90]

While the assassination of George K. Smith was attributed to an organization called the "Buckshots," several contemporary observers extended the blame for his death to the Democratic politicians of the anthracite region.

88. OR, ser. 3, vol. 3, 1,004–6.

89. MJ, January 15, 1879.

90. On Donohue, see MJ, February 23 and April 6, 1867; Coleman, *The Molly Maguire Riots,* 53–54; Dewees, *The Molly Maguires,* 61; on Charles Mulhearn's confession, see MJ, January 15, 1879; "List of Fugitive Mollie Maguires," HSC, Molly Maguire Collection, Photo File.

According to the *New York Times,* the trouble at Audenried and Mauch Chunk emanated from "a riotous crowd of Irishmen who, under the name of *Buckshots* and *Molly McGuires,* have disciplined themselves into an organization, in but few instances dissimilar to the Indian Thug." This organization had introduced "a reign of mob-law . . . full of incidents of riotous brutality, and daily scenes of cold-blooded and deliberate murder." But that the organization existed in the first place was "The Fruits of Copperhead Teaching."[91]

Charlemagne Tower was in full agreement with this political analysis. He forwarded to Washington a letter from an informant claiming that Decatur Nice, a brother-in-law of that "bitter opponent of the Government and the war," Francis W. Hughes, had applauded the killing of Smith and predicted that it marked the "beginning of what we shall see here. There will be a complete revolution here before we are done with it." Along with Cass Township, Tower concluded, the areas around Audenried were "notoriously the receptacles of the worst classes of mining and laboring men."[92]

Benjamin Bannan also connected the events in Audenried with those in Cass, seeing the disloyal teachings of Democratic politicians as the common denominator. The *Miners' Journal* described the whole affair as "a Chapter of Copperhead Tyranny," declaring that the acts of violence executed by "Molly Maguires," "Buckshots," and "other ruffians," along with "every demonstration to impede the operations of the government," were "the fruits of false teachings of copperhead leaders." The people most susceptible to the message spread by disloyal Democrats, the *Miners' Journal* continued, were "the ignorant and prejudiced, of which the mass of the population of Cass Township is a fair sample," and the results were evident "in a tyranny and savage barbarity in the localities where they live, unequalled except by the atrocities of Western savages."[93]

Once the trouble in Carbon County had subsided, a new wave of disturbances broke out in Cass. The *Miners' Journal* of January 2, 1864, reported that the workers in five mines belonging to Heckscher & Company had stopped work, allegedly under the coercion of certain "committee men," who seem to have formed the nucleus of a nascent labor union. When the company found it necessary to close one of its mines, the "committee men" ordered the workers at the other four mines to stop work, "under penalty of summary and severe punishment."[94] The details are shadowy, but it seems that a principal goal of "The Committee" was to halt the production of coal in order to raise its price, thereby bringing about higher wages, shorter working hours, or both.[95]

Benjamin Bannan responded to the events in Cass by insisting that labor activism was merely a cover for brutality and intimidation. In January 1864, the pages of the *Miners' Journal* were filled with stories of "Buckshots" and "Irish Ruffians" from the Cass region assaulting "inoffensive citizens," including an

91. *NYT,* November 7, 1863. Anti-war Democrats were known as "Copperheads."

92. *OR,* ser. 3, vol. 3, 1,004–6.

93. *MJ,* January 23, 1864.

94. *MJ,* January 2, 1864.

95. Long, *Where the Sun Never Shines,* 95; Palladino, *Another Civil War,* 155.

incident in which "they beat a Negro . . . almost to death."[96] In March, the newspaper also printed the following "coffin notice," allegedly posted at a local colliery:

> This is to give you the Gap men a cliar understanding that if you dont quit work after this NOTICE you may prper for your DETH.
>
> You are the damdest *turncoats* in the *State*—there is no ples fit for you bute *Hell* and will soone be there.
>
> MOLLY.
>
> Sind by the real boys this time—so you better loocke oute.[97]

This latest outbreak of disorder drew attention in New York City and Philadelphia as well, where the newspapers identified the activities of "The Committee" with lawlessness in a time of national emergency; in other words, a form of activity that bordered on treason. The newspapers in both cities warned of stern reprisals from the federal level if Schuylkill County proved incapable of putting its own affairs in order.[98]

It is not known who these "committee men" were, but their activities clearly involved the adaptation to local American conditions of a strategy that had long marked social relations in the Irish countryside. Direct, violent action to redress local grievances was the hallmark of this activity on both sides of the Atlantic. Individual mines had their own "committees," but there was no central body to organize their activities, as there would be after the miners' formed a durable trade union in 1868. To the extent that there was any institutional coherence to the events at Cass Township, it probably involved the same "Molly Maguire" organization rumored to have been active there in the late 1850s, which had some affiliation with the Ancient Order of Hibernians. The AOH seems to have taken on a "Ribbonite" function in Cass Township, as Irish immigrant workers struggled for justice in a social system they must have found every bit as oppressive as they one they had left behind in Ireland.

Its violence, as much as its secrecy, explains why the AOH in Cass Township was so vociferously condemned by the Catholic hierarchy. For, once again, the disturbances in Cass Township were suppressed by moral as well as military pressure. Bishop James Frederic Wood of Philadelphia intervened in the disturbances of 1864, just as he had during the first draft riots in Cass Township in October 1862. On January 19, 1864, he issued a pastoral letter against secret societies, which all parish priests in the lower anthracite region were required to read at mass the following Sunday.[99] It was a well-known fact, Wood began, that the church had repeatedly "condemned and censured all secret societies . . . as dangerous to civil society, and injurious to the interests of religion." The

96. *MJ*, January 16, 1864.

97. *MJ*, March 12, 1864.

98. *New York Evening Post*, January 7, 1864; *Philadelphia Evening Bulletin*, January 11, 1864.

99. Copies of the pastoral letter of Archbishop Wood, January 19, 1864, can be found at HML, A 1520, B 979, F, "Memoranda and Papers," and SCBS, Scrapbook on Catholic Archdiocese of Philadelphia, 1864–79.

Church had warned its members, under pain of excommunication, not to associate themselves with such societies, which were clearly "fatal to sound faith, christian piety and good morals." Yet, despite these warnings, "insidious efforts" were being made, not only in this diocese but probably throughout the rest of the country as well, "to blind and deceive the faithful, and to entangle them in the meshes and shackles of these unlawful and forbidden societies."[100]

Wood therefore sternly admonished "all who may have violated this prohibition" to step into line. The societies in question, he continued, included not only groups like the Masons, the Odd Fellows, and the Sons of Temperance, "about whose condemnation no doubt can exist," but also "the 'Fenian Brotherhood,' the 'Molly Maguires,' 'Buckshots,' and others, whose spirit is equally objectionable, and whose names seem to be selected rather to conceal, than to indicate the object of their association." Wood's warning was extended not only to the laity but also the clergy, who were ordered "to instruct and warn their flocks" in the matter of secret societies. "Thus, by the united and harmonious action of Pastors and people," Wood concluded his letter, "we shall neutralize bad influences, which misguided, mistaken and perverse men attempt to force upon us, and shall preserve our faith untainted, our piety active and vigorous, and our morals pure."[101]

The powerful moral sanction of the Catholic church was followed by direct military intervention. On February 16, two Union generals arrived in Cass to make a thorough inquiry into the situation, and by March a portion of the Tenth Regiment of New Jersey had been stationed in Cass Township. Tower arrested seventeen suspected leaders of "The Committee" and charged them with organizing resistance to the draft. But their real crime, as recent historians have suggested, was that they had tried to organize the local mine workers in a struggle for better pay and conditions. Union troops remained in Cass Township for the rest of the war and in this way order was restored in one of the most turbulent places in Pennsylvania. Once the troops had been stationed, Charlemagne Tower felt able to resign his commission; his job, apparently, was done.[102]

Although labor activism had clearly and deliberately been conflated with draft resistance throughout the Civil War, there is no denying that the violence and disorder in the anthracite region were real rather than imaginary. But it is very difficult to disentangle the various strands that went into the violence, from retributive justice to rudimentary trade unionism, and from draft resistance to robbery, intimidation, and drunken brawling. Some combination of these elements made up the pattern of activities that contemporaries labeled "Molly Maguireism." There was clearly a short-lived attempt to organize a labor movement, and this effort, along with all other forms of disorder and crowd

100. Pastoral letter of Archbishop Wood, January 19, 1864.

101. Ibid.

102. Long, *Where the Sun Never Shines,* 95; Palladino, *Another Civil War,* 155, 157; cf. Munsell, *History of Schuylkill County,* 65.

activity, was systematically reported and cataloged by the authorities as evidence of an Irish conspiracy against law, order, and property. In general, it is fair to say that the Molly Maguires during the Civil War were more actively involved in attempts to set up labor organizations than they would be at any point again before the summer of 1875. Their targets were prominent mine officials, and there was an overlap between the strategy of assassination and the strategy of organizing a local labor union known variously as "The Committee," the "Buckshots," and the "Molly Maguires." This intersection of violence with labor organizing distinguished the first manifestation of Molly Maguireism from the version that would emerge in the 1870s, when the Molly Maguires were opposed by a well-organized trade union movement.

Benjamin Bannan, of course, was untroubled by such subtle distinctions. To him the Molly Maguires would always be terrorists, pure and simple. A year before the Civil War ended, a resident of Cass Township wrote to the *Miners' Journal* to ask why the whole population of the township was being blamed "for the lawless actions of a few." In his reply, Benjamin Bannan conceded that the violence was the work of "a few desperate characters who intimidate the peaceably disposed," no more than "one fourth of the miners of any of the lawless districts of this County."[103] This notion of a small, committed conspiracy of terrorist mine workers was soon widely accepted. By the end of the Civil War the term *Molly Maguires* had become a ubiquitous explanation for labor activism, violence, and social disorder. The violence and disorder continued until the end of the 1860s, when the formation of a powerful new trade union inaugurated a new phase in the labor history of the anthracite region.

103. *MJ*, March 12, 1864.

4

The Rise of a Labor Movement

With the return of thousands of demobilized soldiers, a continuing influx of immigrants, and the decline of coal prices and wages after the wartime boom, the immediate aftermath of the Civil War was a period of pronounced social instability in the anthracite region. Four assassinations and numerous beatings, assaults, and robberies were attributed to the Molly Maguires between 1865 and 1868. The extent to which these activities were connected to an organized conspiracy can never be known for certain, though most contemporaries had no hesitation in blaming the Molly Maguires for every incident. Like the events in Audenried and Cass Township during the early 1860s, the Molly Maguire activities in the period 1865–68 make sense only in terms of the general pattern of labor activism and social disorder that marked the history of the anthracite region in the turbulent decade of the Civil War. Much of the violence involved the settling of issues carried over from the war years; most of the rest took the form of robberies and beatings, as order and authority came close to a total collapse in Schuylkill County. But the violence subsided after 1868 for two reasons: the introduction of a new police and judicial system, and the rise of a well-organized, industrywide labor union. There were only two assassinations between October 1868 and October 1874, when the second wave of Molly Maguire violence began. Largely because of the pacifying effect of the labor union, the intervening period was one of relative tranquillity.

While the assassinations of F. W. Langdon and George K. Smith took place during the Civil War itself, the next two Molly Maguire assassinations involved lingering resentment over the enforcement of the draft. The victims, David Muir and Henry H. Dunne, both worked as mine superintendents for the Heckschers, who owned the Forest Improvement Company, the New York and Schuylkill Coal Company, and various other coal-owning interests in Schuylkill County.[1] The Heckschers' superintendents had incurred the enmity of mine workers in Cass Township during the Civil War for their resistance to labor organizing and their cooperation with the officials in charge of conscription.

A native of Scotland, David Muir had come to Schuylkill County in 1845. He settled in Heckscherville, where he worked for the Forest Improvement Company. At the time of his death, he was superintendent at the Otto Colliery in Reilly Township, just west of Cass. He was killed on August 25, 1865, in Foster Township, which bordered Cass and Reilly townships. The president of the New York and Schuylkill Coal Company, O. W. Davis, offered a reward of three thousand dollars for information leading to the arrest and conviction of the assassins, and the Coal Exchange of Philadelphia offered a reward of one thousand dollars. Six months later, Benjamin Bannan was still lamenting that "the murderers—in consequence of the efficiency of the secret, oath bound organization that exists in this County—remain to this day undetected." Nobody was ever arrested for the murder of David Muir. And despite Bannan's certainty that the Molly Maguires were involved, it is by no means clear why Muir was killed. The context and location, however, suggest the settling of scores arising from the wartime turmoil in and around Cass Township.[2]

The second victim was Henry H. Dunne, an Irish Protestant from County Waterford, who had come to Schuylkill County in 1847. He was gunned down by five men on the highway between Heckscherville and Pottsville on January 10, 1866. Once again, it is not clear why he was killed, but it seems to have been a question of revenge rather than robbery, as a sum of money and a watch were found with the body. Like Muir, Dunne had worked as a superintendent at Heckscherville during the disturbances of the Civil War. His employer, O. W. Davis, offered a reward of five thousand dollars for information leading to the arrest and conviction of Dunne's killers but nobody was ever arrested or convicted.[3]

Whatever the uncertainty surrounding the killings of Muir and Dunne, Benjamin Bannan had no hesitation in deciding what needed to be done to remedy the situation. In an editorial on January 13, 1866, he warned that the

1. Munsell, *History of Schuylkill County,* 195–96; NYPL, papers of Charles Heckscher, Moses Taylor Collection; Palladino, *Another Civil War,* 30, 171.

2. Coleman, *The Molly Maguire Riots,* 49; papers of Charles Heckscher, B 588, Clippings, 1863–66, pp. 29, 30; quote from *MJ,* January 13, 1866.

3. Coleman, *The Molly Maguire Riots,* 49; papers of Charles Heckscher, B 588, Clippings, 1863–66, p.33.

Billing Address:

Sheila C. Kramer
441 CLAYHALL ST
GAITHERSBURG, MD 20878-6501
United States

Shipping Address:

Sheila C. Kramer
65 GABLES WAY
JACKSON, NJ 08527-6312
United States

Returns Are Easy!
Visit http://www.amazon.com/returns to return any item - including gifts - in unopened or original condition within 30 days for a full refund (other restrictions apply)

Your order of December 20, 2010 (Order ID:104 – 7243586 – 4210647)

Qty	Item	Item Price	Total
	IN THIS SHIPMENT		
1	**Making Sense of the Molly Maguires** (** P-1-P8E11 **) X0002HD1K3 : X0002HD1K3 bk-071710-071 **Sold by GenuineSeller – (Hardcover)**	$20.78	$20.78
		Subtotal	$20.78
		Order Total	$20.78
		Balance Due	$0.00

This shipment completes your order.

Have feedback on how we packaged your order? Tell us at www.amazon.com/packaging.

(1 of 1)

SDXh0p3JFR

12/DXh0p3JFR/-1 of 1-//1M/second/8987661/1221-17:00/1221-00:33 V3

amazon.com and you're done.

time had come "when protection in Schuylkill County for life and property, must be imperatively demanded." If the local authorities were incapable of dealing with the situation, then they should call on the state to provide "an armed police or military organization." The same issue of the *Miners' Journal* announced that a public meeting was to be held in Pottsville Town Hall that evening to "adopt measures to stop the lawlessness in this County."[4] The following week, a committee appointed by this meeting announced the existence of "an organization of bad men, who are determined, cost what it may, to control the operations of collieries in this County and dictate who shall manage same."[5]

To expedite "the speedy inauguration of law and order in all sections of this Region," Bannan recommended the use of a blacklist. A list of all the workers in the mines, he advised, should be placed in the hands of a central board, so that men discharged from one mine could never be employed again in any other. "The practice of giving employment at collieries to men who have been discharged from other operations for bad conduct, has done much to foster lawlessness," he declared. "This is a very important matter, and if adopted, will compel bad characters, for want of employment, to leave the County or starve."[6] In the meantime, however, the "bad characters" continued to indulge in violence, and the first few months of 1867 were among the most turbulent in the history of the anthracite region.

The following incidents occurred over a period of only five weeks early in 1867 and were chronicled with mounting alarm by Benjamin Bannan in the pages of the *Miners' Journal*. Several adjacent homes at Mount Laffee were robbed by a gang of men on the night of February 9. The same week, "a gang of Irishmen" was alleged to have committed similar "outrages" near Tamaqua, fifteen miles to the east.[7] On February 11 "five Irishmen" entered the home of a coal operator named John C. Northall and fired several shots into the room where he usually slept, in an apparent assassination attempt. The shots attracted a neighbor, an Englishman named Thomas Border, who killed one of the assailants, "Long John" Donohue, rumored to have participated in the murder of George K. Smith. Border was later tried for Donohue's murder and acquitted.[8] On February 16, ten men staged an armed robbery at the Bost Run Colliery, near Ashland, and escaped with $4,500. They were thought to have been Irish and Cornish.[9] On February 25 an elderly English couple, Thomas Edwards and his wife, were robbed and beaten by "ten Irishmen" three miles outside Pottsville. A watch, some clothing, and one hundred dollars were taken.[10] On

4. *MJ*, January 13, 1866.
5. *MJ*, January 20, 1866.
6. Ibid.
7. See Coleman, *The Molly Maguire Riots*, 53.
8. *MJ*, February 23, April 6, 1867; Dewees, *The Molly Maguires*, 61; Coleman, *The Molly Maguire Riots*, 53–54.
9. *MJ*, February 23, 1867.
10. *MJ*, March 3, 1867.

March 2 "three Irishmen" broke into the home of Melder Schmidt, in New Philadelphia.[11]

Two weeks later, the fifth of the assassinations attributed to the Molly Maguires took place. William Littlehales was killed by unknown assailants on the highway from Pottsville to Cass Township on March 15, 1867, two days before St. Patrick's Day. A native of Schuylkill County, he was employed as a superintendent by the Glen Carbon Coal Company. Littlehales usually carried the company payroll with him on the fifteenth of every month, although on this occasion (perhaps expecting trouble) he had sent it by a different route.[12] The Littlehales case was not without precedent. The first highway robbery blamed on the Molly Maguires had occurred two years earlier, on August 10, 1865, when a mine superintendent named William Pollack was attacked and robbed by an armed man on the road between Pottsville and Tuscarora. Though wounded, he had managed to escape with the company payroll. As in so many similar incidents at the time, nobody was arrested in either the Pollack or the Littlehales case.[13] But a document in the Pinkerton archives dating from the late 1870s did list the men suspected of killing Littlehales: John McCloskey, Thomas Boyle, John Casey, John Coniff, Charles Gallagher, and Peter McHugh. Their places of birth are unknown, but Boyle, Gallagher, and McHugh are classic west Donegal names.[14]

Despite the public outcry that followed the Littlehales killing, the violence continued unabated. On March 22 "five Irishmen" unsuccessfully attempted to rob a tavern twelve miles north of Pottsville. The owner killed one of them, Patrick Stinson, and wounded and captured another, Owen McCloskey. The following night, "four Irishmen" attacked the house of a German farmer, Henry Rapp, in Ringtown, but again they were driven off without having taken any money. A few weeks later, "four Irishmen" robbed a man at gunpoint on the road between Locust Gap and Shamokin, in neighboring Northumberland County, and escaped with $1,475. The *Miners' Journal* reported that there had been fourteen murders in Schuylkill County in 1863, fourteen in 1864, twelve in 1865, and six in 1866—all unsolved—and that in the first three months of 1867 there had been five more murders, six assaults, and twenty-seven robberies. Benjamin Bannan had no doubt who was behind most of the trouble. The Molly Maguires.[15]

11. *MJ*, March 9, 1867.

12. *MJ*, March 23, 1867; Coleman, *The Molly Maguire Riots*, 55; Broehl, *The Molly Maguires*, 94.

13. Dewees, *The Molly Maguires*, 53.

14. Undated photostat from the diary of Robert J. Linden, PCA, Molly Maguire Collection; Edward MacLysaght, *The Surnames of Ireland* (1957; Dublin, 1991), 23, 47, 40, 310–12. Peter McHugh was executed on March 25, 1878, for the murder of Alexander Rea. The name McCloskey is commonly found in County Derry, and Casey in County Monaghan, though both names are popular elsewhere in Ireland.

15. *MJ*, March 23, 30, 1867, April 6, 1867.

The *Miners' Journal* of March 23, 1867, carried a strident editorial on "The Terrible State of Affairs in Schuylkill County." The murder of William Littlehales, Benjamin Bannan wrote, had "brought the citizens of the County at last to the conclusion that the bands of assassins and robbers that infest it, must be driven from our midst and protection secured to our people in every section of the Region, or collieries will be stopped, business of every description ruined, capital frightened away and the County depopulated of its best citizens." It was no exaggeration, Bannan concluded, that there was "a reign of terror in Schuylkill County, and that the time has arrived when the ruffians must be brought to justice or driven out, or life and property in this County in the future will not be worth a bauble."[16]

The *Philadelphia Bulletin* joined the chorus, declaring that "it is a blot and disgrace not only upon the people of Schuylkill County, but upon the fair face of the Commonwealth, that such outrages have been committed with such entire impunity." While "such lawlessness" was not surprising in places like Texas or Arkansas or Mississippi, the *Bulletin* declared, it was "a shameful and monstrous thing" in a place as civilized as Pennsylvania, where "terrorism and lawlessness have no proper place." If Schuylkill County could no longer "preserve the lives and property of its citizens," then the state would have to intervene and teach "these scoundrels their duty to society."[17]

Toward the end of March 1867, a committee of fifty "influential citizens" from Schuylkill County went to Harrisburg bearing a petition requesting a new police and judicial system for the lower anthracite region.[18] Up to this point, the region had been policed by a rudimentary force of ineffectual county sheriffs and their constables. Under pressure from Benjamin Bannan and his fellow-petitioners from Schuylkill County, the state legislature now passed a series of laws reforming the judicial and police systems of the Schuylkill region. A new Criminal Court was created with jurisdiction over the counties of Schuylkill, Dauphin, and Lebanon. The judge of this court was to be appointed by the governor until the next election, when he could run for election to a ten-year term in office. Attached to the Criminal Court Bill was a special Jury Bill providing for the appointment of two jury commissioners, one from each political party, to serve until the next election, after which they too would be elected.[19]

The legislative package also included a police bill authorizing the governor to appoint a new police force for those parts of the mining region, such as Schuylkill County, in which one hundred or more residents signed a petition demonstrating that the existing police were incapable of maintaining order and bringing offenders to justice. The new law required the appointment of a marshal of

16. *MJ*, March 23, 1867.

17. *Philadelphia Bulletin*, n.d., quoted in *MJ*, March 23, 1867.

18. *MJ*, March 23, 1867.

19. *MJ*, March 30, 1867; Jeremiah P. Shalloo, *Private Police: With Special Reference to Pennsylvania* (Philadelphia, 1933), 76–78.

police by the governor, and the creation of a police force not exceeding one hundred men. These policemen were to report to the marshal, and the marshal in turn reported to the governor. The force was to be supported by a levy of one cent per ton of coal mined by the coal companies. The new police force was invested with all the authority of the existing sheriff and constables in making arrests. Schuylkill County, one of the most turbulent regions in the United States in the 1860s, had been equipped for the first time with an effective judicial and policing system.[20]

This new system of law and order had an immediate impact on the lower anthracite region. But, in the long term, private police were to make a more important contribution than public police to the demise of the Molly Maguires. The private force of the Reading Railroad played its most significant role in the Molly Maguire story in the mid-1870s, but came into existence on the basis of further legislation passed in the mid-1860s. The state legislature authorized the creation of railroad police in February 1865, allowing the governor to grant police power to any individual for whom the employing railroad petitioned. Under the same law, the "keepers of jails, or lockups, or station houses," were "required to receive all persons arrested by such policemen, for the commission of any offense against the laws of this commonwealth, upon or along said railroads, or the premises of any such corporation, to be dealt with according to law." No time limit was set on the commissions; there were no specific provisions for removal of officers; and there was no charge for commissions until 1870, when a fee of one dollar was levied, payable to the secretary of the Commonwealth. On April 1, 1866, a supplement to the Railroad Police Act was passed, extending its provisions to "all corporations, firms or individuals owning, leasing, or being in possession of any colliery, furnace or rolling-mill, within this Commonwealth."[21]

The term *police* has an inherently public connotation, as it refers to a form of power wielded by the state. In nineteenth-century Pennsylvania, however, the state delegated this power to private corporations and took little or no interest in the matter thereafter. To appoint a police force, the railroad and mining interests simply had to petition the governor to grant commissions to the persons whose names were submitted. The backgrounds and characters of these individuals were not investigated by the state, and the commissions were of unlimited duration. Though the 1866 law did authorize the governor to revoke commissions, there is no evidence that any governor ever did so. As one historian of the subject has observed, "In substance, the practice from 1871 to 1929 was simply a contract between mining companies and the State whereby police power was 'sold' to the industrial establishment. When the commission was issued and the fee paid, together with a subscription of the constitutional oath, which was recorded in the proper county, the State took no further interest." In this way, the state created "islands of police power which were free to float as the employers saw fit."[22]

20. *MJ*, March 30, 1867; Shalloo, *Private Police*, 76–78.

21. Shalloo, *Private Police*, 29, 60.

22. Details and quote from ibid., 61.

Such were the legislative origins of the infamous Coal & Iron Police of the Reading Railroad. At first, their job was simply to guard and protect the mines and mining property. But, given their remarkable autonomy from the state, their function could easily be expanded beyond this protective role. When, in the early 1870s, the Reading Railroad assumed the role not only of the biggest coal carrier but also the biggest landlord and coal operator in the lower anthracite region, the police powers at its disposal were quite awesome. In the climactic year of 1875, the Coal & Iron Police would join forces with the Pinkerton Detective Agency in a new "flying squadron" formed with the specific intention of subduing troublemakers during the "Long Strike" of that year and rooting out the Molly Maguires.

The creation of new public and private police forces in the late 1860s helped to pacify the anthracite region. The peace was broken, briefly but brutally, in October 1868 by the sixth and last Molly Maguire assassination of the 1860s. On October 17, Alexander Rea, a native of New Jersey, was killed by a group of armed men who attacked him on the road between Centralia, in Columbia County, and Mount Carmel, in Northumberland County. The general superintendent of the Locust Mountain Coal & Iron Company, Rea was in charge of the company's payroll, and the motive, once again, appears to have been robbery. Because one of the participants later turned informer, more is known about the circumstances surrounding this crime than any of the other killings blamed on the Molly Maguires in the 1860s. The extent to which the informant's evidence is credible is a moot point, but his statement to the Pinkertons on the Rea murder makes for chilling reading and is worth considering in some detail.[23]

The defendants in the Rea case were convicted only in 1877, primarily on the evidence of one Daniel Kelly, a notorious criminal who was also known as Manus Cull (or Coll) and "Kelly the Bum." Kelly, who was thirty-four years old in 1876, stated in his confession that he had been born in County Donegal, and had come to the United States in June 1865, settling briefly in Wilkes-Barre, Luzerne County. In August of that year he joined the local chapter of the Ancient Order of Hibernians. After spending short periods of time in Canada, Mahanoy City, and Tamaqua, he moved to Mount Carmel, Northumberland County, where he worked for a while on the railroad, before settling in Locust Gap Junction, in the same county. In 1868 he was initiated into the Big Mine Run division of the AOH. The remainder of Kelly's statement offered a detailed account of the planning, execution, and aftermath of the killing of Alexander Rea.[24]

23. According to *SH*, February 9, 1877, Rea was born in Flemington, New Jersey, on May 3, 1821. Details of the Rea case can be found in HML, A 1520, B 979, F, "Statements and Depositions," statement of Manus Cull, a.k.a. Daniel Kelly; another copy at HSP, SC, PNDA, "Synopsis for Mr. Gowen," September 1, 1876. [Town], *Commonwealth v. Patrick Hester, Patrick Tully, and Peter McHugh, Argument of Hon. F. W. Hughes, for Commonwealth;* HML, A 1520, unpublished stenographic reports of the case of *Commonwealth v. Patrick Hester et al.*

24. HML, A 1520, B 979, F, "Statements and Depositions," statement of Manus Cull.

Kelly claimed that on the night before the killing, a Saturday, he and several other Molly Maguires had met in Thomas Donahue's tavern at Ashland, in Schuylkill County. A plan was made to rob Alexander Rea the following morning, though as yet no mention was made of killing him. Present at this meeting were Patrick Tully, Peter McHugh, and Patrick Hester, among others. According to Kelly, all of them spoke Irish. The assassins remained in the tavern drinking, Kelly continued, until just before daylight the following morning. After buying cartridges and loading their weapons, seven men set out to do the deed: Kelly, Patrick Tully, Peter McHugh, Bryan Campbell, James Bradley, John Dalton, and William Muldowney. According to Kelly, Patrick Hester accompanied them as far as the tollgate, but then went home. The other men headed for a water trough on the road between Centralia and Mount Carmel, in Northumberland County, where they arrived just after daybreak and hid in a large bush. The arrangement was that John Dalton, who knew the victim, was to walk out into the road as Rea approached, take off his cap, and salute him.[25]

At about nine-thirty, Rea came along in his carriage, and stopped, as expected, at the water trough. Up to this point, Kelly insisted, "murder had not been talked of." Dalton went to greet Rea; Campbell, Bradley, and Tully jumped out beside the buggy, and Kelly and McHugh approached Rea from the front and ordered him out of the carriage. The men then searched the vehicle, but they could find no money. Rea was asked if he had any cash, and he replied by pulling out his pocket book, which contained only sixty dollars. Tully proposed that they take his watch, and at this point things turned violent. Here is how Kelly told the tale:

> I said, "What do you want the man's watch for? Let him keep his watch." I then said, "What are you going to do with the man?" McHugh said, "I am not going to be hunted around for a living man," and after these words pistols were cocked by nearly all of us. Dalton and I said, "It is too bad to take the man's life for nothing," but it was no use, he had to die. Tully fired the first shot which hit Rae [sic] in the cheek, I think then Rae ran into the bush into Northumberland County. McHugh and the others fired at him and he fell. I was too excited to fire and Dalton took hold of the collar of my jacket and said "this is too hard." Tully went to where Rae was, put his pistol to Rae's ear and fired, that was the last shot fired. We then divided the money and I kept the pocket book and the watch was given to me also. We then left Rae where he fell and struck out for the top of the mountain above the toll gate.

The drinking then resumed, and Kelly eventually disposed of the watch for ten dollars. If this narrative was shocking, the denouement was even more so.

25. HSP, SC, PNDA, "Synopsis for Mr. Gowen," September 1, 1876; report on use of Irish language by Rea's assassins, appended to Cull's statement (HML, 1520, B 979, F, "Statements and Depositions") by Captain Linden. The "List of Members of the A.O.H." (HML, A 1520, B 979, F, "Memoranda and Papers") circulated by the Pinkertons in the mid-1870s reveals that four of the six members of the lodge at Northumberland Junction bore the classic west Donegal name surname Campbell. These Campbells were not implicated in the events of 1868, however, and probably were not present in Northumberland Junction at that time.

"About a week after the murder," Kelly recalled, "I rode up to Ashland from the Gap with Pat Hester. We talked in the buggy about the murder and Hester said it was a great pity, as we had killed the wrong man."[26]

The killing of Alexander Rea was an isolated incident in an otherwise peaceful year. While the new judicial and police apparatus undoubtedly pacified the anthracite region to some extent, the most important reason for the cessation of violence after 1868 was the emergence of an industrywide trade union, the Workingmen's Benevolent Association (WBA). For the first time in the history of the anthracite region, a labor movement emerged that was powerful enough to unite mine workers of different craft and ethnic backgrounds in a single, well-organized trade union favoring negotiations and strikes rather than direct, violent action.

The Workingmen's Benevolent Association of St. Clair was the last of a series of local labor unions founded in the anthracite region in the 1860s. What distinguished it from its predecessors was that it survived for seven years rather than a few months, eventually spreading throughout the anthracite region. The mine workers of Carbon County had formed a brief-lived Workingmen's Benevolent Society in 1864, but the organization was immediately identified with the "Buckshots" and "Molly Maguires," who, the authorities claimed, had been terrorizing that part of the lower region for the previous year and were responsible for the assassination of George K. Smith. Two similar, but equally short-lived, organizations were formed just after the Civil War, the Miners' Benevolent Association of Locust Gap, and the Workingmen's Benevolent Association of Luzerne County.[27] The WBA of St. Clair was founded in February 1868 and received its charter the following June. Branches of the new union were organized throughout the rest of Schuylkill County later that year, and by 1869 there were branches in both the upper and lower anthracite regions.

Molly Maguireism and full-fledged trade unionism represented fundamentally different modes of organization and protest. Given that previous labor movements in the anthracite region had engaged in direct and often violent crowd action, and that labor activism in general had been identified with Molly Maguireism by the late 1860s, the remarkable thing about the trade union that emerged in 1868 is how different it was both from its predecessors and from the Molly Maguires. One of the most important tasks in any attempt to make sense of the Molly Maguires is to do what so many contemporaries so conspicuously and deliberately failed to do: to distinguish between the modes of protest and organization embodied by the WBA and the Molly Maguire violence that existed alongside it.

26. HML, 1520, B 979, F, "Statements and Depositions," statement of Manus Cull.
27. Killeen, "John Siney," 100–103.

One of the few contemporary sources that did make this distinction before the trials and executions of the late 1870s was the newly formed Pennsylvania Bureau of Industrial Statistics. When it issued its first annual "Report on Labor" in 1873, the bureau had no hesitation in distinguishing the labor union from the Molly Maguires. Reviewing the history of the lower anthracite region in the 1860s, the Bureau traced the trouble back to the time of the Civil War, when many men of "vicious and turbulent antecedents" had arrived in the anthracite region, unleashing "a pandemonium of outrage, violence and anarchy, utter disregard of the sanctity of law . . . such as has never been known before in Pennsylvania, and seldom in the nation."[28] But, in the midst of this turbulence, the Bureau was pleased to report, "the more intelligent and thoughtful of the workmen" petitioned the Court of Common Pleas in Schuylkill County for a charter incorporating "The Workingmen's Benevolent Association of St. Clair." Looking back on the five years since the formation of the WBA, the Bureau noted that "the relations existing between employers and employees" had greatly improved. The Bureau attributed this improvement to the stabilizing influence on the work force of the WBA, which had "forced into reformation or removal" the "reckless and turbulent" elements among the mine workers. The union, the Bureau concluded, had brought to an end the "carnival of crime" that had gripped the anthracite region in the 1860s.[29]

The leaders of the WBA were always unequivocally opposed to the Molly Maguires. Given the cultural backgrounds of the men who founded the union, it is not surprising that this should have been so. They came from places in Britain that were already heavily industrialized, they had years of experience in trade unionism and other forms of labor activism, and they arrived in the anthracite region with tried and tested ideas on labor relations. When the court granted the WBA of St. Clair its charter in June 1868, twelve of the sixteen men named as incorporators were English-born, three were Irish-born, and one was Welsh-born. The most prominent of the leaders came from Lancashire, in the heavily industrialized north of England, a county known for its factories, coal mines, and trade unions. All but two of the sixteen founder-members were literate, and several of them came from prosperous mining families. They brought to the labor movement of the anthracite region a culture of working-class organization forged in the British industrial revolution, a culture that was fundamentally different from the modes of protest found in remoter regions of the Irish countryside and practiced by some Irish laborers in the anthracite region. Herein lay the first fundamental distinction between the labor union and the Molly Maguires.[30]

This distinction between two modes of labor organization and protest is not meant to imply that only British workers could become trade unionists. On the

28. PBIS 1, 329–30.

29. Ibid., 330, 363.

30. Ibid., 330; Wallace, *St. Clair,* 288–90; Edward Pinkowski, *John Siney, The Miners' Martyr* (Philadelphia, 1963), 15; Killeen, "John Siney," 110.

contrary, most Irish mine workers belonged to the WBA and roughly half the officers of its executive board in 1872 bore Irish names. But, in addition to the WBA, there existed a loosely organized body of men called the Molly Maguires, whose membership appears to have been exclusively Irish. The founders of the WBA of St. Clair arrived in the anthracite region from a society that was already capitalist and industrial; the Molly Maguires did not, even if some of them had passed through Scotland or England en route to America. The WBA leaders already had experience of coal mining and trade unionism; the Molly Maguires had none.[31]

Both modes of organization, the trade union and the violent secret society, tried to improve conditions of life and labor in the anthracite region. But the strategy of the trade union was indirect, gradual, peaceful, and systematically organized across the entire anthracite region, while that of the Molly Maguires was direct, violent, sporadic, and confined to a specific locality. Trade unionism was a mode of labor organization produced by, and uniquely adapted to, the prevailing social and economic conditions in nineteenth-century Britain and Pennsylvania. Molly Maguireism, by contrast, embodied a form of protest derived in its essentials from a specific part of the Irish countryside.[32]

Nowhere is this argument more valid than in the case of John Siney, the Irish-born labor activist who dominated the WBA from its foundation in 1868 until 1874, when he left the union to become president of a new, national miners' union. Siney was born in Queen's County, in the Irish midlands, in 1831.[33] When his father, a small tenant farmer with a few acres, was evicted in 1835, the family moved to Wigan, an industrial town in Lancashire, England. Three of his brothers went to work in the coal mines as children. At the age of seven Siney was sent to work in a cotton mill, and at sixteen, after refusing to accept a wage cut, he was apprenticed to a brickmaker. In the late 1840s, he experienced the radicalism of the Chartist movement at first hand, and in the early 1850s he went to work as a journeyman in the brickyards of Wigan, where he helped to organize the local brickmakers' union, serving as its president for seven years.[34]

In 1862 Siney's wife died, leaving him with a two-year-old child. A year later the loss of cotton shipments from the American South caused an economic recession in the Wigan region. Siney decided to emigrate to the United States and join some of his old Lancashire associates in St. Clair. John and Levi Orme found lodgings for him with another Lancashire man, Thomas Pilling, whose wife Margaret taught him the rudiments of literacy while he stayed with them.[35] Siney began work at the Eagle Colliery in St. Clair, one of the largest

31. *Anthracite Monitor,* February 3, 1872, and other issues, listed the officers of the WBA.

32. For a broadly similar distinction, see Jon Amsden and Stephen Brier, "Coal Miners on Strike: The Transformation of Strike Demands and the Formation of a National Union," *The Journal of Interdisciplinary History,* 7 (Spring 1977): 587—91.

33. The best study of Siney is Killeen, "John Siney"; the only published book is Pinkowski, *John Siney.* For biographical details, see Killeen, chapter 3.

34. Pinkowski, *John Siney,* 4–10; Wallace, *St. Clair,* 290–91.

35. Killeen, "John Siney," 65.

operations in Schuylkill County, with a work force of 425 men and boys. He was employed first as a laborer and, within a year, as a contract miner working his own "chamber." Like Pilling and the Ormes, John Siney arrived in the anthracite region from the heartland of the British industrial revolution with considerable experience of union activism and with a well-developed position on labor relations. These friends from Lancashire, reunited in Pennsylvania, were the prime movers in the foundation of the WBA in 1868. The new organization exhibited many of the characteristics of its British prototype, particularly in its emphasis on higher wages, a safer work place, and the provision of sick and death benefits. To try and fit John Siney and the Gaelic-speaking laborers from west Donegal into a single category of "Irishness" is clearly more of a hindrance than a help. The cultural differences between them go a long way to explaining the distinction between trade unionism and Molly Maguireism.[36]

John Siney's Workingmen's Benevolent Association was one of several labor organizations in the United States in the late 1860s that rose to power as part of a movement to secure the eight-hour day.[37] It was organized in January and February 1868 during a strike at the Eagle Colliery in St. Clair.[38] The immediate cause of its expansion throughout the anthracite region thereafter was its agitation for the enforcement of an act passed by the Pennsylvania legislature on April 14, 1868, making eight hours "a legal day's work, in all cases of labor or service by the day, where there is no contract or agreement to the contrary."[39] The act carried no compulsory enforcing power and, more importantly, it exempted employers who had contracts with their workers for more than eight hours a day.[40]

On July 6, the Monday directly after the law was to have gone into effect, the men at several collieries in the region of Girardville and Ashland, over the mountain from Pottsville in the Western Middle Coal Field, went on strike to demand the eight-hour day without an accompanying reduction in pay. They adopted tactics reminiscent of the Chartists in England and the labor disputes in Schuylkill County in the 1840s and 1850s, marching to the other collieries in

36. Ibid., 62–64.

37. On the eight-hour-day movement, see David Montgomery, *Beyond Equality: Labor and the Radical Republicans, 1862–1872* (New York, 1967), especially chapters 6 and 8.

38. Killeen, "John Siney," 108; Wallace, *St. Clair,* 288. The Workingmen's Benevolent Association was renamed the Miners' and Laborers' Benevolent Association on March 11, 1870, when its general council received a charter from the state. But it was still popularly referred to as the Workingmen's Benevolent Association, and that name has been employed throughout the present work. Cf. Chris Evans, *History of the Mine Workers of America from the Year 1860 to 1890,* vol. 1 (Indianapolis, n.d.), 21; Marvin W. Schlegel, "The Workingmen's Benevolent Association: First Union of Anthracite Miners," *PH,* 10 (October 1943): 246.

39. PBIS 1, 331; Trachtenberg, *A History of Legislation,* 19.

40. Mine workers who typically worked for ten hours or more a day may have expected the same daily pay for eight hours' work, but in practice the operators found it easy to circumvent the law. All they had to do was insist on the validity of existing contracts; draw up new contracts requiring a longer work-day; or divide wages into hourly rather than daily rates, so that men who worked only eight hours would be paid less than those who worked a full ten-hour day.

Mahanoy Valley and bringing the men out as they passed. Within two weeks, all 140 collieries in Schuylkill County had been shut down. While the stoppage of 1868 resembled that of 1858 in that it originated in the vicinity of Ashland, and involved crowd activity by miners reputedly armed with clubs and other weapons, it differed in its outcome. It ended not in military repression but in the emergence of the first cohesive and systematically organized trade union in the anthracite industry.[41]

On July 23, 1868, the striking mine workers sent delegates to Mahanoy City, to a meeting chaired by John Siney, where it was arranged that the men would vote on the strike and the formation of a union. A resolutions committee was appointed, and the following day the Workingmen's Benevolent Association of Schuylkill County issued its first resolution: "Resolved. That it is the sense of this meeting that 8 hours' labor, 8 hours' rest and 8 hours' sleep are proper divisions of the day in the coal regions, and inasmuch as 8 hours is the workingmen's day on the statutes of Pennsylvania, it ought to be sustained."[42] The first formal convention of the county organization was held in St. Clair on September 3. Twenty-two districts were formed in the network of valleys and slopes where anthracite was mined. With St. Clair as the organizational center, the county organization stretched east to Coaldale, west to Tower City, and north to Ashland and Shenandoah. Each district sent a delegate to the County Executive Board, and these delegates elected John Siney chairman of the Executive Board of the WBA of Schuylkill County at a salary of fifteen hundred dollars a year. With the new organization firmly established in Schuylkill County, Siney went up to Scranton to consult the miners of the upper region, hoping to bring them into a single, industrywide union. As a result of his work, all the local and county unions in the anthracite region were united in a new organization formed at Hazleton on March 17, 1869, the General Council of the Workingmen's Benevolent Association. By the end of the year, thirty thousand of the thirty-five thousand anthracite mine workers belonged to the union.[43]

What Siney had to say to the northern men on the subject of a single, industrywide union offers some important insights on the aims and nature of the WBA at the time of its foundation. Like John Bates twenty years earlier, he was convinced that the most effective way to get fair wages was to control the supply of coal to the market. The operators and the mine workers would both benefit from this strategy, Siney believed, as the former would make more money and be able to pay the latter higher wages. But if the operators were not prepared to cooperate in this joint venture, then the mine workers could enforce their will by striking. According to Siney, this cooperation between

41. PBIS I, 332-34; Wallace, *St. Clair,* 288–92; Broehl, *The Molly Maguires,* 97; Schlegel, "The Workingmen's Benevolent Association," 244; Pinkowski, *John Siney,* 5–33; Long, *Where the Sun Never Shines,* 99–101; Trachtenberg, *A History of Legislation,* 19; Yearley, *Enterprise and Anthracite,* 182–83. The events at Ashland in 1858 are examined in chapter 2.

42. Quoted in Pinkowski, *John Siney,* 18–19; see, also, PBIS I, 333–34.

43. Pinkowski, *John Siney,* 20; Wallace, *St. Clair,* 288–93; Schlegel, "The Workingmen's Benevolent Association," 244–45; PBIS I, 333–34; Killeen, "John Siney," 139, 142.

miners, supplemented by strike activity if necessary, would bring some much-needed stability to the coal industry, ensuring regular profits and wages. As Siney put it in a letter to the workmen of Luzerne County published in the *Miners' Journal* on December 12, 1868, wild fluctuations in wages were

> not known in any other business, and . . . need not be in the coal business after we become united; it is very easy to stop when the market is full, for every ton of coal mined after that deranges the market and creates bad feeling at home and abroad, and to accomplish that end is the main object of the association.[44]

If control over the production and distribution of coal was the primary aim of the WBA, why did it devote so much attention to the eight-hour day? Skilled contract miners, after all, were not paid by time but by the amount of coal they produced; if coal prices were high they were paid well, regardless of how many hours they worked. The eight-hour question was more immediately relevant to laborers who were paid by the day, and to those miners who were paid by wages rather than contract. The agitation by the WBA on this issue suggests that the concerns of laborers and day miners, as well as contract miners, were of central importance to the new union. It would be naive, however, to assume that the intentions of the mining elite who led the WBA were entirely altruistic. In fact, the eight-hour agitation offered the skilled elite of miners the opportunity to exert control over two vital questions. First, limiting the work day to eight hours would enable them to control the amount of coal that was produced and went to market, thereby keeping prices and wages high. Second, entering into an alliance across lines of skill would allow them to control the actions of their laborers. Given the ethnic divisions that corresponded to distinctions of skill within the mine, this was a crucial consideration.[45]

Excluded from the union, the laborers could have formed an organization of their own, calling strikes for better wages and disrupting the union's goal of controlling the production and distribution of anthracite. Disgruntled Irish laborers in the Scranton region tried to do just that in 1871, rejecting the goals of the Welsh miners in the strike of that year and denouncing the Welsh monopoly on skilled positions. The Irish laborers organized a brief-lived union of their own, demanding better pay from the miners who employed them and an end to the discrimination that prevented Irish laborers from graduating to the position of miners with their own "chambers."[46]

In short, there was always an uneasy tension in the strategy of the WBA between meeting the needs of the skilled elite by trying to preserve their privileged craft status, and meeting the demands of the wage-earning mine workers, whose goals and interests were rather different. As these craft distinctions

44. MJ, December 12, 1868; Pinkowski, *John Siney,* 31–32. On the Bates Union and other precursors of the WBA, see chapter 2.

45. Cf. Aurand, "The Anthracite Miner," 468.

46. MJ, May 12, 1871; Aurand, "The Anthracite Mine Workers, 1869–1897," 168. Cf. fig. 4.

corresponded fairly neatly to the differences between British and Irish mine workers, the WBA was a potentially powerful means of transcending divisive questions of status and ethnicity among the mine workers and uniting them in a single labor movement. In this way, craft and ethnic distinctions could be overcome by class solidarity. At times the WBA came close to fulfilling this ideal; at others it was racked by ethnic and status divisions. In general, however, the trade union did a remarkable job in this respect, and the period of its ascendancy neatly divides the first wave of Molly Maguire activities in the 1860s from the second in the mid-1870s.[47]

The rise of the WBA inaugurated a new era in the history of labor relations in the anthracite region. For the first time, the mine workers were represented by a single, powerful organization extending across the region and the industry as a whole. If Molly Maguireism was a mode of protest that sought to redress the mine workers' grievances on a local and individual level, trade unionism involved representatives of one social class meeting representatives of another, in order to devise a mutually acceptable settlement. The declared policy of the trade union was gradual, systematic, and peaceful negotiation; its antithesis, the union leaders repeatedly insisted, was the direct, sporadic, and violent strategy of labor activism embodied by the "Molly Maguires," whose activities could only cause great damage to the trade union movement.

All mine workers, regardless of craft status, national origin, and religious background, were eligible to join the WBA. As a result, the WBA must have included some "Molly Maguires" among its ranks; many of its rank and file were members of the AOH, and there is evidence that some disgruntled trade union members favored violence against the wishes of their leaders, especially in the climactic year of 1875. But there were no Mollys among the leaders of the WBA, who took every opportunity they could to condemn the Molly Maguires and the use of violence as a strategy in the labor struggle. While the membership of the trade union and the secret society undoubtedly overlapped to some extent, they must be seen as ideologically and institutionally distinct.[48]

A central requirement in any attempt to make sense of the Molly Maguires, therefore, is to explain what the trade union stood for, and how its structure, ideology, and strategy differed from the mode of organization and protest embodied by its violent counterpart. The union leaders had a well-developed theory of labor relations that is worth considering in some detail, particularly

47. The anthracite region was not devoid of violence in the intervening period, of course. There were numerous robberies and beatings again in 1870 (cf. Coleman, *The Molly Maguire Riots,* 57–59). But there were only two, unrelated assassinations between October 1868 and October 1874, and the intervening period was a time of relative calm dividing the two principal waves of Molly Maguire activity.

48. On the violence in 1875, see chapter 6; on the position of the WBA on violence, see below.

for its stance on violence, on the potential harmony of interests between labor and capital, and on collective action and third-party politics. Their position on these matters demonstrates the fundamental differences between trade unionism and Molly Maguireism.

Of the various institutions that together made up the social structure of the anthracite region, the Workingmen's Benevolent Association vied with the Catholic church as the most unequivocal opponent of violence. The employers and the state authorities, by contrast, had frequent recourse to violence in the 1860s and 1870s. So, too, did the Molly Maguires. Unlike the Molly Maguires, the leaders of the trade union movement sought to bargain with their enemies rather than threaten, attack, or kill them. In so doing, they were the heirs of a long tradition of British trade unionism.[49] Explicit condemnations of the violent strategy of the Molly Maguires were part of the official policy of the WBA from the beginning. When John Siney went up to Scranton in late 1868 to organize the men of upper Luzerne County, for example, one of his tasks was to allay suspicions that labor activists in the lower region endorsed violence. In a letter published in the *Miners' Journal* on December 5, 1868, he assured his fellow workers in the Scranton area that there was no basis in fact to any rumors they may have heard connecting the WBA to "Molly Maguires, 'Buckshots,' etc., etc." Under the rules of the WBA, Siney insisted, violence was "strictly forbidden," under pain of expulsion.[50]

The most direct source of evidence for the union's position on violence is its newspaper, the *Anthracite Monitor*. Published in Tamaqua, Schuylkill County, by the Miners and Laborers' Publishing Company, the newspaper was wholly owned by individual members of the WBA in shares of twenty dollars each and managed by an elected board. The first editor was "Honest John" Parker, an English-born blacksmith who had worked in the mines at Durham, where he became involved in Chartism, before coming to the United States in 1851.[51] In 1871, C. Ben Johnson, a twenty-four-year-old native of Philadelphia, took over the editorship. Johnson had been a colleague of William H. Sylvis, Andrew C. Cameron, and Richard F. Trevellick in the National Labor Union in the late 1860s, and he continued to advocate their policies in the *Anthracite Monitor* after he settled in Tamaqua in 1871.[52]

The *Monitor's* response to the assassination of Morgan Powell typifies the position of the trade union movement on violence. A native of Wales, Powell was the assistant superintendent of the Lehigh & Wilkes-Barre Coal Company. He was killed at Summit Hill, Carbon County, on December 2, 1871.[53] In

49. Raymond Williams, *Culture and Society, 1789–1950* (New York, 1983), 125.

50. John Siney, letter to the *Scranton Republican,* printed in *MJ,* December 5, 1868.

51. Pinkowski, *John Siney,* 38.

52. The *Monitor* went bankrupt in 1873 and was succeeded by the debt-ridden and sporadically published *Pottsville Workingman.* Siney and Johnson clashed for personal and ideological reasons, and Siney excluded Johnson from the editorship of the *Workingman,* in favor of Robert Morgan. Johnson became editor of the *Workingman* when it was revived in June 1874, by which time Siney had taken up residence in Cleveland as head of the recently formed Miners' National Union.

53. *MJ,* March 29, 1878.

common with all eight Molly Maguire killings between 1862 and 1871, nobody was convicted of this crime at the time. But the *Monitor* was sure that the Molly Maguires were responsible and condemned the assassins in no uncertain terms. On December 9, 1871, the newspaper reported that Powell had been

> murdered in cold blood at Summit Hill, by one of three dastards, who, with a pistol held close to his breast, fired the shot. Mr. Powell is said to have been especially well thought of by the men in the employ of the company; and among the community in which he lived, had many warm friends.

The *Monitor* went on to quote the *New York Sun* that "all talk that this and like crimes are the connection of the Miners' Union is certainly groundless and unjust. It is just as likely to be the work of the Coal Board of Trade, and a thousand times more likely to be the act of miscreants who are the enemies of both." The advertising columns in the December 9 issue of the *Monitor* carried three separate rewards for information leading to the conviction of Powell's killers. "The man who earns this," the *Monitor* commented,

> will likewise earn the lasting friendship of the Miners' Union, which, for the sake of its good name, is interested in seeing brought to justice all who commit such awful crimes in their midst, for by the world, our organization is too frequently held responsible for all such deeds here occurring.[54]

The differences between the union and the Molly Maguires were stated even more clearly by the *Monitor* on January 6, 1872, in an editorial condemning a judge in Northumberland County who had publicly declared that the two organizations were in fact the same. According to the *Monitor,* Judge Rockafellar alleged that "the Miners' Union is a criminal organization guilty of having frequently incited its members to murder, arson, and other crimes, and deserving of rigorous punishment, before it has even been notified that it has been accused." Rockafellar had played the Molly Maguire card in order to be elected, the *Monitor* alleged, and had slandered organized labor by blaming it for the violent acts of a few renegades. The WBA, the newspaper assured its readers, had "not incited to murder, arson, or any other crime, and well Judge Rockafellar knows it." The union was a respectable, chartered organization, the *Monitor* continued, and if it had violated its charter through illegal acts then that charter should be revoked, for the union "should not be made an exception to the rule that all violators of the law are criminal and should be punished."[55]

Nonetheless, in discussing the Rockafellar case, the *Monitor* hinted that some of the WBA's own members were disobeying official policy on violence. "We have no word of commendation for any man who commits any violation of the law, even though it be professedly in the interests of his Union," the *Monitor* warned in January 1872. "On the contrary, we will assist the court, all we can, to bring such a criminal to justice, because we believe that a man who will

54. *Anthracite Monitor,* December 9, 1871.
55. Ibid., January 6, 1872.

commit a crime for his Union is its enemy."[56] This potential division between the leaders and the rank and file was to become much deeper during the "Long Strike" of 1875, when the leadership lost control over a minority of radical union members. But from the inception of the trade union movement in 1868 to its demise in 1875, the leaders of the WBA never wavered from their position on violence.[57]

These explicit denunciations of violence by the leaders of the trade union were part of an overall ideology that posited a harmony of interests between labor and capital. The two sides had a great deal in common, the union leaders argued, and they should sit down and talk rather than attack each other. In this regard, the ideology of the WBA overlapped in some respects, though not in others, with that of Benjamin Bannan, the champion of the small, independent operators. Bannan continued to espouse a version of his antebellum free labor ideology in the 1870s, even as developments in the anthracite region rendered this ideology even less accurate a description of social reality than it had been in the 1850s. From 1870 onward, for example, both Bannan and John Siney criticized the Reading Railroad in much the same way, as the embodiment of corporate tyranny.[58]

Like Benjamin Bannan, the leaders of the WBA and the editors of the *Anthracite Monitor* emphasized the identity of interest between the causes of workers and small mine operators, on the one hand, against financiers, usurers, and corporations, on the other. The *Monitor* supported a national organization called the Labor Reform party in the early 1870s and heartily endorsed its program. That program, as one editorial explained, "teaches that there is no normal difference of interest between employer and employed. . . . On the contrary, we hold that the interests of honest employers and workingmen are at stake in one issue, and that issue is the one which the National Labor Reform Party will soon be asking the suffragers of the people."[59] Bankers and corporate monopolies held the individual mine operators in thrall as well as their employees, the *Monitor* insisted. Under these conditions, "there could be no such thing as prosperity for the honest businessman, and where there is no prosperity for him, there is no prosperity for the workingmen."[60]

What is most interesting here is the manner in which the ideology of the WBA resembles that of Bannan and the small operators.[61] The essential harmony of interests between the operators and their employees was one of the

56. Ibid., January 6, 1872.

57. Related to the question of violence was the question of secrecy. Fearful that the latter might discourage Irish Catholic mine workers from joining the union, the *Monitor* printed a list of the WBA officers on the front page of each issue, and assured its readers that the trade union was not a secret society (see, for example, October 14, 1871). On the "Long Strike," see chapter 6.

58. For Bannan's position on corporate capital in the 1870s, see PBIS 1, "A Few Thoughts on Capital and Labor," 523 ff.

59. *Anthracite Monitor,* January 27, 1872.

60. Ibid., January 27, 1872.

61. For a national parallel, see Montgomery, *Beyond Equality,* chapter 5.

most persistent themes developed by John Siney and other leaders of the WBA. Despite the freight charges imposed by the corporations, Siney wrote to his fellow miners in Scranton in December 1868, the small operators had raised wages over 40 percent since July 1. "Compare that with the fair dealings of corporations," Siney concluded, "and I think you will side with the individual enterprise of our operators, amongst whom the poor man, if he can find a coal vein, will have equal rights to work it, in his own way, and become rich, if successful in the vein he opens."[62] Here was a classic statement of the faith in social mobility that lay at the heart of the free labor ideology. On this issue, if not on others, John Siney and Benjamin Bannan were of a common mind.

The same themes of social mobility and the unity of labor and capital were repeatedly examined in the pages of the *Anthracite Monitor*. The policies of the Labor Reform party, the *Monitor* declared on January 17, 1872, "appeal as earnestly to the reason and conscience of the honest employer as they do to the same springs of wisdom in the employee, and they point to a plan that will enable us to re-establish the natural law of identity of interest between them." That identity of interest had been undermined, according to the *Monitor*, because "individual employers are so completely under the influence and control of usurious rates of interest, and the tyranny of corporations." The same sentiment was expressed in a passage from a newspaper called the *Golden Age*, quoted approvingly by the *Monitor*: "The interests of Labor and Capital are essentially identical. Neither can thrive without the other. Only by harmonizing the two interests can either be promoted or permanently secure."[63] Once again, this emphasis on the identity of interests between productive capital and respectable labor rested on the assumption that skilled miners could eventually become foremen and operators, provided that corporate capital did not stand in their way.

Examining the national labor movement as a whole in the late 1860s, one historian has identified what he calls a "reform syndrome of self-help, free agency, temperance, and the quest for upward social mobility" that many labor leaders shared with the Radical Republicans.[64] Siney and Bannan certainly shared these basic values, and if Bannan had looked a little closer at what Siney and other WBA spokesmen were actually saying in the late 1860s and early 1870s, he would have discovered that he and they had quite a lot in common. This was so not just on the question of violence but also on issues like nativism, the tariff, currency reform, and above all, the identity of interests between honest, respectable labor and honest, productive capital. Despite their increasing mutual antipathy, both sides were espousing a version of the republican ideology shared by most producers in the nineteenth-century

62. *MJ*, December 12, 1868.

63. Quoted in *Anthracite Monitor*, January 17, 1872.

64. Montgomery, *Beyond Equality*, chapter 5, especially 228. The *Monitor* also shared with Benjamin Bannan the view that labor and capital had a shared interest in a high protective tariff (see, for example, the issues of January 27 and February 3, 1872.)

United States, at least until the era of corporate monopoly power from the 1870s onward.[65]

This republican vision of society, in both its trade unionist and its entrepreneurial form, was remarkable for its virtual exclusion of women, African Americans, Chinese Americans, and even unskilled white male workers. The black population of the anthracite region was admittedly tiny: There were only 408 African Americans in Schuylkill County in 1850, out of a total population of 60,713; 357 out of 89,510 in 1860; and 384 out of 116,428 in 1870. The census recorded no Chinese.[66] But this did not prevent Benjamin Bannan and the trade union leaders from framing their separate ideologies in racially identical terms. The racism often implicit in their defense of free white labor was made explicit in their shared detestation of the Chinese.[67] Their position on gender was equally restrictive, even though there were almost as many females as males in the anthracite region by 1870. Women were excluded from the mining business, the trade union movement, the Ancient Order of Hibernians (until 1890), and the execution, if not perhaps the conception, of Molly Maguire violence. This is the social context in which the ideologies of the small producers, the miners, and the Molly Maguires took form.[68]

In their different ways, each of these ideologies rested on a conception of white masculinity that achieved coherence only through the suppression of sexual and racial difference. The trade unionists' conception of work, of union strategy, and of class identity, were clearly defined in exclusionary terms of white masculinity. Their movement, radical though it may have been in toppling the

65. The category of "republicanism" has dominated the last generation of nineteenth-century America labor historiography. The most influential statements of the republican synthesis have been David Montgomery, "Labor and the Republic in Industrial America: 1860–1920," *Le Mouvement Social,* 110 (1980): 250–56; Sean Wilentz, *Chants Democratic: New York City and the Rise of the American Working Class, 1788–1850* (New York, 1984); Wilentz, "Against Exceptionalism: Class Consciousness and the American Labor Movement, 1790–1920," *International Labor and Working Class History,* 26 (Fall 1984): 1–24; Wilentz, "Artisan Republican Festivals and the Rise of Class Conflict in New York City, 1788–1837," in Michael H. Frisch and Daniel J. Walkowitz, *Working-Class America: Essays on Labor, Community, and American Society* (Urbana, Ill., 1983), 37–77. For a timely critique of the category, see Daniel T. Rodgers, "Republicanism: the Career of a Concept," *Journal of American History,* 79 (June 1992): 11–38.

66. For demographic figures, see *Census of the United States: 1850,* 157; *Population of the United States in 1860,* 412; *Ninth Census,* vol. 1, 320.

67. On the shared anti-Chinese sentiment of Bannan and the union leaders, see, for example, *Anthracite Monitor,* October 14, 1871, and April 20, 1872; *MJ,* August 6, 1870.

68. For suggestive critiques of nineteenth-century labor historiography from the point of view of race and gender, see David Roediger, *The Wages of Whiteness: Race and the Making of the American Working Class* (New York, 1991); Ava Baron, "Gender and Labor History: Learning from the Past, Looking to the Future," in Baron, ed., *Work Engendered: Toward a New History of American Labor* (Ithaca, N.Y., 1991); Scott, *Gender and the Politics of History,* especially Parts 1 and 2. Peter Way raises the equally troubling exclusion of unskilled immigrant labor in "Evil Humours and Ardent Spirits," and *Common Labour.* In line with the questions raised by these historians, the term *labor republicanism* has deliberately been avoided in this book, though the miners' leaders clearly exhibited several of the strengths and weaknesses of that ideology as it has been described by historians of nineteenth-century American labor.

barriers of craft and ethnicity, was confined to male, Caucasian workers. It arose, after all, from an underground world based on one of the most ruggedly masculine forms of work. Benjamin Bannan's entrepreneurial producerism, with its emphasis on the dignity of white, male, upwardly mobile labor, was equally exclusionary in terms of race and gender. As for the Molly Maguires, their conception of gender was ambiguous, at least in its cultural heritage of cross-dressing; but their perceptions of racial difference were all-too-evident in their attacks on African Americans during the Civil War and their general opposition to the Union war effort, which presumably entailed hostility to emancipation as much as to conscription.[69]

In terms of race and gender, then, Benjamin Bannan and John Siney had a lot in common. But the broad similarities between their ideologies should not be allowed to conceal the important differences that separated them. If the union leader was firmly committed to collective action in pursuit of his goals, Bannan was an implacable foe of all "combinations," whether of labor or of capital. Thus, while he condemned monopoly capital, Bannan continued to denounce the WBA as well, seeing it as a combination of labor that had inevitably called forth its antithesis, a combination of capital, to the ruin of the independent operators. To complicate matters, he also identified the trade union with the Molly Maguires, despite its leaders' vigorous protestations to the contrary. In this way, he constructed a convenient scapegoat for the variety of ills besetting the lower anthracite region in the era of corporate takeover.[70]

In this respect, Bannan's ideology was more anachronistic than ever, while that of the trade union leaders was a more realistic response to prevailing economic conditions. For, contrary to Bannan's complaints that the union was polarizing society into two antagonistic groups, the WBA had been organized largely in response to the formation of similar collective organizations by the operators.[71] On November 19, 1869, representatives from these various organizations joined forces to form the Anthracite Board of Trade (ABT) of the Schuylkill Coal Region, with William Kendrick as president. The ABT included nearly all the operators in Schuylkill County, and from 1869 onward it was the organization "through which all negotiations and dealings affecting wages and disputes between the operators and the workmen were carried on."[72]

As well as rejecting the very idea of the union on principle, Bannan was

69. Bannan's position on free white labor is discussed in detail in Chapter 3. See *MJ*, January 16, 1864, for an alleged attack by Molly Maguires on an "inoffensive" African American.

70. See, for example, *MJ*, February 25, March 11, 1871.

71. The first operators' association was formed in 1867 when operators north of the Broad Mountain formed the Mahanoy Valley and Locust Mountain Coal Association, which embraced nearly all the collieries in that region. Similar societies were formed in 1868: the Coal Association of the Southern Coal Field of Schuylkill County, at Pottsville; the West End Coal Association, at Tremont, in western Schuylkill County; the Shamokin Coal Exchange, at Shamokin, Northumberland County; and the Mount Carmel Coal Association, at Mount Carmel, Columbia County.

72. PBIS I, 334.

opposed to two of its policies in particular: support for the cooperative movement and third-party politics. While Bannan believed, or clung tenuously to the hope, that miners could eventually move upward in the social scale and become operators, the direct social mobility entailed by cooperative ownership was altogether too rapid for his taste. And, for a committed Republican who had lived through the political turmoil of the 1850s, any fracturing of the two-party system of government was anathema.

One of the more significant ventures proposed by John Siney and the WBA was the formation of cooperative mines. Siney shared a commitment to the cooperative movement with many labor reformers of the time, a commitment based in his case on experiences and models drawn from the Lancashire environment in which the leading figures in the WBA were born and raised.[73] The pages of the *Anthracite Monitor* were filled with stories and examples drawn from the history of labor movements in Britain, including lengthy accounts of the cooperative movement in that country.[74] The founders of the WBA set up "union stores" to sell goods to their members, and in 1870 Siney became involved in plans to start a cooperative mine near Ashland, in Schuylkill County, encouraged in part by local representatives of the iron molders' union, who hoped to bypass the coal carriers and suppliers in acquiring coal to fire their own furnaces.[75]

Though the two sides failed to come to an agreement in this first venture, the *Anthracite Monitor* kept the idea of cooperatives alive throughout the early 1870s. The issue of October 14, 1871, for example, carried an extract from a pamphlet on the cooperative movement, entitled, "The Just Demand of Labor. A More Equal Distribution of Wealth." The author of the pamphlet insisted that, while "wages were fixed and arbitrary . . . a fair share of profits for the laborer must be chargeable according to the success of business enterprises for the time being. In a word, justice demands that labor should be not the employe[e] but the partner of capital." The issue of March 16, 1872, hailed the dawn of the age of cooperation and issued a rallying cry to the workers of the anthracite region:

> Will not mechanics and laboring men take a hint, and instead of selling their labor—the actual capital they own in human sinews and human force—combine it together in Co-operative Unions and so control and receive the full benefit of the labor (of the capital) with which God and nature has invested them[?][76]

If cooperative ownership was much too radical for Bannan's taste, he also parted company with Siney and the *Anthracite Monitor* on the question of party

73. On the national cooperative movement, see Montgomery, *Beyond Equality,* chapter 5 and passim.

74. *Anthracite Monitor,* June 1, 1872.

75. Pinkowski, *John Siney,* 192. The delegates of the WBA voted in favor of this proposition, and Siney was appointed to open negotiations with Colonel James J. Conner, one of the first successful operators in the Mahanoy basin, to turn over two collieries to the union in return for royalties and other fees.

76. *Anthracite Monitor,* March 16, 1872.

affiliation. Bannan remained steadfastly in the Republican fold in the 1870s, even as that party abandoned much of the free labor ideology that had attracted him to it in the 1850s and allied itself with the big business interests that he so distrusted. The WBA and the *Anthracite Monitor,* by contrast, called for a radical restructuring of national politics. "There is no use looking to the old parties," the *Anthracite Monitor* declared on March 16, 1872, "for it is sure to provide only a change of men, not principle—to be a removal from bad to worse." In 1870 John Siney attended the fifth annual convention of the National Labor Union as the delegate from Pennsylvania. He was appointed to a committee that formulated the principles of a new organization, the Labor Reform party.[77] With C. Ben Johnson of the *Monitor,* Siney organized the Schuylkill branch of this party, of which he was appointed president. In the local elections of October 1871, the WBA campaigned on behalf of the Labor Reform ticket, which won an impressive four thousand votes in its first outing in Schuylkill County, though this was not enough to elect any candidates.[78]

As voting patterns were traditionally polarized along ethnic lines in the anthracite region, third-party politics was particularly attractive to the union leaders.[79] The *Monitor* declared that the election "indicates that, at no distant day, the prejudices of workingmen, prejudices that have thusfar been their greatest bane, will be entirely dissipated, that Irish will fraternise with Welsh, English with German, Catholic with Protestant, in a common bond, for the amelioration of the condition of the whole." In this way, the Labor Reform party held out the possibility of overcoming "the differences in religion and nationality that have unfortunately contributed not a little to the defeat of our trade organization as well as this political movement."[80] In local elections in Cass Township the following February, the "People's Reform ticket" won all but one of the contested offices. All the men elected had Irish names, which is not surprising, given the ethnic composition of Cass Township.[81] But the township that had been the center of Molly Maguireism from 1862 to 1867 was now committed to the third-party politics of labor reform. Cass had lost the turbulent and violent character that had made it infamous in the 1860s, and it would not feature at all in the Molly Maguire violence of the 1870s.

Perhaps the most remarkable achievement of the Workingmen's Benevolent Association is the extent to which it overcame the differences of craft and

77. On the National Labor Union and the Labor Reform party, see Montgomery, *Beyond Equality,* passim.

78. *Anthracite Monitor,* October 14, 1871.

79. On voting patterns, see Gudelunas and Shade, *Before the Molly Maguires,* passim.

80. *Anthracite Monitor,* October 14, 1871. The full platform of the National Labor Reform party was printed in the issue of April 20, 1872.

81. *Anthracite Monitor,* March 16, 1872.

national origin that were a fact of life in the anthracite region. The absence of Molly Maguire violence after 1868 is a powerful testament to the success of this effort; so, too, is the resurgence of Molly Maguire violence after the defeat and collapse of the union in 1875. The mine workers overcame most of their differences in a larger struggle for goals they all believed in. Chief among these from the outset were higher wages, welfare for sick and crippled miners, and safer working conditions. The struggle for welfare and safety, in particular, brought all mine workers together in a single, unified labor movement.

In addition to an ever-present risk of injury and fatality, mine workers faced a series of occupational hazards. The most debilitating of these hazards was "miners' asthma" or "black lung disease," a variety of fatal pulmonary disorders caused by the inhalation of coal dust, powder, smoke, and underground gases. Thousands died from it, including John Siney in 1880. Miners who became ill could hope for little in the way of medical care, especially in the lower region. In the upper region, the Delaware, Lackawanna, & Western Railroad ran its own hospital in Scranton, and in 1872 citizens of Wilkes-Barre established the City Hospital. But the rest of the anthracite region lacked hospitals at this time. Injured miners in the Eastern Middle Coal Field, for example, were hospitalized at Bethlehem, the local mental asylum.[82]

In Schuylkill County, the *Miners' Journal* had been calling for a county hospital since the 1840s. In 1868 the WBA took up the fight, and two years later the legislature passed an act incorporating the Miners' Hospital and Asylum of Schuylkill County. The hospital would provide free medical care to anyone injured while mining or transporting coal, financed by a tax of one cent per ton of coal transported in Schuylkill County. A board of directors elected by the borough councils would govern the hospital. But twelve years passed before the hospital finally opened. The last leader of the then-defunct WBA, John Welsh, successfully led the drive to complete construction, and the hospital opened at Fountain Springs, near Ashland, in 1882. A separate act of 1879 provided for a regional hospital to house miners from all the anthracite counties. These were among the crowning accomplishments of the labor movement inaugurated by the Workingmen's Benevolent Association in 1868.[83]

The greatest hazard mine workers faced in their daily lives was the risk of death or injury. One of the events they feared most was a large fall of coal or rock, which could kill men directly or block the passage of air, with fatal consequences, especially when the pillars failed and the roof caved in. Accidents of this type were often preceded by the buckling of pillars prior to the collapse of the roof. They were known as "squeezes," as the pillars emitted a creaking sound that might warn the men. Another warning sign was sudden movement away from the coal face by the thousands of rats who lived in the mines. The workers also faced the ever-present threat of explosions or asphyxiation caused

82. Aurand, "The Anthracite Mine Workers, 1869–1897," 323.

83. *MJ*, November 29, 1845; June 20, 1846; October 23, 1858; Aurand, "The Anthracite Mine Workers, 1869–1897," 325–26; Trachtenberg, *A History of Legislation*, 97–98.

by the variety of noxious gases underground, including "stinkdamp" (hydrogen sulphide), "firedamp" (methane), "blackdamp" (carbon dioxide), and "whitedamp" (carbon monoxide).[84]

Most accidents in the mines killed one or two men, though some killed dozens. One major hazard was flooding, which might be caused by the collapse of strata under a river, or by miners tapping an unsuspected body of water. But the most lethal accidents involved a combination of fire and gas. The worst of these occurred at the Steuben Shaft at Avondale, just outside the town of Plymouth, in Luzerne County in September 1869. Operated by the Delaware, Lackawanna, & Western Railroad, the Steuben Shaft was 327 feet deep and employed two hundred men. Directly on top of the shaft stood a wooden coal breaker, and halfway down the shaft a furnace had been installed to provide ventilation. This single shaft was the sole means of entry and exit for the mine workers; the accompanying upcast and downcast carried air, not men. On the morning of September 6, 1869, sparks from the wood used to ignite the furnace, possibly combined with some gas in the upcast, set fire to the timbering in the shaft, which in turn set fire to the breaker above. The breaker tumbled down through the shaft, blocking the only possible exit from the mine and starting a fire that rapidly consumed all the oxygen and spread various poisonous gases. One hundred and ten men were asphyxiated. It took a rescue party two days to find all the bodies.[85]

Three days after the tragedy, John Siney addressed a large crowd of mine workers and their families at Avondale. The crowd was composed of men, women, and children, miners, laborers, and slate pickers of Welsh, Irish, German, and American extraction. Disasters of this magnitude generally transcended divisions of class, status, and ethnicity in mining communities. Nonetheless, some witnesses at the coroner's inquest blamed the disaster on the Irish. The fire, they claimed, was the culmination of mounting class and ethnic hostilities between Irish and Welsh mine workers. The Avondale Shaft had reopened on September 2, after a three-month strike. Apparently the Welsh, who held most of the best mining jobs, had been eager to end the strike, while the Irish, most of whom worked as laborers, wanted to stay out. It was openly alleged at the inquest that the Irish had started the fire deliberately to settle their scores with the Welsh. Tensions were exacerbated by the fact that most of the Irish mine workers had taken off the day of the disaster for a funeral, so that only six of the men who died were Irish. The jury discounted these allegations, and blamed the fire on sparks from the furnace.[86]

The origins of some of the more conspiratorial theories about the Molly

84. For a good description of the dangers of life underground, see the exhibit at the Anthracite Museum, Ashland. For a vivid report of a "squeeze," see [Hudson Coal Company], *The Story of Anthracite,* 172–74. Cf. Long, *Where the Sun Never Shines,* 35.

85. Blatz, "Ever-Shifting Ground," 66–71; Pinkowski, *John Siney,* 5–53; Trachtenberg, *A History of Legislation,* 37–39.

86. NYT, September 15, 1869; *New York Herald,* September 11, 12, 14, 1869; *New York Evening Post,* September 15, 1869; Blatz, "Ever-Shifting Ground," 67.

Maguires lay in the politics of safety. The struggle for safer working conditions occasionally divided the mine workers among themselves but more often united them in opposition to the mine owners and operators, who invariably blamed accidents on the carelessness of the workers and minimized their own responsibility, determined as they were to attribute the problems of the coal trade to anyone but themselves. At first, mine workers in general were blamed for all accidents; but this general criticism was soon focused on a specific group. By the 1870s all fires, floods, and accidents were liable to be classed as acts of terrorism committed by a hard core of radical miners, the Molly Maguires. Every faction fight, assault, or murder that occurred in the anthracite region was already being blamed on the Mollys, and every explosion or mishap underground could now be interpreted as industrial sabotage and attributed to the same nefarious organization.[87]

But only the most diehard enemy of the Irish could believe that they had deliberately plotted the Avondale disaster. Governor John W. Geary of Pennsylvania was much closer to the mark when he declared that the real culprit was neither the faulty furnace nor Irish arson, but the grossly negligent operators. The failure of the operators to provide the mine workers with the safety they needed and deserved, Geary continued, "renders our mining system worse than that of any other country, whilst our mining interests are unequalled by those of any other part of the world." Governor Geary had a point. Historians have estimated that the rates of injury and fatality in the anthracite mines of Pennsylvania were three times as high as in Britain. And Schuylkill County, the center of Molly Maguire activities, was always the most dangerous area in the anthracite region, losing 556 dead and 1,667 maimed and injured between 1870 and 1875.[88]

The tragic irony of Avondale is how easily the disaster might have been prevented. Since the 1850s, the mine workers had been fighting for a comprehensive safety law, with the fear of just such a disaster very much in mind. The WBA had put safety at the top of its agenda from the beginning, forming a committee that went to Harrisburg in 1869 with a petition fifteen feet long, bearing more than three thousand signatures. Under WBA pressure, the Pennsylvania legislature debated a new mine safety act in the spring of 1869. The law provided for adequate ventilation in every mine as well as the appointment of a mine inspector (from the ranks of the skilled miners) to oversee safety. But the Democratic senator from Luzerne County, George Turner, objected strenuously to the proposal that this law be applied to the anthracite region as a whole. As a result, when the act became law on April 12, 1869, it applied only to Schuylkill County.[89]

87. Wallace, *St. Clair,* 273.

88. Geary, quoted in Trachtenberg, *A History of Legislation,* 38–39; Wallace, *St. Clair,* 250–51; *Annual Report of the Secretary of Internal Affairs for the Commonwealth of Pennsylvania, 1875–76. Industrial Statistics* (Harrisburg, n.d.), 475.

89. *MJ,* May 6, 1854, letter from "John Morris, a Miner"; Wallace, *St. Clair,* 249–313; Blatz, "Ever-Shifting Ground," 69–71; Trachtenberg, *A History of Legislation,* 23–37.

Though the 1869 law did not explicitly require separate means of entry and exit from the mines, it did require the construction of furnaces in such a way as to prevent fires below ground. The furnace and breaker at Avondale would scarcely have survived the scrutiny of a rigorous mine inspector. But, thanks in large part to the efforts of Senator Turner, the new safety law did not apply to Luzerne County, so the mines at Avondale were not affected. After the disaster, Turner himself led the legislative movement for a new law, though as usual it was a committee of miners who did the initial lobbying at Harrisburg. The law, passed on March 3, 1870, applied to the entire anthracite region, explicitly prohibiting the employment of men underground unless two outlets from each coal mine were constructed within four months of the passage of the act. A year later the *Anthracite Monitor* was still complaining that "at very few collieries are provisions of the law being fully complied with." Throughout the early 1870s, the *Monitor* continued to run a weekly column entitled "What it Costs to Mine Coal," listing recent casualties and deaths. Mining anthracite remained a remarkably dangerous way to make a living.[90]

The Mine Safety Act of 1870 was a significant victory for the labor movement, a striking illustration of the power of collective action. But the victory was distinctly double-edged, as it took a considerable amount of control over the work place away from the miners, placing it more directly in the hands of the operators and their "inside bosses." The introduction of stringent safety regulations in 1870, therefore, had a somewhat paradoxical effect. The mine workers benefited from the fact that the burden of safety had been shifted back to their employers. Many lives were saved as a result. But the mines also became more disciplined places to work in, and the skilled mine workers in particular lost some more of their much-valued autonomy.[91]

On matters of safety, wages, and interethnic unity, the WBA had won a series of impressive victories during the first years of its existence. In its "Report on Labor" in 1873, the Pennsylvania Bureau of Industrial Statistics gave due praise to the WBA for the transformation of labor relations in the anthracite region over the previous five years. But the report ended on a somber note, pointing to an ominous cloud on the horizon: the rapid absorption of coal lands and collieries by the Reading Railroad, "which many look upon with dread anticipations of remorseless monopoly in the future."[92] Those who had most to dread were the leaders of the Workingmen's Benevolent Association. For their existence was a fundamental obstacle to the designs of the Reading Railroad and its president, Franklin B. Gowen.

90. Wallace, *St. Clair,* 249–313; Blatz, "Ever-Shifting Ground," 69–71; Trachtenberg, *A History of the Legislation,* 23–37; *Anthracite Monitor,* October 14, 1871.

91. Wallace, *St. Clair,* 296; Papers of Charles Heckscher, B 588, Clippings, 1863–66, p.54, handbill setting out the "Rules and Regulations Established by the New York and Schuylkill Coal Company" in 1865.

92. PBIS 1, 363.

5

The Reading Railroad Takes Control

Franklin B. Gowen, the president of the Philadelphia & Reading Railroad, has aptly been described as "one of the great architects of industrial capitalism in America."[1] The rise of the Reading under Gowen's presidency provides the essential background for understanding the reemergence of the Molly Maguires in the 1870s. In his struggle to win control of the Schuylkill anthracite industry, Gowen faced two main sources of opposition, independent coal operators and organized labor. By defeating the small operators, the trade union, and the Molly Maguires, he eventually secured control of the coal industry of the lower anthracite region for the Reading Railroad.

Unlike the upper anthracite region, Schuylkill County was still a bastion of small-scale enterprise as late as 1870. For Gowen's plan to succeed, the independent operators had to be driven out of business; so, too, had the independent middlemen who controlled the marketing of coal in Philadelphia. As for organized labor, at the heart of the strategy developed by the Workingmen's Benevolent Association was an effort to control the production and hence the distribution of coal. By limiting the amount of coal that was mined and sent to market, the union hoped to keep coal prices high; wages, in turn, were linked to the price of coal, so this strategy would benefit both the mine workers and the

1. Wallace, *St. Clair,* 411.

operators. Franklin B. Gowen had very different ideas on the subject. Corporate control of the industry would guarantee stable wages and prices, he claimed, but the best way for the railroad to make a profit was to send as much coal to market as possible. This would also benefit consumers, by lowering prices. But what about the producers? Conflict between the trade union and the railroad was inevitable.[2]

By 1873 Gowen had removed the threat of the independent operators and their retailers, clearing the way for the railroad to control not only the transportation but also the production and distribution of Schuylkill coal. By manipulating freight rates and purchasing tens of thousands of acres of coal lands, Gowen drove the independent operators out of business; by marketing his own coal as well as producing and transporting it, he eliminated most of the independent coal merchants of Philadelphia. Hand-in-hand with his campaign against the small entrepreneurs, he developed a strategy for undermining the position of the WBA, insisting that the Reading Railroad, not the workers, should control the amount of coal produced. Gowen established himself as the chief arbiter of labor relations in the anthracite region. He proposed company welfare and benefits schemes designed to undercut the union. And, as part of this same campaign against the WBA, he repeatedly identified trade unionism with Molly Maguireism, insisting that there was no substantial difference between the two.

After spending the early months of 1869 organizing in all six anthracite counties, John Siney attended the first General Council of the WBA at Hazleton in March 1869. Present were four delegates each from Schuylkill County and Luzerne County, three from Carbon County, two from Columbia County, and one from Dauphin County. The meeting was presided over by Thomas M. Williams, an English-born miner from Luzerne County. But Siney, as a founder-member of the original WBA of St. Clair and the representative of some fifteen thousand mine workers in Schuylkill County, was the dominant presence. The delegates agreed to make plans for a general suspension of work in order to raise the price of coal. A delegate named George Corbett explained the theory behind this decision in a letter to the *Miners' Journal*. "Have we not a right to ask a price for coal that will give us a price in wages?" he asked. "What other class of men is there that does not ask a price for what he has to sell, and if the buyer will not give the price he asks, what follows? Why, he withholds it and puts it back to the stock to remain until he can get his price."[3]

At a second meeting on April 20, 1869, the WBA delegates voted in favor of a general suspension to begin on Monday, May 10. This was the first general

2. See, for example, PGA, 17.

3. Letter from George Corbett to the *Philadelphia Public Ledger*, quoted in Pinkowski, *John Siney*, 35. See, also, PBIS I, 334; Schlegel, "The Workingmen's Benevolent Association," 245–46.

strike by the mineworkers of the anthracite region. The order was obeyed throughout the coal fields, except in the part of the upper region around Scranton and Pittston. There the collieries were owned by the three so-called "Scranton companies," the Delaware, Lackawanna & Western Railroad Company, the Delaware & Hudson Canal Company, and the Pennsylvania Coal Company. Some of the employees of the first two companies joined the strike, but the Pennsylvania Coal Company men refused to quit their jobs, enticed by an offer of higher wages.[4]

After five weeks' suspension, the General Council assembled again at Mahanoy City on June 9 and voted for a resumption of work the following week. The men in each region were given the intervening time to negotiate individual settlements with their employers. The intention of the strike, as the wording of the General Council's order to resume work demonstrates, had been to control the production and marketing of coal in order to raise prices and wages. On behalf of the WBA, John Parker and Thomas M. Williams declared that "the object of our doing so [i.e., suspending work] has been to a great extent accomplished, to-wit, the reduction or depletion of the surplus of coal already in the market, together with the preventing if possible of the enormous oversupply that was going to the market." The leaders of the WBA had no desire to inflate the price of coal, Parker and Williams continued; all they wanted was "a steady, healthy market, which will afford to the operators and dealers fair interest on their investments, and at the same time that we may receive a fair day's wages for a fair day's work."[5]

The union leaders believed that the best way to ensure fair and regular wages in the future, without work stoppages and contract negotiations every few months, was to tie the price of labor to the price of coal. They proposed a "sliding scale" whereby fluctuations in the price of the commodity produced by miners would be reflected in the remuneration they received. They also insisted on a minimum basis beyond which wages could not fall. The Schuylkill men reached an agreement that included these provisions on June 16, 1869, and the Lehigh men on July 1; but the operators in the Wyoming region refused to grant a sliding scale, and the northern men stayed out until September 1, when they gave up their demands for an adjustable wage in return for a one-time advance in pay.[6]

For the Schuylkill region, the minimum basis for wages was to be set according to the price of coal at Port Carbon, the principal shipping point from the lower anthracite region. When coal sold at three dollars a ton at Port Carbon, outside laborers would receive eleven dollars per week, inside laborers twelve dollars, and miners on wages fourteen dollars. Wages would increase by 5 percent with every rise of twenty-five cents in the price of coal; but they

4. Schlegel, "The Workingmen's Benevolent Association," 246; PBIS 1, 336.

5. PBIS 1, 336–38, 339 (quote); Evans, *History of the United Mine Workers of America,* vol. 1, 19. See, also, Schlegel, "The Workingmen's Benevolent Association," 246.

6. Schlegel, "The Workingmen's Benevolent Association," 247.

would not decrease if the price of coal fell below three dollars a ton. In other words, the new scale would slide upward but not downward. This was a big concession to labor, and it would be summarily rescinded by the operators the following year. In the Lehigh region the minimum basis was set at five dollars per ton of coal, the price at its distribution center in New Jersey. This higher price reflected the cost of transportation from the mining region (roughly two dollars per ton). Wages on the five-dollar basis in Lehigh were set at roughly the same levels as those for the three-dollar basis in Schuylkill. But the Lehigh men suffered the disadvantage that their wages would fluctuate with freight rates as well as with the price of coal before it left the mining region.[7]

Independent contract miners were included in the new agreement as well as wage workers. They were to receive an agreed-upon price for the amount of coal they freed, from which the employer would deduct the wages of the miner's laborer (unless the miner paid his helper himself), along with charges for powder, oil, and equipment. Pay scales per wagon or yard of coal freed were to slide upward in the same proportion as the rates set for wage workers. But rates for contract miners also depended on the width of the coal seam and the difficulty of the work. Because of the variety of tasks the contract miners performed, and the varying conditions they worked in, contemporaries were never quite sure how much they earned. Most appear to have made about what twice what miners on wages did, though a minority of independent contractors made considerably more than this by opening new mines and maintaining existing ones. The great majority of contract miners, however, were engaged almost exclusively in mining and earned between $100 and $125 a month. Moreover, by the 1870s most contract miners had to work at least part-time for wages in order to make ends meet. In terms of both tonnage rates and wages, then, all miners were parties to the new sliding scale.[8]

The sliding scale worked very well for labor during its first year in operation. Coal prices remained above three dollars per ton at Port Carbon from mid-June through November 1869, partly because of the continuing strike in upper Luzerne County. As a result, wages in the Schuylkill region were an average of 12.5 percent above the base rate. Then, from December 1869 to May 1870, prices and wages remained at the minimum basis. And, even if the price of coal had fallen below three dollars, the men knew that they would still have been paid the minimum wage. As a result, labor relations in the lower anthracite region were remarkably harmonious in the twelve months following the agreement of June 1869.[9]

7. Andrew Roy, *A History of the Coal Miners of the United States* (1905; Westport, Conn., 1970), 75; PBIS 1, 336, 344; Schlegel, "The Workingmen's Benevolent Association," 247–48; Broehl, *The Molly Maguires,* 100.

8. See, especially, Long, *Where the Sun Never Shines,* 60; Schlegel, "The Workingmen's Benevolent Association," 248.

9. Roy, *A History of the Coal Miners in the United States,* 75; PBIS 1, 336, 344; Schlegel, "The Workingmen's Benevolent Association," 247–48; Broehl, *The Molly Maguires,* 100; *MJ,* January 13, 1873.

Though the wage negotiations of 1869 implied de facto recognition of the trade union, the operators still refused to grant formal recognition. When the operators' organization, the Anthracite Board of Trade (ABT), made its resumption proposal to the WBA in June 1869, it warned that the collieries would remain idle if "outsiders" threatened mine operators or officials. For the operators, the term "outsiders" clearly meant anything beyond individual, one-on-one negotiation between employer and employee. Their position, as described by the Pennsylvania Bureau of Industrial Statistics, was that "any pressure brought to bear upon their workmen individually, affecting the question as to how, when or for what wages he should work, by any combination of other workmen, was a violation of individual rights and an act of conspiracy." The leaders of the WBA, on the other hand, claimed that they had the same right as the ABT to organize for mutual protection. If all actions by the union to determine conditions or wages were to be construed as conspiracy, then the union had no right to organize at all. The WBA accepted the wage proposal offered by the ABT but rejected the operators' position on the right of the union to interfere in the workings of the mines.[10]

Even without formal recognition by the operators, however, the union had won a significant victory. A sliding pay scale with a minimum wage was a major achievement for the mine workers. Above all, it recognized a connection, for wage workers as well as contract miners, between what was produced and how its producers were paid. This connection lay at the heart of the skilled miners' sense of craft and independence. With their wages tied directly to production, they hoped to be spared the fate of contemporary factory workers, whose labor power and its renumeration were being separated entirely from the productive process and the ability to control it. And, thus far at least, the union men were in basic agreement with their employers that the best way to keep prices and wages at an optimal level would be periodic stoppages in production.

If the operators shared with the mine workers a desire for high prices, they were less enamored of the prospect of correspondingly high wages. In its offer of a new contract for 1870, the Anthracite Board of Trade proposed a drastic reduction in wages. With a ton of coal now selling for less than three dollars ($2.74 in December), the operators insisted that the pay scale be adjusted to allow wages to slide downward as well as upward, with a new base of two dollars per ton of coal. With coal selling at this price at Port Carbon, outside laborers were to receive $7.50 a week compared to $11 in 1869, inside laborers $8.50 compared to $12, and miners on wages $10.50 compared to $14. Rates for contract work were to be slashed by 40 percent. When the price of coal reached $2.50, wages would increase by 5 percent, and by another 5 percent if the price reached $3.00. Thereafter, wages would rise by 4 percent for every increase of twenty-five cents in coal prices. But when the price of coal fell, wages would decrease in the same proportion down to the new basis of two dollars. The proposal for 1870 therefore represented a potential pay cut of 33 percent.[11] As a

10. PBIS I, 338; cf. Schlegel, "The Workingmen's Benevolent Association," 249–50.

11. PBIS I, 347; Schlegel, "The Workingmen's Benevolent Association," 248.

result, it "was not formally rejected, but was received with such indignant contempt by the men that they did not even give it consideration." The union leaders demanded retention of the three-dollar basis and insisted that wages should not fall below this basis, even if the price of coal did.[12]

On February 18, 1870, the Anthracite Board of Trade responded with a compromise offer, proposing a basis set at $2.50 per ton of coal instead of $2.00, which would raise the rates for outside laborers to nine dollars a week, for inside laborers to ten dollars, and for miners on wages to twelve dollars. Rates for contract work were to be reduced by 30 percent instead of the 40 percent originally proposed. Under the new proposal, wages would advance at a rate of 20 percent for every rise of one dollar in the price of coal and would slide downward to the $2.50 base, but not beyond. When the WBA met in convention at Summit Hill, Carbon County, it rejected this compromise proposal, demanding the retention of the 1869 wage levels on a three-dollar basis with no downward movement. Seventy-six operators and coal company representatives then convened at Union Hall, Pottsville, on March 15, and decided to stick by their offer. They delivered an ultimatum to the union: accept the compromise by April 2, or face a general suspension. The union refused to yield, and the shutdown of operations in the lower region began on schedule. The stoppage proved to be prolonged and bitter, causing considerable privation among the mine workers. It was entering its fourth month when, amid rumors that some operators were about to resume on the 1869 basis, Franklin B. Gowen intervened. The resulting "Gowen Compromise" marked a turning point in the history of the lower anthracite region, the first of a series of moves by which the Philadelphia & Reading Railroad eventually won control of the Schuylkill coal industry.[13]

Franklin B. Gowen was appointed acting president of the Philadelphia & Reading Railroad in 1869, at the age of thirty-two. The son of Episcopalian Irish immigrants, he was born in 1836 in Philadelphia, where he attended Beck's Boys Academy. At the age of thirteen, his father sent him to work with a merchant in Lancaster County. After joining his older brother, Thomas, in a coal retailing company at Shamokin, Northumberland County, Gowen went into partnership in a coal mine at Mount Laffee, just north of Pottsville, in 1858. Like many such mining operations in the Schuylkill region, the company dissolved within a year. Two of Gowen's older brothers had already become lawyers, and after reading law in a Pottsville lawyer's office in the winter of 1859–60, Gowen was admitted to the Schuylkill County bar. In 1862, at the age

12. PBIS 1, 348 (quote). Rounded daily figures for 1870 and 1869, assuming an average of nine months (or 216 days) worked, would have been $1.75 compared to $2.33 for miners on wages, $1.42 compared to $2.00 for inside laborers, and $1.25 compared to $1.83 for outside laborers. The respective annual figures were $504 reduced to $378, $342 reduced to $306, and $396 reduced to $270. Figures compiled from PBIS 1, 344–48.

13. PBIS 1, 344–49; Schlegel, "The Workingmen's Benevolent Association," 247–51. Mines in the upper anthracite region remained open.

of twenty-six, he was elected district attorney for Schuylkill County on the Democratic ticket. His two-year period of service in this position coincided with the peak of the Molly Maguire activities during the Civil War. Gowen resigned in November 1864 to devote himself full-time to his expanding private law practice.[14]

Soon after quitting politics in 1864, Gowen was appointed head of the legal department of the Philadelphia & Reading Railroad. He returned to Philadelphia to take up his new job, and quickly rose through the ranks, replacing the ailing Charles E. Smith as acting president in 1869. The following year he became president in his own right. Having already taken over the Schuylkill Canal and the feeder railroad lines in Schuylkill County, the Reading had by this time achieved a virtual monopoly on transportation in and out of the lower anthracite region. But it still did not control the marketing of anthracite, let alone its production. Unlike the northern transportation companies, the Reading Railroad did not yet own any coal mines; indeed, it was prohibited by its own charter from doing so, a prohibition that Gowen would soon take measures to remedy.[15] Before it began to mine its own coal, most of the railroad's profits came from hauling anthracite. Gowen therefore had a vital interest in the negotiations between the trade union and the operators. He was particularly opposed to the WBA's efforts to maintain high wages by holding coal at the three-dollar level. If coal prices could be brought down to $2.50 a ton, Gowen claimed, the anthracite industry would be stabilized, bringing greater prosperity to all. Lower prices would increase consumption, so that profits would not fall; and miners and laborers would be guaranteed stable wages at a reasonable level.[16]

On July 18, 1870, with the suspension in its third month, Gowen offered his services as a mediator between the union and the operators. Under Gowen's proposal, pay rates would slide downward as well as upward, with a new basis set at two dollars, just as the operators wanted. If coal sold for three dollars a ton, the men would make the same as in 1869; if the price of coal went up or down, wages would rise or fall at the rate of 8.25 percent (instead of the 5 percent proposed by the operators) for each change of twenty-five cents in the cost of a ton of coal. And pay cuts for contract miners would be graduated according to income, with reductions of between 10 and 40 percent. The former rate would apply to those who made less than $125 a year (the majority), while those with higher incomes would suffer correspondingly higher reductions, up to a maximum of 40 percent for the small elite who made more than $200 annually. For reasons that remain obscure, the WBA decided to accept this offer. The concession to the contract miners was certainly an important inducement; and Gowen may have persuaded the men that coal prices were likely to stay closer to three dollars than two dollars a ton in the coming year. The most

14. Schlegel, *Ruler of the Reading,* 1–11.
15. Ibid., 33; Broehl, *The Molly Maguires,* 121.
16. Schlegel, *Ruler of the Reading,* 19.

convincing explanation for the union's capitulation, however, is simply that its members were in danger of being starved into submission and had to settle for what they could get. But the great danger of the "Gowen Compromise" was that it allowed wages to fall with coal prices by as much as 33 percent, precisely the figure proposed by the operators in the initial round of negotiations in December 1869. In retrospect at least, it is clear that the union leaders had more to lose than to gain by accepting Gowen's offer. But it is equally clear that the union had little choice in the matter.[17]

It is therefore quite surprising that the Anthracite Board of Trade initially rejected Gowen's proposal, claiming that the railroad president had departed from his original instructions. The small operators were evidently concerned about the precedent of a corporation dictating policy in the lower anthracite region. But when the more independent among them, like Benjamin Thomas, threatened to break ranks and resume work, the ABT accepted the "Gowen Compromise." On July 29, 1870, representatives of the Anthracite Board of Trade and the Workingmen's Benevolent Association signed the first written contract in the United States between miners and operators. While the settlement of 1870 was primarily concerned with setting the basis for wages, it also included the following significant clause: "It is agreed that the Workingmen's Benevolent Association shall not sustain any man who is discharged for incompetency, bad workmanship, bad conduct, or other good cause; and that the operators shall not discharge any man or officer for actions or duties imposed on him by the Workingmen's Benevolent Association."[18] Within two years of its formation, the WBA had received formal recognition from its counterpart among the operators.

No sooner had the agreement for 1870 been reached, however, than the double-edged character of the adjusted sliding scale was revealed. Mining resumed in the lower anthracite region on August 1, but during the strike the producers in the north had greatly increased their production and taken over most of the market usually supplied by the Schuylkill region. As a result, the Schuylkill operators found themselves temporarily without consumers, and, as the price of coal plummeted, wages declined accordingly. In August, the miners suffered a pay cut of 8.25 percent, and John Siney's request that the wage question be reopened was summarily rejected by the ABT. Coal dropped to $2.50 a ton in September and October, which meant that wages were reduced by another 8.25 percent. In November and December the price of coal averaged $2.25, leading to a third reduction in wages. By the end of the year, wage rates in the Schuylkill region stood 24.75 percent below the guaranteed minimum that had been paid in 1869.[19]

17. PBIS 1, 347–51; Schlegel, "The Workingmen's Benevolent Association," 249–50.
18. Quoted in PBIS 1, 351; Evans, *History of the United Mine Workers of America,* vol. 1, 20–21.
19. PBIS 1, 352; Schlegel, "The Workingmen's Benevolent Association," 251.

Though his railroad did not yet own any coal mines, Franklin B. Gowen had emerged as the arbiter of labor relations in the anthracite region. The basis of his power was that he controlled the transportation of coal from the lower anthracite region. But his command of the region's coal trade could not be considered complete until the Reading Railroad entered the business of mining more directly. Accordingly, Gowen's next task was to find a way to purchase mines for the railroad and to eliminate the small entrepreneurs who dominated the production and marketing of coal. His ambition was to duplicate the situation in the upper anthracite region, where a few large corporations controlled not only the transportation of coal but its production and distribution. To achieve this goal, the first thing that had to be done was to find a way to circumvent the railroad's charter, which prevented it from owning coal mines. Special legislation would be needed to remove this impediment.[20]

With public criticism of railroads on the increase, Gowen presumably realized that openly asking the legislature for an amendment to the Reading's charter would not be wise. Instead, he tried to obtain a charter for a new corporation, with a proviso in the small print granting landowning rights to the Reading Railroad. Accordingly, in January 1871 he applied to the Pennsylvania legislature for a charter for the Franklin Coal Company. But when the bill for incorporation came up, the anti-monopoly Senator Esaias Billingfelt repeatedly demanded to know which company was backing it, and the sponsor of the bill finally had to admit that Gowen was behind the plan. The clause empowering the Reading was struck out, rendering the bill useless.[21]

Six months later Gowen succeeded in his plan to incorporate a landowning subsidiary for the Reading Railroad, using exactly the same tactics. To understand how the railroad president achieved this goal, his actions must be considered in tandem with two other important developments in the coal industry in the first six months of 1871, the negotiations for a new wage contract and an investigation by the Pennsylvania legislature into the anthracite coal industry. Together, these three rather complicated developments consolidated the control of the Reading Railroad over the lower anthracite region, setting the stage for Gowen's final campaign against the trade union and the Molly Maguires in the mid-1870s.

On November 7, 1870, committees representing the ABT and the WBA met in Pottsville to arrange the basis for the Schuylkill region in the coming year. Both parties agreed to a basis set at the price of $2.50 per ton at Port Carbon, with outside wages at nine dollars a week, inside wages at ten dollars, miners on wages at twelve dollars, and rates for contract work to be reduced by 16.5 percent from their existing level. But, just as this agreement was reached, the corporations of the upper region announced a reduction in wages which their employees decided to resist. John Siney and the other leaders of the WBA faced

20. Schlegel, *Ruler of the Reading,* 33; Broehl, *The Molly Maguires,* 121.

21. Schlegel, *Ruler of the Reading,* 33–34; Broehl, *The Molly Maguires,* 122.

a serious dilemma. Should they join the strike called by the northern men, in the interest of union solidarity? Or should they adhere to the agreement just made, for fear of discrediting the union in the eyes of the operators?[22]

The General Council of the WBA met to consider this issue, and though the Schuylkill delegates voted against a strike, they were outvoted by the council as a whole. A general suspension in the anthracite industry was ordered to begin on January 10, 1871. Reluctantly, Siney decided to go along with the wishes of the majority. When he wrote to Gowen informing him that the Schuylkill men would join their Luzerne brethren on strike, the railroad president replied: "I feel that it will be a great injury to the workingmen of Schuylkill County. It appears to me that the workingmen of Schuylkill are being used entirely in the interests of the men of other regions; that whenever there is to be a strike in one region only, it must be in Schuylkill County, but whenever the Wyoming and Lackawanna regions suspend Schuylkill County must stop also."[23] Gowen was clearly playing on regional tensions and resentments, for the previous summer the men of the upper region had continued to work when the Schuylkill mine workers were on strike.

Gowen's letter, written on December 30, 1870, got to the heart of his differences with John Siney. "I am very firmly convinced that the results of a strike are always disadvantageous to the workingmen," Gowen wrote, "more especially when the strike is intended to raise the price of coal by diminishing its production." Whereas Siney, along with most of the smaller operators, wanted to curtail production in order to raise prices, Gowen argued that the best policy, for the union, operators, railroad, and consumers alike, was to increase demand rather than decrease supply. "The real interests of the men," he insisted, "are to be served by increasing the demand for coal, but the present design seems to be to diminish its production." According to Gowen:

> To increase the consumption is to secure a lasting benefit, by the natural and legitimate operation of those laws which govern trade throughout the world. To lessen the production . . . is to obtain a present temporary benefit (by means which are not only unwise, but actually criminal) at the expense of the whole future of the trade.[24]

Siney, of course, would scarcely have regarded the logic here as inexorable. The supposedly immutable laws of trade, and the supposedly shared interests of the various people involved in the coal business, were clearly the laws and interests of the corporation, not those of the union or the small operators.

Though the union leaders were at best ambivalent, the strike began on January 10, 1871. Later that month, the majority of the districts of Schuylkill County voted in favor of a $3.00-basis, against the wishes of their leaders, who still felt bound by their tacit agreement with the ABT to accept a new basis of

22. PBIS I, 353–55; Schlegel, "The Workingmen's Benevolent Association," 252.
23. PGA, 17.
24. Ibid., 17.

$2.50. Placing regional solidarity and the wishes of the rank-and-file before their own interests, the leaders of the Schuylkill County WBA resolved to hold out for a three-dollar basis "if the men of the northern counties cooperated with them; if not, they would make the best terms for themselves they could."[25] This was the third year in a row that coal production had been halted in the lower region. Several Schuylkill operators faced bankruptcy if the strike continued, and there was serious dissension among them on the question of conceding the union's demands. With the unity of the ABT broken, some of the operators prepared to resume work at a basis of $2.50, or even $3.00. At this point, Franklin B. Gowen intervened again in a dramatic way, hoping to curtail the power of both the union and the operators and to bring coal prices and production more firmly under the Reading's control.[26]

As the mine workers were now clearly united in a powerful union, Gowen attempted to coerce the operators into a similar combination under his control. This new organization, he hoped, would prevent individual operators from settling with the union on their own terms. Gowen proceeded to call a meeting of the Schuylkill mine owners in Philadelphia on February 2, 1871, where it was arranged that all anthracite-carrying and -producing interests would convene in New York City the following month. Representatives of the Reading Railroad, the Lehigh Valley Railroad, the Lehigh Coal & Navigation Company, and the three Scranton coal-mining and coal-carrying companies met in New York on February 14, along with independent operators from the upper and lower regions. After a committee was appointed to determine a uniform wage scale for all anthracite workers, Gowen unveiled a new set of freight rates, which were to remain in effect until the striking miners accepted the committee's offer. These had evidently been worked out with the other railroads in advance, without consulting the independent operators.[27]

Because of the Reading's stranglehold on transportation in and out of the lower region, Gowen could draw the operators into line by raising transport rates to a level where it would no longer be profitable to mine coal. In an unprecedented move, the rates were doubled, so that it now cost four dollars instead of two to transport a ton of coal from Schuylkill County to Philadelphia. At this time, coal was priced at about three dollars a ton at Port Carbon, its departure point from the anthracite region. When Colonel Cake, one of the more independent operators affiliated with the ABT, tried to resume production even under these new rates, Gowen responded by raising the rates by another two dollars, and the other carriers followed suit. At these rates it was pointless to try and move coal out of the anthracite region.[28] In the past, the miners and the operators had tried at different times to halt production in order to drive up

25. PBIS I, 354.

26. Schlegel, "The Workingmen's Benevolent Association," 252–53.

27. Schlegel, *Ruler of the Reading,* 24–25; Schlegel, "The Workingmen's Benevolent Association," 253–54.

28. Schlegel, *Ruler of the Reading,* 24–25; PBIS I, 355.

prices, wages, or both. Now they wanted to resume production but were prevented from doing so by a third party, the Reading Railroad. Neither the workers nor their employers could afford a lengthy stoppage. But the corporation was sufficiently wealthy and powerful to delay the resumption of production for as long as it took to break the power of the small operators. Four years later, during the climactic "Long Strike" of 1875, Gowen would engineer an even longer work stoppage as part of his final campaign to break the labor movement.

Unaware of Gowen's secret meetings with the operators, the General Council of the WBA had resolved to return to work on February 15. But even if the operators had wanted to resume work they could no longer have done so, as the new freight rates made it pointless to mine coal. Thus, when a committee of the Schuylkill County WBA approached the ABT with an offer to return to work on the minimum basis of $2.50 proposed the previous November, the ABT refused even to meet the union delegates. Gowen had full control of the situation and was "planning to settle the strike in his own way."[29] When John Siney published a letter complaining that Gowen was making war upon the trade union, Gowen responded: "I have no disposition, even if I had the power, to attack or injure your organization in the least." He went on to inform Siney that his only demand "is that you shall not insist upon wages so high as to make it impossible to produce coal at the prices which it will bring in the market, and that you shall not resort to strikes and suspensions in order to produce a scarcity of coal and force prices beyond what manufacturers and consumers can afford to pay."[30] In other words, Gowen was prepared to tolerate the trade union only if it would forsake the very cause to which it owed its existence: some degree of control over the production and distribution of coal, and hence over the destiny of the labor force at the mines.

On February 23 the operator's wage committee delivered its report in Philadelphia, recommending that the Schuylkill men be offered the terms agreed upon the previous November. Pay in the Lehigh region was to be reduced by 10 percent to bring it into line with Schuylkill, and the three Scranton companies were to reissue the offer that had precipitated the strike in the first place. The committee's offer on wages was not, in itself, all that unreasonable; the terms were the same ones requested by the WBA when the operators had refused to meet them the previous week. But the operators unequivocally declared their opposition to any control by workers over production, resolving unanimously "that we are united in opposing any interference by the workmen or their association with the management or control of our works, and will insist upon the abandonment of their claims to such control."[31]

Still outraged at Gowen's dictatorial manipulation of the freight rates, and

29. Schlegel, *Ruler of the Reading,* 25; Schlegel, "The Workingmen's Benevolent Association," 253–55 (quote, 253).

30. *MJ,* February 23, 1871.

31. *MJ,* February 24, 1871.

incensed by the high-handed tone of the operators, the leaders of the WBA decided to reject this compromise offer. The *Miners' Journal* of February 27, 1871, ran an editorial denouncing "the tyranny and oppression" of the union leaders and calling for drastic measures, including martial law. "If any of these leaders should interfere in any way," Bannan demanded, "arrest, try and punish them on the spot."[32] Undaunted by Bannan's hyperbole, the general council of the WBA met on March 1 and voted to hold out for the 1869 basis. Three days later, the *Miners' Journal* retorted that the effect of the policies favored by "the Grand Council of Conspirators" was to "crush business interests and damage labor more than any other single cause that can be named."[33]

Bannan's accusations of conspiracy and anarchy were an important step in the process by which trade unionism was gradually identified by its detractors with Molly Maguireism. In an article entitled "The Tyranny in Schuylkill County," Bannan announced that "few people have an adequate conception of the tyranny which exists in Schuylkill County at the hands of the prominent leaders of the W.B.A. . . . Men dare not work, and their families must starve. In the meetings of the Association, a man who would even attempt to complain or express an independent opinion, would be hooted down and cowed into silence." The great question of the day, Bannan concluded, was how much longer "this system of terrorism and tyranny" would be permitted to continue.[34] The Molly Maguires were not mentioned by name, but to Benjamin Bannan there was clearly no difference between the secret society and the trade union; both were run by terrorists. Franklin B. Gowen could not have agreed more. Over the coming months, the champion of small enterprise and the champion of corporate power found common cause in their opposition to organized labor, as trade unionism was identified with terrorism more emphatically than ever before.

Some of the almost-bankrupt small operators may have approved of the Reading Railroad's intervention, hoping that it would bring some much-needed stability to the industry. But others denounced it with great bitterness, sensing the demise of individual free enterprise in the lower anthracite region.[35] Outside the mining region public sentiment was leaning sharply against the railroad rather than the miners. Gowen's draconian freight rates drew national attention. The *Harrisburg State Journal,* for example, pointed out that "the precedent, if established, will be one of the most dangerous infringements on personal rights ever inflicted on the people of this State or nation." If the railroads were to be permitted to raise and lower their transportation charges at will, the editors

32. *MJ,* February 27, 1871.

33. *MJ,* March 4, 1871.

34. *MJ,* February 25, 1871.

35. PBIS 1, 355; see also the discussion of Benjamin B. Thomas later in this chapter.

concluded, "then there is not an industrial operation in the State that may not be destroyed in a month."[36] Faced with a series of petitions demanding controls on the franchises of the coal carriers, Governor John White Geary of Pennsylvania authorized the Senate to conduct an investigation on the right of railroad companies "to impose exorbitant freights on anthracite coal."[37]

When the investigation opened at Harrisburg on March 8, 1871, the striking mine workers had high hopes. But the senators chose to restrict themselves to what they called two "purely legal" matters: the narrow question of whether the railroad companies had violated their charters in "charging their present rates" and the more substantive question of whether their general policy on freights amounted to "an abuse of their privileges under the charters."[38] On the first question, the committee ruled that the Reading was authorized by its charter "to adopt such rules and regulations in relation to the transit of merchandise, etc., as they deem expedient" within a limit of four cents per ton per mile.[39] But the committee chose to avoid the second and crucial question altogether, pleading that it was beyond the purview of the legislature. These findings were supplemented by a recommendation that "a system of boards of arbitration and conciliation" be adopted; and an acknowledgment of the right of workingmen to organize collectively, "*provided they use none but lawful means, and aim at none but lawful ends*."[40]

The findings of the committee made no practical difference to life in the anthracite region, particularly as they side-stepped the main issue, corporate power and its limits. The historical significance of the investigation, however, lies not in its findings but in the manipulation of its proceedings by Franklin B. Gowen. Gowen pushed the investigation far beyond the points of law the committee had met to consider, transforming it into a general inquiry into labor-capital relations, conducted from his own point of view. In his testimony before the committee, he dismissed the legal questions in a single sentence, claiming that the Reading was entitled by its charter to charge whatever rates it pleased. He also bluntly denied the existence of "an organization among the operators to keep up prices." Whereas the Lehigh region did have such a board, which met once a month, Gowen testified, "There are 171 collieries in our region, and there is no board that regulates the price . . . in our region it is a scrimmage; everybody sells out at what they can get."[41]

Cross-examined by the committee, Gowen denied point blank that he had threatened the Schuylkill operators in February 1871 that he would raise rates so high that they could ship no more coal.[42] Asked whether he had stated to

36. Quoted in Schlegel, *Ruler of the Reading*, 27.
37. PGA, 9.
38. Ibid., 9.
39. Ibid., 9.
40. Ibid., 11, 4; italics in original.
41. Ibid., 25.
42. Ibid., 44.

the assembled operators that he should "absolutely prohibit them from getting it shipped," Gowen replied, "Never anything of the kind to anybody!"[43] With a straight face, he informed the committee that the rates had been increased from two dollars to six dollars a ton, not to restrain trade, but to cover operating expenses. He insisted that his statements in Philadelphia and New York that he would raise rates had been "merely incidental to the meeting" and that "there was no attempt or design to interfere with the association of the workingmen."[44] Asa Packer, the president of the Lehigh Valley Railroad, corroborated Gowen's testimony, denying that the rates had been raised in order to "drive the Workingmen's Benevolent Association to terms," and further denying that he had "any arrangement with the president of the Reading railroad." There was no "bargain," Packer insisted, "no arrangement." The representatives of six railroads had simply come together and, as good businessmen, said in each other's presence that each railroad would raise its rates if the others did.[45]

Having dispensed with the legal formalities, Gowen devoted most of his testimony to the WBA. The real issue, he insisted, was the power of the union to damage the coal business by its actions. "The result was farcical," as his biographer has noted. "Gowen, supposedly the defendant, turned himself by means of his brilliant legal talent, into prosecuting attorney, and the committee found itself conducting an inquisition into the WBA."[46] The climax of the investigation was an eloquent speech by Gowen, in which he described the problems of the coal industry and laid much of the blame on the WBA. Without mentioning the Molly Maguires by name, he delivered a fierce indictment of the WBA, insinuating that the labor union and the secret society were, if not one and the same organization, so closely allied as to make no difference.

A small, conspiratorial band of radicals, Gowen insisted, dominated the honest majority of workingmen in the lower anthracite region. The order for a suspension of work on January 10, 1871, he claimed, had been brutally enforced. Everyone had to stop work, and "if they disobeyed they knew what their doom would be. It made no difference if a man knew that he must go home to find his wife and children starving for want of bread. The order was obeyed as literally as ever any order of the Khan of Tartary was obeyed." Thus, the Reading Railroad "was thrown out of business" and "20,000 or 30,000 of these poor men were thrown idle by the order of three of four men who met and determined that they should do no work." Had the Schuylkill men been permitted to vote on the issue by secret ballot, Gowen asserted, most would have voted to stay at work.[47]

All of this flagrantly contradicted the facts. When the WBA members in the lower region had voted to support the striking northern men in January 1871,

43. Ibid., 44.

44. Ibid., 52, 8.

45. Ibid., 50.

46. Schlegel, "The Workingmen's Benevolent Association," 255.

47. PGA, 19.

they had done so against the wishes of their leaders, who had already come to a tacit agreement on wages with the ABT. When the leadership of the Schuylkill County WBA had resolved to hold out for the three-dollars-a-ton basis, they were bowing to the dictates of the rank-and-file. But the theory of a small, committed conspiracy leading the honest majority astray was central to Gowen's association of the WBA leadership with the Molly Maguires. "There has never been, in the most despotic government in the world, such a tyranny, before which the poor laboring man has to crouch like a whipped spaniel before the lash, and dare not say that his soul is his own," Gowen declared. He proceeded to assert the existence of "an association which votes in secret, at night, that men's lives shall be taken, and that they shall be shot before their wives, murdered in cold blood, for daring to work against the order." And he concluded that "the only men who are shot are the men to disobey the mandates of the Workingmen's Benevolent Association."[48]

Gowen's skillful manipulation of the investigation threw the representatives of the WBA onto the defensive. In their testimony to the committee, Siney and other union officials spent so much time defending themselves against Gowen's allegations that they had no time to state their own case, let alone question the powers of Gowen's corporation, which was ostensibly the issue under investigation. Virtually the sole subject of Siney's questioning by the committee was the violence in Schuylkill County and the possible existence of a secret society. Siney objected strenuously that the WBA had been "stigmatized as a band of assassins," and he insisted that, though he had "heard say" that such a society existed, he knew not "a solitary man belonging to it."[49] But, despite Siney's protestations, the overall impression given by the legislative investigation was that the WBA was indeed a violent conspiratorial organization.

Following Gowen's testimony before the committee, Benjamin Bannan made the connection between the union and the Molly Maguires explicit. Objecting to an assertion in the *New York Herald* "that the Molly Maguires do not belong to the W.B.A.," Bannan stated bluntly that "this is not true; they all belong, because they could not get any work whatever if they did not. There are but two classes in this Region—members of the W.B.A., or what they term blacklegs." As all mine workers belonged to the union, Bannan argued, so too did the Molly Maguires. The *Herald* had alleged that "the 'Buckshots' and 'Molly Maguires' are the self-constituted detectives and judges for the Workingmen's Benevolent Association, though not members of the order." But Bannan insisted on a different distinction, identifying the unruly elements in the union with the will of its leaders, and the orderly element with those honest miners who were forced to follow their leaders' commands. The Molly Maguires, he concluded, were "the Danites of the leaders, and whenever the Monitor, the organ of the leaders, denounce any person, the Danites are ready

48. Ibid., 18.
49. Ibid., 33.

to execute the order."[50] Like Gowen, Bannan reversed the relation between the leadership, who were strenuously opposed to violence, and the rank-and-file, who presumably included some elements that supported more direct and drastic action.

Even as Gowen and Bannan were accusing the WBA of Molly Maguireism in March 1871, the miners and operators were still trying to agree on the wage basis for the coming year. After their resounding defeat at the legislative investigation, the union leaders were more anxious than ever for a settlement. Finally, both sides agreed to the novel idea of arbitration. Arbitrators from each side, representing Carbon, Luzerne, Schuylkill, Columbia, and Northumberland counties, met on April 17, 1871, at Mauch Chunk. Judge William Elwell of Bloomsburg was chosen as umpire. When the two sides failed to reach agreement, the matter was handed over to Judge Elwell.

Before deciding the issue of wages, Elwell delivered a series of dicta on what he considered the most equitable relations between labor and capital. The right of management and control of the mines was reserved exclusively to the operators, he ruled. "It is the undoubted right of men to refuse to work," he conceded, "except upon such terms as shall be agreeable to them." But he warned that a boycott of operators who fired union men, or who employed nonunion men, was "contrary to the policy of the law, and subversive of the best interests of the miners and their employers." He also denounced all violence, threats, and coercion designed to prevent employees from working where they pleased or to deter operators from employing whom they pleased, at wages agreed between them and their employees. At the same time, he cautioned the operators that they "ought not in any manner to combine against persons who belong to the Miners' and Laborers' Benevolent Association," and that they were not justified in refusing to hire men simply on the grounds that they were connected to the union.[51]

As for wages, Judge Elwell split the difference between the two sides, setting the basis at $2.75, rather than the $3 proposed by the WBA and the $2.50 offered by the ABT. Wages for outside labor were set at ten dollars a week, inside labor at eleven dollars, and waged miners at thirteen dollars, again splitting the difference between the demands of the workers and the offer of the employers. Wages would rise or fall by 1 percent for every 3 cents increase in the price of coal above $2.75 and decrease down to, but not beyond, $2.25.[52] This decision was something of a victory for the union; even if the WBA failed to win a basis of $3, the ABT had initially offered a basis of only $2. But the legislative investigation had been a disaster for the trade union, and by the summer of 1871 it was clear that the real power in the lower anthracite region lay firmly with the Reading Railroad.

50. *MJ,* March 11, 1871. Bannan was referring to the *Anthracite Monitor;* by the "Danites" he presumably meant the secret society of Mormons thought to have been founded in the late 1830s.

51. PBIS 1, 355–56. The Miners' and Laborers' Benevolent Association was the official name of the WBA from March 1870 onward.

52. Compiled from PBIS 1, 357–59.

At the same time as he was overseeing the wage settlement in the anthracite region and using the legislative investigation to denounce the WBA and the Molly Maguires, Franklin B. Gowen had been proceeding with his plans to purchase coal lands. Soon after Senator Billingfelt had thwarted his attempt to incorporate the Franklin Coal Company in January 1871, Gowen came up with another plan. On March 28, 1871, the same day the investigation into the railroad's affairs ended, Gowen's allies again approached the legislature, this time with a new front company, the Laurel Run Improvement Company. The bill passed the House unchanged, but in the Senate Esaias Billingfelt once again exposed the Reading's vested interest, and the key clause (granting coal-mining rights to the railroad) was struck out by a vote of 17 to 15. What happened next can never be known for certain, but three of the bill's opponents were mysteriously absent after lunch, and another had changed his mind. A motion was introduced to reconsider the morning's vote, and over Senator Billingfelt's strenuous objections, the key clause was restored and the bill passed. Governor Geary signed the bill without comment. The Reading Railroad had finally acquired a coal-owning subsidiary.[53]

By the end of 1871 the Reading Railroad, through its Laurel Run satellite (soon renamed the Philadelphia & Reading Coal & Iron Company, or PRCI), had purchased 65,605 acres of coal land. In 1872, an additional 15,000 acres were purchased, and the PRCI reported that it controlled over 80,000 acres of coal land, including ninety-eight collieries. The largest twenty-seven of these mines were run directly by the company, while the remaining seventy-one were leased. Veteran operators like Roland Luther, William Williams, Thomas Croxton, and John M. Wetherill quickly sold out, and became land agents or colliery superintendents for the Philadelphia & Reading Coal & Iron Company. William Kendrick, who as head of the ABT had initially opposed the monopolistic designs of the Reading, also took a salaried job in Gowen's new coal-owning company. By 1874 the Reading Railroad would own over 100,000 acres of coal land and dominate the mining industry of the lower anthracite region.[54]

By the end of 1871, the Reading Railroad was rapidly assuming control over the production of anthracite in the Schuylkill region. It also monopolized the transportation of coal from Schuylkill to Philadelphia. But the marketing of coal in Philadelphia remained a problem, and Franklin B. Gowen now turned his attention to this question. With the nation at the height of its post-Civil-War prosperity, demand for coal was higher than ever. But abundant production

53. Broehl, *The Molly Maguires,* 123; Schlegel, *Ruler of the Reading,* 34–35.

54. U.S. House of Representatives, *The Reports of the Committees of the House of Representatives for the Second Session of the Fiftieth Congress, 1888–89.* Report no. 4147, *Labor Troubles in the Anthracite Regions of Pennsylvania, 1887–1888* (Washington, 1889), lxiii; Broehl, *The Molly Maguires,* 126; Yearley, *Enterprise and Anthracite,* 208–9.

simply led to a fall in coal prices, and consequently in wages. By March 1872, coal had fallen to $2.25 a ton at Port Carbon, which was about the cost of getting it to the consumer in Philadelphia. By August, the price had fallen to $1.92, and many local collieries chose to shut down rather than continue losing money.[55] To Gowen, the reason was unsystematic management of the marketing of coal. The problem, as he saw it, was caused by the coal "factors," or middlemen, who retailed coal in Philadelphia, making a handy profit of twenty-five cents per ton of coal. Gowen decided to set up large retail yards to bypass the factors and sell coal directly to the consumer. The railroad would sell its own coal, and it offered to sell the coal of independent operators at a fee of ten cents a ton instead of the usual twenty-five cents charged by the factors.[56]

Gowen summoned a group of fifteen Philadelphia coal factors who owned their own independent collieries to attend a meeting with him on December 21, 1872. The meeting took place at the headquarters of the Reading Railroad, 227 South Fourth Street, Philadelphia. The operators' delegation was led by Benjamin B. Thomas, a Welsh-born entrepreneur who owned several mines in Schuylkill County and was one of the principal coal factors in Philadelphia. A committed opponent of the monopolistic designs of the Reading Railroad, Thomas exchanged a series of letters with Gowen in the aftermath of the meeting on December 21, which he later published in an inexpensive paperback edition as part of an effort to publicize the cause of the embattled small operators.[57]

Gowen opened the meeting with the operators by suggesting that they abandon individual enterprise and join him in "having all the coal from our collieries reaching Port Richmond and going through the Delaware and Raritan Canal, under the control of one central hand."[58] Outraged by this proposition, the operators rejected it out of hand. At Gowen's request, they then held a meeting "to suggest some plan by which we could work in harmony with the large mining interests." Determined to resist corporate power, they resolved at this meeting to continue managing their own business according to "the natural laws of supply and demand."[59] In their exchange of letters, Gowen informed Thomas that, far from attempting to bully the small operators into submission, the Reading Railroad was acting in their best interests. As the railroad already had "a very large number of collieries of its own," it believed "that it could materially aid the owners of other good coal in disposing of their product at good prices," and so "thought it proper to present to the owners of these collieries the opportunity of uniting their product with that of the company." The whole affair, Gowen concluded, was "a simple business proposition, made in a spirit of

55. Broehl, *The Molly Maguires,* 170.

56. Schlegel, *Ruler of the Reading,* 39.

57. B. B. Thomas, *The Coal Monopoly: Correspondence Between B. B. Thomas and F. B. Gowen* (New York, 1873).

58. Ibid., 3.

59. Ibid., 3.

kindness."[60] Thomas replied to Gowen by objecting to his "defiant and threatening" posture at the meeting of December 21, charging that the coal-mining power of the railroad had been "obtained through bribery, fraud and corruption, and therefore should be regarded as of no binding force."[61] When Gowen objected to these charges, and especially to the accusation of bribery, Thomas responded in a letter dripping with irony: "Whilst I believe the majority of our legislators are not proverbial for their mental acumen, I never supposed they were such a set of consummate asses as to confer such extraordinary privileges, so sadly subversive of the interests of their constituents, upon corporations without any compensation to themselves."[62]

Thomas's objections went beyond his own interests as an independent operator, to an appraisal of the threat posed to republican society by the concentration of power in corporate hands. In the erosion of free competition he detected a threat not just to economic freedom but to political freedom as well. Not only were the railroads about to eliminate the small operators and to subjugate "the laboring man"; they were "availing themselves of rights never contemplated by the people, in their encroachments upon individual enterprise and personal rights."[63] The Reading Railroad and the Pennsylvania legislature, he claimed, were "insidiously in conjunction with other corporations, sapping the very vitals of the nation, crushing individual enterprises, subsidizing the press, and rendering the idea of representative government a scoff and a byword."[64] But Thomas's objections were to no avail. Gowen's new system transformed the coal-retailing trade of Philadelphia, placing it firmly under the control of the Reading Railroad.

A potentially more serious problem than retailing anthracite was how to control the amount of coal sent to market in the first place. Here, Gowen had to contend with the influence of the corporations that controlled the upper anthracite region, selling their coal on the New York market. In January 1873, he went to New York to meet the rail and coal company presidents who had been involved with him in the freight embargo of 1871: Asa Packer of the Lehigh Valley, Thomas Dickson of the Delaware & Hudson, George Hoyt of Pennsylvania Coal, and Samuel Sloan of the Lackawanna. They reached an agreement to fix coal at an average of five dollars a ton, wholesale, in New York City. This was the first case of industrywide price fixing in the history of the United States.[65] A month later the group met again and set a tonnage limitation. Each company could mine as much as it wanted, but was allowed to ship only a certain amount to market. The Reading was to have 25.85 percent of the market, the Hudson 18.37 percent, the Jersey Central 16.15 percent, the Lehigh

60. Ibid., 4.
61. Ibid., 6.
62. Ibid., 11.
63. Ibid., 7.
64. Ibid., 6.
65. Broehl, *The Molly Maguires,* 171.

15.98 percent, the Lackawanna 13.80 percent, and the Pennsylvania Coal Company, though not formally a party to the arrangement, a quota of 9.85 percent. In this way, "America's first major pool was born."[66]

While these corporate agreements signaled the demise of individual free enterprise in Schuylkill County, they also brought to an end, temporarily at least, the instability that had always characterized the industry of the lower region. The anthracite producers had a profitable year in 1873. Wages, tied to a sliding scale, remained relatively high. And relations between the employers and the mine workers were uncharacteristically stable. At the office of the *Miners' Journal,* Benjamin Bannan greeted these developments with considerable ambivalence. He welcomed the promise of social and economic stability, yet it now seemed clear that the scenario he had long dreaded had come to pass. With the small operators in decline, a powerful combination of labor found itself ranged against a powerful combination of capital. In place of a republican commonwealth in which labor and capital existed in ostensible harmony, Bannan now saw a society divided into selfish and irreconcilable interests. In 1873 he was asked to submit an essay on the current situation by the Bureau of Industrial Statistics, which was in the process of compiling its first annual report on the condition of labor. The result was a nine-page work entitled "A Few Thoughts on Labor and Capital," in which he reiterated the republican, free labor ideology from which he had scarcely wavered since the early 1850s, despite the momentous changes in the economic and social structure of the lower anthracite region.[67]

Bannan began with the familiar theme that there was no real conflict between labor and capital. But he now divided capital into two types, productive and nonproductive, and placed much of the blame for the current situation on the latter. "The great contest now waging, not only in this, but in many other countries, between the producers and laborers," he argued, "is caused by this antagonism in which the non-producing monied interests are striving to gain the ascendancy." According to Bannan, more money was now being made from trading in currency and stocks, from speculation and high rates of interest, and from corporate maneuvers, than from honest production. Producers and their employees needed to realize that they were "in the same boat," that their interests were identical, and that "they must be united to triumph over the power of non-productive capital, which is always aggressive and must and will triumph over the laborers and producers if they are not united."[68]

This idea of a harmony of interests between honest productive labor and honest productive capital was more of a pipe-dream than ever in the 1870s. By the middle of that decade the society of the lower anthracite region was split along lines that are best described in terms of class, precisely the form of social cleavage that Bannan had always feared most. Rigid divisions between working

66. Ibid., 171.

67. Benjamin Bannan, "A Few Thoughts on Capital and Labor," PBIS 1, 523 ff.

68. PBIS 1, 523–25.

class and middle class, and between the interests of capital and labor, are much more evident in the United States after the Civil War than before. In the industrial society of the post-Civil War era, as the leading historian of nineteenth-century America has noted, "the mobility of the age of the independent producer, whose aspiration was economic self-sufficiency, was superseded by the mobility of industrial society, in which workers could look forward to a rising standard of living, but not self-employment."[69]

At the heart of this transformation was a shift from small-scale to large-scale economic enterprises, and from self-employment to wage labor. While these processes led to the degradation of skilled labor, they also eroded divisions between skilled and unskilled workers, bringing about greater unity among workingmen and women. And workers found solidarity in the face of a second misfortune, the national economic depression that began in 1873. One third of the workers in Pennsylvania were idle in 1874, and the state Bureau of Industrial Statistics commented that "the community has suffered a degree of demoralization that twenty years of war could not have effected."[70] As "the mass of the working class" sank ever deeper into "poverty, hopelessness and degradation," the Bureau noted, "the line dividing them from the employing class . . . was widened day by day, until they were completely separated in feeling, habit of thought, purposes, interest and sympathy as if they were separate peoples in race and civilization."[71]

The chief culprits, according to the Bureau of Industrial Statistics, were the new corporations that had replaced the skilled workmen and small entrepreneurs. The corporations had been granted "one extraordinary privilege after another," so that industry was now characterized by "immense capitals." As a result, "the avenues to successful enterprise have nearly closed against the individual operator with small means."[72] The history of the lower anthracite region offers a stark example of this process. And, given that the takeover by the Reading Railroad was completed in the context of an economic depression, the chances of successful resistance were slight.

Although the small operators had been defeated by the end of 1873, the Reading Railroad still faced the threat posed by organized labor. At some point soon, Franklin B. Gowen would have to address the problem of the Workingmen's Benevolent Association. For the present, however, he was preoccupied with another form of labor organization; in 1873, rumors had begun to circulate that the Molly Maguires were active once again. In the early months of that year, a number of mine superintendents in Schuylkill County were threatened and

69. Foner, *Free Soil, Free Labor, Free Men,* 33.

70. PBIS 2, 439.

71. PBIS 1, 327; see, also, PBIS 2, 436–39, 452–53.

72. PBIS 2, 438–39.

beaten, several railroad cars were derailed, and there was a series of suspicious fires at coal mines. Gowen decided to hire America's foremost detective, Allan Pinkerton, to get to the bottom of the matter once and for all.[73]

Allan Pinkerton was born in Glasgow, Scotland, on August 25, 1819. His father, William, was a sergeant in the local police force. At the age of twelve, Pinkerton was apprenticed to a cooper, and he became an independent craftsman seven years later. Ironically, he was an active supporter of Chartism as a young man, just like the leaders of the Workingmen's Benevolent Association, which was to be infiltrated by his agents in the 1870s. Pinkerton came to the United States in 1842 and settled in the Scottish colony of Dundee, Illinois, forty miles from Chicago, where he took up his old trade of coopering. In 1855 he opened a private detective agency, and for the next five years the bulk of the agency's work involved spying on railroad conductors and other employees.[74]

The turning point in Allan Pinkerton's career, as in so many other aspects of the Molly Maguire story, came during the Civil War. "By 1860," as the most recent historian of the detective agency has observed, "Pinkerton headed a midwestern regional police force of growing repute. The Civil War acted as a springboard and Pinkerton was able to create his National Detective Agency. He became America's national and even international policeman."[75] In February 1861 Pinkerton moved to Philadelphia with five of his operatives, to supervise railroad protection services for the Wilmington & Baltimore Railroad, one of the few remaining links between Washington and the northern United States. While working on this contract, Pinkerton discovered an apparent plot to assassinate Abraham Lincoln in Baltimore, on the way to his inaugural in Washington, D.C. After ensuring that Lincoln arrived in Washington safely, Pinkerton was hired to do detective work for the Union army by George B. McClellan, the president of the Ohio & Mississippi Railroad, who was now the general in charge of the Ohio Department. Under the pseudonym E. J. Allen, Pinkerton headed the Union's military secret service from May 1861 until November 1862, when both McClellan and Pinkerton lost their jobs.[76]

With the money he earned from government and railroad contracts, Pinkerton expanded his agency into a national operation. After the war, he opened offices in New York (1865) and Philadelphia (1866). In 1873 he published a pamphlet, *General Principles of Pinkerton's National Detective Agency,* which offers some insights into the operating principles of the new agency.[77] "The profession of the Detective is a high and honorable calling," Pinkerton declared in his guidebook. "Few professions excel it. He is an officer of justice, and must himself be

73. Broehl, *The Molly Maguires,* 145.

74. Frank Morn, *The Eye that Never Sleeps: A History of the Pinkerton National Detective Agency* (Bloomington, Indiana, 1982), 19–33.

75. Ibid., 34.

76. Ibid., 39–45.

77. PNDA, *General Principles of Pinkerton's National Detective Agency* (Chicago, 1873).

pure and above reproach." As such, the detective must not use criminal methods to catch his prey. Nonetheless, the detective generally had to employ devious and covert means in his attempt to enforce justice: "It cannot be too strongly impressed upon Detectives that secrecy is the prime condition of successes in all their operations." The detective also had to be something of an actor, possessing "the player's faculty of assuming any character that his case may require, and of acting it out to the life, with an ease and naturalness which shall not be questioned." Part of this acting inevitably involved playing the role of the criminal: "It frequently becomes necessary for the Detective, when brought into contact with Criminals, to pretend to be a Criminal." Judged by these standards, James McParlan turned out to be an excellent detective.[78]

Pinkerton agents had first been employed by the Reading Railroad to spy on its conductors as early as 1863. Franklin B. Gowen hired them in the same capacity in 1870; and early in 1873, the Pinkerton operatives working for the Reading in Schuylkill County turned their attention toward social disorder and crime in general, rather than incidents of dishonesty among railroad employees. When a large coal tipple was burned at Glen Carbon, a few miles west of Pottsville, Pinkerton superintendent Benjamin Franklin wrote to Gowen on October 9, 1873: "The operatives report the rumored existence at Glen Carbon of an organization known as the 'Molly Maguires', a band of roughs joined together for the purpose of instituting revenge against any one of whom they may take a dislike."[79]

This first mention of the Molly Maguires in a Pinkerton report coincided with a meeting in Philadelphia between Allan Pinkerton and Franklin B. Gowen, some time in the first two weeks of October 1873. No reliable record of this meeting has survived, though Pinkerton began his book on the Molly Maguires with a six-page account of his conversation with Gowen.[80] Like many elements of Pinkerton's narrative, this conversation then made its way into subsequent works of history, despite the fact that Pinkerton's book was clearly semifictional. The Molly Maguires, Gowen allegedly informed Pinkerton, were "a noxious weed" of "foreign birth," which had arrived in the United States from Ireland at some point in the previous twenty years. "Wherever anthracite is employed is also felt the vise-like grip of this midnight, dark-lantern, murderous-minded fraternity," Gowen continued. "Wherever in the United States iron is wrought, from Maine to Georgia, from ocean to ocean—wherever coal is used for fuel, there the Mollie Maguire leaves his slimy trail and wields with deadly effect his two powerful levers: secrecy—combination." Declaring that he saw it as "a sacred duty" to bring the Molly Maguires to justice, Gowen then announced his desire to send in an undercover detective, and Pinkerton set to work.[81]

78. Ibid., 6–10.

79. Broehl, *The Molly Maguires,* 145.

80. Pinkerton, *The Molly Maguires and the Detectives,* 13–18.

81. Ibid., 14–16.

While it is difficult to imagine anybody actually talking like this outside a black comedy, the rhetoric was not all that different from the type employed by Gowen in the showcase trials of 1876, and even in some of his correspondence.[82] A conversation between Pinkerton and Gowen on the subject of the Molly Maguires undoubtedly did take place sometime in early October 1873. The two men agreed to send a Pinkerton detective into the anthracite region undercover to try and infiltrate the Molly Maguires. The man chosen for the job was James McParlan. A native of County Armagh, in the province of Ulster, McParlan had worked in a Belfast linen warehouse and a chemical factory in Durham, England, before emigrating to America in 1867. He found employment first in a grocery store in New York City, then in a dry goods store in Medina, New York, and then in a series of odd jobs in the Great Lakes region. After working for a short time as a "preventive policeman" for a small detective agency in Chicago, he joined the Pinkertons in 1871.[83]

Of all the aspects of the Molly Maguire story, McParlan's exploits are the best known. These exploits, indeed, have been celebrated over and over again, providing the plot for most stories on the Molly Maguires from Allan Pinkerton's best-selling work of semifiction in 1877 through the various popular and scholarly histories published over the following century. McParlan's activities in the anthracite region need only be briefly summarized here, as the job of reconstructing his movements has already been done well and often. On October 8, 1873, he was asked by Allan Pinkerton to draw up a report on secret societies in Ireland. On October 27 he left Philadelphia for Pottsville, and he spent the next two and a half years in Schuylkill County accumulating evidence against the Molly Maguires, under the alias James McKenna.[84]

After his arrival in Pottsville, McParlan apparently spent most of his time at Pat Dormer's saloon, where he claimed to have heard lots of stories about the Molly Maguires, who were concentrated "over the mountain" in Girardville, Shenandoah, and Mahanoy City. On January 30, 1874, he arrived in Shenandoah, where he "played the part of an Irish laborer, and actually worked for some time at Indian Ridge Shaft, at Shenandoah." On April 14, 1874, he was initiated into the Shenandoah division of the AOH at Michael "Muff" Lawler's tavern; and on July 15 he was elected secretary of this division, apparently because the other members were illiterate. As an officer of the AOH in Shenandoah during the next two years, McParlan claimed to have observed and participated in the planning of several Molly Maguire killings. In March 1876, he finally fled the anthracite region; two months later

82. See the discussion of Gowen's courtroom rhetoric in chapter 8; and the exchange of letters between Gowen and Archbishop James Frederic Wood during the first Yost trial (SCBS, Papers of Archbishop Wood, FBG to Wood, May 11 and 14, 1876).

83. Dewees, *The Molly Maguires,* 79–83.

84. HML, A 1520, B 979, F, "Memoranda and Papers," report of JMCP to AP, October 10, 1873. This report is discussed in chapter 1. As noted in the introduction to the present work, Coleman is the only historian of the Molly Maguires who has tried to break the narrative mould set by Allan Pinkerton and James McParlan.

he appeared as the chief witness for the prosecution at the first of the showcase trials in Pottsville.[85]

McParlan was not the only Pinkerton detective working under cover for the Reading Railroad in the anthracite region. In 1874, operative P. M. Cummings was sent to investigate and infiltrate the WBA. A Scotsman who had worked in the Dublin police force, Cummings had settled in Dundee, Illinois, in the 1850s, where he met Allan Pinkerton. He had experience as a mine worker, and the plan was that he would work in the Schuylkill mines and infiltrate the trade union. Cummings arrived in Philadelphia on February 23 and reported to Benjamin Franklin at the Pinkerton office. On February 25 he left Philadelphia for St. Clair, where he made his first contact with John Siney at a cock-fight three days later. Cummings reported that he told Siney he had been victimized for his union activities in Illinois, and Siney soon found work for Cummings as a laborer in Wadesville, for thirteen dollars a week.[86]

As a mine worker, Cummings automatically joined the WBA, but his early reports must have been discouraging to his employers. He noted, for example, the view of one local resident that before the existence of the trade union "the miners were a very rough class," but that "since the advent of the union they had mended very much." Cummings attended several union meetings in February and March, but invariably had nothing to report other than the details of district meetings, by-laws, and committee work. If his task was to collect incriminating information on the labor movement, his early reports were singularly unsuccessful; he could find no evidence whatsoever that the union was involved in violence.[87]

Although the Pinkertons could find no evidence implicating the trade union in Molly Maguire activities, organized labor still represented a considerable threat to Franklin B. Gowen. Both the railroad and the union laid claim to control over the production of coal; a showdown between them was all but inevitable. The WBA was the chief target of Gowen's campaign to eliminate the power of organized labor, but the victory could not be considered complete unless the Molly Maguires were eliminated as well. In their different ways, the Mollys and the WBA stood in the way of Gowen's plans to impose order and stability on the lower anthracite region. What better way to destroy these coexisting movements—the one systematic and coherently organized, the other sporadic and intermittent—than to insist that they were one and the same? The defeat of one would then entail the defeat of the other. Herein lies the key to understanding the rise and fall of the Molly Maguires in the mid-1870s.

85. [Miners' Journal], *Among the Assassins! The Molly Maguires and their Victims* (Pottsville, 1876), 7 (quote); HSP, SC, PNDA, reports of JMCP, January 26, 1874, to May 4, 1874; Broehl, *The Molly Maguires,* 152–69, 174–77.

86. HSP, SC, PNDA, report of BF to FBG on the work of Detective Cummings, March 27, 1874.

87. All details from HSP, SC, PNDA, report of BF to FBG on the work of Detective Cummings, March 27, 1874. For additional reports by Cummings, see LC, Pinkerton MS, Miscellaneous Section, report of BF to FBG, October 29, 1874.

6

The Return of the Molly Maguires

The final confrontation between the Reading Railroad and the Workingmen's Benevolent Association took the form of the "Long Strike," which lasted from January to June 1875. The battle was fought in the context of a national economic depression. It was one of several desperate and unsuccessful efforts by organized labor in the United States to preserve the considerable gains won in the late 1860s and early 1870s. All over the United States, labor was on the defensive. The defeat of Pennsylvania's anthracite mine workers was the most spectacular and violent of a series of similar defeats for American labor during the great depression of the 1870s, including those of the cigarmakers of New York City and the textile workers of Fall River, Massachusetts.[1]

The defeat and collapse of the Workingmen's Benevolent Association was the immediate precondition for the sudden wave of six assassinations that gripped the lower anthracite region in the summer of 1875. With the miners' union under concerted attack, signs of fragmentation and disunity had become evident within the ranks of organized labor from 1873 onward. Severe ethnic

1. John R. Commons et al., *History of Labour in the United States,* vol. 2, part 5, (1935–36; New York, 1966), chapter 5, especially 175–85; Eric Foner, *Reconstruction: America's Unfinished Revolution* (New York, 1988), 512–15; Herbert G. Gutman, *Work, Culture and Society in Industrializing America* (New York, 1977), part 4.

tensions emerged between the Welsh and Irish residents of northern Schuylkill County. And, for the first time since 1868, there was a significant upsurge in violence. Rumors circulated that the Molly Maguires were active once again. Exploiting these rumors to the full, Franklin B. Gowen and Robert Ramsey, the new editor of the *Miners' Journal,* systematically identified the miners' union with the Molly Maguires throughout the first half of 1875. The union leaders, though they continued to condemn violence, seem to have lost control over some of the more radical and unruly members of the rank and file, especially in the last, turbulent months of the Long Strike. All of this was grist to the mill of Gowen and Ramsey, who insisted that the task of defeating the labor movement could not be considered complete until the Molly Maguires had been brought to justice.[2] One response to these developments was the emergence of the Catholic church as a powerful condemnatory voice within the Irish community. This cultural conflict among the Irish took place in the context of a wider struggle to determine the social and economic future of the anthracite region. Together, these two related developments go a long way toward explaining the nature and meaning of Molly Maguireism in the 1870s, both as a form of violence and as a concept in a pattern of ideological representation.[3]

The Molly Maguire conflict in Pennsylvania has generally been portrayed by historians as a matter of Irish Catholics fighting ancient battles with British Protestants on new soil.[4] Because the Molly Maguires were Irishmen, it has generally been assumed that they must therefore have been Catholic nationalists. This rather one-dimensional account of Irish and Irish-American history is badly in need of revision. Among other things, it ignores the hostility between the Molly Maguires and the Catholic church in Ireland and the condemnation of the Molly Maguires by the Catholic hierarchy on both sides of the Atlantic.[5]

There was undoubtedly a strong element of anti-Irish Catholic nativism at work in the case of the American Molly Maguires, as well as a concerted campaign against organized labor. But one of the most striking aspects of the episode is the extent to which it involved a struggle within the Irish-American community of the anthracite region to define the meaning and limits of ethnicity. This intraethnic dimension of the Molly Maguire episode has been

2. Robert Ramsey became owner-editor of the *Miners' Journal* in February 1873.

3. For the position of the Catholic church, see Kenny, "The Molly Maguires and the Catholic Church"; James Edmund Roohan, *American Catholics and the Social Question: 1865–1900* (New York, 1976), 161–84.

4. Broehl, *The Molly Maguires,* 1.

5. Cf. Beames, *Peasants and Power,* 78; Connolly, *Priests and People,* chapter 6; Donnelly, "Irish Agrarian Rebellion: The Whiteboys of 1769–97," 322; Donnelly, "The Rightboy Movement," 163–71.

ignored in previous accounts of the subject. The most visible arena of conflict was religion, particularly in terms of its relation to ethnic identity. At stake were the souls of tens of thousands of men and women who were neither "Irish" nor "American" but both, and the crucial question was how to determine the content of their hybrid ethnic identity.[6]

In the lower anthracite region, just as in the United States as a whole, the definition of Irish ethnicity involved a power struggle between rival, if sometimes overlapping, groups and institutions. The major players in the drama, both locally and nationally, were politicians, saloon keepers, labor activists, a slowly emerging middle class, and the Catholic church. Of these various forces and institutions, it can plausibly be argued that, in the anthracite region at least, a specific Catholic definition of Irishness emerged victorious in the 1870s. While this version of Irishness did not go entirely unchallenged thereafter, the case of the Molly Maguires offers an excellent (though quite distinctive) example of the general pattern of middle-class formation delineated by historians of Irish-America. In the anthracite region, this process of ethnic definition involved the eradication of less acceptable versions of Irishness, especially the wild alternative embodied by the Molly Maguires.[7]

The struggle between the Molly Maguires and the Catholic church is best seen as a transatlantic strand of the "Devotional Revolution" that historians have detected in postfamine Ireland, in which the wilder elements of Irish religiosity were purged. In this respect, the religious struggles considered here are part of a broad transatlantic movement involving the Romanization of Irish Catholicism through the enforcement of more regular devotional practices and the eradication of residual cultural forms. The latter included various forms of local custom and folk belief and the transparently unorthodox practices involved in wakes. On both sides of the Atlantic, this devotional revolution was intimately bound up with processes of middle-class formation. Even had they not turned to violence, the people of west Donegal would almost certainly have found themselves in a profound cultural conflict with the American Catholic hierarchy.[8] The argument here, it should be emphasized, is not that the Molly Maguires were pre-Catholic or even necessarily anti-Catholic. Rather, to the limited extent that their religious consciousness can be inferred from the campaign waged against them by the Church, they seem to have practiced a version of Catholicism markedly different from the one propagated by the hierarchy in Rome, Dublin, and Philadelphia. Both the Mollys and their clerical opponents were Irish Catholics; but the meaning of Irish Catholicism, far

6. On nativism, see Kenny, "Nativism, Labor, and Slavery"; for a more elaborate version of the argument of religion and ethnicity presented in this chapter, see Kenny, "The Molly Maguires and the Catholic Church."

7. On Irish-American middle-class formation, see Miller, "Class, Culture, and Immigrant Group Identity in the United States," 124.

8. Larkin, "The Devotional Revolution in Ireland, 1850–75"; Miller, "Irish Catholicism and the Great Famine."

from being self-evident, was contested and disputed throughout the nineteenth century.[9]

The frequent condemnations of the Ribbonmen and Whiteboys in Ireland provided the Catholic hierarchy in the United States with certain precedents in its campaign against the Molly Maguires. Apart from their violence, the aspect of the agrarian societies most objectionable to the Irish hierarchy was the requirement that members swear a secret oath of fidelity to a secular authority outside the orbit of both church and state. The same two objections were leveled by the hierarchy against the AOH in Pennsylvania, but the uncertainty about the name and nature of the organization meant that there was considerable room for diversity within the hierarchy. At the discretion of the bishop in question, the condemnation of the Ribbonmen in Ireland could be interpreted as an existing condemnation of the AOH, so that the matter need not be referred to Rome for clarification, and the Molly Maguires could be condemned and even excommunicated. On the other hand, as neither the Molly Maguires nor the AOH had been condemned by name, a bishop could choose to tolerate rather than condemn them.[10]

The Catholic hierarchy in Pennsylvania, as a result, did not adopt a unified stance against the Molly Maguires and the AOH. While Bishop James Frederic Wood of Philadelphia was a committed opponent of the Molly Maguires from the early 1860s onward, his counterpart in Scranton, Bishop William O'Hara, did not come out publicly against the AOH until 1877. In Pittsburgh, Bishop Michael Domenec refused to join Wood in condemning the AOH, and the diocesan newspaper, the *Catholic Republican,* openly supported the organization. Only in April 1876 did Domenec's successor, Bishop Tuigg, issue a circular against the AOH.[11] In retrospect, the reason for the reluctance of the other bishops to join Wood is quite clear. Although there were AOH lodges in all the Pennsylvania dioceses, only the Philadelphia diocese was directly involved in the Molly Maguire affair. The Southern Coal Field and the Western Middle Coal Field, where the Molly Maguires were active, were both in the Philadelphia diocese, while the upper anthracite fields were part of the diocese of Scranton, organized in 1868. The centers of Molly Maguire activity, in other words, were both in the territory under Wood's control, while the more quiescent north was in O'Hara's diocese.

Of the two Catholic bishops with power over the anthracite region, James Frederic Wood played by far the more significant role in the Molly Maguire

9. The evidence on this point is confined to what Catholic clergymen did and said, rather than what their parishioners thought and believed. Virtually no evidence has survived on the specific folk beliefs and religious practices of the Molly Maguires in Pennsylvania.

10. Cf. Connolly, *Priests and People,* 116–17, 128–29, 229–30, 239–50, 308–9; Donnelly, "Irish Agrarian Rebellion: The Whiteboys of 1769–97," 322; Donnelly, "The Rightboy Movement," 163–71; Kenny, "The Molly Maguires and the Catholic Church," especially 345–51.

11. For O'Hara's position, see *SH,* February 13, 1877, and *Catholic Standard* (Philadelphia), February, 17, 1877; for Tuigg's position, see SCBS, papers of Archbishop Wood, letter from Tuigg to Wood, April 19, 1876.

story. Born in 1813 and converted to Roman Catholicism in 1836, Wood was appointed bishop of Philadelphia in 1860 and archbishop in 1875. His English Protestant background has often been cited as a factor in his hostility toward the Molly Maguires, though it is difficult to interpret what impact, if any, his upbringing had on his interpretation of Catholic doctrine. But, whether because of ethnic animosity or doctrinal orthodoxy, he was a committed opponent of the Molly Maguires from 1862 onward, when he first intervened in the troubles in Cass Township.[12]

His ethnic and cultural heritage aside, there can be no doubt that Wood was quite out of touch with the sentiments of ordinary Irish men and women in the anthracite region, let alone the Molly Maguires themselves. In this respect, his position was in marked contrast to the local clergy in the coal fields, most of whom were Irish and Irish-American. Catholic churches were built and parishes were formed wherever the Irish settled. These churches tended to be ethnically exclusive, with Irish and German Catholics each building their own. In Schuylkill County, Irish Catholic churches were built at Pottsville in 1828 (followed by a cathedral dedicated in 1838), Tamaqua in 1836, Minersville in 1846, Port Carbon in 1847, Ashland in 1857, Heckscherville in 1858, St. Clair in 1864, New Philadelphia in 1867, Shenandoah in 1872, Mahanoy City in 1873, Gilberton in 1874, Girardville in 1876, and West Mahanoy in 1880. The pattern of church building mirrored the pattern of settlement and migration in Schuylkill County, as the last five churches named were in the turbulent area to the north of the county, which was undergoing rapid and volatile expansion in the 1870s and became the center of Molly Maguire activity in that decade. Priests like Fr. Daniel O'Connor of Mahanoy Plane, Fr. Daniel McDermott of New Philadelphia, and Fr. Henry F. O'Reilly of Shenandoah were responsible for enforcing at the local level the decrees of the hierarchy issued in Philadelphia, Baltimore, and Rome.[13]

Catholic condemnations of the Ancient Order of Hibernians rested partly on the fact that the AOH was a secret organization, partly on the assumption that it was a cover organization for the Molly Maguire conspiracy. One person who strenuously rejected this assumption was no less a figure than John Kehoe, the head of the AOH in Schuylkill County and the alleged "kingpin" of the Molly Maguires. In a letter written to the *Shenandoah Herald,* Kehoe pointed out that the AOH was "a chartered organization, recognized by the Commonwealth, and composed by men who are law-abiding and seek the elevation of their members." He complained that "nothing can be more unjust than to charge the order with any acts of lawlessness." The "firing of firearms throughout

12. Biographical sketch of James Frederic Wood in SCBS, Scrapbook on the Archdiocese of Philadelphia, 1864–79; John J. Delaney, *Dictionary of American Catholic Biography* (Garden City, N.Y., 1984), 603–4; Broehl, *The Molly Maguires,* 79.

13. The Germans organized churches at Pottsville in 1840, St. Clair in 1852, Minersville in 1855, Ashland in 1857, Mahanoy City in 1864, and Shenandoah in 1874. The first Polish Catholic church in the region was founded in 1874. Compiled from Munsell, *History of Schuylkill County,* passim.

the county, and other minor deeds of lawlessness," Kehoe concluded, "are committed by men who are the drones of society."[14]

Kehoe had a point. The preamble to the constitution of the AOH declared that "all members must be Roman Catholics, and Irish or of Irish descent, and of good and moral character, and none of your members shall join in any secret societies contrary to the laws of the Catholic Church, and at all times and at all places your motto shall be: 'Friendship, Unity, and True Christian Charity.'"[15] The initial intentions of the AOH, when it was founded in 1836, were to provide some protection to Catholics in a time of intense nativist hostility, and for this reason Bishop John Hughes of New York City appears to have tolerated the organization, though he condemned secret societies in general in a pastoral letter of 1842.[16] The organization quickly grew into an international fraternal society, with branches not only across the United States but also in Britain and in Ireland, where, according to some sources, it was presided over by a shadowy body known as the Board of Erin.[17]

There was nothing particularly ominous about the AOH. It was simply the Irish Catholic equivalent of Protestant fraternal groups like the Odd Fellows and the Knights of Pythias, complete with initiation rites, handshakes, signals, passwords, and toasts. Like all of these societies, it dispensed aid to its dues-paying members in times of need and operated as a clearing house for advice and favors. But the AOH required a secret oath of its members, and this requirement, in itself, was sufficient to ensure its condemnation under prevailing Catholic doctrine. Moreover the association of the AOH with violence in the lower anthracite region meant that by the 1870s it had become a thoroughly unrespectable society, widely condemned by the hierarchy in Philadelphia and the clergy in Schuylkill County. Contrary to the courtroom rhetoric of the prosecuting attorneys at the Molly Maguire trials, the notion that the Ancient Order of Hibernians was part of a vast international conspiracy is transparently absurd. But some Irishmen did apparently use its lodges to plan acts of violence; and there may even have been a loosely organized inner circle of Molly Maguires, as James McParlan and the prosecuting attorneys charged, operating under the cover of an outwardly harmless fraternal organization.

Before 1875 all Catholic clergymen in Schuylkill County, in their public declarations at least, were hostile to the Ancient Order of Hibernians and the Molly Maguires. More ambivalent clerical declarations on the Mollys, including attempts to explain (though not to justify) their violence in historical and sociological terms, came only after the trials of 1876 and, especially, in the wake

14. Kehoe's letter was written in October 1875 and printed in *SH*, June 8, 1876.

15. Quoted in O'Dea, *History of the Ancient Order of Hibernians,* vol. 2, 885.

16. Ibid., vol. 1, 89–91; vol. 2, 887.

17. Bergin, *History of the Ancient Order of Hibernians,* 35; *RCK,* 176; John T. Morse, Jr., "The 'Molly Maguire' Trials," *American Law Review* (January 1877): 233–60 ("Board of Erin," 237); Broehl, *The Molly Maguires,* 38–39. In Ireland, the Ribbonmen were said to be presided over by a Board of Erin.

of the mass executions of 1877. The most significant interventions by a parish priest against secret societies in the period before 1875 were those of Fr. Daniel McDermott of New Philadelphia, who established a reputation as the most outspoken clerical opponent of the Molly Maguires in the anthracite region. On July 26, 1874, McDermott delivered a sermon in New Philadelphia on the subject of "The Church and the Forbidden Societies." All secret societies, McDermott declared, were "evil of their very nature," and "opposed to the law of God." They were "anti-Christian," and membership in them was "an act of apostasy." The AOH, he charged, had "sympathized with and aided murders *after the fact,*" and "contributed to their defense not only by money, but by suborning witnesses." Why, despite repeated clerical condemnation, had the AOH continued to organize and attract new members? The answer, for McDermott, lay in man's fundamentally depraved nature. "Men love darkness more than light for their works are evil," he warned his listeners, and most men were too weak to resist the temptation of joining the AOH. "These societies are, then, in favor of the idle, the improvident, the unskillful—of all those who hope to succeed in this world without personal merit," McDermott concluded. "They are a conspiracy against men of industry, skill and genius—a conspiracy against the souls of men, against our neighbor, against our country, against religion, against Christ." As a bulwark against temptation, two basic institutions needed to be reinforced: the state and the family. The AOH, McDermott claimed, was contrary to the interests of both.[18]

A week after publishing McDermott's sermon, the *New York Freeman's Journal* published the "Declaration of the Seven Pastors," the most cogent statement produced by the clergymen of the anthracite region of their opposition to the Molly Maguires. Six of the seven priests involved were pastors in the Western Middle Coal Field, always the most turbulent area in the anthracite region, and the center of Molly Maguire activity. The "Declaration" was also printed in the Philadelphia *Catholic Standard* on October 17, 1874, at the request of Bishop Wood. The pastors listed ten objections to the secret societies, mentioning the AOH and the Ribbonmen by name, though not the Molly Maguires. The condemnation of secret societies in Ireland, they argued, applied equally to their counterparts in Pennsylvania. Irrespective of the high-minded claims of its constitution, the AOH was controlled by "men of notoriously infamous character," who had repeatedly broken "the commandment 'thou shalt not kill.'"[19]

The timing of the declaration can be interpreted, in part, as a sign that

18. The sermon was published in the New York diocesan newspaper, the *Freeman's Journal and Catholic Register,* on October 3, 1874, and the Philadelphia diocesan newspaper, the *Catholic Standard,* on October 17, 1874.

19. "Declaration of the Seven Pastors," Philadelphia *Catholic Standard,* October 17, 1874. Fr. Michael Sherman of Ashland, Fr. Henry F. O'Reilly of Shenandoah, Fr. Daniel O'Connor of Mahanoy Plane, and Fr. Joseph Bridgman of Girardville all lived in northern Schuylkill County; Fr. E. T. Field was pastor at Centralia, just across the border from Schuylkill, in the coal-mining section of Columbia County; and Fr. Joseph Koch was pastor at Shamokin, in Northumberland County.

violence was once again on the upsurge in the parishes of northern Schuylkill County. By the end of that month the violence had spilled out into yet another killing, that of George Major at Mahanoy City on October 31, 1874, which led to a greater outcry than ever against the Irish secret society. The background to Major's assassination offers some important insights into what Molly Maguireism was about in the mid-1870s, in particular the element of interethnic gang warfare between the Welsh and the Irish that was so marked a feature of life in the more turbulent areas of northern Schuylkill County.

Born in 1841 at Delaware Farm, between Pottsville and Minersville, George Major was elected in 1874 to the position of chief burgess of Mahanoy City, a post equivalent to that of mayor in other cities. Mahanoy City was one of the new towns in the heart of the most turbulent part of the anthracite region, the area "over the mountain" from Pottsville in the Western Middle Coal Field. Incorporated in 1863, its population had reached 5,533 in 1874, the year George Major was assassinated.[20] The immediate cause of his death was violent conflict between the Welsh and Irish populations of Mahanoy City. The WBA always had a difficult time defusing ethnic conflicts among mine workers; in the case of northern Schuylkill County at least, John Siney's dreams of the brotherhood of all mine workers were utopian.

Mahanoy City was segregated along ethnic lines. Main Street divided the Irish section of the town from the British section. Like most of the surrounding territory, the city was the scene of sporadic fighting between rival ethnic groups. Besides the "Molly Maguires," there were the "Modocs" and the "Sheet Iron Gang." These gangs found themselves in frequent conflict, with the Molly Maguires generally doing battle with both the Modocs and the Sheet Iron Gang. The Sheet Iron men (also known as the "Iron Clads," the "Iron Shields," and the "Chain Gang") were composed mainly of skilled Irish coal miners from Kilkenny, many of whom were apparently Protestant. The Modocs, who were primarily Welsh, for some reason chose to fight under the name of an American Indian people with a reputation for indomitability, based in the borderlands of California and Oregon, against whom a bloody war had begun in 1873.[21]

20. Munsell, *History of Schuylkill County,* 228.

21. McParlan frequently reported incidents of conflict between the Modocs, Molly Maguires, and Sheet Iron Gang in 1874, as well as identifying their ethnic background and mentioning the use of term *soup drinkers.* See especially HSP, SC, PNDA, reports of JMcP, February 2, 4, 7, 8, 12, 18, 21, 1874; March 1, 3, 7, 14, 15, 20, 22, 27, 30, 1874. The "Sheet Iron Men" are also mentioned in a report from JMcP, March 1, 1875 (HML, A 1520, B 1001, report of BF to FBG, March 31, 1875); and a report of November 27, 1874, by P. M. Cummings (HML, A 1520, B 1001, report of BF to FBG, December 12, 1874). For an account of conflict between the Modocs and the Molly Maguires in December 1874, see LC, Pinkerton MS, Miscellaneous Section, report of BF to FBG, January 24, 1875. For gang violence in Mahanoy City involving Molly Maguires, Modocs, and the "Sheet Iron Boys," see Munsell, *History of Schuylkill County,* 240–41; *SH,* April 17, 1876; *New York Herald,* September 23, 1876.

Map 1. Most of the American Molly Maguires emigrated from nine counties in north-central and northwestern Ireland: Monaghan, Cavan, Fermanagh, Longford, Leitrim, Roscommon, Sligo, Mayo, and Donegal.

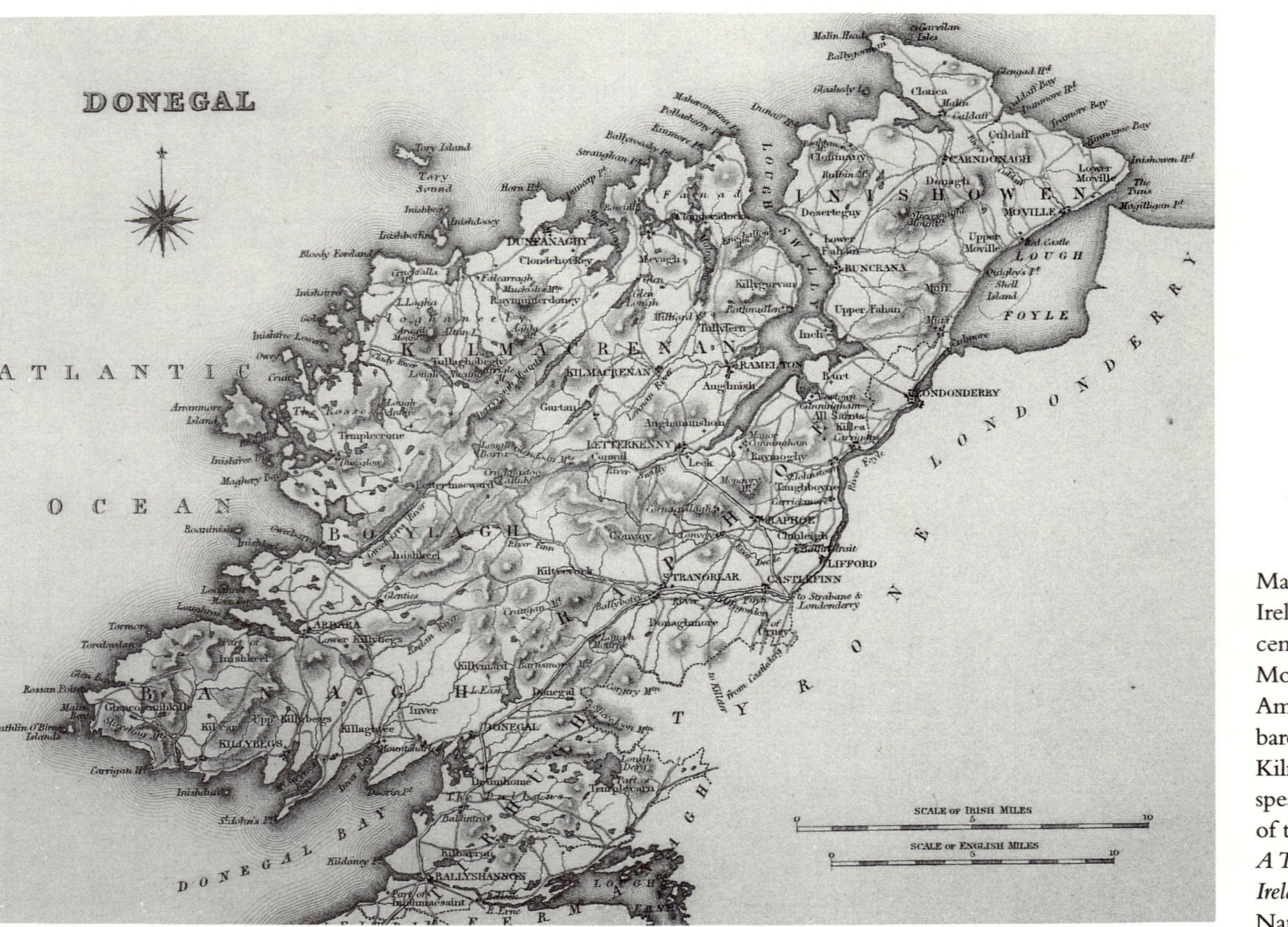

Map 2. County Donegal, Ireland, in the mid nineteenth century. The nucleus of the Molly Maguire leadership in America came from the baronies of Boylagh and Kilmacrenan in the Irish-speaking western portion of the county. Samuel Lewis, *A Topographical Dictionary of Ireland*. Courtesy of the National Library of Ireland.

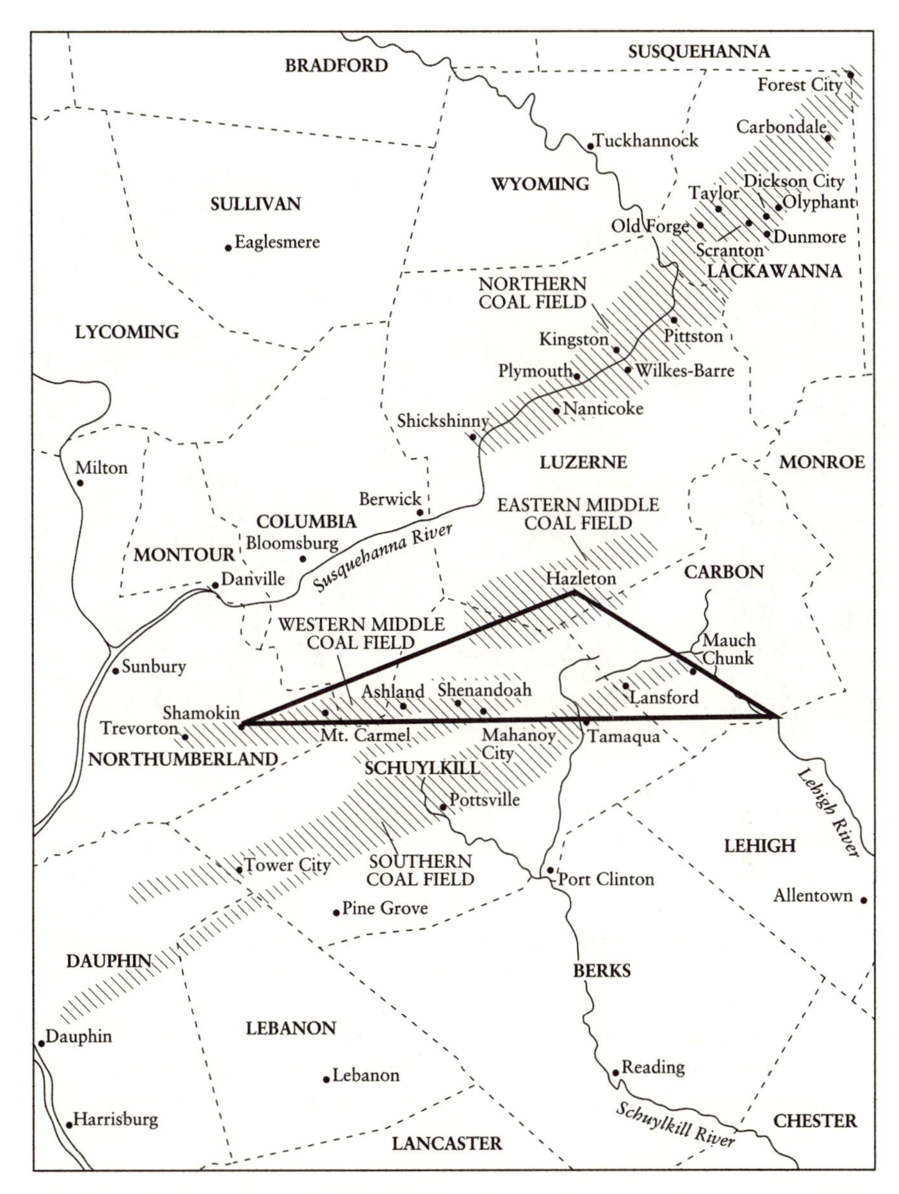

Map 3. The Pennsylvania anthracite region in the mid nineteenth century. The Molly Maguires were based in the area between Mauch Chunk and Tamaqua, at the eastern end of the Southern Coal Field; along the borders of Luzerne, Carbon, and Schuylkill counties, in the vicinity of Hazleton; and in the territory extending westward across the Western Middle Coal Field from Mahanoy City through Shenandoah and Ashland to Mount Carmel and Shamokin.

Figure 1. "The Strike in the Coal Mines—Meeting of 'Molly McGuire' Men." In this famous engraving from *Harper's Weekly*, the Molly Maguires appear uncharacteristically respectable. The scene can be read as labor's Sermon on the Mount, with the Molly Maguires assembled to hear their leader declaim on social justice. The seated figure behind the orator has sometimes been taken as James McParlan in the role of Judas; but this is anachronistic, as the detective's identity was not known until 1876. The figure stands out because he wears no hat, has a peculiar facial expression, and is noticeably younger than the other men. But none of these characteristics necessarily signifies guilt or deception; together, they may instead suggest John the Beloved Disciple, seated next to his revered teacher. Paul Frenzeny and Jules Tavernier, *Harper's Weekly*, January 31, 1874. Courtesy of the Perry-Castañeda Library, the University of Texas at Austin.

Figure 2. "A Marked Man." In the turbulent decades of the late nineteenth century, labor violence was frequently equated with savagery and untamed femininity. Molly Maguire is represented here in the figure of a virago, brandishing her fist at a mounted passerby and thereby marking him for death. Joseph Becker, *Frank Leslie's Illustrated Newspaper*, April 10, 1875. Courtesy of the New York Public Library.

Figure 3. "Riots Near Scranton." Bosses often tried to keep their mines open during strikes. Here, two bosses trying to bring some coal out of a mine are greeted by striking workers armed with sticks and stones. Joseph Becker, *Frank Leslie's Illustrated Newspaper*, April 29, 1871. Courtesy of the New York Public Library.

Figure 4. "The Coal Riots." Tensions between Welsh miners and Irish laborers were at the heart of the Molly Maguire story. Here, a group of "Welsh miners and their wives" disrupts a meeting of Irish laborers in the Scranton region. The laborers had organized a brief-lived union of their own in May 1871, demanding better pay from the miners who employed them and an end to the Welsh monopoly on skilled positions. Joseph Becker, *Frank Leslie's Illustrated Newspaper*, May 27, 1871. Courtesy of the New York Public Library.

Figure 5. "Miners' Homes." A typical mine patch in 1874. Joseph Becker, *Frank Leslie's Illustrated Newspaper*, December 12, 1874. Courtesy of the Perry-Castañeda Library, the University of Texas at Austin.

Figure 6. "Miners' Homes Near Mine Hill Gap." The large structure in the background is probably company-built housing. Joseph Becker, *Frank Leslie's Illustrated Newspaper*, February 6, 1875. Courtesy of the New York Public Library.

Figure 7. "Blacklegs in Mahanoy City." To keep their mines in operation during strikes, the bosses often imported replacement labor. Here, strikebreakers are confronted by supporters of the trade union. Joseph Becker, *Frank Leslie's Illustrated Newspaper*, March 25, 1871. Courtesy of the New York Public Library.

Figure 8. "Rioters Chalking up Threats and Warnings Against the 'Blacklegs.'" Organized labor is represented here as turbulent and threatening, erasing any distinction between trade unionism and Molly Maguireism. Note the simian features of the figure standing at the top (left center), and next to him the man sketching the coffin, with the words "The Next thing You Will be all Shut in . . ." Joseph Becker, *Frank Leslie's Illustrated Newspaper*, May 6, 1871. Courtesy of the New York Public Library.

Figure 9. "Horrors of the Mine—After the Explosion." American anthracite mining in the nineteenth century is believed to have been the most dangerous form of coal mining in the world. Paul Frenzeny and Jules Tavernier, *Harper's Weekly*, May 31, 1873. Courtesy of the Perry-Castañeda Library, the University of Texas at Austin.

Figure 10. "The Last Loaf." In this hostile depiction of a scene from the Long Strike of 1875, women and children face starvation as their menfolk carouse irresponsibly in the background. Joseph Becker, *Frank Leslie's Illustrated Newspaper*, March 13, 1875. Courtesy of the New York Public Library.

Figure 11. "Pay-Day in the Mining Regions." The arrest of a wild Irishman forms the obligatory centerpiece. Joseph Becker, *Frank Leslie's Illustrated Newspaper*, September 4, 1875. Courtesy of the New York Public Library.

Figure 12. *Clockwise from top left:* James Carroll (c.1837–77), hanged on Black Thursday for the murder of Benjamin Yost; Michael J. Doyle (c.1850–77), hanged on Black Thursday for the murder of John P. Jones; mine foreman Thomas Sanger (1842–75), assassinated on September 1, 1875; mine superintendent John P. Jones (1832–75), assassinated on September 3, 1875. Barclay & Co., *The Lives and Crimes of the Mollie Maguires*. Courtesy of the New York Public Library.

Figure 13. *Clockwise from top left:* Four Molly Maguires hanged on Black Thursday: Thomas Duffy (c.1852–77), for the murder of Benjamin Yost; Thomas Munley (1845–77), for the murders of Thomas Sanger and William Uren; James Roarity (1845–77), for the murder of Benjamin Yost; and James Boyle (c.1852–77), for the murder of Benjamin Yost. Barclay & Co., *The Lives and Crimes of the Mollie Maguires*. Courtesy of the New York Public Library.

Figure 14. Clockwise from top left: Alexander Campbell (1833–77), hanged on Black Thursday for the murders of John P. Jones and Morgan Powell; Hugh McGehan (c.1852–77), hanged on Black Thursday for the murder of Benjamin Yost; policeman Benjamin Yost (1841–75), assassinated on July 5, 1875; and Edward Kelly (c.1855–77), hanged on Black Thursday for the murder of John P. Jones. Barclay & Co., *The Lives and Crimes of the Mollie Maguires*. Courtesy of the New York Public Library.

Figure 15. Mine foreman Frank W. Langdon, assassinated on June 14, 1862; and Jack Kehoe (1837–78), the alleged mastermind of the Molly Maguire conspiracy, executed on December 18, 1878, for Langdon's murder. Barclay & Co., *The Lives and Crimes of the Mollie Maguires*. Courtesy of the New York Public Library.

Figure 16. Franklin B. Gowen (1836–89), President of the Reading Railroad; and the informer, Jimmy "Powder Keg" Kerrigan (c.1845–98). *Scribner's*, 18 (July 1895): 82. Courtesy of the Library of Congress. Reprinted with permission.

Figure 17. Allan Pinkerton (1819–84). *Harper's Weekly*, July 12, 1884. Courtesy of the Library of Congress. Reprinted with permission.

Figure 18. James McParlan (1844–1919). *Scribner's*, 18 (July 1895): 82. Courtesy of the Library of Congress. Reprinted with permission.

Figure 19. "Executions of the 'Mollie Maguires' at Mauch Chunk," June 21, 1877. Barclay & Co., *The Lives and Crimes of the Mollie Maguires*. Courtesy of the New York Public Library.

Figure 20. "The March to Death," Pottsville, June 21, 1877. Nine Molly Maguires were executed in the yard of Pottsville Prison between 1877 and 1879. Joseph Becker, *Frank Leslie's Illustrated Newspaper*, July 7, 1877. Courtesy of the New York Public Library.

In Mahanoy City these interethnic conflicts found expression in a ubiquitous nineteenth-century ethnic organization, the volunteer fire company. In the 1870s, the city had two fire companies, the Humane Fire Company, No. 1, founded by the Irish in 1868, and the Citizen's Fire Company, No. 2, staffed mainly by Welshmen and organized in 1870. George Major was elected foreman of the second company.[22] Each company served its own side of the town, but problems arose when a fire broke out in the center of the city: Both sides rushed to the scene and inevitably clashed, usually after the fire was extinguished, though sometimes before. Indeed, there is evidence that some fires were started deliberately in order to bring the rival companies face to face.[23]

When a fire broke out in the center of Mahanoy City just before midnight on Saturday, October 30, 1874, the two companies rushed to the scene and a major brawl ensued. According to the *Miners' Journal,* "It is the public belief that the purpose of the fire was to get up a fight between the two fire companies."[24] That this incident took place on the weekend of Halloween was surely no coincidence; the celebration of the Celtic festival no doubt added to the existing ethnic tensions, not to mention the boisterousness of payday and the Saturday-night revels that typically accompanied it.[25] Shots were soon exchanged and several people had already been injured when, just after midnight, George Major attempted to impose order by stepping out on the street and brandishing his pistol. Somebody in the crowd then shot Major and, before he fell, he fired off two more bullets. Daniel Dougherty, a young Irishman who had been shot in the head, was arrested on the assumption that Major had fired at him in retaliation.[26]

The newspapers were exultant. Robert Ramsey, the editor of the *Miners' Journal,* concluded that Dougherty had been caught red-handed and, as Dougherty was a member of the AOH, Ramsey characterized the crime as yet another outrage by the Molly Maguires. The Molly Maguires must be rooted out, he insisted, and an example should be made of Dougherty: "One good, wholesome hanging, gently but firmly administered, will cure a great deal of bad blood, and save a great many lives in this community."[27] Dougherty, in imminent danger of being

22. Munsell, *History of Schuylkill County,* 230–31.

23. Pinkerton operative P. M. Cummings, for example, reported from Mahanoy City in November 1874 that "another fire will be gotten up by the Sheet Iron Gang, at which they will go around and clear the MM's out." Quoted in Broehl, *The Molly Maguires,* 181.

24. *MJ,* November 6, 1874.

25. Halloween was originally a Celtic festival for the dead, celebrated on the last day of the Celtic year, October 31. Elements of the festival were incorporated into the Christian holiday of All Hallows' Eve, the night preceding All Saints' (Hallows') Day. Bonfires were traditionally built on this day to ward off malevolent spirits. The British, however, celebrated "Bonfire Night" six days later, on November 5, the anniversary of Guy Fawkes's alleged attempt to blow up parliament in a Catholic conspiracy in 1605. In Ireland, October 31 was also the day on which half-yearly rents fell due and rural violence reached one of its peaks. The timing of the assassinations of George K. Smith (late on November 5, 1863) and George Major (early on October 31, 1874) may not have been entirely arbitrary.

26. *MJ,* November 6, 1874; Broehl, *The Molly Maguires,* 181–83.

27. *MJ,* November 6, 1874.

lynched if he remained in the vicinity of Mahanoy City and Shenandoah, was removed to Pottsville to await trial. When the trial began, on March 28, 1875, feeling ran so high in Schuylkill County, both for and against the defendant, that the venue was changed to the town of Lebanon, in the farming area of neighboring Lebanon County. When the case was finally heard, in late April 1875, the prosecution produced a string of witnesses against Dougherty, but the defense produced an equal number of witnesses who testified that the murderer was one John McCann, who had since returned to Ireland.[28]

The case ended under dramatic and unexpected circumstances, when a doctor removed the bullet that had lodged in Dougherty's head the night Major was killed. The defense demonstrated that the bullet could not have come from Major's pistol; Dougherty could not therefore have been shot by Major, and the prosecution's case collapsed. Amid a rowdy demonstration by his supporters, Dougherty was acquitted and released.[29] But the killing of George Major had unleashed a degree of hysteria against the Molly Maguires that had not been seen in Schuylkill County since 1868. And the timing of Dougherty's acquittal could not have been worse, for the climactic Long Strike of 1875 was by then entering its fifth, bitter month, and violent incidents were on the upsurge.

The innocence or guilt of Daniel Dougherty is not really the issue here. Indeed, in a later trial, McParlan testified that Dougherty was certainly innocent, but that he had stood trial, knowing that he would be acquitted, to help his friend John McCann to escape.[30] But what, if anything, did this Saturday-night drunken violence have to do with the Molly Maguires? Was it necessary to invoke the Molly Maguires in order to explain the violence? Or was it simply a case of ethnic and gang rivalry, heavy drinking, and the usual boisterousness of payday intensified by the celebration of Halloween? Dougherty was a member of the AOH, and that was sufficient evidence of his guilt in the eyes of Robert Ramsey and the prosecuting attorneys. A dangerous precedent was being set here. In the trials of 1876 and 1877 mere membership in the AOH was taken to be a crime, the AOH itself was put on trial, and its members were held to be automatically guilty by association. The AOH lodges in the Mahanoy Valley of Schuylkill County did fulfill a role of ethnic self-defense, especially those of them that had been adapted to "Ribbonite" purposes by immigrants from north-central and northwestern Ireland. Nonetheless, it is difficult to see how the crime attributed to Daniel Dougherty was connected in any way with an organized conspiracy.

A few weeks after Major was killed, the *New York World* published an account of the "reign of lawlessness in the coal regions," reporting that two men had been murdered the previous day, and one had been crucified and left to die.[31]

28. Broehl, *The Molly Maguires,* 195–98.

29. Ibid.

30. Ibid., 197; cf. the discussion of McParlan's testimony and possible role as an agent provocateur in chapters 7 and 8 of the present work.

31. *New York World,* November 18, 1874.

But, when a reporter from the *New York Tribune* arrived to investigate "the startling and incendiary reports relative to the alleged serious riots, outbreaks and murders in the Schuylkill and Luzerne districts," he concluded that "the printed accounts were grossly exaggerated, having no resemblance whatever to truth." The reporter had indeed heard numerous stories of violent and murderous men. But he "found that all this 'Molly Maguire' sensationalism is purely imaginary. The idle, shiftless people who have been named 'Molly Maguires' are not organised in bands, and while they have committed depredations, their work is not more startling than the ordinary police cases generally found on the dockets of any alderman in the larger cities."[32]

This sober assessment evidently had some influence on Robert Ramsey of the *Miners' Journal,* which quoted the *Tribune* article with approval on November 25. In a subsequent issue, the *Miners' Journal* complained that the recent events had been blown out of proportion. Despite his own attacks on Dougherty only a few weeks earlier, Robert Ramsey now announced that he was no longer convinced that the Molly Maguires existed as an organized conspiracy. "We have contended all along," he wrote, "that the false reports of lawlessness in the Pennsylvania coal regions, spread broadcast by the New York papers, are calculated to injure our good name and change our reputation." Newspapers "all over the Union" were saying that Schuylkill County was "over-run by a species of Ku-Kluxism which goes by the name of Molly Maguireism"; but Ramsey insisted that "as a rule Schuylkill County is quite dull and it is only now and then that here and there law is broken."[33]

There was an element of provincial pride here, a defense of Schuylkill County against its metropolitan detractors. Yet, within a few months, Ramsey was in full agreement with the sentiment that Schuylkill County was "over-run with . . . Molly Maguireism." He changed his mind because of the events that occurred during the Long Strike of 1875, which was marked by a level of violence and disorder reminiscent of the mid-1860s. By the time this violence occurred, rumors of the Molly Maguires had already resurfaced in Schuylkill County, particularly in the Major case. Hence, the labor union and the Molly Maguires were lumped together into a single, conspiratorial category and, more than ever before, the defeat of one entailed the defeat of the other.

The argument here is not that the violence was simply invented, nor that the Molly Maguires did not exist. But the general disorder in Schuylkill County during the economic depression of the mid-1870s, and the upsurge of violence from 1873 onward, made it possible to condemn all striking mine workers and all labor activists as terrorists, thereby obliterating the very real differences in ideology and strategy that had always separated Molly Maguireism from the trade union leaders. To understand how this happened, it is necessary to turn to the history of labor relations in the anthracite region in the climactic year of

32. *New York Tribune,* November 24, 1874.

33. *MJ,* December 21, 1874.

1875. The campaigns waged by the Reading Railroad against the Workingmen's Benevolent Association and the Molly Maguires in the mid-1870s are best seen as twin aspects of a single policy designed to consolidate the control of the railroad and impose a specific vision of economic and social order on the lower anthracite region. In this respect, the "Long Strike" of 1875 was the decisive moment.

Compared to previous years, labor relations in the anthracite region in 1872 and 1873 had been quite tranquil. The Reading Railroad had enforced a new stability on the region, and there were no significant work stoppages. The wage negotiations for these two years were straightforward. Under pressure from Franklin B. Gowen, the ABT and WBA reached an amicable agreement on January 6, 1872. Wages were set according to a basis of $2.50 per ton of coal, which would be allowed to slide downward to $2.25, but only for two months. Under this agreement, work continued quite steadily throughout the year, with no general suspensions and only a few work stoppages. Average wages in 1872 were only 1.375 percent below the basis. On January 18, 1873, committees of the WBA and ABT agreed to keep wages substantially the same as for the previous year, except that they were not to go below a minimum level set at the price of $2.50 per ton of coal.[34] Under this arrangement, production was more regular and labor relations more harmonious than at any time since the formation of the WBA.

One of the hallmarks of John Siney's maturing theory of labor relations was his reluctance to use strikes as a weapon in labor negotiations. The WBA had never taken strikes lightly: "Workingmen know and have always known," as the *Anthracite Monitor* put it on October 14, 1871, "that strikes are expensive, that they frequently bring suffering, and sometimes trials grievous to be borne, upon those who look to them as a means of escaping the tyrannies of capital." "Strikes are wars," the *Monitor* warned. "All wars are expensive."[35] This cautious approach to strikes was one of the defining characteristics of a new national miners' organization that Siney helped create toward the end of 1873, the Miners' National Association (MNA). Like the WBA, the MNA was founded on the principles of industrial unionism, in that it was open to all men who worked in and around the mines, not just the skilled elite.[36] As the MNA constitution put it in a rousing preamble: "'In union there is strength,' and in knowledge of union there is power. . . . Single-handed we can do nothing, but united there is no

34. PBIS 1, 361, 363; Schlegel, "The Workingmen's Benevolent Association," 258–59.

35. *Anthracite Monitor,* October 14, 1871.

36. Evans, *History of the United Mine Workers of America,* vol. 1, 26–31; Pinkowski, *John Siney,* 102–40. As Evans notes (p.7), the first national miners' union, the American Miners' Association, had been founded by miners from Illinois and Missouri at St. Louis, Missouri, on January 28, 1861.

power of wrong we cannot openly defy."[37] The new organization was based at Cleveland, Ohio, and John Siney was nominated to the post of president, at a salary of twelve hundred dollars a year.[38]

The MNA embodied Siney's conviction that strikes were dangerous, futile, and counterproductive. This opposition to strikes rested on the assumption that the proper relation between labor and capital was one of harmony rather than conflict. The constitution of the MNA committed the union "to remove, as far as possible, the causes of all strikes, and adopt wherever or whenever it is possible, the principle of arbitration."[39] Thus, the very same month that Franklin B. Gowen embarked on his plan to infiltrate the Molly Maguires and the WBA with Pinkerton agents, John Siney was organizing a new labor union that was opposed not only to violence but also to strikes.

For almost six months after he became president of the MNA, Siney retained the presidency of the WBA of Schuylkill County. He was succeeded as president by Thomas F. Williams of Locust Dale, who served for only one year before being replaced by John F. Welsh, the man who would lead the union in the Long Strike of 1875. Welsh was a native of Ireland whose background closely resembled that of Siney. Born of Catholic parents in County Down, he had moved to England with his family to escape the famine of the 1840s. He began working underground as a boy in the mines at Durham, in northeastern England. At the age of sixteen, already experienced in coal mining and trade unionism, he emigrated to the United States. At first he headed west in search of gold, but he soon returned to the East to work as a coal miner in Schuylkill County. During the Civil War he enlisted in a New York regiment and served for three years. After the war he paid a visit to Ireland, where he married a literate woman who taught him to read and write when the couple settled in Schuylkill County in 1866. Involved in the WBA from the beginning, Welsh was a close friend of Siney, whose ideas he generally favored. Siney remained active in the affairs of Schuylkill County after he resigned the WBA presidency, and with Welsh as his successor, he had high hopes that the men of the lower anthracite region would be among the first to join his new organization.[40]

But, while John Welsh was generally supportive of the MNA, most rank-and-file members of the WBA evidently were not. The majority of the bituminous miners in western Pennsylvania quickly joined the new union, but Siney experienced considerable opposition in recruiting his erstwhile colleagues in the anthracite region, where rival lodges of the WBA and the MNA were formed. The latter took root mainly in the upper region, where the WBA had always been weak. The chief source of opposition to the MNA in the anthracite region involved questions of strategy, especially the use of strikes. Pinkerton operative P. M. Cummings reported several times in 1874 on the unpopularity of John

37. Constitution of the MNA, quoted in PBIS I, 532.

38. Pinkowski, *John Siney,* 108.

39. Constitution of the MNA, quoted in PBIS I, 533.

40. Killeen, "John Siney," 261–62.

Siney and the MNA among the men of Schuylkill County, noting that the local miners "speak very badly of Siney" and "will never vote for him for any political office." Many local union men blamed him for deserting the WBA and opposing the use of strikes.[41]

Meanwhile, Franklin B. Gowen had taken steps to try to undermine the position of the WBA, while at the same time preparing for the last, decisive confrontation with the union. In 1873, he had proposed that the Philadelphia & Reading Coal & Iron Company set up its own benefit plan for its workers, even though the union already administered a plan of its own. Under Gowen's plan, the company would contribute one day's worth of its earnings to start a benefit fund, and the mine workers would contribute their wages from one day's work. Presumably aware that Gowen's principal intention was to undercut the appeal of the union, the mine workers paid little attention to his plan.[42]

At the beginning of 1874, the last contract between the WBA and the ABT was signed, holding wages at much the same level as the previous year. But this was merely a prelude to the coming showdown between the corporation and the labor movement. By the end of the year, Gowen had organized the operators into the Schuylkill Coal Exchange, a pooling system that agreed to control the production and distribution of anthracite. This system was a direct attack on the union, as the power of the WBA rested on its ability to exercise the same type of control over the coal industry. Who was to exercise this control in the future, the WBA or the Reading Railroad and its affiliate operators? This was the central question in the dispute that began in December 1874 and ended six months later in the final defeat and collapse of the Workingmen's Benevolent Association.

During the autumn of 1874, the operators and the railroad stockpiled enough coal to last through the winter. With the necessary preparations made for a long stoppage, the operators in the Schuylkill, Lehigh, and Wyoming regions announced simultaneous wage offers for 1875. The terms were very harsh. In the Lehigh region, laborers' pay was cut 10 percent and that of miners on wages by 15 percent. In the Schuylkill region, the pay cuts were 10 percent for laborers and 20 percent for miners. Worse still, the minimum basis on the sliding scale was to be abolished. Wages were to be reduced by 1 percent for each fall of 3 cents in the price of coal below $2.50 a ton, and would continue to fall as long as coal prices did. Even the *Miners' Journal*, scarcely a friend of organized labor, declared that it had "no hesitation in saying that these wages are too low for mining." And without a guaranteed minimum basis, there was every

41. LC, Pinkerton MS, Miscellaneous Section, Cummings's reports of July 25, August 17, August 20, 31, 1874, in report of BF to FBG, October 29, 1874 (quote, August 20). After a promising start, the MNA collapsed within a couple of years amid financial troubles and internal dissension. By April 1876, John Siney was back in St. Clair, a defeated man. See Killeen, "John Siney," 269–70, 348–61.

42. Roy, *A History of the Coal Miners of the United States*, 77; Virtue, "The Anthracite Mine Laborers," 770; Blatz, *Democratic Miners*, 32.

prospect that wages would fall still lower in the future. But the operators insisted that these terms were not negotiable, and the mine workers had to choose between accepting the terms or losing their jobs.[43]

The operators must have known that the union would reject this draconian proposal. Clearly, they wanted to provoke the union into a protracted strike, with the intention of finally breaking its power. As expected, the men in the Schuylkill and Lehigh regions, where the WBA was strongest, rejected the new terms out of hand, agreeing to work only for operators who would pay the basis of 1874 (a purely symbolic gesture, as no independent operator could afford to defy Franklin B. Gowen in this way). Pottsville's Democratic newspaper, the *Standard,* warned against calling a strike in the midst of a severe economic depression. The WBA leaders, who had always regarded strikes as a last resort, were perfectly aware of the perils of going on strike during the depression and the resulting hardships for the members. But, if the union was to survive at all, they apparently felt they had no option but to proceed.[44]

By the beginning of January 1875, production in the Lehigh and Schuylkill regions was almost completely suspended and the Long Strike was underway. Among the local mine workers who expressed a keen interest in the progress of the strike was the Pinkerton operative P. M. Cummings, by then vice president of the St. Clair local of the WBA; and James McParlan, who attended several meetings of the Shenandoah local. Over the coming months, two more operatives were sent in to spy on the union: William McCowan, who became an officer of the WBA in Shamokin, Northumberland County, and operative "WRH," who was based at Frackville. Various journalists also assisted the Pinkertons, among them H. B. Hanmore and Joseph Becker. Hanmore furnished Gowen with reports on the trade union and other matters in return for occasional payments by check. Becker, who produced a series of famous engravings of life and labor in the anthracite region for *Frank Leslie's Illustrated Newspaper,* subsequently claimed to have cooperated with an unnamed Pinkerton operative in the hunt for evidence on the Molly Maguires.[45]

More than ever before, the strike of 1875 depended on regional solidarity. For the strike to succeed, all the men in the upper and lower regions had to come out. In the Lehigh section of lower Luzerne County (the Eastern Middle Coal Field), the men quickly joined the striking mine workers of the two

43. *MJ,* January 4, 1875 (quote); Schlegel, *Ruler of the Reading,* 63–64; Schlegel, "The Workingmen's Benevolent Association," 260; Broehl, *The Molly Maguires,* 184–85.

44. *Pottsville Standard,* December 19, 1874.

45. HML, A 1520, B 1001, F1, report of JMCP, December 5, 1874, and F2, expense accounts of Pinkerton operatives, April 10, 1875. I am grateful to Josh Brown for the information on Becker, whose engravings of the anthracite region appeared in *Frank Leslie's Illustrated Newspaper,* September 25, 1869; March 25, April 15, 22, 29, and May 6, 27, 1871; December 12, 1874; February 6, March 13, April 10, and September 4, 1875; June 16, 30, and July 7, 1877. Cf. Joshua Brown, "*Frank Leslie's Illustrated Newspaper*: The Pictorial Press and the Representations of America, 1855–1889" (Ph.D. diss., Columbia University, 1993). The best of Becker's illustrations have been reproduced in the present work.

Schuylkill fields. But the workers in the Northern Coal Field, in upper Luzerne County, were divided. Most of the men in the lower section of the field, around Wilkes-Barre and Pittston, initially accepted a pay cut. But in February the Lehigh district council of the WBA voted to join the strike, calling on those of its members who had accepted the new terms to stop working. In the upper section of the Northern Field around Scranton, by contrast, most of the mine workers had abandoned the WBA after the strike of 1871 and now belonged to the MNA. Accepting a pay cut of 10 percent, the Scranton men continued to work throughout 1875, thereby greatly diminishing the prospects of a victorious strike in the lower region.[46]

By April, the Lehigh and Schuylkill mine workers were entering the fourth month of their strike. The WBA had won the support of some Pennsylvania newspapers, though more in terms of hostility to corporate power than approval of the union. The *Harrisburg Patriot,* which had long been worried about Gowen's monopolistic designs, declared that the WBA provided the mine workers with necessary protection against corporate power.[47] The *Scranton Republican,* too, condemned the greed of the corporations, and their ruthlessness in dealing with labor.[48] But this hostility to corporate power came only from newspapers outside the striking regions. The principal newspapers in Pottsville, the *Miners' Journal* and the *Standard,* outspokenly condemned the striking men, especially as the level of violence increased toward the end of the strike. Because of this violence, the WBA was increasingly identified with the Molly Maguires. By characterizing the labor union as a terrorist organization, powerful commentators like Franklin B. Gowen and Robert Ramsey ensured its destruction. At the same time, the identification of the union with the Molly Maguires encouraged the idea that the latter was equipped with a powerful institutional structure, belying its sporadic and disorganized nature and paving the way for its destruction as a necessary sequel to the defeat of the union. The accusation that the trade union and the Molly Maguires were the same organization was made repeatedly, and it quickly entered local lore and history.[49]

This was a highly effective ideological strategy, but its content needs to be unraveled if the Molly Maguires are to make any sense. For, while a small minority of union members undoubtedly supported and committed acts of direct violent action, the union leaders continued to condemn all such activities throughout the strike. One astute observer who noticed this was the editor of the *Pottsville Standard.* While the *Standard* conceded that the WBA had a right to

46. Schlegel, "The Workingmen's Benevolent Association," 261.

47. *Harrisburg Patriot,* April 17, 1875.

48. *Scranton Republican,* April 22, 1875.

49. A typical example was the first general history of Schuylkill County, compiled at the end of the 1870s. Reviewing the events of the middle of the decade, Munsell's *History of Schuylkill County* (p. 70) blamed the "mad conspirators" of the WBA for the "stubborn and prolonged contest" of 1875, during which the "conspirators" had resorted to their usual tactics "of intimidation, violence, outrage, incendiarism, and assassination," unleashing a "reign of terror . . . throughout the coal fields."

organize for better wages and conditions, it warned the union leaders that they had no right "to interfere with the companies or to dictate to them whom they shall employ or what wages they shall pay." The responsibility for such "lawlessness," the *Standard* concluded, lay with a "turbulent" minority: "We are satisfied that the better and more intelligent class of miners have taken no part in these acts of violence, and we know from personal observation that many of them condemn them in the strongest terms." But the big risk for the trade union was that the acts of a violent minority would tarnish the union's reputation and undermine its cause. In New York City, *Frank Leslie's Illustrated Newspaper* made the same point. Alongside illustrations of simian Irishmen, coffin notices, and ominous, brooding landscapes of the anthracite region, it warned that the "miners who shield those who have committed outrages must not feel aggrieved if they are classed with the 'Molly Maguires' who gained for the Schuykill [sic] coal regions an unenviable name."[50]

In the last few months of the strike, the leadership appears to have lost control over those elements of the rank and file who favored direct and violent action over gradual negotiation. The extent to which this violence involved "Molly Maguires" is unclear, but the adoption of violence as a tactic by striking miners provided Gowen and Ramsey with further evidence of the union's identity with the secret society. A series of violent incidents occurred from February 1875 onward. When one of the shafts of a mine being constructed for the Reading Railroad on the Mammoth Vein (just north of Pottsville) was destroyed by fire, Gowen offered an extravagant reward of ten thousand dollars for the arrest and conviction of the culprits, though it was by no means certain that arson was involved. He also offered protection to informants, the implication being that the mine workers were terrorized into silence by their leaders. When a second fire broke out, the Executive Board of the WBA joined in the condemnation of suspected arsonists. Throughout March 1875, there were frequent reports of arson, of loaded coal cars being dumped off sidings, of locomotives being derailed, and of armed and masked "Molly Maguires" assembling at night to intimidate blacklegs. On March 31, mine workers commandeered a coal train in Heckscherville and staged a demonstration in Ashland, in support of a brief-lived strike by employees of the Reading Railroad.[51]

In addition to newspaper accounts, the chief sources of evidence on the violence during the strike are the reports of the Pinkerton operatives. On

50. *Pottsville Standard,* April 3, 1875; *Frank Leslie's Illustrated News,* April 10, 1875.

51. *New York Tribune,* March 11, 14, 22, 31, 1875; *Philadelphia Press,* March 30, 1875; Schlegel, *Ruler of the Reading,* 65, 69–70; Schlegel, "The Workingmen's Benevolent Association," 261–63. In March 1875, maintenance workers on the Reading Railroad formed a union, the Mechanics and Workingmen's Benevolent Association (MWBA), which sought affiliation and exchanged membership cards with the WBA. Gowen dismissed those of his employees who joined the union, and when the MWBA called a strike he replaced them with strikebreakers, whom the mine workers of Heckscherville and Ashland attempted to drive out of the region. Hopes that the railroad workers' strike might help the cause of the mine workers soon dwindled, however, as the strike ended within a couple of days and the MWBA collapsed.

March 14, 1875, for example, James McParlan reported that Fr. O'Reilly of Shenandoah "in speaking about the Molly Maguires the other day said he was glad they were going to parade on St. Patrick's Day, as it would give him an opportunity of seeing all the cut-throats in the county. He also said that night God's curse, and his curse, rest on all the Molly Maguires and their families." A week later, after the parade was held in Mahanoy City, McParlan reported that "a number of MM names were read out in church," including his own name, and that "Father O'Reilly asked the members to pray for the Molly Maguires."[52]

McParlan also reported several conspiracies to destroy bridges, breakers, and other property belonging to the Reading Railroad and individual operators. In one such incident, he told how he had thwarted an attempt to destroy the high trestle bridge near Ringtown, on the Catawissa Branch of the Reading Railroad. The conspirators, according to McParlan, were two men named Brennan and Welch. Neither of them, he claimed, belonged to the Molly Maguires. Indeed, McParlan reported, they had approached him because he was a well-known "Molly Maguire" himself, and they wanted to know what the leaders of the secret society thought of their plan. McParlan promised to ask his fellow "Molly Maguires" and he invited Brennan and Welch to meet them at Shenandoah. When a group of "Mollys" met at Number Three Hill, Shenandoah, the detective reported, some of those present approved of the plan; but McParlan argued that Brennan and Welch were trying to set them up. Frank McAndrew, the leader, or "bodymaster," of the Shenandoah lodge of the AOH, agreed with him. Brennan and Welch, in any case, did not turn up for the meeting, and there the matter ended.[53]

On the basis of the reports he received from the Pinkertons, Franklin B. Gowen compiled a ten-page "List of Outrages" and a catalogue of "Coffin and Pistol Notices" posted in Schuylkill County from December 1874 to July 1875. After presenting this material as evidence to an investigative committee of the Pennsylvania legislature in July 1875, he published it in a pamphlet later the same year, along with his testimony before the committee. Most of the threatening letters were unsigned and featured a sketch of a coffin or a pistol, along with a crudely scrawled note. They included general warnings like these:[54]

> Mr. John Taylor.—Please leave Glen Carbon or if you dont you will suffer, by the order of the B.S.H. WE will give you one week to go but if you are alive on next Saturday you will die. Remember and leave.

> Notice you have Caried this as far as you can By cheating thy men you three Bosses Be Carefull if the Above dont Be your home in a short time. From a Stranger he nowes you.

There were also orders to mine workers or operators to stop working:

52. HML, A 1520, B 1001, F2, reports of JMcP, March 14, 21, 1875.

53. *Among the Assassins!*, 13.

54. All of these "coffin notices" were printed as part of an appendix to FBG 1875.

> Notice is here given to you men the first and last notice that you will get for no man will go down this slope. After to night if you Do you Can Bring your Coffion Along With you for by the internal Crist We Mean What this notice says you Drift man stop at home and Cut no more Coal let him go and Get Coal himself I Dont mean Engineer Or forearms let them mine there one work now men the Next Notice you will get I Dont mean to Do it With my Pen I will Do it with that there Rolver I Dont want no more Black legs at this Collary.

The orthography suggests that these notices were authentic, though there is no way of knowing for certain. But it is remarkable how many of the notices dealt directly with the enforcement of the strike. Here are some examples:

> Take notice Avery Black Leg that will Take Aney Eunnion man plac you will have A hard Road to travel you will Rot in this shape [picture of a coffin] if you wish to Escape this home.—By a stranger.

> Any blackleg that takes a Union Mans job while He is standing for His Rights will have a hard Road to travel and if he dont he will have to suffer the consequences.

> Any man starting to work in the rail road now going to begin under the basis will have to stand the consequences. So black legs to notice.
> —M.M.N.

> Black Legs Take Notice—
> that you are in dang er of your Life by working in the mines without the Consent of the union men of Swatara Branch 14 Dis at Middle Creek Mines.

> Black legs if you dont leave in 2 days time you meet your doom their will Bee an open war immeatley.

> from the gap Daniel Patch
> remember you will be running in this coal ragion at night you took on nother mans engin we will give you fair warning in time and some more.
> V.L.
> —M.M. H.S.T.

If these notices were authentic, then it would appear that the Molly Maguire tactic of threatening retributive justice was being employed by at least some trade unionists toward the end of the strike. But this does not change the fact that the union leaders remained unequivocally opposed to violence. There were undoubtedly some Molly Maguires in the union, and toward the end of the strike some of them may well have seen themselves as its unofficial, enforcing arm. Though the transition cannot be documented, it is probable that an Irish ethos of direct violent action was being transformed into an ethos of industrial trade unionism through direct experience in a protracted labor dispute. But the result was a fusion of trade unionism with the earlier strategy, so that violence was not simply replaced by negotiation, as the leaders of the WBA wanted. Instead, trade unionism, at least as it was practiced by certain striking mine workers, was becoming more violent.

By April 1875 the union and the strike were in serious trouble. In early April the miners at Hyde Park, in upper Luzerne County, again voted not to join the strike. On April 10, WBA president John F. Welsh decided "that the time has arrived when a change of our programme is necessary." Even though he believed the men were "willing and able to hold out at least two months longer if necessary," Welsh recommended that a meeting be held in each district to vote on returning to work for any operators who wished to resume production, at whatever terms the operators saw fit. But no coal was to be shipped from collieries owned by the Reading Railroad, Welsh insisted, until a final settlement had been reached between the railroad and the WBA.[55]

There was a large element of wishful thinking in Welsh's proposal. As Gowen and the operators were fully aware, the union was on the verge of collapse. And even if the independent operators had wanted to resume production, they could not have afforded to defy the Reading Railroad. Thus, when the union submitted a proposal for arbitration on April 21, the operators did not bother to reply. Finally, on May 14, a committee of Schuylkill operators agreed to meet with union representatives. The union men arrived at the meeting with the radical proposal that all sliding scale and contract wages be eliminated in favor of a single, flat rate of fifteen dollars for a week of six eight-hour days. The operators agreed to consider this proposal; but, aware that the balance of power had now swung irrevocably away from the mine workers, they never issued a response. As it turned out, this was to be the last meeting between the operators and the WBA. By the time the WBA next approached the Coal Exchange a month later, the strike had been broken and the union was on the verge of disintegration.[56]

Late in May, the operators decided to reopen the mines unilaterally, offering the 1874 basis to whomever came to work, and guaranteeing protection to those who did. After six months without pay, in the midst of a severe economic depression, most workers and their families could hold out no longer. Andrew Roy, an official of the Miners' National Association, recalled that in the last days of the strike, "hundreds of families rose in the morning to breakfast on a crust of bread and a glass of water. . . . Day after day men, women, and children went to the adjoining woods to dig roots and pick up herbs to keep body and soul together." Early in June, the men began to drift back to work and by the end of the month most of the collieries in the Schuylkill region were open once again.[57]

Throughout the month of June, however, some radical workers rejected the union leaders' call to return to work. The center of opposition was the area

55. HML, A 1520, B 979, letter to the Miners' and Laborers Benevolent Association of Schuylkill County from John F. Welsh, April 10, 1875. The MLBA was still popularly known as the WBA.

56. Schlegel, "The Workingmen's Benevolent Association," 264–66.

57. Roy, *History of the Coal Miners of the United States*, 99. Cf. fig. 10.

between Shenandoah and Mahanoy City, the heart of Molly Maguire country. The tactics employed were reminiscent of many previous labor disputes in the anthracite region, a mixture of crowd action with intimidatory behavior. On the morning of June 2, Captain Heisler of the Reading Railroad's Coal & Iron Police arrived in Shenandoah with more than one hundred men, all armed with repeating rifles and ready to take whatever measures were considered necessary. Later that day, over a thousand people assembled and marched in a parade through the town, Irish and British mine workers together, along with their families. Hundreds of mine workers gathered for a labor picnic at Number Three Hill, Shenandoah. Plans were made to hold a parade the following day, and the miners slept out on the hillsides overnight.[58]

The next morning a procession of about seven hundred mine workers marched out of Shenandoah to Mahanoy City. At the Reading Railroad's West Shenandoah Colliery, which had reopened on June 1, they stopped to persuade the men to quit. But they were met at the mine by a phalanx of heavily armed policemen, led by the Pinkerton operative Robert Linden, who had secretly been deputized as a captain in the Coal & Iron Police the previous month. Among the crowd of demonstrators was James McParlan. Turned back by the police at West Shenandoah, the crowd proceeded to Mahanoy City, bringing out the men at three collieries along the way. When they got there, several hundred miners from Hazleton had already arrived, shutting down six mines in the area. The crowd, now a thousand strong, next approached the Little Drift Colliery, where they were met by the sheriff, who read them the riot act. One of the sheriff's posse fired into the crowd, apparently by accident. A general melée followed, with stones and bullets flying through the air. Nobody was killed, and the mine workers returned to Shenandoah. State militia were stationed in Shenandoah and all the collieries that had been closed were reopened the following day, June 4.[59]

In the face of this new outbreak of violence, the *Miners' Journal* unleashed a bitter attack on the mine workers and their union. "It seems to us that five months is long enough to bear with insolence, oppression and tyranny, but we should be content to wait and let the struggle wear itself out, if it were not for the violence which has now been resorted to," Robert Ramsey complained. Thankfully, "military power" had now "been called to aid the civil authorities" in preserving "the rights of persons and property" and to help eradicate "anarchy." If defensive military action proved inadequate, Ramsey urged, then "let the troops act on the offensive. Let the leaders of these riots be hunted down

58. HSP, papers of Owen Hunt, chronology of the period between July 3, 1874, and July 7, 1876; Schlegel, *Ruler of the Reading,* 72; Schlegel, "The Workingmen's Benevolent Association," 265.

59. For an account of the events of June 2 and 3, see *MJ,* June 11, 1875; LC, Pinkerton MS, Miscellaneous Section, report of Captain Robert Linden, June 24, 1875, in report of BF to FBG, July 26, 1875. The best secondary account is Schlegel, *Ruler of the Reading,* 72–73. On Captain Linden, the Coal & Iron Police, and the formation in May 1875 of a "flying squadron" to root out the Molly Maguires, see chapter 7.

and arrested." If "the ruffians" of northern Schuylkill County "will learn tolerance only by being shot down, it is better to shoot them down than to let them shoot others."[60]

Ramsey pointed to recent events in the mining county of Clearfield, in central Pennsylvania, as a model of justice for Schuylkill County. John Siney and Xingo Parks, a fellow-organizer from the Miners' National Association, had recently been arrested there in connection with a labor dispute. They were charged with conspiracy and incitement to cause riot. Twenty-six local trade unionists were also arrested, and in early June 1875 they were convicted on conspiracy charges. In passing sentence, the judge was reported to have declared: "I find you, Maloney, to be president of the union, and you, Joyce, to be secretary, and, therefore, I sentence you to one year's imprisonment."[61] Two other union men received the same sentence, thirteen were fined twenty-five dollars plus costs and sent to prison for sixty days, and the remainder received suspended sentences.[62]

This was just the sort of treatment the *Miners' Journal* now recommended for the recalcitrant mine workers of Schuylkill County, especially John Siney, who had begun all this trouble in the first place. "If ever a man deserved the penitentiary for the villainy that he has set in motion and produced—the injury he has done the miners and the laborers, and the destruction of business caused by his rascality in deceiving the miners and using them for his own purposes to advance his own interests, and to put money in his own pocket, that man is John Siney!" The "villains" and "scoundrels" who led the union in Schuylkill County should all be arrested, Ramsey demanded, just as they had been in Clearfield.[63]

And who, exactly, were these "villains" and "scoundrels?" They were, Ramsey declared, a "herd of ruffians connected with the leaders in all the Divisions, four-fifths of whom were Irishmen—in fact the whole strike has been practically run by the Irish element for several months past."[64] While Ramsey generally placed Siney and Welsh into an undifferentiated category of Irishness alongside the Molly Maguires, his attack on the Irish in this case contained an important insight. In recent months, the strike had indeed been controlled by "the Irish element," in the sense that the primarily British or anglicized union leaders had lost control over some of their members, including those who

60. *MJ*, June 11, 1875.

61. Quoted in Killeen, "John Siney," 325.

62. On the Clearfield conspiracy case, see *MJ*, June 11, 1875; *Pottsville Workingman*, June 19, 1875; Evans, *History of the United Mine Workers*, vol. 1, 74–80; Pinkowski, *John Siney*, 154–77; Killeen, "John Siney," 310–46. When Siney finally went on trial in late September 1875, he was acquitted, largely through the efforts of a defense team that included two of Pottsville's best lawyers, Lin Bartholomew and Francis W. Hughes, the county's leading Democratic politician. The following year, Hughes would play a leading role for the prosecution in the Molly Maguire trials, while Bartholomew appeared for the defense.

63. *MJ*, June 11, 1875.

64. Ibid., June 11, 1875.

favored a strategy of direct, violent action. To this extent, Molly Maguireism was the unofficial, violent enforcing arm of trade unionism in 1875, though its strategy was far removed from that promoted by the union leaders since 1868. Ramsey failed to see these differences, or chose to ignore them, blaming all the trouble on the Irishman who had founded the WBA eight years earlier, even though Siney was no longer active in union affairs in the anthracite region at the time of the Long Strike.

The union leaders were quick to respond to attacks of this type. "Those who charge the inculcating of violence or the encouragement of the employment of force on trade unions are . . . utterly ignorant of the doings of such associations," declared the union newspaper, the *Pottsville Workingman*.[65] In "their desire to serve capital and gratify their aristocratic hate of workingmen," such people were willing to perpetrate "the meanest and foulest slanders." The *Workingman* admitted that the union leaders had lost control over some of the rank and file, who "have committed acts of violence against those who have broken through the rules which the workingmen have deemed necessary to the protection of their interests." Here, in a nutshell, was the ethic of Molly Maguireism: direct retributive action against those who transgressed a specific vision of what was just and moral. But the *Workingman* sharply dissociated the WBA from such tactics, and reported that the union had gone "so far as to denounce the acts of these individuals, and even offers to furnish . . . the necessary police to prevent the perpetration of acts violative of the rights of property."[66]

Hoping to keep their disintegrating organization intact, the WBA Executive Board met at Pottsville on June 8, 1875. The union leaders announced that they would make a direct appeal to Franklin B. Gowen for a compromise settlement. But when Gowen read about this plan in the newspapers the following day, he wrote to John F. Welsh rejecting the possibility of compromise. "I think it is my duty to the workingmen to protest against the use of my name for the purpose of prolonging the strike," Gowen wrote. "I am not a member of the Coal Exchange, appointed to take charge of the subject of wages, and therefore, I cannot consent to have any conference whatsoever with your Association upon that question." He also denied the right of the WBA to "interfere in any manner in the establishment of freight and tolls to be charged by this company, or in determining the price of coal." Adding insult to injury, Gowen concluded the letter by stating that, "apart from the general reasons above given, my own sense of self respect forbids me having any personal intercourse whatever, with either you, or Mr. C. B. Johnson."[67]

65. The *Workingman* had succeeded the *Anthracite Monitor* as the official organ of the WBA in 1873. In 1876, the *Workingman* relocated to Wilkes-Barre, where it soon ceased publication.

66. *Pottsville Workingman,* June 19, 1875.

67. Letter from FBG to John F. Welsh, June 9, 1875, published in *MJ,* June 10, 1875. C. B. Johnson was the editor of the miners' newspapers, the *Anthracite Monitor* and the *Pottsville Workingman.* On the last days of the Long Strike, see Schlegel, "The Workingmen's Benevolent Association," 265–66.

Faced with Gowen's intransigence, the union leaders turned to members of the Coal Exchange. Arguing that half the men were still prepared to stay out in opposition to the proposal of January, but that they would return to work if a less severe wage cut were offered, the leaders proposed a meeting with the operators at Shenandoah to discuss terms. But, when the union leaders arrived in Shenandoah for the meeting on June 12, there was nobody there to greet them. On June 14, 1875, the Executive Board admitted defeat. In a defiant final circular to the members, the WBA leaders authorized the men to accept the end of the strike "under protest," and to return to work "upon the best terms that can be secured." The leaders also pointed out to Gowen and the other "autocrats" that it was only "the keen pangs of hunger" that had driven the men "into a reluctant acceptance of terms which, under other circumstances, they could never have been induced to accept."[68]

Within a week of the WBA's final declaration, all the Schuylkill men had returned to work, and the state militia had left the county. By July 1, 1875, the Long Strike was over. At least one superintendent found his employees too weak to work, for want of food, and he had to request emergency provisions from his superior.[69] The WBA never recovered from its defeat in the Long Strike; within a few months it had collapsed. In the Lehigh region, the mine workers were at least able to sign a collective contract on the new terms, thereby maintaining the principle of negotiation. But in Schuylkill County, the men returned to work on terms set by their individual employers, just as they had before the existence of the WBA. They were also forced to accept a wage schedule 26.5 percent below the 1869 level. With the union defeated, wages continued to fall over the coming years until, in 1877, they were 54 percent below the 1869 level.[70]

Joseph Patterson, who served as secretary of the WBA during the Long Strike, later recalled the agony of defeat. "How bitter, how very humiliating was the defeat sustained by the miners in 1875 is hard to impress upon those who did not experience it," Patterson recalled. "The pain of having to yield was only exceeded by the hunger and suffering produced by a struggle of six months, during which time nothing was earned to provide bread for the miners' families. Famine drove men into submission."[71] "The struggle is over," the *Miners' Journal* of June 18, 1875, exulted. "The war between Capital and Labor is ended, and Labor is not victor. It is not even the drawn battle signified by compromise: it is an unconditional surrender, a capitulation of all the army, and relinquishment of all the claim for which it fought."[72] As a miners' ballad lamented:

68. *MJ*, June 17, 1875, and *Pottsville Workingman*, June 19, 1875. Cf. Schlegel, "The Workingmen's Benevolent Association," 256–66.

69. Roy, *History of the Coal Miners of the United States*, 99.

70. Evans, *History of the United Mine Workers of America*, vol. 1, 36.

71. Joseph Patterson, "Old W.B.A. Days" (Pottsville, 1909), Publications of the Historical Society of Schuylkill County, 2, 382–83.

72. *MJ*, June 18, 1875.

"Well, we've been beaten, beaten all to smash, And now, sir, we've begun to feel the lash, As wielded by a gigantic corporation, Which runs the Commonwealth and ruins the nation."[73]

In the day-to-day lives of the miners, the most noticeable result of the railroad's victory was a tightening of discipline in the workplace. Like most miners, the anthracite workers of eastern Pennsylvania were not accustomed to working under rigidly controlled, factory-style conditions. The distinctive physical and social geography inside the mines had always militated against this. So, too, had the traditionally small-scale and decentralized character of mining operations in the lower anthracite region. Moreover, work was frequently interrupted, often for long intervals. Accidents, fires, and floods were one source of interruption; another was the frequent strikes and suspensions after 1868.[74]

The now unchallenged control of the Reading Railroad over the industry of the lower region changed the nature of work in the mines. Corporate control by one owner allowed for greater discipline in the workplace than in the era of small enterprise. The Philadelphia & Reading Coal & Iron Company (PRCI) posted rules at all its newly acquired collieries, ensuring strict compliance with the safety laws and regimenting the use of time by its nine thousand employees. Access to the mines was controlled in such a way that all workers, including contract miners, were required to work for ten hours a day.[75] By 1875 only 17 of the 153 mines in the lower anthracite region as a whole employed fewer than 75 men. Practically all of them were owned or leased by corporations, and most were controlled by the Reading Railroad.[76] With the trade union in disarray, the PRCI proposed a new benefits plan, which went into effect in 1877. Greater control over the work force, as much as corporate benevolence, was the motive.[77] Because of the distinctive geography of their workplace, miners retained considerably more independence than factory workers throughout the nineteenth century. But the miners of the lower anthracite region were noticeably less independent in 1880 than they had been in 1850.

A correspondent for the *New York Labor Standard* vividly captured the conditions in the new industrial order when he visited the Hickory Colliery, just outside St. Clair, in 1877. "The entrance to the mines is from the top of a precipitous hill, which, covered with the black refuse of scores of years, bears the semblance of a mountain of coal dust," he wrote.

> From the doors and open windows of the colliery buildings a great cloud of black dust is ever streaming, settling on everything. . . . The interior of the

73. Quoted in Korson, *Minstrels of the Mine Patch,* 225–26.

74. PBIS 1, 343.

75. Wallace, *St. Clair,* 425–26.

76. Long, *Where the Sun Never Shines,* 59.

77. Roy, *The Coal Mines,* 248; Virtue, "The Anthracite Mine Laborers," 770–73; Blatz, *Democratic Miners,* 32–33; Ray Ginger, "Company-sponsored Welfare Plans in the Anthracite Industry before 1900," *Bulletin of the Business Historical Society,* 27 (June 1953): 113.

> building is a cloud of hazy blackness; and the black silent men, as they appear and disappear in the dust, seem like so many evil genii floating in the dark storm clouds.

At this mine, three hundred men and boys were employed, and each had his own clearly regulated task:

> Each one had his routine to go through, and he went through it just as a steam engine or a clock. And when quitting time came each one went back to his home in the regular groove, just as the steam goes out of the boiler when its work is done, and then dropped off into sleep, his only pleasure. I have seen far more cheerful bodies of men in prisons. It may be their black and dreary surroundings; it may be their knowledge of constant and terrible danger; it may be the strain of great physical labor—I know not what it is, but something there is about these mines that wears the life and soul out of the men, leaving only the weary, blackened shell.[78]

This depressing description, with its prominent mechanical imagery, was a far cry from the dignity and independence of the miner celebrated throughout Schuylkill County over the previous three decades. The era of free labor and small-scale enterprise in the lower anthracite region had come to an end.

In a fitting phrase, the anthracite region in the immediate aftermath of the Long Strike has been described in terms of "The Rise of the Company State." By 1876,

> the Reading system . . . held an unchallenged, near-perfect monopoly of the Schuylkill coal trade. It produced most of the coal in its own collieries, carried all of it on its own railroads or its own canal, delivered it at Port Richmond to its own wharves, ships and dealers.

The railroad maintained the prices it wanted through pooling combinations with other corporations. Its economic power was supplemented by police power over Schuylkill County, in the form of its own private police force, assisted by Pinkerton operatives working undercover. The Reading also wielded formidable power in state politics, with extensive influence over the governor and the legislature at Harrisburg.[79]

The power vested in the railroad was now brought to bear on the Molly Maguires, the final obstacle standing in the way of Franklin B. Gowen's grand design for a stable, productive Schuylkill County. The identification of the WBA with the Molly Maguires during the last few months of the Long Strike meant that the task of defeating labor could not be considered complete until the Molly Maguires had been arrested and brought to trial. When the Pennsylvania legislature carried out a second investigation into the affairs of the Reading Railroad in July 1875, therefore, the subject of the Molly Maguires was very much on Gowen's mind. Having illustrated the altruistic and patriotic designs

78. New York *Labor Standard,* March 17, 1877.

79. Wallace, *St. Clair,* 425.

of the corporation in the first part of his testimony to the committee, Gowen proceeded to launch a blistering attack on labor in the second, casting the union leaders as a small band of terrorist conspirators. He began his attack by denying that he was "reflecting in any manner on the laboring class" in general. He admitted that "ninety-five out of every one hundred of the men employed about the mines" were "decent, orderly, law-abiding, respectable men." But among these decent folk was "a class of agitators," a small group of "men brought here for no other purpose than to create confusion, to undermine confidence, and to stir up dissension between the employer and the employed."[80] His task, Gowen claimed, was to weed out this pest, on behalf of the majority of workmen, who wanted nothing more than to be allowed to work: "I stand here as the champion of the rights of labor—as the advocate of those who desire to work and who have been prevented from doing so."[81]

In a dramatic flourish, Gowen then produced for the committee a ten-page "List of Outrages in Schuylkill and Shamokin Region, from December 13, 1874 to July 15, 1875." This list was appended to the published copy of Gowen's argument, along with a series of threatening letters and "coffin notices" allegedly posted in the anthracite region in the same period. Nearly all of these "outrages," he claimed, were committed, not "to injure the property of the employer," but "to intimidate the workingmen themselves from going to work."[82] The list mentioned one assassination, one attempted assassination, nine cases of threatening letters or notices, several burglaries, and scores of cases of arson, assault, and industrial sabotage.[83] Striking a poignant note, Gowen concluded that "when the father of the starving family and the husband of the emaciated wife goes forth to earn his daily bread, he is met by the pistol of the assassin and the torch of the incendiary, and driven back to his home to starve."[84] Moving easily from poignancy to patriotism, he ended his address by reminding the committee that, in a year's time, they would be celebrating the centenary of the American Republic. Let us not forget, he warned, that "almost within the shadow of Independence Hall, tens of thousands of citizens are subject to a tyranny and a despot such as neither Khan nor Caliph ever exercised, and such as in the wildest dream of power was ne'er conceived by Sultan or by Czar."[85]

In this way, the labor union and the Molly Maguires had at last been made to appear as one. Trade unionism had certainly become more violent in 1875. But the union leaders had remained steadfast in their denunciation of violence. And the differences between trade unionism and Molly Maguireism, on which the

80. FBG 1875, 76.

81. Ibid., 76–77.

82. Ibid., 77. See appendix 4.

83. Ibid., 99–109. The assassination was that of Benjamin Yost on July 5, 1875; the victim of the attempted assassination was William "Bully Bill" Thomas. Both cases are discussed in chapter 7 of the present work. See, also, appendix 4.

84. Ibid., 78.

85. Ibid., 79.

leaders of the WBA had always insisted, were to be dramatically revealed in the immediate aftermath of the Long Strike. The defeat of the WBA was followed by a remarkable three months of violence, which included the last six assassinations attributed to the Molly Maguires. In the first half of 1875 two separate modes of labor protest and organization had been firmly identified as one; but now their fundamental difference was to be revealed. In the second half of 1875, with the WBA in ruins, the mine workers of Schuylkill County searched for an alternative strategy. Some of them turned to violent action, and the result was the second wave of Molly Maguire assassinations.

7

Rough Justice

By the mid-1870s, the violence in the lower anthracite region was once again drawing national attention, just as it had a decade earlier. The single year from October 1874 to September 1875 was the most concentrated period of Molly Maguire activity. In this period, eight more assassinations were attributed to the organization—the same number as in the previous twelve years. Two of the assassinations took place late in 1874; the other six were committed in the four months immediately following the Long Strike. Although it was castigated as mindless barbarity by contemporaries, much of the Molly Maguire violence of the 1870s involved the enforcement of a specific type of retributive justice. The victims varied from Welsh gang members to miners, mine superintendents, and public officials. But the strategy of revenge employed in each case was much the same: direct, violent, and lethal. Elements of greed, dishonesty, and brutality entered into the picture, as they often do in human affairs; some of the participants in the Molly Maguire violence were not fighting for social justice in any meaningful sense, being animated instead by strictly individual grievances. But most of the violence bore either a primary or a secondary connection to labor relations, the assassination of mine officials in the most direct sense, and the assassination of public officials and Welsh miners and gang members because it was part of a general interethnic conflict that had its material basis in patterns of discrimination in the workplace.

This conflict was greatly exacerbated by the collapse of the Workingmen's

Benevolent Association in June 1875. For seven years the union had enabled the mine workers of Schuylkill County to overcome their craft and ethnic differences and fight together in a common cause. It had also effectively discouraged the use of violence as a strategy in labor disputes, so much so that the two principal waves of Molly Maguire activity were neatly divided in time by the period in which the trade union had flourished. The collapse of the union not only opened the way for a resumption of ethnic and labor violence; it removed the one organization that had protected the mine workers as a whole from the dictates of the employers, especially the Reading Railroad. In the summer of 1875, a minority of Irish workers turned to violence as the sole remaining strategy for winning some sort of rudimentary justice in the mines. The Molly Maguires, in other words, temporarily filled the vacuum left by the defeat of the Workingmen's Benevolent Association. Given the presence in the anthracite region of an increasingly brutal Coal & Iron Police, supplemented by a "flying squadron" of policemen and undercover Pinkerton agents, this drift toward violence on the part of labor is scarcely surprising. It had begun in the last months of the Long Strike and would reach its peak between June and September 1875.

While most of the violent incidents reported in the press were blamed on the Molly Maguires, the violence was a many-sided process. It took a variety of legal and extralegal forms, and the line that divided these forms was arbitrary. Violence was employed against the Molly Maguires as well as by them, starting with the use of force by the state during the Civil War, and continuing thereafter in various direct and indirect ways. These included the general pattern of gang warfare between the Welsh and the Irish; the sale of police power to the private sector; the deployment of local militias and the National Guard during labor disputes; the formation of vigilante committees in Schuylkill County; and ultimately the employment by the state of the legalized form of violence known as execution by hanging. Both the legal and the extralegal forms of violence—from military power and executions on the one hand, to vigilante action, gang warfare, and Molly Maguire assassinations on the other—were used to enforce competing visions of social justice. The struggle between these different visions provides the key to understanding the Molly Maguires in the 1870s.

In the late 1870s, more than fifty suspected "Molly Maguires" were indicted on sixteen counts of murder and multiple counts of conspiracy. All the defendants belonged to the Ancient Order of Hibernians. The figure of sixteen murders includes only those killings for which "Molly Maguires" were indicted during the showcase trials of the 1870s. Rumors of "Molly Maguire" involvement had surrounded several other murders in the mid and late 1860s, by which time the term had already become a ubiquitous explanation for violence in the lower anthracite region. But very little is known about these incidents, except that some Irishmen were involved. Only the eight killings of the 1860s for which indictments were handed down in the following decade have been included in the discussion here, along with the eight committed in the 1870s.[1]

Of the sixteen men allegedly killed by the Molly Maguires between 1862 and 1875, only one was a mine owner. The absence of mine owners among the victims strikingly resembled the pattern of agrarian violence in Ireland, where landlords were rarely killed, and the main victims were land agents, middlemen, small farmers, and figures of local authority. In both Ireland and Pennsylvania, the people at the top of the social hierarchy tended to be absentees, and they might rarely if ever be seen. The violence was deflected onto the nearest available target, the people with whom the perpetrators were in daily contact—middlemen, agents, small farmers or mine superintendents, local officials, and people from their own social background (mine workers in Pennsylvania, tenants and laborers in Ireland) who had somehow incurred their enmity. Five of the men allegedly killed by the Molly Maguires in Pennsylvania were mine superintendents, four were mine foremen, two were miners, one was a mine owner, one a mine watchman, one a policeman, one a burgess, and one a justice of the peace. Though they came from different social and ethnic backgrounds, they all had one thing in common. They were victims of a form of direct, retributive justice derived from a specific part of rural Ireland and adapted for use in a specific part of the anthracite region.

On the basis of contemporary newspaper reports, trial testimony, and informers' confessions, a typology of the Molly Maguire killings can be constructed. These sources are heavily biased; but it is nonetheless possible to divide the killings into five overlapping categories. The first of these was the assassination of mine officials under the peculiar conditions of the Civil War and its immediate aftermath. The second category appears to have involved mainly profit or gain, taking the form of highway robbery, and occurring in the late 1860s. The third involved revenge, either to settle individual grievances or to defend the honor of one ethnic group against another. It occurred mainly in the mid-1870s and involved gang warfare and interethnic faction fighting. The fourth type of violence emerged only in 1875: the killing of figures of authority, including policemen and justices of the peace. The fifth, which also appeared in 1875, involved the assassination of mine officials once again, though this time without the provocation of the military draft. Instead, it was a matter of certain Irish workers turning to more desperate tactics in the wake of the disastrous Long Strike. Examining the crimes in this way, it becomes apparent that many contemporaries did not, or would not, realize the complexities of what they

1. The other incidents of the 1860s in which the Molly Maguires were implicated included the killings of James Shields in 1864 and William Williams in 1865, both in Blythe Township. See the pamphlet published by Eveland & Harris, *The Molly Maguires* (Tamaqua, n.d., ca. 1876), 6, 18–19. These killings did not feature in the trials of the 1870s. Various acts of industrial sabotage were also attributed to the Molly Maguires, but here it is even more difficult to know what was going on and who was responsible. See, for example, the incidents involving rail tracks on July 15 and 20, 1875, reported in HSP, chronology of the period from July 3, 1874, to July 7, 1876, papers of Owen Hunt.

were describing. Behind the distortions of ideological representation there was indeed a long tradition of Irish violence. By attempting to see that violence in its various forms, instead of as an undifferentiated manifestation of social evil, various patterns can be detected. Within the monolithic evil portrayed by contemporaries, in other words, there were several different levels of activity (see Table 7.1).

The first wave of Molly Maguire activities, from 1862 to 1868, involved four assassinations specific to the Civil War, along with two committed in the course of highway robberies. In the case of the latter, the status of the victims as mine officials arguably made them legitimate targets in the eyes of the Molly Maguires. But robberies and killings committed by Irishmen for personal gain sometimes took on the color of Molly Maguireism only on the basis of subsequent judicial or ideological developments. The assassination of Alexander Rea in 1868, for example, does not appear to have been connected in any

TABLE 7.1. Types of Molly Maguire Killings

Type	Date	Victim	Occupation	Nationality
Civil War	1862	F.W. Langdon	Foreman	n.a.
	1863	George K. Smith	Mine owner	n.a.
	1865	David Muir	Superintendent	Scottish
	1866	Henry H. Dunne	Superintendent	Irish
Highway Robbery	1867	William Littlehales	Foreman	American
	1868	Alexander Rea	Superintendent	American
Revenge, ethnic conflict, gangs	1871	Morgan Powell	Superintendent	Welsh
	1874	George Major	Burgess	Welsh
	1875	Gomer James	Miner	Welsh-American
Government officials	1874	George Major	Burgess	American
	1875	Benjamin Yost	Policeman	American
	1875	Thomas Gwyther	Justice of Peace	American
Mine officials	1862	F.W. Langdon	Foreman	n.a.
	1863	George K. Smith	Owner	n.a.
	1865	David Muir	Superintendent	Scottish
	1866	Henry H. Dunne	Superintendent	Irish
	1867	William Littlehales	Foreman	American
	1868	Alexander Rea	Superintendent	American
	1870	Patrick Burns	Foreman	n.a.
	1871	Morgan Powell	Superintendent	Welsh
	1874	Frederick Hesser	Watchman	n.a.
	1875	Thomas Sanger	Foreman	Cornish
	1875	William Uren*	Miner	Cornish
	1875	John P. Jones	Superintendent	Welsh

n.a.: information not available

*Uren has been included in the category of mine officials because he was killed during the assassination of Thomas Sanger.

way with the activities of the "Molly Maguires" or the Ancient Order of Hibernians elsewhere; whisky and money were its central motifs. The four killings connected to the Civil War, by contrast, involved the intersection of labor organizing with hostility to the military draft. They were part of a general, loosely organized pattern of resistance to employers and the state authorities in the context of the wartime emergency.[2]

The next two assassinations attributed to the Molly Maguires occurred in 1870 and 1871, during the period of relative stability inaugurated by the rise of the Workingmen's Benevolent Association. The first of these was the killing of Patrick Burns, foreman of the Silver Creek Colliery in Tuscarora. Burns was killed on April 15, 1870; but, as in the previous six assassinations, nobody was arrested for this killing at the time. The incident was traced to the Molly Maguires only in the late 1870s, when Martin Bergin was convicted and executed on the evidence of an informer, James McDonnell. McDonnell claimed that John Kane, the Irish-born outside boss at the mine in question, was the man behind the murder. Kane had apparently been involved in an ongoing dispute with Burns, his immediate superior, over wages and other issues.[3] The nature of these "issues" was not specified at the trial, though they presumably involved some notion of justice for Irish mine workers. Bosses like Kane were generally ex-miners who had a close relationship with the work force, as distinct from superintendents, who typically belonged to a distinct managerial class. McDonnell, however, quickly added a second motive for the assassination, which was much more in line with the prosecution's characterization of the Molly Maguires as gangsters who murdered for gain or for sport. Burns had discovered that Kane was robbing the company, he testified, and Kane had arranged with him to have Burns killed. McDonnell, in turn, had appointed Martin Bergin to do the job.[4]

The second assassination in this transition period between 1868 and 1874 was that of Morgan Powell, at Summit Hill, Carbon County, on December 2, 1871. Once again, Welsh discrimination against Irish mine workers was at the heart of the matter. A native of Wales and a skilled miner, Morgan Powell had risen through the ranks to become a superintendent at the Lehigh &

2. These first six assassinations are discussed in chapters 3 and 4. Rea's killers belonged to the AOH, but the murder occurred in the course of a highway robbery and had no evident connection with the AOH or the "Molly Maguires." One of the convicted killers, Patrick Tully, stated in his confession that "It wasn't so much the Order (referring to the Ancient Order of Hibernians) as it was whisky led me into it." *MJ,* March 28, 1878.

3. On the trials of Bergin and McDonnell, see chapter 9 of the present work, and the stenographic reports at the HML. Cf. Schlegel, *Ruler of the Reading,* 146–47.

4. The "List of Members of the AOH." (HML, A 1520, B 979, F, "Memoranda and Papers") compiled by the Pinkertons in the 1870s, included a Jerry Kane, bodymaster of the Mount Laffee lodge of the AOH. Kane was also included in the "List of Fugitive Mollie Maguires" published by the Pinkertons in 1879 (HSC, Molly Maguire Collection, Photo File). This may well be the same individual referred to as John Kane by McDonnell. Michael J. Doyle and Edward Kelly, who were later convicted of assassinating John P. Jones, were also members of the Mount Laffee lodge of the AOH.

Wilkes-Barre Coal Company. Though nobody was arrested at the time, Alexander Campbell, John "Yellow Jack" Donahue, and Thomas Fisher were convicted of the crime in 1876. According to a report in the *Miners' Journal* in 1878, the Powell killing was "an assassination participated in by almost an entire lodge at the instance of a single member, who considered himself aggrieved and not properly treated by Powell." The member in question was Alexander Campbell, who allegedly wanted Powell killed because he had refused to give Campbell his own coal face at the mine, favoring his Welsh compatriots instead. There was considerable tension between the Welsh and the Irish in this part of Carbon County, corresponding to craft distinctions and discrimination in the mines.[5]

With the exception of the Burns and Powell cases, and some scattered violence in 1870, there was little by way of Molly Maguire activities again until 1873, the year James McParlan entered the anthracite region. By the end of 1873, violence was on the upsurge in the Schuylkill region, and by the end of the following year there had been two more Molly Maguire killings. Little is known about the second of these, the killing of the mine watchman Frederick Hesser at Shamokin, Northumberland County, on December 1, 1874. The case was attributed to the Molly Maguires only in 1878, when Peter McManus was convicted of first-degree murder.[6] The other case, the assassination of George Major on October 31, 1874, was a clear indication of the type of ethnic tensions afflicting northern Schuylkill County in the mid-1870s.[7]

The Major case was one of a series of violent clashes between the Welsh and Irish residents of northern Schuylkill County in 1874 and 1875. On August 2, 1874, for example, a group of Irish mine workers was attacked by a large force of Welsh and German miners at Connors Patch, Schuylkill County, and one of the attacking group was shot dead. On August 20, two Irish mine workers were attacked by a group of Welsh and German workers, and one of the Irishmen was killed.[8] The shooting of Major, during a drunken fight between rival Welsh and Irish fire companies in Mahanoy City early on the morning of Halloween 1874, was the next incident in this escalating pattern of interethnic violence. The violence reached its peak during and directly after the disastrous Long Strike of 1875. Though not all the victims were mine workers or officials, the material basis of the conflict was the pattern of discrimination in the workplace by which the best jobs were reserved for the British, and especially the Welsh. The response of some Irishmen to this situation was to resort to direct, retributive action, up to and including assassination. As the labor movement of the lower anthracite region fragmented in 1874 and 1875, ethnic violence of this sort became endemic, a development that makes sense only if it is recalled that the WBA had

5. MJ, March 29, 1878 (quote); Campbell, *A Molly Maguire Story,* 141–42. Whether the men actually convicted were guilty is another matter. See the discussion of their trial in chapter 8.

6. Schlegel, *Ruler of the Reading,* 147.

7. The Major case is discussed in chapter 6.

8. HSP, chronology of the period from July 3, 1874, to July 7, 1876, papers of Owen Hunt.

attempted, with considerable success, to transcend the differences of status and ethnicity that divided Irishmen and Welshmen in the coal fields.

The trouble in the summer of 1875 began in Mahanoy City, as part of the continued hostilities emanating from the killing of George Major the previous October. After Daniel Dougherty had been acquitted of killing Major in April, the Welsh "Modocs" had apparently sworn revenge. Late in May, Dougherty was attacked and shot by two men; the bullet passed through his clothing and he survived the attack unscathed.[9] According to McParlan's trial testimony, John Kehoe then called a convention of the AOH to avenge the assassination attempt on Dougherty. The convention met in Mahanoy City on June 1, 1875—just as the Long Strike was ending, amid scenes of violence and crowd protest in the Mahanoy Valley. Three men were blamed for the attack on Dougherty, two kinsmen of George Major (William and Jesse Major) and their fellow Welshman, William "Bully Bill" Thomas.[10]

McParlan, who was present at the meeting as de facto head of the Shenandoah division, testified that the following plan was agreed upon. As the Majors had by then left Mahanoy City and were working at a mine in Tuscarora, the AOH bodymaster (or division leader) in that region, John "Yellow Jack" Donahue, was assigned to take care of them, while the Shenandoah division would handle "Bully Bill" Thomas. McParlan testified that he notified Thomas Hurley, John Gibbons, and Michael Doyle of the plan. These three men then apparently decided to carry out the Thomas killing the following day. But troops had just been stationed in the Mahanoy Valley, following the disturbances over the weekend, and McParlan claimed to have dissuaded the men from carrying out their plan.[11] The return of the Shenandoah bodymaster, Frank McAndrew, relieved McParlan from the responsibility of planning the assassination. Hurley, Gibbons, and a mine worker named John Morris finally attempted to kill Thomas in a stable at Shoemaker's Patch, near Shenandoah, on the morning of June 28, 1875. Thomas was shot twice, but survived. At no point did McParlan make an attempt to warn him. At the trial of the defendants in the Thomas case, the defense cross-examined the detective on this point at length, seeking without success to portray him as an agent provocateur.[12]

The miner Gomer James was the next victim in the ongoing dispute between the Welsh and Irish residents of the Mahanoy Valley. American-born of

9. *MJ*, May 28, June 11, 1875.

10. See McParlan's testimony in RCK, 27–28, 58, 63–64, 82.

11. See McParlan's testimony in RCK, 27–28, 58, 63–64, 82. In November 1875 Thomas Hurley was arrested and charged with the attempted murder of "Bully Bill" Thomas and James Johns. Released on bail provided by McParlan, he disappeared and was never captured. During the trials of 1876, he was accused by McParlan of being the assassin of Gomer James. In a "List of Fugitive Mollie Maguires" (HSC, Molly Maguire Collection, Photo File) circulated by Pinkerton's National Detective Agency in 1879, Hurley (described as a twenty-five-year old miner, once resident in Shenandoah) was listed as the "Murderer of Gomer Jamas" [*sic*].

12. See McParlan's testimony in RCK, 27–28, 58, 63–64, 82. On the accusations during the trials that McParlan was an agent provocateur, see chapter 8.

Welsh parents, James had been acquitted of the murder of an AOH member, Edward Cosgrove, in Shenandoah in 1873. He was no doubt a marked man thereafter. As in the case of George Major, the immediate precondition for his assassination was an event involving a fire company. On August 14, 1875, James was tending bar at a picnic for the Rescue Hook and Ladder Company at Glover's Grove, just outside Shenandoah, the *Miners' Journal* reported, when a man armed with a revolver walked up to the bar and shot him dead. Though the killing occurred in broad daylight, the assassin apparently disappeared into the crowd, and nobody was arrested. The story that emerged at the trials the following year was that a "Molly Maguire" named Thomas Hurley had done the shooting, and that he had later approached the AOH for a reward. According to McParlan, the matter was discussed at a convention of the Schuylkill County AOH held at Tamaqua on August 25. On this evidence, seven Molly Maguires were convicted, in August 1876, of conspiracy to reward Thomas Hurley for murder.[13]

Gomer James was assassinated on what turned out to be the single most violent day in the summer of 1875. The *Miners' Journal* lamented the events of this drunken and violent payday with a banner headline: "A Bloody Night North of the Mountain. Squire Gwyther of Girardville Assassinated—Gomer James of Shenandoah Butchered at a Picnic—Fight in Mahanoy City and a Man Fatally Shot—'Bully Bill' in a Row and Comes to Jail—Man with an Oyster Knife in His Back."[14] In Girardville, the newspaper reported, gangs of armed men had roamed through the streets "absolutely rampant and defiant of lawful restraints." When a fight broke out at one of the town's taverns, the victim went to the office of Thomas Gwyther, justice of the peace, and swore out a warrant for the assailant's arrest. But, when Gwyther stepped out on the porch of his office to serve the warrant, he was shot dead. A man named Thomas Love was arrested for murder, but he was soon released on the grounds that the assassin had been his brother William, who had since fled the region.[15]

The final incident on this "Bloody Saturday" involved the Welshman "Bully Bill" Thomas, once again. This time, he engaged in a shoot-out with an Irishman named James Dugan on the main street of Mahanoy City, in which an innocent German bystander was hit by a stray bullet and killed.[16] Thomas was arrested for the assault on Dugan, but no charges were brought for the killing, presumably because Thomas decided to cooperate with the Coal & Iron Police, who needed evidence against the Molly Maguires. In August 1876 nine prominent AOH leaders were tried for conspiracy to murder Thomas; but Thomas himself, despite his violent reputation, never faced any charges. Not for the

13. *MJ*, August 20, 1875. Cf. the discussion of the trials in Chapter 8; Broehl, *The Molly Maguires*, 229–30, 328.

14. *MJ*, August 20, 1875.

15. Ibid.; William Love was named in the "List of Fugitive Mollie Maguires" circulated by the Pinkertons in 1879 (HSC, Molly Maguire Collection, Photo File).

16. *MJ*, August 20, 1875.

first time, many of the Irish residents of the anthracite region must have wondered whether there was one standard of justice for themselves, another for the Welsh.[17]

Although the last of the "Molly Maguire" assassinations was committed in September 1875, interethnic violence remained endemic in northern Schuylkill County for the remainder of the year. When, for example, the newspapers reported a "Night of Terror" at Shenandoah on October 9, 1875, the events in question bore a striking resemblance to many previous Saturday nights in the Mahanoy Valley, especially the ones on which George Major and Thomas Gwyther had been killed. On this single violent night in Shenandoah, an Irishman named John Heffron attempted to shoot Daniel Williams, a Welsh bartender at the National Hotel; another Irishman, Richard Finnen, was shot by an unknown assailant in Couch's Saloon, the bullet lodging in his head above the right eye; and at eleven o'clock a Welshman named Reese Thomas was arrested and jailed for firing a shot from his revolver. Over the next hour, shots were heard all over town. James Johns, a Welshman, was shot and had his throat cut; by midnight the streets were filled with crowds of men, and fifteen shots were fired into "Muff" Lawler's Irish tavern. On Sunday, the deputy sheriff issued a proclamation, and that night "the town was patrolled by one hundred special policemen, composed of the leading citizens of the place. Quiet was again restored."[18]

Here, once again, were the conditions in which countless Molly Maguire "outrages," including several killings, had been committed over the previous year. All of these incidents, and scores of other drunken scrapes and vendettas like them, were part of the general pattern of interethnic gang warfare that characterized the Mahanoy Valley in the mid-1870s. To dismiss this violence as drunken brawling, or as the settling of purely individual and personal grievances, is to ignore its relationship to the structure of work, society, and culture in the lower anthracite region. Ultimately, the violence makes sense only against the background of a general pattern of discrimination in the mines, along with the emergence of bitter divisions between the Welsh and the Irish as the labor movement fragmented in 1875.

Part of the conflict appears to have involved a power struggle within the ranks of organized labor over strategy, especially over the use of violence. This struggle had first become evident in the closing months of the Long Strike. By the summer of 1875, the inchoate, sporadic, and violent strategy embodied in "Molly Maguireism" had once again become the sole means of organization available to Irish mine workers. For the first time since the 1860s, the Molly Maguires could claim to be the voice of organized Irish labor, even if that voice was most unwelcome to many erstwhile trade unionists. Not by coincidence, the summer of 1875 was marked not only by ethnic feuding but by the

17. On the Thomas conspiracy trial, see chapter 8.

18. Dewees, *The Molly Maguires,* 235–37.

assassination of mine officials and public authority figures. A policeman, a justice of the peace, and two mining officials were assassinated, indicating that there was much more to the Molly Maguire violence of 1875 than ethnic conflict. Drawing on tactics first devised in the Irish countryside, a minority of Irish mine workers evidently tried to fill the vacuum left by the collapse of the trade union by turning to more desperate forms of resistance against their employers and the authorities.

On July 14, 1875, a policeman named Benjamin Yost was assassinated in Tamaqua. Born in Schuylkill County in 1841 of German parents, Yost had settled in Tamaqua in 1873, where he was appointed to the position of policeman by the borough council.[19] At the trials in Pottsville in 1876, a graphic narrative of the assassination was provided by Jimmy "Powderkeg" Kerrigan, the most infamous of the Molly Maguires to turn informer. A member of the Tamaqua division of the Ancient Order of Hibernians, Kerrigan turned state's evidence after he was arrested in connection with the assassination of the mine superintendent, John P. Jones, in which he freely admitted his own complicity.[20]

Kerrigan claimed that the killing of Benjamin Yost had been arranged by another member of the Tamaqua AOH, Thomas Duffy, who had been arrested and beaten up by the policeman. According to Kerrigan, the motive was revenge, pure and simple. Duffy had allegedly approached James Roarity, bodymaster of the nearby Coaldale lodge, offering him ten dollars to kill Yost, which Roarity accepted. James Carroll, a saloon-keeper who served as secretary of the Tamaqua lodge, was also involved in the plan, along with Hugh McGehan and James Boyle, two AOH members from Summit Hill and Storm Hill in Carbon County, a few miles east of Tamaqua.[21] According to Kerrigan's story, McGehan and Boyle waited at the local cemetery until Yost and his fellow-constable, Barney McCarron, arrived. Then, as Yost and McCarron were extinguishing the gas street lamps, McGehan and Boyle approached and shot Yost. Kerrigan stood in the cemetery watching from a distance of sixty or seventy yards. James McParlan corroborated Kerrigan's testimony in part, telling the court that McGehan had confessed his role in the murder and had implicated James Boyle and Jimmy Kerrigan. On this evidence, Carroll, Roarity, Boyle, McGehan, and Duffy were convicted of first-degree murder in 1876.[22]

The killing of a policeman is a serious matter, with serious consequences. It was surely not entered into as lightly as Kerrigan and McParlan claimed. Kerrigan admitted his own part in the assassination, and it is more than likely that he

19. *SH*, June 16, 1877.

20. For a concise account of the testimony of Kerrigan and McParlan in the Yost trial, see *Among the Assassins!*

21. *Among the Assassins!*, 6, 11–12, 18–21.

22. Ibid., 6, 11–12, 18–21. The trials are discussed in chapter 8.

twisted the story to meet the needs of the prosecution and to save his own neck. His own wife publicly denounced him as a liar, and testified in court that he had told her he had shot Yost himself.[23] The exact manner in which Kerrigan distorted the facts can never be known, but his testimony certainly enabled the prosecution to portray the Molly Maguires as gangsters, ready to kill at the slightest provocation. Yet, no doubt unwittingly, Kerrigan's story also contained some important information that suggests the outlines of a more concerted ideology and strategy, one which had much more to do with winning justice for Irish immigrant workers than with matters of personal aggrandizement or revenge.

Though it is impossible to know for certain what the assassins intended, Kerrigan's story about them contained two striking parallels with the pattern of violence in rural Ireland. The prominence of a saloon-keeper in the plot, and the use of men from a neighboring lodge to carry out the assassination, were frequently reported in contemporary accounts of other Molly Maguire crimes, and they provide important links with the pattern of agrarian protest in nineteenth-century Ireland. Together, they place the Molly Maguire violence of 1875 in a rather different light from the one shed upon the subject by detectives, informers, and courtroom orators, not to mention subsequent historians.

The institution of the tavern played a central role in the conspiracy described by Jimmy Kerrigan. McGehan, Duffy, Boyle, and Carroll had allegedly met at Carroll's saloon on the night of the murder. Carroll had asked Kerrigan to go and get a pistol from a neighboring saloon. But the other saloon-keeper was unable to furnish the gun, and McGehan and Boyle eventually left Carroll's saloon with a pistol provided by James Roarity (who was absent that night, as his wife was ill).[24] In his widely publicized confession, made a month before the Yost trial began in May 1876, Kerrigan explained how Carroll's saloon had once been owned by Alexander Campbell, the alleged Molly Maguire ringleader in Carbon County, who now kept a tavern at Summit Hill. He claimed to have been inducted into the AOH in the Tamaqua saloon at the time Campbell owned it, without suspecting that the AOH (as he now asserted) was simply the Molly Maguires under another name.[25]

Within the AOH, Kerrigan claimed, there was an inner ring of leaders, or bodymasters, most of whom were saloon- and tavern-keepers, who made up the nucleus of the Molly Maguires. A striking number of the men convicted of Molly Maguire crimes, including all the alleged ringleaders, kept taverns or hotels: Alexander Campbell (Storm Hill), James Carroll (Tamaqua), Thomas Fisher (Summit Hill), Patrick Hester (Locust Gap Junction), John Kehoe (Girardville), Michael "Muff" Lawler (Shenandoah), and Hugh McGehan (Summit Hill). At the trials, prosecuting attorneys like General Charles Albright distinguished between the "outer" and "inner" rings of the Molly Maguires, the top-brass of

23. See Mrs. Kerrigan's testimony in *MJ*, May 12, 1876.

24. *Among the Assassins!*, 6, 11–12, 18–21.

25. See Kerrigan's confession, *Philadelphia Inquirer*, April 6, 1876.

saloon-keepers and the pawns who carried out their orders.[26] The prominence of tavern-owners among the alleged Molly Maguire leaders adds a significant twist to the crusade against alcohol initiated by Benjamin Bannan in his nativist phase in the 1850s and joined in the 1870s by the Catholic church.[27]

At first sight, the crucial role of tavern-keepers might support the contention that the Molly Maguires were simply small-time gangsters devoid of any connection or solidarity with the mass of exploited mine workers. But this is surely to miss the point. Along with the Catholic church and the trade union, the tavern was one of the three central institutions in the lives of the Irish mine workers. And the tavern-keeper was one of the most powerful members of the immigrant community. It is scarcely surprising that assassinations would have been planned in taverns; nor is it surprising that tavern owners were among the alleged leaders of the conspiracy. Even if these men had never set foot in the mines, it seems fair to assume that they would have shared bonds of solidarity with their fellow countrymen, and especially their fellow countymen.

But the striking fact about the tavern-keepers in question is that most of them had worked in the mines before going into the liquor business. Alexander Campbell worked underground for a year and a half before opening the Columbia House in Tamaqua in 1870. Thomas Fisher worked in the mines at Summit Hill, Carbon County, before opening the Rising Sun Hotel there in 1872. John Kehoe was a miner before he opened his first tavern in Shenandoah in 1870. Hugh McGehan opened his tavern in Summit Hill only after he had been blacklisted by John P. Jones, a mine superintendent who was to be assassinated in Lansford, Carbon County, on September 3, 1875. And James Carroll kept the tavern in Tamaqua where the Yost killing had allegedly been planned. These men had bitter memories of their own days underground and they maintained intimate links of class and ethnicity with the mine workers who frequented their taverns. Unless this is understood, the Molly Maguire violence of 1875 makes little sense.[28]

This argument becomes all the more persuasive in light of the second hint on the organization of the Molly Maguires that emerges from the Yost killing, namely the tactic of reciprocity whereby favors were exchanged among the various lodges of the Ancient Order of Hibernians. Both McParlan and Kerrigan linked the Yost killing with the assassination of John P. Jones. The detective and the informer both testified that McGehan and Boyle, who were members of the AOH in that area, had participated in the Yost murder in order to secure the participation of Tamaqua men in the subsequent assassination of Jones. The alleged Molly Maguire ringleaders in the two areas in question were

26. Albright, *The Great Mollie Maguire Trials,* 31.

27. On Catholic support for temperance, see the Pottsville monthly *Emerald Vindicator,* June 1876.

28. For biographical details and sources, see appendix 1. Neither Carroll nor Hester appears to have worked in the mines. Nor does "Muff" Lawler, the Shenandoah tavern-keeper who turned state's evidence to save his neck.

the tavern-keepers James Carroll and Alexander Campbell. After Campbell's men had killed Yost, Kerrigan testified, the Tamaqua division was supposed to return the favor by killing Jones, who had already been marked for death by Campbell.[29] Thus, even if the Yost case is written off as a murder with no motive other than revenge, it takes on a different meaning when the tactic of reciprocity is borne in mind. Yost's assassination may have had no direct relation to conditions in the mines; but his killers expected that the members of the Tamaqua division of the AOH would return the favor by assassinating Jones, a Welsh mine superintendent who was hated by the Irish mine workers of Carbon County.

The existence of a reciprocal relationship between the AOH lodges was central to the prosecution's case at the trials, as it suggested a tightly meshed conspiratorial network stretching across the anthracite region. This idea soon made its way into contemporary newspaper accounts as well. In the words of the *Philadelphia Press:* "Under the Mollies' code, it was only necessary for the 'Body Master' or president of one Lodge to will a man's death. He could then call upon the Body Master of any other Lodge to furnish the assassins, and it was only common courtesy to grant the request."[30] Early histories of the Molly Maguires repeated this claim.[31] Though the extent of the conspiracy was exaggerated, this idea of reciprocity was not simply invented by the enemies of the Molly Maguires. Reciprocity has always been considered one of the hallmarks of agrarian violence in Ireland, the chief advantage being that killers brought in from outside would not be recognized.[32]

Immigrants from Donegal, in particular, clearly maintained close ties of kinship and community in the anthracite region, with the tavern functioning as a central institution in this respect. Here the tavern owners, who had often themselves worked in the mines in the recent past, listened to the immigrant workers' tales of life, labor, and discrimination underground. In some cases, they evidently organized direct action in response. This certainly seems to have been so in the related assassinations of Yost and Jones, which together get to the heart of the Molly Maguire conspiracy of 1875, such as it was. It never approached the heights of sophistication or the depths of evil attributed to it by others; but it was a deadly and desperate form of violence nonetheless.

The assassination of John P. Jones on September 3, 1875, was one of two similar incidents that brought the cycle of Molly Maguire assassinations to a close, the other being the killings of Thomas Sanger and William Uren two days earlier. Sanger and Uren were shot dead by a group of five men who attacked them on their way to work. The incident occurred at Raven Run, a mile

29. See Kerrigan's confession, *Philadelphia Inquirer,* April 6, 1876; and the summary of his evidence in the Yost trial in *Among the Assassins!,* 18–21.

30. *Philadelphia Press,* June 21, 1877; see, also, *New York Herald,* September 23, 1876.

31. See, for example, Rhodes, *History of the United States, 1850–1896,* vol. 8, 54; Rhodes, "The Molly Maguires in the Anthracite Region of Pennsylvania," 548.

32. See, for example, Beames, "Rural Conflict in Pre-famine Ireland," 278.

north of Girardville, Schuylkill County. Born at Germae, Cornwall, in 1842, Sanger had emigrated to the United States with a small group of his townsmen in 1861. After working as a miner in Northumberland County, he went to California in 1866 to work in the gold mines. He soon returned to the anthracite region, where he found employment as a skilled miner in Girardville. In September 1873 he was appointed inside boss at Heaton's Colliery in Raven Run. Sanger had already received several "coffin notices" before he was killed. Uren, the young Cornish miner who was killed with him, boarded with the Sanger family and accompanied Sanger to work most mornings. He was presumably killed to prevent him from identifying Sanger's assassins. "It is one of the gravest charges against the secret society known as the 'Molly Maguires,'" the *Miners' Journal* reported on September 2, "that its members do this kind of work as a part of their society's 'business,' without a scruple or compunction."[33]

The motive in the Sanger-Uren case was never determined. Sanger was not killed for his money; nor does revenge appear to have been an issue. The attack was probably related to the enforcement of some desired code of operation at the mine where Sanger worked, but there is no way of knowing for certain. McParlan named Michael Doyle, James McAllister, and two brothers, James and Charles O'Donnell, as the assassins. McAllister and the O'Donnells lived at Wiggans Patch, a small mine patch near Mahanoy City, which later that year went down in local history as the site of a brutal attack by vigilantes.[34]

The final assassination attributed to the Molly Maguires was that of the mine superintendent John P. Jones. Born at Shenhowe, Wales, in 1832, Jones came to the United States with his parents in 1852 and settled in Tamaqua. He worked first as a laborer for his sister's husband, a miner named Daniel Carrington. Then, like most Welshmen in the region, he became a full-fledged miner. After an unsuccessful trip to California in search of gold, he returned to Schuylkill County and worked as a miner in Centralia, and then in Ashton, where after a few years he was promoted to the rank of mine superintendent.[35] McParlan claimed to have been appointed as one of the "Mollys" who would kill Jones, along with Thomas Munley, Michael Darcy, and John McGrail. Then, late on the night before the assassination, he learned that Jimmy Kerrigan and two other men had already left to carry out the assassination. Kerrigan, who had turned informer by the time the trial began, confirmed this story, admitted his own part in the assassination, and named his two accomplices as Michael J. Doyle and Edward Kelly, both of them members of the AOH in Mount Laffee.

33. *Pottsville Evening Chronicle,* September 1, 1875; *MJ,* September 2, 1875; [Barclay & Co.], *The Lives and Crimes of the Mollie Maguires* (Philadelphia, 1877), 30–33 (hereafter referred to as Barclay, *Lives and Crimes*).

34. James "Friday" O'Donnell and Michael Doyle were also named as the killers of Sanger and Uren in the "List of Fugitive Mollie Maguires" circulated by the Pinkertons in 1879 (HSC, Molly Maguire Collection, Photo File). On McParlan's views on the case, see Broehl, *The Molly Maguires,* 231–33.

35. Barclay, *Lives and Crimes,* 21–22.

Unlike most of the other Molly Maguires, Kerrigan, Doyle, and Kelly were American-born; but, by dint of the connection of the Jones case with the assassination of Benjamin Yost, they were part of a reciprocal network controlled by men from County Donegal.[36]

According to Kerrigan's testimony, the three assassins spent the night before the assassination drinking at the saloons of Alexander Campbell and Hugh McGehan, before killing Jones at Lansford railway station the following morning. Kerrigan, Doyle, and Kelly were arrested shortly afterward in some nearby woods by a local posse and brought back to Lansford. A large crowd gathered, and as the *Pottsville Evening Chronicle* reported, "They wanted to get hold of the prisoners to hang them without trial. In the minds of the people they were already found guilty and could the mob have gained access to the prisoners, they would have been strung up like dogs." For their own safety, the prisoners were removed to Mauch Chunk, the county seat, to await trial.[37]

John P. Jones was a superintendent for the Lehigh & Wilkes-Barre Coal Company, the same position that Morgan Powell had held when he was assassinated four years earlier. According to the *Miners' Journal,* indeed, some of the conspirators in the Powell case in 1871 had wanted to kill Jones instead.[38] In each case a prominent Welsh mining official was killed because he discriminated against Irish workers. Morgan Powell had allegedly favored Welshmen over Alexander Campbell, who swore revenge; Jones had blacklisted Hugh McGehan, who then participated in the murder of Benjamin Yost in Tamaqua in July, so that the Tamaqua lodge would furnish the men to kill Jones.[39] In this way, the Yost killing had been caught up in a larger conspiracy that directly involved conditions of labor in the mines. The Jones assassination may also have had an indirect link with the killing of Gomer James two weeks earlier.[40]

Serious questions surround the role of James McParlan in the assassinations of Sanger, Uren, and Jones. He clearly knew of the plot to kill Sanger at least one day in advance. McParlan named the men assigned to kill Sanger in a report dated August 31, 1875, the day before the assassinations took place. Apparently, the report was not received by Benjamin Franklin in Philadelphia until September 2, the day after Sanger and Uren were killed.[41] Why, then, did McParlan not notify Captain Linden or warn Sanger directly? His failure to act in the Jones case is even more troubling, as the plans for this assassination were known long in advance. Several reports by Captain Linden in July and August

36. See the summary of the Yost and Jones assassinations in *Among the Assassins!*

37. *Pottsville Evening Chronicle,* September 4, 1875.

38. *MJ,* March 29, 1878. On the Powell case, see chapter 4.

39. See the evidence of McParlan and Kerrigan in the Yost trial, as summarized in *Among the Assassins!*

40. The same AOH county convention at Tamaqua on August 25 that discussed Thomas Hurley's claim to a "reward" for killing Gomer James allegedly laid the final plans for the assassination of John P. Jones.

41. Cf. Broehl, *The Molly Maguires,* 231.

confirm that the Pinkertons had received advance warning of the plan from McParlan. On July 31, for example, Linden reported that "the Summit Hill assassination has been postponed." On August 5 he reported that "Jones is the boss who will be assassinated, but it has been postponed until the last of the month, and after the Molly Maguire convention which is to be held at Tamaqua, on the 25th inst." On August 13 he noted that "it has been decided that the Jones affair shall take place immediately after the M.M.'s convention on the 25th," and on August 27 he reported that "operative J.McF. had volunteered to accompany them and was accepted."[42] Did McParlan allow Sanger and Uren to be killed so that he could accumulate evidence against the Molly Maguires? Was the detective an agent provocateur?

Like so much else in the Molly Maguire story, these questions cannot be answered definitively. Even without McParlan, there would have been plenty of violence in the anthracite region, especially in the wake of the Long Strike. The assassinations committed in the 1870s were not contingent on the presence or absence of a single Pinkerton detective. Their origins are to be found in wider social developments, especially the defeat and fragmentation of the labor movement. Yet, there is no doubt that McParlan participated in the planning of some of the Molly Maguire assassinations, that he knew about several of them in advance, and that he did little to prevent them or to warn the victims. The weight of the evidence in the Sanger, Uren, and Jones cases is that McParlan let these killings go ahead in order to accumulate evidence. Strictly speaking, that may not make him an agent provocateur, but it speaks volumes about the measures that were taken to bring the Molly Maguires to justice in the violent summer of 1875.[43]

The collapse of the trade union early that summer had opened the way for the reemergence of the Molly Maguires, who briefly and violently became the unofficial voice of labor in the lower anthracite region. Further evidence to support this argument can be found in a letter published in the *Shenandoah Herald* a month after the second wave of Molly Maguire assassinations had ended. On October 2, 1875, Thomas J. Foster published a letter from "A Molley" in Mahanoy City explaining why the violence had taken place. If this letter is genuine (and there is no reason to suppose that it is not), it is a uniquely valuable piece of historical evidence.[44] Virtually all the other contemporary accounts of the Molly Maguires were written by hostile observers, except for a few confessions signed by informers and convicts and a letter by John Kehoe

42. HML, A 1520, report of BF to FBG, October 20, 1875, reports of Captain Linden on July 31, August 5, 13, 27, 1875.

43. On McParlan's possible role as an agent provocateur, see Broehl, *The Molly Maguires,* 175–76, 211–17, 265, 299–300, 302, 308–9, 326–27.

44. It is difficult to see why Thomas J. Foster of the *Herald* would have fabricated this letter, given that it maintained what he so steadfastly denied: that the Molly Maguires had a motivation and justification.

denying that the AOH and the Molly Maguires were the same organization.[45] The letter published by the *Herald* is the only source that provides a direct insight into the motivation of the Molly Maguires at the time the violence was occurring.

According to the "Molley" who wrote to the *Herald,* he and his brethren were attempting to win the goals of the trade union, but through different means. "i am against shooting as mutch as ye are," he informed Foster. "But the union is Broke up and we Have got nothing to defind ourselves with But our Revolvers and if we dount use them we shal have to work for 50 cints a Day." As for "the other nationalateys," they would also have adopted the same tactics as the Molly Maguires, "onley that they are to Damd cowardley." The aims of the Molly Maguires were simple: just wages and fair working conditions. In the "Molley's" own words: "i have told ye the Mind of the children of Mistress Molly Maguire, all we want is a fare Days wages for a fare Days work, and thats what we cant get now By a Long shot."[46] The same phrase, "a fair day's work for a fair days pay," was used by the leaders of the WBA and the Molly Maguires, even if their strategies for achieving this goal were starkly different. Only the trade union had come close to acquiring respectability, but the invocation of "Mistress Molly Maguire" stakes a claim to a similar level of legitimacy for the Irish tradition of violent protest.[47] And it is particularly interesting that the letter closes on a defiant, insurgent note, rather than a defensive one, warning that the children of Mistress Maguire will "make it Hot as Hell" for the employers if they continue to violate the Molly Maguires' sense of justice.

The six killings of 1875 took place under different circumstances, but they had certain features in common. Chief among these was the tactic of enforcing retributive justice directly. If the Molly Maguires wanted to improve conditions at a mine, or to challenge the prevailing system of policing and justice, or to avenge an insult from a Welshman, they were likely to do so by construing the opposition in individual rather than collective terms, by attacking or killing a single, immediate enemy rather than embarking on a program of systematic change. Here the contrast with the trade union movement could not be greater. Not only had the union leaders advocated a systematic vision of labor relations, they had unequivocally eschewed the use of violence as a strategy in labor disputes. Even after the defeat of the Long Strike and the collapse of the union, they remained steadfast in their denunciations of violence.

On September 4, 1875, for example, the *Pottsville Workingman* denounced

45. The confessions, which are discussed in chapters 8 and 9, typically blame the Molly Maguire violence on some combination of evil, alcohol, and atheism. For Kehoe's letter, see SH, June 8, 1876.

46. SH, October 2, 1875.

47. The phrase, as used by the union men, is excerpted from an official notice issued in Mahanoy City, June 9, 1869, signed by John Parker and Thomas M. Williams; quoted in Evans, *History of the United Mine Workers of America,* vol. 1, 19.

the killings of Sanger and Uren as a "terrible deed, the perpetrators of which should be hunted down and punished; not by Lynch Law but by the proper tribunal, in the courts of Schuylkill County."[48] Ninety-nine percent of the workers in the county were honest and law-abiding, the *Workingman* insisted; far from applauding or sheltering the murderers of Sanger and Uren, they "lent their services willingly and fearlessly to the pursuit of them." The "recent outbreak of outlawry north of the mountain," the *Workingman* concluded, was the result of "'nationality disputes' fomented in large part by the enemies of the Union." By contrast, when the union had prospered, it had been "a most effective conservator of law and order."[49]

Even Robert Ramsey, who had castigated the leaders of the WBA as a group of violent terrorists the previous June, now finally admitted that the WBA and the Molly Maguires were very different organizations. "The two societies are distinct, and in a measure, though not wholly, independent of each other," the *Miners' Journal* conceded on September 10, 1875; "they may be distinguished by the character of their actions—the W.B.A. strikes at the pocket, the Molly Maguires at the heart."[50] Even if some of their immediate goals were the same, the ideology and strategy of trade unionism and Molly Maguireism had always been fundamentally different. With the collapse of the WBA in the summer of 1875, Molly Maguireism briefly and violently emerged, for a minority of Irish mine workers, as an alternative mode of protest and organization. But the forces arrayed against the Molly Maguires were soon to prove overwhelming.

Ultimately, the activities engaged in by the Molly Maguires in 1875 make sense only in terms of violence being met by violence. If direct retributive justice was a matter of taking the law into one's own hands, the Molly Maguires had a counterpart among citizens of the anthracite region who soon proved to be more than their match. Violent tactics employed against the Irish mine workers ranged from the legal (public police) to the quasi-legal (private police) to the extralegal (vigilante committees). Indeed, the distinctions between these tactics were quite arbitrary, and a concerted combination of all three was used to counterattack the Molly Maguires in 1875. Private detectives were deputized into the Coal & Iron Police and provided information to vigilante committees, who used it to deadly effect. Rights of assembly by workingmen were severely curtailed in the last months of the Long Strike. Workingmen could demonstrate only under pain of arrest, and troops were stationed in Hazleton, Shamokin, and the Mahanoy Valley of northern Schuylkill County between

48. *Pottsville Workingman,* September 4, 1875.

49. Ibid.

50. *MJ,* September 10, 1875.

April and June 1875.[51] By 1876 the full force of the local judicial apparatus would be arrayed against the Molly Maguires as well.

Those who write the history of violence and public disorder need to remember, as one historian of labor has observed, that in the evidence "certain kinds of violence are singled out for attention—mostly on administrative, legal, political or moral grounds *by the authorities or the upper classes*." On these grounds, an arbitrary distinction between violence and nonviolence can be justified.

> The crucial criterion would be the distinction not between force and non-violence, but between different kinds of force or violence, and the crucial variable not the miners' willingness to use force, but the employers' or the authorities' determination to resist strikes and the means they were prepared to use.[52]

In the anthracite region in the 1870s the Workingmen's Benevolent Association stood out as one of the few institutions that unequivocally opposed violence. A minority of Irish immigrant workers, by contrast, turned to violence in desperation; and the employers and the state authorities were more than willing to respond in kind.

In 1875 the most important weapon in the counterattack against labor violence was private police power, supplemented by the services of Pinkerton's National Detective Agency. One reason why private detectives were employed in the anthracite region was that the Coal & Iron Police, who were required to wear badges and uniforms, could not be used for undercover work. On the other hand, the detectives had no powers of arrest and detention. Some combination of these two forms of policing was needed, and in May 1875 just such a combination was created as the Long Strike drew to a bitter and violent close. On April 28, with the strike about to enter its fifth month, Allan Pinkerton came to Philadelphia to consult Franklin B. Gowen. Plans were made for a "flying squadron" of police to be set up to patrol the coal fields.[53] This squadron was to consist of seven Pinkerton agents, along with an equal number of men picked from the ranks of the Coal & Iron Police. The squadron was to be commanded by a Pinkerton operative, and for this job Allan Pinkerton called on one of his most trusted agents, Captain Robert J. Linden, who had been with the agency since shortly after the Civil War.

After meeting with Benjamin Franklin and Allan Pinkerton in Philadelphia, Linden went to the coal fields on May 3, 1875. He stopped first at Schuylkill Haven, where he was met by James McParlan. The next day, in Pottsville, Linden went to see General Henry Pleasants, the veteran of the "Battle of the

51. See the proclamations of Sheriff Werner of Schuylkill County (April 1, 1875) and Governor Hartranft of Pennsylvania (April 3, 1875), both in *Pottsville Standard,* April 3, 1875. See, also, *MJ,* June 11, 1875; Munsell, *History of Schuylkill County,* 241; Schlegel, *Ruler of the Reading,* 70; Schlegel, "The Workingmen's Benevolent Association," 263.

52. Eric Hobsbawm, *Workers: Worlds of Labor* (New York, 1984), 10–11; italics in original.

53. Schlegel, *Ruler of the Reading,* 105; Broehl, *The Molly Maguires,* 192.

Crater" who commanded the Coal & Iron Police. A "flying squadron" was organized, consisting of seven Pinkerton agents, including Linden, and seven non-Pinkertons headed by Captain W. J. Heisler. The Pinkerton agents were sworn in as members of the Coal & Iron Police at Pottsville courthouse, Linden assuming the rank of captain. The "flying squadron" was then dispatched to several locations in the vicinity of Ashland, in northern Schuylkill County.[54] This infusion of Pinkerton agents transformed the Coal & Iron Police from a force of mine guards into an effective policing agency. By the time the Coal & Iron Police and the Pinkertons joined forces in May 1875 the striking mine workers were on the point of submission. The new force therefore played only a limited role during the Long Strike, which had little more than a month to run. But the force was organized with longer-term goals in mind, specifically the accumulation of concrete evidence on the basis of which Molly Maguires could be arrested, convicted, and hanged once the WBA had been broken.[55]

In addition to accumulating evidence, the Pinkertons and their "flying squadron" became involved in one of the most controversial incidents in the history of the anthracite region, the vigilante attack at Wiggans Patch on the morning of December 10, 1875. Given the general turbulence in the anthracite region in the 1860s and 1870s, it is perhaps not surprising that there were frequent calls for the formation of vigilante committees. Newspapermen like Benjamin Bannan and Thomas J. Foster had been discussing the merits of vigilantism in occasional editorials since at least 1870. The very first issue of Foster's *Shenandoah Herald,* on May 28, 1870, had announced that "crime is getting to be as common in this county as in California, in the days of Vigilance Committees," adding that "perhaps, if things continue this way long, the talk of them here, a few weeks ago, may prove to be something more than mere talk."[56] Benjamin Bannan had taken a tentative step in the same direction the following year, hinting that if the authorities failed to act there existed an alternative. "Nobody can justify Lynch law, except under very peculiar circumstances but such circumstances sometimes occur," Bannan warned. "It did in San Francisco, and a number of scoundrels were tried on the spot, and hung by a Vigilance Committee." Such desperate measures had been justified, he insisted, as they alone could "remove the evil" and restore "peace and quietness" to San Francisco.[57]

These vague threats grew more intense and focused in 1874 and 1875. A week after the killing of George Major on October 31, 1874, for example,

54. HML, A 1520, B 1001, F2, reports of Captain Linden, in report of BF to FBG, June 15, 1875.

55. Broehl, *The Molly Maguires,* 194.

56. *SH,* May 28, 1870.

57. *MJ,* March 25, 1871. The repeated references to San Francisco in the calls for a vigilante movement are particularly interesting, as the vigilante movement in California had in part been a pogrom directed at Irish Catholic immigrants. See Miller, *Emigrants and Exiles,* 323; Patrick Blessing, "Culture, Religion, and the Activities of the Committee of Vigilance, San Francisco, 1858," Working paper, Series 8, no. 3, Cushwa Center for the Study of American Catholicism.

Robert Ramsey of the *Miners' Journal* called for "one good, wholesome hanging, gently but firmly administered," and he clearly had a specific person in mind: Major's alleged killer, Daniel Dougherty.[58] Ramsey did not specify whether the hanging was to be legal or extralegal, but at the time he wrote, Dougherty was in imminent danger of being lynched in Mahanoy City jail and had to be removed to Pottsville for protection. By September 1875, after six more Molly Maguire killings in only four months, calls for vigilantism were being made quite openly. In Tamaqua, the editors of the *Courier* announced that "desperate diseases require desperate remedies." "What is to be done?" the *Courier* asked on September 4, 1875. The answer: "Something that will strike terror into their base hearts and make them flee before an outraged community. . . . Who can blame the friends of the victims if they demanded an eye for an eye, a tooth for a tooth and blood for blood. Something *must* be done; that something must be *sure*, swift and terrible."[59]

When a coal breaker was burned shortly afterward, the *Pottsville Evening Chronicle* suspected arson and blamed the Molly Maguires. "The outrage season is not yet over," the *Chronicle* reported, "and though but a short time has elapsed since the 'Mollies' perpetrated their last fiendish work of deviltry, they are again at it." As the men who set the fire were strangers who would never be found, and as there was "not a single doubt that it was the work of the 'Mollie Maguires,'" the *Chronicle* recommended that "we must have some kind of a vigilance committee, and the sooner it is organized the better for the whole region. These men deserve no mercy, and should be strung up wherever they are caught."[60]

Thomas Foster of the *Shenandoah Herald* issued the most intemperate calls for vigilante action. Shenandoah was the reputed center of Molly Maguireism in the anthracite region, and while Foster was generally quite sympathetic to the WBA, he outspokenly opposed the Molly Maguires. On September 4, 1875, in the aftermath of the assassinations of Jones, Sanger, and Uren, Foster declared that "this state of affairs has lasted too long, and something has got to be done immediately. A remedy that will strike terror into the hearts of such cowardly assassins, is what is wanted and must be had." To end the "reign of terror," the "ruffians" of Schuylkill County must be shown that "'law is right, and right is might.'" Lest there be any doubt about what Foster had in mind, he cited with approval the case of a "vigilance committee" in California and announced that "we are forced to take the same course." The first Molly Maguire "strung up" would "strike terror into the hearts of his cowardly associates."[61]

Foster continued to publish remarkably intemperate editorials throughout September and October 1875. The "day of cowardly assassinations," Foster warned, was about "to close with a sunset of bloody hue, but it will be followed

58. *MJ*, November 6, 1874.

59. *Tamaqua Courier*, September 4, 1875.

60. *Pottsville Evening Chronicle*, October 6, 1875.

61. *SH*, September 4, 1875.

by a sunrise in a purer, better and much more safe moral and social atmosphere."[62] It is impossible to determine how much Foster knew and the extent to which he was personally involved, but it is clear from the evidence that vigilante committees had already been established in Schuylkill County by this time, with the direct collusion of the Pinkertons. The Pinkertons, of course, were no strangers to vigilantism. They had apparently cooperated with vigilantes in the lynching of nine members of the Reno gang, including the three Reno brothers, in Indiana in 1868.[63] And, in the case of the James gang in 1875, they adopted tactics that, despite the institutional cover of a registered detective agency, were indistinguishable from vigilantism.[64]

The tactics employed by the Pinkertons elsewhere in the United States in 1875, and the frame of mind exhibited in Pinkerton's letters at this time, provide the context for understanding the events that unfolded in Schuylkill County in the latter part of that year. After Benjamin Yost was killed in Tamaqua on July 5, 1875, local citizens formed a committee to track down his killers. The committee was led by Michael Beard, a close friend of Yost's, and Daniel Shepp, a brother-in-law of Mrs. Yost. They apparently turned to the Pinkertons for help, writing to Benjamin Franklin at the agency's Philadelphia office. Unknown to them, Franklin was the man in charge of the undercover agents already operating in the anthracite region. He accepted the commission, and within a few days McParlan was in Tamaqua investigating the Yost killing, though it is highly unlikely that Shepp and Beard knew anything about him.[65]

What is known for certain is that the Pinkertons were providing information to vigilantes in Schuylkill County, and that Allan Pinkerton had come out in favor of desperate measures by the end of the summer of 1875. The most persuasive evidence for this assertion is a letter from Allan Pinkerton to George Bangs, dated August 29, 1875. Pinkerton began this extraordinary letter by quoting from a "dispatch" he had already sent to Bangs: "If Linden can get up vigilence [sic] committee that can be relied upon, do so. When M.M's meet, then surround and deal summarily with them. Get off quietly. All should be securely masked." Pinkerton proceeded to inform Bangs that "the M.M.'s are a species of Thugs. . . . The only way then to pursue that I can see is, to treat them in the same manner as the Reno's were treated in Seymour, Indiana. After they were done away with, the people improved wonderfully and now Seymour is quite a town." In the same way, Captain Linden's new "vigilence [sic]

62. SH, September 17, 18, 25, 1875; October 2, 9, 16, 23, 30, 1875; quote, October 2.

63. Morn, *The Eye That Never Sleeps,* 78; Broehl, *The Molly Maguires,* 239–40. For references by Allan Pinkerton to the Seymour case, see LC, Pinkerton MS, Letterpress Copybook iv: AP to George Bangs, April 17, 1874; AP to Alfred Gaither, November 1, 1874; AP to A.P. Charles, November 4, 1874.

64. LC, Pinkerton MS, Letterpress Copybook iv, AP to George Bangs, April 17, 1874; AP to Mrs. Askew, May 11, 1875.

65. Broehl, *The Molly Maguires,* 222–23. On the possible involvement of the informer James Kerrigan with the Pinkertons and vigilantes long before his confession of April 1876, see Campbell, *A Molly Maguire Story,* 104–7.

committee" should "pounce upon the M.M's . . . , take the fearful responsibility and disperse."[66]

Another significant piece of evidence is a list of names and addresses of suspected Molly Maguires drawn up by the Pinkertons and addressed to "The Vigilance Committee of the Anthracite Coal Region."[67] The report is undated, but it can have been written only between September 3 and December 10, 1875. It gives details on the "outrages" of 1875 and names the men considered responsible. Thomas Hurley was named as the chief culprit in the Thomas shooting and as the assassin of Gomer James. Hugh McGehan, James Boyle, and Jimmy Kerrigan were named as the killers of Benjamin Yost. William Love was named as Thomas Gwyther's assassin, and Michael Boyle [sic], Edward Kelly, and Jimmy Kerrigan as the assassins of John P. Jones. The killers of Sanger and Uren were named as James "Friday" O'Donnell, his brother Charles O'Donnell, Thomas Munley, Charles McAllister, and Mike Doyle.[68]

The addresses of the suspects were also listed, along with their rank in the Ancient Order of Hibernians. The O'Donnells and McAllister were listed as living at Wiggans Patch, a small mine patch near Mahanoy City. The household was presided over by the widow Margaret O'Donnell, who lived there with her sons Charles and James, and her daughter Ellen, along with Ellen's husband Charles McAllister, and their infant child. A second daughter of Margaret O'Donnell, Mary Ann, was married to John Kehoe, the Schuylkill County delegate of the AOH and the alleged kingpin of the Molly Maguires. Another "Molly Maguire," James Carroll, had married one of Mrs. O'Donnell's nieces. Natives of Gweedore, the O'Donnells were one of many extended families in northern Schuylkill County that had come to the anthracite region from west Donegal. There were four paying guests in the household, Tom Murphy, John Purcell, James Blair, and James McAllister (a brother of Charles).[69]

Intriguingly, a first cousin of the four O'Donnell siblings, Patrick O'Donnell of Gweedore, was soon to gain notoriety in Ireland in one of the best-known political assassinations of the century, the killings of Lord Frederick Cavendish and T. H. Burke in Dublin on May 6, 1882. One of the suspected assassins, James Carey, turned informer, and on his evidence five men were hanged for the assassination in May 1883. Two months later, Carey set sail for Africa; on board, he

66. LC, Pinkerton MS, Letterpress Copybook iv, AP to George Bangs, August 29, 1875.

67. PCA, Molly Maguire Collection, report "To the Vigilance Committee of the Anthracite Coal Region and All Other Good Citizens Who Desire to Preserve Law and Order in Their Midst," n.d.

68. The report included details on all the killings of 1875 up to September 3. Charles O'Donnell, James "Friday" O'Donnell, and Charles McAllister were listed as living at Wiggans Patch, but by the evening of December 10 Charles O'Donnell had been killed and the other two men had fled.

69. The Pinkerton report misspelled the location as "Weigan's Patch." Margaret O'Donnell's husband, Manus, had emigrated with the family and was present in the anthracite region at the time of his daughter's marriage to Kehoe in 1866. By 1875, however, he was apparently no longer living. Cf. McCarthy, *The Great Molly Maguire Hoax*, 101.

became involved in an altercation with Patrick O'Donnell, who produced a revolver and shot him dead. In November 1883 O'Donnell was convicted of murder, and on December 17 he was hanged in London.[70] The exact nature of O'Donnell's motivation is unknown, but he is commemorated in Gweedore today by a well-known ballad and a public monument. Like so many other men from Donegal, he had left his native county for America in the late 1850s. Born in 1840, he spent some or all of the time between 1857 and 1882 in the United States, and there is some evidence that he lived with his brother Michael in Wiggans Patch, the same mining patch where his cousins resided. Evidently, he returned to the British Isles just in time to kill Carey.[71]

With its extended family network and paying boarders, the O'Donnell household in Wiggans Patch was quite typical of domestic arrangements among mine workers in the anthracite region. What distinguished it was that it was home to three alleged "Molly Maguires" who had been named by the Pinkertons as the assassins of Sanger and Uren the previous September. At three o'clock on the morning of December 10, 1875, a party of more than thirty armed and masked men descended on the household. Charles McAllister was able to escape into the house next door through a wooden partition in the cellar. But his mother-in-law, Mrs. O'Donnell, was pistol-whipped, and his pregnant wife, Ellen, was shot dead as she came downstairs. Thomas Murphy was questioned but left unharmed; John Purcell was tied to a bedpost; James Blair was taken downstairs and had a noose placed round his neck, before being released when he gave his name. James McAllister and the two O'Donnell brothers were taken outside to the yard, where they broke free and tried to run away. James O'Donnell managed to escape, as did McAllister, though he was hit by a bullet in the arm as he fled. Charles O'Donnell was not so lucky. He was shot at least fifteen times in the head. A piece of paper was found near the body, with the following words scrawled on it: "You are the murderers of Uren and Sanger."[72]

Who was responsible? Most contemporaries acknowledged that vigilantes had conducted the attack at Wiggans Patch, though some contended that the incident had stemmed from faction fighting among rival Irish gangs, or even a feud within the Molly Maguires. One theory was that the Molly Maguires had killed some of their own men in order to silence them. In Boston, for example, the *Pilot* reported that "the shooting grew out of a previous shooting affair, the facts of which the O'Donnells were aware of, and it is as though the murderers

70. Ó Gallchobhair, *History of Landlordism in Donegal,* chapter 5.

71. For this information I am indebted to Máirín Seoighe of Scannáin Dobharchú Film and Television Production, Machaire Clochair, Na Doirí Beaga, County Donegal.

72. *SH,* December 10, 11, 1875; *Pottsville Evening Chronicle,* December 10, 11, 1875; *MJ,* December 11, 1875; *Pottsville Standard,* December 11, 1875; *Philadelphia Evening Telegraph,* December 11, 1875; *Philadelphia Evening Telegraph,* December 11, 1875; *NYT,* December 11, 1875.

found it necessary to silence them for fear of damaging evidence in their possession."[73] The *Pottsville Standard* reported that "some old grudge is at the bottom of this trouble and that threats of violence have frequently been made against the O'Donnell family, who were possessors of certain ugly secrets in regard to some of the recent acts of lawlessness in that locality."[74]

This idea also resurfaced during the trials when an informer, John Slattery, accused John Kehoe of organizing the killings in order to silence the men who had killed Sanger and Uren.[75] But, since Kehoe was married to the sister of Charles and James O'Donnell and Ellen McAllister, this theory always seemed far-fetched, even to those who believed in the diabolical nature of the Molly Maguires.[76] As for the theory that a rival gang was involved, the *Miners' Journal* and the *Philadelphia Evening Telegraph* reported rumors that the O'Donnell family had recently been in a fight with a gang in Gilberton, and that the Gilberton gang had now taken its revenge.[77] But neither newspaper found these rumors particularly convincing, and both concluded that it was much more likely that the attack had been committed by vigilantes in revenge for the killings of Sanger and Uren. The *Pottsville Evening Chronicle* insisted that "a Vigilance Committee" was responsible.[78] Fr. Daniel McDermott, in an article written in 1877, complained that the men responsible for the vigilante killings at Wiggans Patch had still not been arrested. "With very little effort on the part of the authorities these offenders could long since have been brought to justice," McDermott claimed. "Who counselled, abetted and committed the Wiggans massacre has long been an open secret."[79] He did not choose to reveal their names, however, and they cannot be deduced from the surviving evidence.

A more equivocal opinion on Wiggans Patch can be found in an unpublished memoir by Thomas J. Foster of the *Shenandoah Herald*. "When it became clear that available courts and police were inadequate to deal with the situation, and that organized opposition was futile," Foster wrote, "then, under the name of the Committee of Safety, was formed an oath-bound society of preventers and avengers whose planning was as hidden and whose purpose was as indomitable as was the procedure of the organization against which they were aligned." But, according to Foster, the Committee of Safety was not responsible for the "bloody reprisals" at Wiggans Patch, which had instead been committed by an "unofficial" vigilante committee.[80] This distinction between an official

73. *Boston Pilot,* December 18, 1875.

74. *Pottsville Standard,* December 11, 1875.

75. Broehl, *The Molly Maguires,* 263.

76. Dewees, *The Molly Maguires,* 239–40.

77. *MJ,* December 11, 16, 1875; *Philadelphia Evening Telegraph,* December 11, 1875.

78. *Pottsville Evening Chronicle,* December 11, 1875.

79. *Catholic Standard* (Philadelphia), June 30, 1877.

80. PCA, Molly Maguire Collection, vol. 1, Miscellaneous Publications, typed copy of a thirty-thousand-word manuscript on the Molly Maguires by Foster. The manuscript was apparently dictated by Foster to a Mr. Dennis Crolly of Wilkes-Barre, shortly before Foster's death in the late 1930s. Crolly sent a copy to the Pinkertons in 1941.

and an unofficial vigilante committee is rather too fine to be convincing. The Committee of Safety was itself a vigilante committee; and vigilante committees, whether official or unofficial, exist to circumvent the law and to enforce justice directly.

Finally, the man who might have had most to lose in admitting the role of vigilantes was remarkably forthright on the subject. Allan Pinkerton's book, *The Molly Maguires and the Detectives*, included a chapter, "Violence for Violence," which described the events at Wiggans Patch as follows: "Between two and three o'clock, the morning of the day mentioned, occurred an outrage of which it was supposed citizens of the neighborhood were perpetrators, the Mollies taking, for the very first time, the place of the victims." It was a case of "fighting fire with fire," Pinkerton explained. "The people, stung to madness by the rapidly succeeding murders of the summer and fall, were, it appeared, taking the law into their own hands and giving payment for assassination in similar coin." He concluded that it was "natural that this should be so," that it was "in the interests of humanity and the law," and that it "had a wonderfully tranquilizing effect upon the society" of the mining region.[81]

While Pinkerton freely admitted that vigilantes were responsible for the killings at Wiggans Patch, in no way did he admit the complicity of his own agents in the incident. The extent to which the Pinkertons were indeed involved can never be fully determined. It is clear that they furnished the names and addresses of the Molly Maguires of Wiggans Patch to the vigilantes, and accused them of killing Sanger and Uren. And the attack was so well-organized it resembled a paramilitary operation. The men were masked and heavily armed, and they were dressed in long oilskin coats. This evidence, in itself, dispenses with the theory of a faction fight; it also suggests that the men had been trained or at least advised by somebody like Captain Linden. Though he was not present at Wiggans Patch on the evening in question, Linden had presumably followed his orders from Pinkerton to organize a vigilante committee to meet force with force. But, while it is highly probable that the Pinkertons helped organize the vigilantes, and certain that they provided them with information, it can never be known whether they participated in the attack directly.

One final piece of evidence implicating the Pinkertons in the planning of the attack, if not its actual execution, is a letter written by James McParlan.[82] In anguished tones, McParlan reported how he had heard about the attack on Wiggans Patch early on the morning of December 10. "Now as for the

81. Pinkerton, *The Molly Maguires and the Detectives,* 457–58.

82. PCA, Molly Maguire Collection, Letter from J. McF, Pottsville, December 10, 1875. The document in question is a handwritten copy of a letter written on December 10, 1875, the same day as the early-morning killings at Wiggans Patch. At the top of the letter are the words "Copy of Report of J.McF." Broehl (*The Molly Maguires,* 264–65) questioned the provenance of this document. But McParlan was always referred to as "JMCF" in the Pinkerton reports and there can be little doubt that he wrote the letter. Cf. James Horan and Howard Swiggert, *The Pinkerton Story* (New York, 1951), 152–53.

O'Donnell's I am satisfied they got their just deservings," he wrote; after all, they had killed Sanger and Uren. But McParlan was apparently outraged that women had been beaten and killed. "Now I wake up this morning to find that I am the murderer of Mrs. McAllister," he wrote. "What had a woman to do in this case[?] Did the Sleepers [i.e., Molly Maguires] in their worst time shoot down women[?] If I was not here the vigilant committee would not know who was guilty. And when I find them shooting women in their thirst for blood, I hereby tender my resignation to take effect as soon as this message is received." It was not "cowardice" that had prompted him to resign, McParlan insisted, but his conviction that the vigilantes were no better than the "Molly Maguires," that "one is the same as the other and I am not going to be accessory to the murder of women and children."[83] The response of his employers to this letter is unknown, but McParlan was to remain in the anthracite region for another three months.

While there had been frequent calls for vigilante committees over the years, the general reaction to the events at Wiggans Patch was one of revulsion. "It seems incredible that such a crime as this could have been committed in a region that pretends to be civilized," Robert Ramsey wrote in the *Miners' Journal*, even if "the house assaulted was a favorite head quarters of the Mollie Maguires" and "its inmates were among the worst characters in the region."[84] But this revulsion was matched by a remarkable reluctance to take measures against the perpetrators of the attack. Denouncing the incident as "a foul blow on the fame of the Mahanoy Valley," Ramsey declared that the reputation of Schuylkill County could be restored "only by promptly finding the murderers and delivering them to justice."[85] Nothing was ever done in this respect, however, except for the arrest of a butcher from Mahanoy City named Frank Wenrich, who was quickly released without charge.[86]

The immediate effect of the incident at Wiggans Patch was renewed criticism of the Molly Maguires, rather than a wave of sympathy for the victims. Without them, so the theory went, there would have been no vigilantes in the first place. The *Miners' Journal* clearly laid much of the blame for the attack on the Molly Maguires, a sentiment echoed in the *Philadelphia Public Ledger*, which denounced "lynch law" and "kukluxism" and warned the residents of Schuylkill County that the mining regions were too important to the welfare of Pennsylvania "to allow that they shall be governed either by 'Molly Maguires' or vigilants, or any other organized band of lawless men."[87] On a similar note, the *Pottsville Standard* described the O'Donnell household as "a place of resort for desperate characters" and noted that "all the parties implicated are doubtless of the very worst class of a heterogeneous population."[88]

83. PCA, Molly Maguire Collection, letter from J.McF, Pottsville, December 10, 1875.
84. *MJ*, December 11, 1875.
85. Ibid., December 11, 1875.
86. Ibid., December 11, 1875; Broehl, *The Molly Maguires*, 261–63.
87. *Philadelphia Public Ledger*, quoted in *MJ*, December 16, 1875.
88. *Pottsville Standard*, December 11, 1875.

In Philadelphia, Archbishop Frederic Wood responded to the events at Wiggans Patch by formally excommunicating the Molly Maguires. He reissued the pastoral letter against secret societies he had first published in 1863, editing it in one significant detail. After the words "Mollie Maguires," he inserted the phrase "otherwise the Ancient Order of Hibernians."[89] In Irish Catholicism, excommunication was very much a social as well as a religious punishment. The laity were instructed by the clergy to shun the excommunicate, who was cast out of society as well as the Church. This was clearly the case in the anthracite region after December 1875.[90] After reading Wood's letter from the pulpit of his church at Mahanoy Plane, for example, Fr. Daniel O'Connor instructed his listeners as follows. "Beware of the Molly Maguires. If you have a brother among them, pray for his repentance but have nothing further to do with him—and remember that he is cut off from the Church." This society, along with the "Hibernians, Buckshots, or whatever else they may choose to call themselves," had been "excommunicated," O'Connor reiterated, and he advised the congregation not to "show sympathy for these men, for they are cut off from all connections with the Church. Let them fight their own battles, for you have a conscience, and they have none. They are scum and a disgrace to us as Irishmen and American citizens."[91] Long denounced as un-American in the nativist and anti-labor press, the Molly Maguires were now placed firmly beyond the pale of respectable Irish society as well.

To complement the powerful moral sanction of the Catholic church, Robert Ramsey called for the proper enforcement of the law in Schuylkill County. Both the Molly Maguires and the vigilantes, he argued, were operating under the assumption that the law was impotent. "Writing 'Thou shalt not kill' upon the statute book will not prevent murder," Ramsey warned. "It must be written on the hearts and consciences of men." The people of Schuylkill county must choose, and choose quickly, Ramsey concluded: "If they will not enforce the laws peaceably the vigilantes will do it for them by violence."[92] But the vigilante phase of activities was now at an end. The following month, the first of the great Molly Maguire trials began.

89. Wood's letter was published in *NYT*, December 23, 1875.

90. Cf. Connolly, *Priests and People*, 124–29.

91. Excerpts from O'Connor's sermon were published in *SH*, December 23, 1875, and *NYT*, December 23, 1875.

92 *MJ*, December 16, 1875.

8

The Molly Maguires on Trial

The trials of the Molly Maguires began in January 1876 and ended in August 1878. They bordered on a travesty of justice. The trials were conducted under conditions of enormously hostile publicity. The defendants were arrested by private policemen and convicted on the evidence of a detective who was accused of being an agent provocateur. The detective's evidence was supplemented by a series of informers who turned state's evidence. Irish Catholics were excluded from the juries as a matter of course. Most of the prosecuting attorneys worked for railroads and mining companies; the star prosecutor at the great showcase trials in Pottsville was none other than Franklin B. Gowen. As one historian has aptly put it: "The Molly Maguire investigation and trials marked one of the most astounding surrenders of sovereignty in American history. A private corporation initiated the investigation through a private detective agency, a private police force arrested the supposed offenders, and coal company attorneys prosecuted—the state provided only the courtroom and hangman."[1]

Some of the men convicted in the Molly Maguire trials were probably innocent of the crimes they were charged with, though there is no way of knowing

1. Aurand, "The Anthracite Mine Workers, 1869–1897," 57.

for certain at this point. Thomas Duffy, James Roarity, and Jack Kehoe, for example, surely ought not to have been convicted as charged. But even those who were wrongly convicted may well have been involved in other, similar activities. Many of the men who stood trial had engaged in violence, up to and including assassination. To deny this, and to argue that the Molly Maguires were the entirely innocent victims of a diabolical plot against the Irish or against the labor movement, is to replace one form of conspiracy theory with another. Inherently evil nativists and capitalists take the place of inherently evil Irishmen, and the old mythology is simply turned on its head. There was a very real pattern of violence in the anthracite region in the 1860s and 1870s, and much of it was committed by the Irish. The task of historians is to try and explain why, and the best explanation is the adaptation and transformation in the anthracite region of a pattern of retributive violence that had its roots in the Irish countryside.[2]

That some Irish immigrant workers engaged in beatings and assassinations, then, is beyond question. But that they did so as evil terrorists in the type of conspiracy portrayed by the prosecution at the trials is beyond credibility. Despite the allegations of the prosecution, it is clear that most members of the Ancient Order of Hibernians had nothing to do with the Molly Maguires, even in the anthracite region. The Ancient Order of Hibernians had lodges throughout the United States, Britain, and Ireland. The great majority of these lodges had no connection with violence. But the mid-1870s was no time for such subtleties. In the anthracite region, the Ancient Order of Hibernians, and not just its members, was put on trial.

The first of the great Molly Maguire trials took place in Mauch Chunk, Carbon County, in late January 1876. It involved the assassination of John P. Jones at Lansford on September 3, 1875. Shortly after the assassination, Michael J. Doyle, Edward Kelly, and James Kerrigan had been arrested in the woods nearby. The three men asked for separate trials, and Doyle's was called first.[3] Doyle was a member of the AOH in Mount Laffee, where he had been born of Irish parents twenty-seven years earlier. He worked in the mines for the Lehigh & Wilkes-Barre Coal Company, the biggest employer in Carbon County and lower Luzerne County. John P. Jones was employed as a superintendent by the same company. The company's lawyer, Charles Albright, led the case for the prosecution, noting that his employer, Charles Parrish, had "determined to spare neither effort nor money to bring the murderers of John P. Jones to punishment."[4] As a mine owner in

2. MacCarthy's *The Great Molly Maguire Hoax,* for example, argues quite unconvincingly that the Molly Maguires were the entirely innocent victims of anti-Catholic oppression, thereby ignoring the fact that they were responsible for a considerable amount of violence in the anthracite region, including a series of assassinations.

3. The stenographic reports on the Doyle trial are at the Pottsville Free Library, Schuylkill County. See, also, *MJ* for the last week in January 1876.

4. Albright, *The Great Mollie Maguire Trials,* iv.

Carbon County in 1863, Albright had written to Abraham Lincoln, informing him of the existence of the Molly Maguires (whom he called "Buckshots").[5] He went on to become a general in the Union army, and during the trials he appeared in court in full uniform complete with sword, reinforcing the notion that the Molly Maguires were treasonous and un-American.

The trial of Michael J. Doyle began on January 26, with Judge Samuel Dreher presiding. It ended on February 1 in a verdict of guilty of murder in the first degree. Though neither McParlan nor any of the Molly Maguire informers testified for the prosecution, the trial set some important precedents. The jury included no Irishmen and was manned primarily by German-speakers from the periphery of Schuylkill County, some of whom knew little or no English.[6] The prosecutors worked for railroad or mining companies: District Attorney E. R. Siewers was assisted by Francis W. Hughes for the Reading Railroad, Allen Craig for the Lehigh Valley Railroad, and Charles Albright for the Lehigh & Wilkes-Barre Coal Company. The defense consisted of local lawyers like Daniel Kalbfus, Edward Mulhearn, Lin Bartholomew, John W. Ryon, and J. B. Reilly. As might be expected, defense attorneys like Reilly, Ryon, and Kalbfus were prominent in the local Democratic party. But the defense also included Republicans like Bartholomew, while the prosecution included leading Democrats like Gowen and Hughes. Hughes, indeed, was so outspokenly critical of the Molly Maguires during the trials that he may well have been compensating for the charges of disloyalty that had been leveled against him during the upheaval of the early 1860s.[7]

Doyle's trial also set the tone for the remarkable coverage by the press that would characterize the Molly Maguire trials as a whole. As the trial began, for example, a reporter for the *New York Evening Post* applauded the "intrepidity" of the authorities in bringing the suspects to court "in the face of the possibility that a band of their comrades three or four thousand strong may, on any day, march into town, attack the Court House, release the criminals, and shoot down all opponents."[8] And, if the discursive conditions surrounding the trial were not already unfavorable enough, a bizarre twist was added when two of the leading publishers of pulp fiction in New York City began to serialize

5. *OR,* ser. 3, vol. 3, 1,008–9. See chapter 3.

6. Albright, *The Great Mollie Maguire Trials,* v; Pinkerton, *The Molly Maguires and the Detectives,* 464; Coleman, *The Molly Maguire Riots,* 105; Broehl, *The Molly Maguires,* 272.

7. The four prosecutors in the Doyle case were to appear at all the important trials in Mauch Chunk over the coming months. So, too, were Doyle's defense attorneys, with the exception of J. B. Reilly, who was replaced by E. T. Fox after the first trial. In the principal trials held in Pottsville over the coming year, Albright and Hughes were joined by Franklin B. Gowen and Guy E. Farquhar, while Bartholomew, Ryon, and Kalbfus were joined by Martin M. L'Velle. On Hughes's antiwar sentiment, and rumors concerning his position on the assassination of George K. Smith, see chapter 3. Though Gowen and Hughes were Democrats, neither of them was an Irish Catholic. Hughes was of Welsh and Huguenot descent, while Gowen was the son of an Irish Episcopalian.

8. Quoted in *MJ,* January 28, 1876. See, also, *Pottsville Evening Chronicle* February 1, 10, 1876; *MJ,* February 2, 1876.

competing stories on the Molly Maguires. The stories ran from March to July 1876 in the *Fireside Companion* and the *New York Weekly Story Teller,* complete with fictitious threatening letters and "coffin notices" allegedly sent to the publishers by the Molly Maguires.[9] If ever there was an aspect of the Molly Maguire story where fact merged easily into fiction it was in the case of these two popular novels. The story papers vied with each other for the most outlandish plots and the most depraved acts of violence; significantly, however, the world of popular fiction also allowed for greater nuance and ambiguity than the one-sided hostility of the national press. At certain points, as their plots twisted and turned with new developments, these ambivalent stories came close to portraying the Molly Maguires as working-class heroes rather than terrorists and criminals.[10]

As Doyle's trial was proceeding, Edward Kelly and Jimmy Kerrigan were being held in solitary confinement, awaiting trial for the same crime, the murder of John P. Jones. Just before Doyle's conviction, Kerrigan apparently decided to confess, and he told his story of how the Yost and Jones murders were connected, implicating Thomas Duffy, James Roarity, Hugh McGehan, Alexander Campbell, and James Carroll in the plot, along with Doyle and Kelly. As the bodymaster of the Tamaqua division of the AOH, Kerrigan freely admitted his own role in the killings of Yost and Jones. After turning informer he testified in several trials and was evidently promised immunity in return, as he never stood trial for any crime.[11]

On the basis of information provided by Kerrigan, a series of arrests was made by the Coal & Iron Police directly after the trial of Michael J. Doyle. On February 4, Captain Linden organized a posse to round up James Carroll, James Roarity, Thomas Duffy, Hugh McGehan, James Boyle, and Alexander Campbell, the six suspects in the killings of Yost and Jones. On February 10, a second posse was organized to arrest the suspects in the killings of Sanger and Uren. McParlan had already identified the assassins as Charles and James "Friday" O'Donnell, James McAllister, Thomas Munley, and Michael Doyle of Shenandoah (not to be confused with Michael J. Doyle of Mount Laffee). But Charles O'Donnell had been killed by vigilantes at Wiggans Patch the previous December, and his brother James had fled the anthracite region after the attack, as had McAllister and Doyle. At 6 A.M. on February 10, the Coal & Iron Police seized Thomas Munley at Gilberton, and an hour later they arrested Charles McAllister at Mahanoy City, apparently mistaking him for his brother, James.[12] In Mauch Chunk,

9. Albert Aiken, "The Molly Maguires; or, The Black Diamond of Hazelton" [sic], in *Fireside Companion,* March 6 to June 5, 1876; Daniel Doyle, "Molly Maguire, The Terror of the Coal Field, in *New York Weekly Story Teller,*" March 13 to July 3, 1876.

10. Kevin Kenny, "The Molly Maguires in Popular Culture," *Journal of American Ethnic History,* 14 (Summer 1995): 27–46; Michael Denning, *Mechanic Accents: Dime Novels and Working-Class Culture in America* (New York, 1987), especially chapter 7.

11. See Kerrigan's confession, as printed in the *Philadelphia Inquirer,* April 6, 1875, along with his testimony in the Yost trial, *Among the Assassins!,* 18–21; Broehl, *The Molly Maguires,* 274–75; Coleman, *The Molly Maguire Riots,* 111–14; cf. Campbell, *A Molly Maguire Story,* 104–19.

12. *Pottsville Evening Chronicle,* February 10, 1876; Broehl, *The Molly Maguires,* 276.

the *Democrat* celebrated that a blow had finally been struck against the Molly Maguires, who had exerted "a reign of terror" throughout the mining region "for the last twenty-five years." The *Democrat* congratulated Archbishop Wood for his recent excommunication of the Molly Maguires and declared that "we may assume that this denunciation has materially aided the course of justice." It was now time for all Irishmen to live up to Wood's expectations, "to aid in sustaining the laws—to help the course of justice," and in so doing to end the stigma of violence attached to name of "Irishman" and "Catholic."[13]

On February 23, three weeks after his conviction in the Jones case, Michael J. Doyle was sentenced to be hanged, the first capital conviction of a Molly Maguire. At the end of the following month, twenty-four-year-old Edward Kelly faced trial in Mauch Chunk for the murder of John P. Jones.[14] Like Doyle, Kelly was born of Irish parents in Mount Laffee, where he had joined the local branch of the AOH. After Doyle's trial, he stood little chance of escaping the hangman's noose, and what chance he had was ended by the confession of Jimmy Kerrigan. With the same judge and prosecution, substantially the same defense team, and a jury again dominated by German-Americans and lacking a single Irishman, the trial began on March 29. It ended on April 6 with a verdict of guilty of murder in the first degree. Six days later Kelly was sentenced to be hanged.[15]

Following the conviction and sentencing of these first two Molly Maguires in Mauch Chunk, attention shifted to Pottsville, where a series of showcase trials was staged in the summer of 1876. The first of these highly publicized proceedings began on May 4, with James Carroll, Thomas Duffy, James Roarity, Hugh McGehan, and James Boyle facing trial for the murder of Benjamin Yost. James McParlan and Jimmy Kerrigan had both linked the Yost killing to the Jones case, and of all the alleged Molly Maguire crimes, the Yost-Jones conspiracy was the one in which the Donegal connection was most pronounced. Carroll, who was born in Wilkes-Barre of Irish parents in 1837 or 1838, had married a niece of Margaret O'Donnell, matriarch of the extended Donegal-born family of Wiggans Patch. He settled in Tamaqua in 1872, where he operated a saloon and was secretary of the local lodge of the AOH. Duffy, a native of Donegal who had come to Schuylkill County with his parents as a child, was also a member of the Tamaqua division. He worked at the Buckville Colliery, operated by the Philadelphia & Reading Coal & Iron Company, two miles outside Tamaqua. Roarity, born in Donegal in 1845, was bodymaster of the Coaldale division. McGehan, another native of Donegal, had once worked at the mine run by John P. Jones, who had blacklisted him. He was a member of the AOH at Summit Hill, where he kept a tavern. Boyle, also a member of the

13. *Mauch Chunk Democrat*, February 19, 1876.

14. The stenographic reports on the Kelly trial are available at the Pottsville Free Library, Schuylkill County. See also *MJ* for the first week in April 1876.

15. *SH*, April 1, 1876; Coleman, *The Molly Maguire Riots*, 111.

Summit Hill division, was born in Schuylkill County of parents from Donegal (see Appendix 1).

The Summit Hill lodge lay in the heart of territory allegedly controlled by two other men born in Donegal, the AOH delegate for Carbon County, Thomas Fisher, and the AOH treasurer at Storm Hill, Alexander Campbell. Fisher was later found guilty of the murder of Morgan Powell, along with John "Yellow Jack" Donahue; and Campbell was convicted of the murder of Powell and of John P. Jones, both of whom had worked as superintendents for the Lehigh & Wilkes-Barre Coal Company. Of the ten men eventually hanged for their part in the Powell-Yost-Jones murders, five were born in west Donegal (Campbell, Duffy, Fisher, McGehan, and Roarity), one was born in the anthracite region of parents from west Donegal (Boyle), another (Carroll) had married into a family from west Donegal, two (Doyle and Kelly) were American-born but belonged to a reciprocal network dominated by immigrants from Donegal, and the nativity of the tenth is unknown.[16]

A panel of three judges presided at the Yost trial: Cyrus L. Pershing (Democrat), Thomas H. Walker (Democrat), and David B. Green (Republican). Once again, the jurors were primarily of German extraction. One juror, Levi Stein, admitted, "I don't understand much English"; another, William Becker, asked to be questioned "in Dutch as I am light on English . . . I would not understand the witnesses." Both men were accepted as jurors.[17] In his opening speech, District Attorney Kaercher caused a sensation in the courtroom by announcing that James McParlan would appear as the chief witness for the prosecution. McParlan had fled the anthracite region on March 7, when he learned from Fr. Daniel O'Connor that he was suspected of being a detective.[18]

The drama was heightened when, toward the end of Kaercher's opening statement, ten more Molly Maguire prisoners were led past the courthouse in chains to Schuylkill County prison, having just been arrested. They included John Kehoe, the AOH delegate for Schuylkill County and the alleged ringleader of the Molly Maguires. "The news of the latest 'catch' spread through the town like wildfire, gathering in a short time an immense concourse of excited citizens all anxious to learn the details," the *Shenandoah Herald* reported. "Poor fools! They imagined themselves sharp and capable of committing any deviltry without being followed—not to mention captured by that justice which sleeps, but never dies." Now at last, the *Herald* exulted, the Mollys were about to be "swept from the face of the earth."[19]

16. See appendix 1. For a summary of the alleged Powell-Yost-Jones conspiracy, see *Among the Assassins!*

17. Albright, *The Great Mollie Maguire Trials,* v; Broehl, *The Molly Maguires,* 296.

18. See McParlan's testimony in the Yost trial, *Among the Assassins!,* 16–17; and, for a fuller account, see his testimony in RCK, 92–98. Cf. Pinkerton, *The Molly Maguires and the Detectives,* 497–508; Dewees, *The Molly Maguires,* 252–74; Broehl, *The Molly Maguires,* chapter 11.

19. *SH,* May 8, 1876.

Late on Saturday, May 6, just after Kaercher's opening speech, James McParlan entered the Pottsville courtroom for the first time, accompanied by Captain Linden and two Pinkerton bodyguards. On the first day of his testimony, McParlan described his relation to the Yost case, how he had heard firsthand confessions from Carroll, Roarity, and Kerrigan, and how Duffy was the mastermind behind the whole affair. This evidence, on its own, might have convicted the defendants, but on Monday the prosecution extended its case into a general indictment of the Ancient Order of Hibernians, otherwise known as the "Molly Maguires," and McParlan offered minute details of the inner workings of the conspiracy. Much of his testimony was corroborated by the informer Jimmy Kerrigan.[20]

With the prosecution poised for a major victory, the trial was suddenly disrupted on May 18, when Levi Stein, one of the German-speaking jurors selected by the prosecution, fell ill. The case was suspended, and when Stein died on May 25, apparently of pneumonia, the judge was forced to dismiss the jury and declare a mistrial. The setback for the prosecution was only temporary, however. There was little doubt in anybody's mind that the testimony offered by McParlan and Kerrigan had doomed the five defendants. All that was needed was to arrange a new trial. In the meantime, the defendants in the Yost case were remanded in custody.

McParlan's revelations made great copy. The newspapers, both locally and nationally, had a field day, reporting the Yost trial with near-hysterical zeal. The *Miners' Journal,* for example, denounced the Molly Maguires as "lawless wretches" who, in pursuit of their "diabolical crimes," had "thrown aside all restraint, all respect for law and for the opinion of mankind . . . and given themselves up to the unrestrained indulgence of their own passions."[21] The *Shenandoah Herald* referred to the Molly Maguires as "scum" and warned them that the time was "close at hand" when they would be "swept from the face of the earth."[22] "Death to all 'Mollies' is the cry from one end of the coal region to the other," the *Herald* announced, "and never let it be silent until the devilish order is irretrievably dismembered and its members scattered." For the Molly Maguires, "murder was but child's play, arson but a pleasure, and wickedness of all kinds but the natural outpourings of vile and devilish hearts."[23]

While this sort of reaction was scarcely surprising from committed opponents of the Molly Maguires like Robert Ramsey and Thomas J. Foster, the language of the metropolitan newspapers of the East Coast was scarcely more temperate. "When the inner history of the Mollie Maguires shall have been written," the *Philadelphia Inquirer* announced on May 20, "it will embody the harrowing details of a conspiracy such as the world has rarely known. This history has been making itself through years of lawlessness, bloodshed, plunder

20. *MJ,* May 5 to May 18, 1876; *Among the Assassins!,* passim.
21. *MJ,* May 19, 1876.
22. *SH,* May 8, 1876.
23. *SH,* May 25, 1876.

and general anarchy." The Molly Maguires had all but ruined the anthracite region, the *Inquirer* continued:

> What Providence intended for a harvest of peace and plenty the devilish ingenuity of banded cut-throats turned into a harvest of death and rapine. . . . Capital was fettered, honest labor held by the throat, and Red-Handed Murderers, Reeking with the blood of their victims, held high carnival over the prostrate form of Justice, blind and bleeding.[24]

In much the same vein, the *New York Times* announced that

> the revelations of the doings of the Mollie Maguires . . . uncover a state of brutish ignorance and superstition which one might think could not exist in this Republic. The Pennsylvania authorities owe it to civilization to exterminate this noxious growth, now that its roots have been discovered.[25]

It is difficult to see how the defendants could have got a fair trial in these circumstances. As defense attorney James Ryon objected in one trial later that summer: "When men are to be tried before courts and juries by public opinion instead of the law and evidence, then has the right of trial by jury fallen indeed."[26] But these were the conditions in which the Molly Maguires were tried, once the first convictions had been secured.

In June, Alexander Campbell was brought to trial in Mauch Chunk for the murder of John P. Jones, for which two men had already been convicted and sentenced to death. Edward Kelly and Michael Doyle, however, had merely been members of the AOH; Campbell was the treasurer of the Storm Hill lodge and he was suspected of being the leader of the Molly Maguire conspiracy in Carbon County. Judge Samuel S. Dreher presided, having already sentenced Kelly and Doyle for the same crime. While Kelly and Doyle had been convicted of doing the actual shooting, Campbell was charged as an accessory before the fact, accused of having planned the crime. The assassins had allegedly spent the night before the killing in his tavern at Storm Hill. The jury in Campbell's trial was made up of Germans and Welshmen, and it included no Irish Catholics.[27] Several witnesses testified that Kelly, Doyle, and Kerrigan had not visited Campbell's tavern on the night before the murder. But, after a trial of eleven days, the jury quickly reached a verdict of guilty of murder in the first degree. On August 28, Campbell was sentenced to death. Given that Campbell had not been present at the crime, and given his standing within the AOH, this verdict represented a major triumph for the prosecution and an ominous precedent for the other Molly Maguires awaiting trial.[28]

24. *Philadelphia Inquirer,* May 20, 1876.

25. *NYT,* May 14, 1876.

26. RCK, 204.

27. Coleman, *The Molly Maguire Riots,* 137.

28. The stenographic reports on Campbell's trial are at Pottsville Free Library, Schuylkill County. See, also, *MJ* for the last week in June 1876; and Campbell, *A Molly Maguire Story,* 104–139.

Before Campbell's trial had ended, a second trial was already underway in Pottsville. On June 27, Thomas Munley and Charles McAllister were brought to court to face charges of murdering Thomas Sanger and William Uren at Raven Run the previous September. McAllister was granted a separate hearing. Munley stood trial at Pottsville from June 27 to July 12, with Judge D. B. Green presiding. The jury, once again, included no Irish Catholics and was predominantly German-American. As James Kerrigan knew nothing of the affair, the prosecution's case rested on the testimony of McParlan, who had named the suspected killers of Sanger and Uren in his field reports.[29] Other than the detective's testimony, there was no evidence to implicate Munley in the Sanger-Uren case. The big question for the prosecution was whether the detective's uncorroborated testimony would stand up in court. Eventually, one witness (a woman from Raven Run named Jeanette Williams) claimed to have seen Munley at the scene of the killing with a pistol in his hand. But Munley's father, brother, sister, and several friends testified that he had been at home on the morning of September 1, and it was evident that one side was lying. The way was opened for perjury charges in the event of Munley's conviction. Despite the testimony of the defense witnesses, the jury took only one hour to find Munley guilty of first-degree murder. A native of County Mayo, Munley had emigrated to the United States in 1864. Like Alexander Campbell, he was sentenced to death on August 28.[30]

Six days before Munley was convicted, the second Yost trial had opened in Pottsville, taking up where it had abruptly left off in May. Thomas Duffy requested and was granted a separate trial, which took place the following September. The other four defendants were tried between July 6 and July 22, with the same panel of three judges and the same prosecution and defense attorneys as before, but a new jury. This time the prosecution was not to be frustrated. On July 22 McGehan, Boyle, Carroll, and Roarity were found guilty of first-degree murder. All four men were sentenced to be hanged.

The conviction of the defendants in the Yost case was followed by a series of showcase trials in Pottsville over the coming months. Though the first of these trials involved lesser crimes than the Yost and Jones cases, the defendants included almost the entire leadership of the Ancient Order of Hibernians in the

29. For the testimony in the Munley trial, see *MJ* and *SH*, June 28 to July 13, 1876. See, also, Pinkerton, *The Molly Maguires and the Detectives*, 509; Broehl, *The Molly Maguires*, 231.

30. According to Barclay, *Lives and Crimes* (p.37), Munley was born in Tallaughn, parish of Kilcommon, County Mayo in 1845, and emigrated to the United States in 1864, "being the last of the family to leave the sod." From the record of the trials and executions, it is evident that his father, brother, and sister lived in Schuylkill County. He also had relatives in the region of Ennis, County Clare (see the undated letter from Michael Munnelly et al. in SCBS, Molly Maguire Collection).

lower anthracite region. The trials of John Kehoe were the most highly publicized. The extent to which Kehoe was actually involved in the crimes he was accused of cannot now be determined with any certainty. But his eventual conviction of the first-degree murder of Frank W. Langdon is unquestionably the most dubious of all the verdicts handed down to the Molly Maguires.

John Kehoe was a powerful and reasonably wealthy man in the Irish community of northern Schuylkill County, having worked his way up from immigrant mine worker to tavern-keeper and local politician. Born in County Wicklow in 1837, Kehoe had come to the United States with his parents, brothers, and sisters at the age of thirteen, settling in Tuscarora. In the mid-1850s, the family lived in Middleport, Blythe Township, and Kehoe worked in a mine at St. Nicholas. At the age of twenty he got a job at the No. 2 Breaker Colliery of J. B. McCreary & Co., in Audenried, where he eventually became a miner. It was in this area, much to Kehoe's subsequent misfortune, that George K. Smith and Frank W. Langdon were assassinated during the Civil War.[31]

Kehoe was one of thousands of Irish mine workers who moved to northern Schuylkill County from the mid-1860s onward, when the coal business took off there. He settled first in Mahanoy City, where he married Mary Ann O'Donnell, the daughter of Manus and Margaret O'Donnell, immigrants from west Donegal. In 1870, Kehoe and his family moved to Shenandoah, another of the new mining towns in the Mahanoy Valley, where he opened his first tavern. Late the following year, he moved with his family to an area known as Foulketown, in Butler Township, which was chartered as Girardville Borough on June 4, 1872. Kehoe set up business as proprietor of the Hibernia House, a tavern, and was elected high constable of Girardville for two consecutive terms.[32]

Kehoe's biography suggests an atypically successful Irish immigrant, who had survived and prospered through the various hardships and frequent relocations experienced by most Irish mine workers in this period. He was the leader of the Irish community in Girardville, and he clearly had political ambitions. His great misfortune, at least in retrospect, was that he had been elected to the post of Schuylkill County delegate of the Ancient Order of Hibernians in August 1874. According to McParlan and the prosecution, the AOH and the Molly Maguires were the same, evil organization. Victory over the Molly Maguires could not be considered complete, therefore, until "Black Jack" Kehoe had been convicted of a capital crime.[33]

In his first trial, Kehoe was accused, along with eight other prominent members of the AOH, of conspiring to kill William "Bully Bill" Thomas. The list of

31. McCarthy, *The Great Molly Maguire Hoax,* 90, 101–3.

32. Ibid., 101–3.

33. Kehoe succeeded Bernard "Barney" Dolan as county delegate after Dolan was expelled from the Order for embezzlement. Cf. Broehl, *The Molly Maguires,* 167, 176, 186.

defendants at this trial read like a roster of the leaders of the Ancient Order of Hibernians in Schuylkill County.[34] The plot to kill Thomas had allegedly been hatched at an AOH convention in Mahanoy City on June 1, 1875, attended by the defendants along with the chief witness for the prosecution, James McParlan. The presence of John Kehoe, the prominence of the defendants, and a remarkable speech by Franklin B. Gowen, made this trial the most highly publicized of all the trials staged in the anthracite region in 1876. The proceedings opened on August 8, with judges Pershing, Green, and Walker presiding. As usual, the jury was composed almost exclusively of German-Americans, and it included no Irish Catholics. On the evening of August 12, the jury took only twenty minutes to find the defendants guilty as charged, recommending mercy for Frank McHugh, who had turned state's evidence during the trial. The remaining defendants were later sentenced to the maximum possible term, seven years in prison.[35]

Two days after being convicted, most of the defendants in the Thomas case were indicted for a second crime, conspiracy to kill William and Jesse Major. John Kehoe, Dennis Canning, Christopher Donnelly, Michael O'Brien, James Roarity, John "Yellow Jack" Donahue, and Frank McHugh were accused of having plotted the murder at the same AOH convention where the attack on "Bully Bill" Thomas had been planned. Judge Green presided, though a new jury was sworn in. McParlan and Kerrigan testified for the prosecution. The trial lasted only two days; on August 15 all the defendants were found guilty as charged. Kehoe and Canning were later sentenced to a further seven years in prison, and the other defendants to lesser terms.[36]

On the same day, another mass trial began in Pottsville. O'Brien, Donnelly, Donahue, and Roarity were arraigned for "aiding and assisting to reward Thomas Hurley, for the murder of Gomer James," along with three new defendants, Patrick Dolan, Sr. (AOH bodymaster, Big Mine Run), Francis O'Neil (AOH bodymaster, St. Clair), and Patrick Butler (AOH bodymaster, Lost Creek). John Kehoe was also arraigned in this case, but he was to receive a separate trial. The chief witness was McParlan, who claimed to have attended the AOH convention at Tamaqua on August 25, 1875, at which Hurley's claim for a reward was supposedly discussed. Up to this point, none of the defendants in any of

34. The defendants were John Kehoe (AOH delegate, Schuylkill County); Dennis F. Canning (AOH delegate, Northumberland County), Christopher Donnelly (AOH treasurer, Schuylkill County), James Roarity (AOH bodymaster, Coaldale), John "Yellow Jack" Donahue (AOH bodymaster, Tuscarora), Michael O'Brien (AOH bodymaster, Mahanoy City), Frank McHugh (AOH secretary, Mahanoy City), John Morris (AOH member, Shenandoah), and John Gibbons (AOH member, Shenandoah). Morris and Gibbons were charged with doing the actual shooting, under orders from the other seven defendants, who were charged with planning the crime.

35. For the names of the jurors, see *SH*, August 11, 1876.

36. See McParlan's testimony in RCK, 27–28, 58, 63–64, 82, and appendix; *MJ* and *SH*, August 15 to 18, 1876. The Majors were not killed, so the indictment was for conspiracy to murder, rather than murder or attempted murder. The convention where the crime was supposedly planned met at Mahanoy City on June 1, 1875.

the Molly Maguire trials had testified on the witness stand. This tactic was adopted for the first time in the Hurley conspiracy trial. But, when Patrick Butler was called as a witness for the defense he broke down on the stand and admitted his guilt. The trial lasted a few more days, and on the evening of August 22 the jury took only fifteen minutes to reach a verdict of guilty in all cases (with a recommendation of mercy for Butler). Donnelly, Butler, O'Brien, and O'Neil were later sentenced to two years in prison, and Dolan to eighteen months.[37]

In September, the momentum of the Molly Maguire trials continued unabated, as five new cases were tried in Pottsville. Thomas Duffy, the sole remaining defendant in the Yost case, was brought to trial on September 6. The mainly German jury had no hesitation in reaching a verdict of guilty of murder in the first degree, and Duffy became the fifth and final Molly Maguire to be sentenced to death for the murder of Benjamin Yost.[38] On September 21, the Shenandoah saloonkeeper and AOH bodymaster, Michael "Muff" Lawler, was arraigned as an accessory before the fact in the killings of Sanger and Uren. Lawler turned state's evidence and, as a result, the jury failed to reach a verdict. His decision to become an informer was long remembered in the anthracite region in a bitter miner's ballad called "Muff Lawler the Squealer." But, in November, Lawler was tried for a second time in the Sanger-Uren case, convicted of second-degree murder, and sent to prison.[39]

Two days after Lawler's first trial had opened on September 21, another mass trial began in Pottsville in the case of conspiracy to kill William and Jesse Major. John Slattery, John Stanton, Michael Doolin, Charles Mulhearn, Ned Monaghan, Frank O'Neil, and Pat Dolan, Sr., were arraigned, and all but Stanton were found guilty. Slattery and Mulhearn turned state's evidence, and their sentences were postponed, along with that of Michael Doolin. Monaghan was later sentenced to seven years in prison, O'Neil to five years, and Dolan to one year. The convictions aside, the most interesting aspect of this trial was that Slattery implicated John Kehoe in the murders of Sanger and Uren.[40]

The fifth and final trial of September 1876 was the case of the *Common-*

37. *SH*, August 18, 25, 1876; Broehl, 328–29; Pinkerton, *The Molly Maguires and the Detectives*, 543. Roarity had already been sentenced to death for the murder of Benjamin Yost; and, by the time the defendants were sentenced, Donahue had been sentenced to death for the murder of Morgan Powell. Perhaps because of these prior convictions, Roarity and Donahue do not appear to have received additional sentences in the Hurley case.

38. *SH*, September 8, 15, 1876.

39. Lawler was tried and convicted on November 13, 1876; see *SH*, November 17, 1876. For the ballad on Lawler, see George G. Korson, *Minstrels of the Mine Patch* (Philadelphia, 1938), 267–68. In another trial, Charles McAllister was brought to court on September 21 and charged with the murder of Sanger and Uren, but the case was dropped when the prosecution was forced to admit that the defendant had been mistakenly arrested in place of his brother, James, who had fled the anthracite region after the attack on Wiggans Patch. On November 26, in a second case, McAllister was convicted of the attempted murder of James Riles and sent to prison; see *SH*, December 1, 1876.

40. *SH*, September 23, 25, 29, 1876; *MJ*, September 23, 25, 29, 1876.

wealth v. Bridget Hyland et al.[41] The defendants were accused of perjuring themselves in testimony delivered on behalf of three men already convicted of murder, Thomas Munley, James Boyle, and Thomas Duffy. Mrs. Hyland was arraigned for perjury in the Munley trial; sixteen-year old Kate Boyle and her brother Barney were arraigned for perjury in the Yost trial, along with James Duffy. The defendants were quickly found guilty. On October 16 they received their sentences, along with fifteen other Molly Maguires who had been convicted in the Thomas and Major conspiracy cases. All nineteen convicts were brought into Pottsville courtroom chained together, for a single, mass sentencing. It was a remarkable show of power by the authorities, a spectacle that was not to be surpassed until the following June 21, when ten Molly Maguires were executed on a single day.[42]

All of the Molly Maguire trials from January to September 1876 involved killings committed in the violent summer following the collapse of the Long Strike. By October, the main suspects had been convicted in four of the six Molly Maguire killings of 1875, those of Yost, Sanger, Uren, and Jones. Nobody was ever convicted of the other two assassinations committed in 1875 (Thomas Gwyther and Gomer James), nor of the assassination of George Major in 1874. But, as late as October 1876, the eight Molly Maguire killings committed between 1862 and 1871 remained unsolved. The authorities now turned their attention to these cases, extending their inquiries back in time to the killings of Morgan Powell (1871) and Alexander Rea (1868), and eventually to what they regarded as the very root of the Molly Maguire conspiracy, the assassinations of F. W. Langdon and George K. Smith during the Civil War.

Over the next two years, there were eight more Molly Maguire trials. Only one of these trials involved a killing committed during the second wave of Molly Maguire activities, the conviction of Dennis Donnelly in November 1877 as an accessory before the fact in the assassinations of Sanger and Uren. The other seven trials were part of a mopping-up operation involving the Molly Maguire assassinations committed from 1862 to 1871. Four of these trials took place in the period between the mass sentencings of October 16, 1876, and the mass executions of June 21, 1877; the other four were conducted after the executions had begun.[43]

The first case to be called was the *Commonwealth v. John Donahue et al.* for the murder of Morgan Powell, which opened at Mauch Chunk on October 19, 1876. John "Yellow Jack" Donahue, Thomas Fisher, Patrick McKenna, Patrick O'Donnell, Alexander Campbell, and John Malloy were charged with the

41. The trial lasted from September 25 to September 30, and was reported in *MJ* and *SH* between those dates.

42. Coleman, *The Molly Maguire Riots,* 157; Dewees, *The Molly Maguires,* 330. Barney Boyle was sentenced to three years in prison, Kate Boyle, James Duffy, and Bridget Hyland to two and a half years each.

43. The trials conducted between November 1877 and August 1878 are considered in chapter 9.

murder of Morgan Powell in 1871. Accused as well as the defendants in court was Matthew Donahoe, who had not yet been arrested. Once again, the Donegal connection was prominent. Fisher and Campbell were both natives of that county; O'Donnell is one of the classic names of Donegal; Cornelius T. McHugh, an informer who testified for the prosecution, bore a surname most commonly found in west Ulster, especially Donegal. Witnesses for the defense included the monolingual Irish speaker Celia O'Donnell, whose testimony was translated by John McGinley. O'Donnell and McGinley are classic west Donegal surnames.[44]

The Powell case was the most important and best-publicized of all the trials in Carbon County. While O'Donnell, McKenna, and Malloy were mere members of the AOH, the other three defendants belonged to its upper echelons. Thomas Fisher was the AOH delegate for Carbon County. Campbell headed the AOH in Storm Hill and was suspected of being the Molly Maguire ringleader in the county. Donahue was the bodymaster of the Tuscarora division, just across the border in eastern Schuylkill County. Judge Samuel S. Dreher presided, having already handed down death sentences to three Molly Maguires (Doyle, Kelly, and Campbell) for the murder of John P. Jones, Morgan Powell's successor at the Lehigh & Wilkes-Barre Coal Company. The jurors, as usual, were mainly German-Americans, and Irish Catholics were excluded. Donahue, Fisher, and Campbell were convicted of first-degree murder in separate trials, and later sentenced to be hanged. McKenna and O'Donnell were convicted of second-degree murder and sent to prison; Malloy, who was able to substantiate an alibi, was acquitted.[45]

With the conviction of the leading figures in the Ancient Order of Hibernians in Carbon County, the authorities once again turned their attention to John Kehoe. Without his conviction on a capital offense, victory over the Molly Maguires could not be considered complete. As the Powell trials were being conducted in Mauch Chunk, the Pinkertons and the Coal & Iron Police had been accumulating information on the assassination of F. W. Langdon in 1862. Nobody had been charged with the killing in 1862. But on November 24, 1876, six men were arraigned at Pottsville Courthouse: Neil Dougherty, John Campbell, Columbus McGee, Michael McGee, John Chapman, and John Kehoe. Once again, the Donegal connection is evident. Like Kehoe's wife, the McGee brothers came from west Donegal. Columbus McGee had been a witness at Kehoe's wedding in Mahanoy City in 1866. He had also been suspected of assaulting an enrollment officer during the draft resistance in Schuylkill County in 1863, when his name was mentioned in official military dispatches from the anthracite region to Washington. John Campbell bore a sur-

44. See *SH*, December 29, 1876.

45. HML, A 1520, V 1744, stenographic reports of the case of *Commonwealth v. John Donahue et al.*; *SH*, December 8, 22, 1876; Pottsville Free Library, stenographic reports of the Campbell, Fisher, and McKenna trials. The trials also received extensive treatment in *MJ and SH*: Donahue (October 19–25), Fisher (December 6–18), and Campbell (December 19–22).

name typical of west Donegal, and the name Dougherty is also found more commonly in west Ulster than elsewhere.[46]

Separate trials were granted, and the case of Neil Dougherty was called first. Dougherty was found guilty of second-degree murder on November 30, 1876, and later sentenced to nine years in prison. John Campbell was convicted of second-degree murder on January 9, 1877, and sent to prison for five years. Michael McGee was acquitted on May 17, and the charges against Columbus McGee and John Chapman were eventually dropped. But the main target of the prosecution was John Kehoe, whose trial opened amid considerable publicity on January 9, the day Campbell was convicted. Having already been sentenced to two seven-year terms in prison in the Thomas and Major cases, Kehoe was now finally charged with first-degree murder, a capital offense. Franklin B. Gowen returned to Pottsville for the occasion, to appear for the prosecution.[47]

It is difficult to imagine how, under normal conditions, a verdict of guilty could have been reached in this case. But the conditions in Schuylkill County were not exactly normal. There had been eighteen highly publicized Molly Maguire trials before the case came to court; and Kehoe had recently been accused not only of being directly involved in the Sanger-Uren murders, but also of being the mastermind of the entire Molly Maguire conspiracy.[48] A number of witnesses did present circumstantial evidence against Kehoe. One testified that a few weeks before Langdon was assaulted, Kehoe had told him that Langdon was a "son of a bitch," whom he would kill because he was "robbing the people and docking wages." Another said that Kehoe had spat on the American flag during the altercation with Langdon, and had again threatened to kill him. But there was no evidence that Kehoe had directly participated in the attack on Langdon, and one witness testified that he had not even been present at the scene of the beating.[49]

The defense lawyers were therefore able to construct a plausible case for their client. They argued that Langdon had died, not as a result of the beating, but because of the over-zealous treatment administered by his doctor. He had walked home after the assault and had died only the following day. The defense attorneys attempted to demonstrate that his doctor had improperly administered stimulants, causing a fatal stroke. They also maintained that Kehoe had not been present at the beating; and that, even if he had been, the assault was spontaneous rather than premeditated. Langdon was not attacked with the

46. SH, December 1, 1876; McCarthy, *The Great Molly Maguire Hoax,* 101; OR, ser. 3, vol. 3, 332; Coleman, *The Molly Maguire Riots,* 40; Broehl, *The Molly Maguires,* 90–91.

47. MJ, November 25 to December 1, 1876, January 5 to 12, 1877; SH, November 25 to December 1, 1876, January 5 to 12, 1877, May 25, 1877.

48. HML, A 1520, B 979, F, "Statements and Depositions." In separate statements to the Coal & Iron Police, Patrick Butler (September 24, 1876), John J. Slattery (September 28, 1876), and Dennis Canning (May 4, 1877) all implicated Kehoe in the Sanger-Uren killings.

49. Reports of the trial proceedings can be found in SH, January 9 to 16, 1877; MJ, January 9 to 16, 1877; see, also, [E.D. York], *Report of the Case of the Commonwealth v. John Kehoe, January 9, 1877* (n.p., 1877).

intention of killing him, so Kehoe could be liable for second-degree murder at worst. The defense also complained that the entire investigation had been carried out by the Coal & Iron Police, rather than the public authorities.[50] But Judge Pershing went to some trouble to make the jury understand, first, that the prosecution claimed Kehoe was actually present at the crime; and, second, that they claimed he had planned the murder in advance, so that even if he had not been present he was still guilty.[51] The jury evidently agreed, and on January 16 John Kehoe was found guilty of first-degree murder. Conviction of second-degree murder might have been expected; but the verdict of guilty of murder in the first degree is, in retrospect at least, quite remarkable. On April 16 Kehoe was sentenced to be hanged. It was the prosecution's greatest triumph.

The scene now shifted to Bloomsburg, the seat of Columbia County, which hosted the last of the great trials before the mass executions of June 1877. Though Bloomsburg lay in the heart of farming country, the Western Middle Coal Field ran across the southern tip of Columbia County, and it was in this territory that Alexander Rea had been killed in 1868. Two of the three defendants lived across the border in Northumberland County, but the killing had occurred just inside the Columbia side of the border, so the trial was held in that county. In November 1876, Daniel Kelly, otherwise known as Manus Cull or "Kelly the Bum," produced a chilling confession, implicating Patrick Hester, Peter McHugh, Patrick Tully, and others in the Rea killing, as well as admitting his own role. Like Jimmy Kerrigan, he never had to stand trial himself.[52]

On the basis of Kelly's confession, Hester, McHugh, and Tully were brought to trial in Bloomsburg in February 1877. Just as John Kehoe allegedly headed the Molly Maguire conspiracy in Schuylkill County and Alexander Campbell in Carbon County, Patrick Hester was suspected of being the mastermind in Northumberland County. Born in County Roscommon in 1825, Hester had come to the United States in 1846, when the Molly Maguires were active in his home county. He settled first at Minersville, Schuylkill County, but soon moved to Locust Gap Junction, Northumberland County, where he opened a hotel and tavern, the Junction House. Active in local Democratic politics, Hester was bodymaster of the Northumberland Junction division of the AOH, and in that capacity had been arrested in 1868 and charged with the murder of Alexander Rea. After being held in jail for six months, he was released without trial, as the authorities were unable to put together a case against him.[53] Hester's

50. [York], *Report of the Case of the Commonwealth v. John Kehoe,* passim.

51. See Pershing's charge to the jury in [York], *Report of the Case of the Commonwealth v. John Kehoe,* 436–42.

52. HML, 1520, B 979, F, "Statements and Depositions," statement of Manus Cull, a.k.a. Daniel Kelly; another copy at HSP, SC, PNDA, "Synopsis for Mr. Gowen," September 1, 1876.

53. *MJ,* March 29, 1878; HML, A 1520, V 1745–48, stenographic reports of the case of the *Commonwealth v. Hester et al.,* 4; [Town], *Commonwealth v. Patrick Hester, Patrick Tully, and Peter McHugh, 1877. Argument of Hon. F. W. Hughes for Commonwealth.* Thomas Donahue of Ashland, John Duffy of Mahanoy City, and Michael Prior of Branchdale were also arrested, but when their cases came to trial they were acquitted.

codefendants in 1877, Peter McHugh and Patrick Tully, were also Irish-born. McHugh was born in 1834, probably in west Donegal, and had come to the United States in 1864 by way of England. He was the AOH delegate for Northumberland County.[54] Patrick Tully, who was born in County Cavan in 1830, had moved to Scotland as a teenager and came to the United States in either 1854 or 1863. In 1865, he settled in Centralia, in the mining section of Columbia County. According to Daniel Kelly, all of Rea's killers spoke Irish.[55]

The trial opened on February 8, with Judge Elwell presiding. The jurors, as usual, were mainly German-American. The procedure was much the same as at the previous trials and, after a year filled with Molly Maguire convictions, the defendants stood little chance of acquittal. Kelly's evidence was corroborated, in part, by that of another informer, "Muff" Lawler of Shenandoah. On February 24, Hester, Tully, and McHugh were convicted of first-degree murder. All three men were sentenced to death, joining the twelve other Molly Maguires who were awaiting execution.[56]

While it would be facile for a historian to set himself up as judge and jury over the Molly Maguires, it is quite obvious that they were tried under remarkably adverse conditions. If the composition of the juries and the prosecution teams stand out as particularly questionable, so too do the role of informers and the possibility that James McParlan was an agent provocateur.

The case presented by the prosecution relied to a remarkable extent on the testimony of informers who had once been members of the Ancient Order of Hibernians. The most notorious of these informers were Daniel Kelly and Jimmy Kerrigan, whose characters and backgrounds ought to have called their evidence into serious question. Kelly, otherwise known as "Manus Cull" or "Kelly the Bum," had already been convicted of a range of crimes, including highway robbery in 1869. He was known locally as a drunken and dangerous character, and he freely admitted his own part in killing Alexander Rea. In November 1874 he had been convicted of grand larceny and sentenced to three

54. The name McHugh is typical of west Donegal, where the McHughs today say that one of their ancestors was hanged as a Molly Maguire (interview with Patrick McHugh, Dungloe, County Donegal, June 23, 1993).

55. PCA, Molly Maguire Collection, typed copy of the "Confession of Patrick Tully made to Capt. Aldersen at Bloomsburg on March 18, 1878" states that Tully "came to this country in 1863 and joined the A.O.H. in Centralia[,] Columbia Co., Columbus McGee, Bodymaster." *MJ*, March 28, 1878, contained two more "confessions" by Tully, one dating his arrival in the U.S. to 1854, the other to 1863. Tully implicated Columbus McGee and Patrick Hester in the Rea killing, and admitted his own guilt. He also named the killers of William Littlehales, among them McGee, and Tully's fellow-defendant in the Rea case, Peter McHugh. On Rea's killers as Irish speakers, see HSP, SC, PNDA, "Synopsis for Mr. Gowen, September 1, 1876," statement of Manus Cull, dated August 22, 1876.

56. *SH*, February 16, 1877.

years in Pottsville prison. It was there that Captain Linden found him in November 1876 and extracted a lengthy confession. On January 6, 1877, Governor Hartranft signed a pardon for Kelly on the larceny charge, and a month later he appeared as the chief prosecution witness at the Bloomsburg trial.[57]

Secrecy was one of the defining characteristics of Molly Maguireism in Pennsylvania, just as it had been in Ireland. As a result, there was no surer way to rupture solidarity than to turn informer and betray one's colleagues. Informers have had a long, ignoble record in Irish history, and to become a turncoat was to engage in a particularly hated form of betrayal. In rural Ireland, the punishment for informers was severe: beating, mutilation, or death.[58] Much of this distaste for turncoats was also evident among the Irish in the anthracite region. As Francis P. Dewees put it in 1877: In the eyes of this "ignorant, prejudiced, and romantic people" to "*inform of a crime* has in many instances come to be considered *as great a wrong as the crime itself.*" Jimmy Kerrigan's own wife denounced him as a liar and a traitor; she called him "a dirty little rat" from the witness stand, and she refused to visit him in prison. Kerrigan and his wife were later reconciled; but like Kelly, they had to leave the anthracite region. They lived in exile in Richmond, Pennsylvania, and then in Manchester, Virginia, where Kerrigan adopted his wife's surname. For long afterward, his betrayal was remembered in a miners' ballad, "Jimmy Kerrigan's Confession." Kelly the Bum reportedly received one thousand dollars from "the good citizens of Columbia County," with which to leave the country.[59]

In addition to Kelly and Kerrigan, at least eight other accused Molly Maguires turned informer during the trials. Frank McHugh turned state's evidence in the Thomas conspiracy case, Patrick Butler in the Gomer James conspiracy case, "Muff" Lawler in the Sanger-Uren case, Charles Mulhearn and John J. Slattery in the Major conspiracy case, and Cornelius T. McHugh in the Morgan Powell case. As for the trials conducted after the mass executions of June 1877, Dennis Canning, who had been convicted in the Thomas and Major cases, turned informer and received a pardon in exchange for testifying against Dennis Donnelly in November 1877; and James McDonnell, who was sentenced to death for killing George K. Smith, helped convict Martin Bergin of the murder of Patrick Burns, in an unsuccessful attempt to have his own sentence commuted.

It is impossible to know how truthful these informers were. Kelly and Kerrigan were self-confessed killers who would scarcely have hesitated to bend their evidence in the direction the Pinkertons required, in return for immunity from

57. On Linden's discovery of Kelly, see *SH,* November 10, 1876.

58. Beames, *Peasants and Power,* 166–67; for a strikingly similar conception of informers in rural India, see Guha, *Elementary Aspects of Peasant Insurgency,* 198.

59. Dewees, *The Molly Maguires,* 12; italics in original; *Pottsville Evening Chronicle,* May 17, 1876 (quote from Mrs. Kerrigan); *MJ,* May 12, 1876. Kerrigan died in Manchester, Virginia, on October 1, 1898 (*MJ,* October 5, 1903). The ballad about him can be found in Korson, *Minstrels of the Mine Patch,* 250. On the payment to Kelly, see Broehl, *The Molly Maguires,* 354.

prosecution. The defendants who turned state's evidence were in an equally precarious position; some faced the possibility of long terms in prison or the death penalty, while others had already been convicted and sentenced, and hoped for mercy. All of them were under considerable pressure to comply with the demands of the prosecution. For example, in the Morgan Powell case, Captain Linden was cross-examined by the defense and forced to admit that the choices he had offered Charles Mulhearn and Cornelius T. McHugh were rather stark: Either testify for the prosecution or face trial and possible execution. Linden also admitted that both men were promised their freedom in return for cooperating, and that he had provided their families with money as they awaited trial in prison.[60]

The validity of evidence provided by informers was questioned repeatedly by the defense attorneys. The trial of Thomas Duffy was a case in point. Duffy had requested a separate trial when the second Yost trial opened in July, and there was some reason to believe he would be acquitted. McParlan was unable to testify against Duffy, as he had never met him. The sole source of evidence was Jimmy Kerrigan, who had admitted his own participation in Yost's assassination. And the only real evidence Kerrigan provided was the allegation that Duffy had offered James Roarity ten dollars for Yost's death, to satisfy the grudge he had borne since Yost had beaten him up.[61]

This was very flimsy evidence, and Judge Thomas J. Walker warned the jury to proceed with considerable caution. Given that an accomplice like Kerrigan had strong motives for falsifying his testimony, Walker advised the jurors not to return a verdict of guilty on the basis of Kerrigan's uncorroborated testimony alone. In other words, they had to determine whether the prosecution had corroborated Kerrigan's evidence in presenting its case. If there was any doubt about Duffy's guilt, then "that doubt should be cast in his favor."[62] As the *Shenandoah Herald* reported, Walker's final remarks to the jury had "leaned toward the side of mercy." There was "hardly a soul in the courtroom but was satisfied Duffy's chances of acquittal were more than even."[63] Yet the jury did not hesitate to reach a verdict of guilty of murder in the first degree. Given the paucity of the evidence, and the tone of Walker's warning to the jury, this was a remarkable decision. But such was the momentum of events in the anthracite region.

If the testimony of informers was suspect, this was even more true of the evidence provided by the Pinkerton detective, James McParlan. Although he knew nothing of the crimes committed before 1874, McParlan provided most of the evidence regarding the second wave of Molly Maguire assassinations in 1874 and 1875. During the Yost trial, the *Pottsville Workingman* pointed out that

60. Stenographic reports of the Campbell case, Pottsville Free Library; Campbell, *A Molly Maguire Story,* 140–44.

61. For the testimony in the Duffy trial, see *MJ* and *SH,* September 7 to 20, 1876.

62. HSC, Papers of Thomas J. Walker, n.p.

63. *SH,* September 21, 1876.

in the seven years before McParlan's arrival in the anthracite region there had been very little violent crime, whereas the two and a half years he spent there were remarkably violent. Eight assassinations were attributed to the Molly Maguires in this short period. The obvious question, for the *Workingman*, was whether McParlan had been sent into the anthracite region to instigate crimes and accumulate evidence.[64] In other words, was he an agent provocateur? The defense attorneys argued repeatedly that McParlan's evidence should be discounted on the grounds that he had instigated several of the Molly Maguire crimes. Taken with the admitted complicity of the informers, this argument was potentially a powerful one.

In the first Yost trial, for example, defense attorney Daniel Kalbfus argued that McParlan had instigated and participated in much of the violence, and that he could have prevented some of the killings had he wanted to, especially the assassination of John P. Jones. McParlan countered that he had not informed Linden or Franklin about the Jones murder on the night before he knew it was to take place because to have done so would have been to risk revealing his identity and losing his life. He gave the same justification for not having tried to prevent the attempted murder of William "Bully Bill" Thomas. An alternative explanation, of course, would be that McParlan let the plans go ahead in order to accumulate evidence. But the jury accepted McParlan's version of events, and the defense had little success in shaking his testimony.[65]

In the trial of Alexander Campbell for the murder of John P. Jones, McParlan was questioned repeatedly on why he had not been able to save Jones's life, given that the assassination plot was known of so long in advance. As one defense attorney put it: "If he saved a thousand lives it would not atone for the one he took."[66] The prosecution successfully countered this attempt to portray McParlan as an agent provocateur by putting Pinkerton superintendent Benjamin Franklin on the stand. Franklin testified that McParlan had indeed notified him of the plan, that Jones had been warned, and that a local committee had been formed to protect him.[67]

The possibility that McParlan was an agent provocateur was also raised repeatedly at the Thomas conspiracy trial. Before he left the witness stand, McParlan was cross-examined by Martin L'Velle, who accused him of instigating and participating in many of the crimes he blamed on the Molly Maguires. When L'Velle pressed McParlan to directly answer the question of whether he had participated in the crimes or not, the following exchange took place in the courtroom:

Q. Did you or did you not [participate]?
A. I seemed to; it was not a fact that I was.

64. *Pottsville Workingman,* May 27, 1876.

65. Cf. Broehl, *The Molly Maguires,* 299–300.

66. *MJ,* June 23, 1876.

67. Stenographic reports on Campbell's trial, Pottsville Free Library; *MJ* for the last week in June 1876; Campbell, *A Molly Maguire Story,* 104–39.

Q. Did you or did you not? I want an answer.
A. Of course I did not, so far as I was concerned; so far as the members were concerned they thought so.
Q. Then you were not the party that Mr. Kehoe authorized to get men to kill Bully Bill, were you, or were you not?
A. Certainly I was the party.
Q. Did you deem that participation?
A. No; I did not deem it participation. I went there for the purpose of finding out what they were going to do.[68]

L'Velle also forced McParlan to admit that he had known that Daniel Dougherty had been innocent even as he stood trial in April 1875 for the murder of George Major. The other defense attorneys at the Thomas conspiracy trial also argued that McParlan had been either an accomplice or a provocateur during his years undercover in the anthracite region. But it was unlikely that McParlan was an accomplice, Judge Walker advised the jury, because accomplices generally testified in order to mitigate their own punishment, whereas McParlan was charged with no crime and had nothing to gain. The jury evidently agreed, and the accusation that McParlan was an agent provocateur fell on deaf ears.[69]

All attempts to portray the Molly Maguires as an omnious conspiracy, rather than a loosely organized pattern of violence, rested on their identification with some other institution. Clearly, the prosecution could not build a convincing case that the Molly Maguires were simultaneously the force behind the Workingmen's Benevolent Association and the Ancient Order of Hibernians, as the trade union and the fraternal society were quite distinct organizations. The trade union, in any case, had collapsed by the time the trials began; and its defeat in 1875 had been followed by the reemergence, not the disappearance, of the Molly Maguires. The idea that the trade unionists were terrorists gradually diminished, as the prosecuting attorneys admitted that the WBA and the Molly Maguires were very different forms of labor activism. At the same time, they developed a powerful conspiracy theory that the Ancient Order of Hibernians was merely the Molly Maguires under another name. In this way, mere membership in the AOH could be construed as evidence of guilt. While the argument that the AOH as a whole was engaged in Molly Maguire activities was scarcely credible, the reputation of the national organization was far from being untarnished. This was especially so after its involvement in the Orange riots in New York City in 1870 and 1871, in which sixty-eight people died and hundreds were injured. This association of the

68. RCK, 39.
69. RCK, argument of L'Velle, 85–86; arguments of Garrett, L'Velle, and Ryon, 134–36, 195, 216; remarks of Judge Walker, 237.

AOH elsewhere in America with violence greatly strengthened the case of the prosecution in Pennsylvania.[70]

The chief source of the allegation that the AOH and the Molly Maguires were the same organization was James McParlan. When he appeared on the witness stand for the first time in May 1876, McParlan revealed the inner workings of the Ancient Order of Hibernians, lending credence to the notion that the Molly Maguires were a vast, well-organized conspiracy.[71] On the basis of his testimony, the prosecution was able to demonstrate, to the satisfaction of the jurors at least, that the AOH and the Molly Maguires were the same organization. McParlan described his early movements in the anthracite region, his initiation into the AOH at Shenandoah, the system of passwords and grips, the organizational network, the trading of "jobs" between the different branches on a reciprocal basis—in short, the whole paraphernalia of a vast conspiracy. Each individual crime the Molly Maguires stood accused of could therefore be construed as part of an ominous criminal network.[72]

McParlan gave his most detailed account of the inner workings of the AOH at the highly publicized trial of John Kehoe and his codefendants for conspiracy to murder William "Bully Bill" Thomas. After describing his early adventures in the coal region, he described how he had been initiated into "the Ancient Order of Hibernians, more commonly called Mollie Maguires."[73] He also described the various passwords and signs, known colloquially as "the goods," used by the society. Here is one example of a password: "The Emperor of France and Don Carlos of Spain, They unite together and the pope's right maintain." And the response: "Will tenant right in Ireland flourish, If the people unite and the landlords subdue?" These open declarations on land and religion would hardly have been conducive to secrecy, but at night a more oblique set of words was used: "The nights are very dark," followed by the answer "I hope they will soon mend." McParlan also gave these details of a sign commonly used among the members: "The sign is to touch the right hand to the corner of the right eye. The answer is to catch the lappel [sic] of the vest with the little finger and thumb of . . . the left hand." The language and gestures are reminiscent of Ribbonism in nineteenth-century Ireland, though the elements of French republicanism evident in the Irish version have been replaced here with Bourbon absolutism and Catholic orthodoxy.[74]

The identification of the Molly Maguires with the Ancient Order of Hibernians was the principal theme of the remarkable speeches delivered by the prosecuting attorneys at the trials. The highlights of the Yost trial, the Munley

70. See Michael A. Gordon, *The Orange Riots: Irish Political Violence in New York City, 1870 and 1871* (Ithaca, N.Y., 1993).

71. See the editorials in *MJ,* May 19, 1876.

72. The testimony and arguments in the Yost trial were reported in *MJ* and *SH,* May 5 to May 18, 1876. The testimony of McParlan and Kerrigan is summarized in the pamphlet *Among the Assassins!*

73. RCK, 16.

74. Quotes from RCK, 19, 20.

trial, and the Thomas conspiracy trial, indeed, were Franklin B. Gowen's histrionic speeches for the prosecution on the conspiracy hatched by the AOH, also known as the Molly Maguires.[75] In the first Yost trial, for example, Gowen explained how the AOH had been transplanted from Ireland to the United States, drawing heavily on W. Steuart Trench's *Realities of Irish Life* as his source.[76] The AOH, Gowen argued in the Thomas trial, existed for the sake of crime, profit, and power. "The purpose was to make the business of mining coal in this country a terror and a fear; to secure for the leading men in this society profitable positions, and the control of . . . every colliery." Unchecked, the society would soon have transformed the anthracite region into a "desert," and a "pest-house," "the lazar-house of the United States, controlled and ruled by a class of men to whom human life was no more sacred than the life of the worm they trod beneath their heel." Though it had only "five or six hundred" members in Schuylkill County at present, Gowen asserted, its membership would soon have swelled to twenty or thirty thousand. Throughout history, he concluded, there had never existed "in any society claiming to be civilized," such an "infernal tribunal" with "instruments of vengeance as ghastly and horrible" as those wielded by the Ancient Order of Hibernians.[77]

The prosecuting attorneys repeatedly presented mere membership in the Ancient Order of Hibernians as damning evidence of guilt by association. Gowen was unequivocal on this point. In the Yost trial, for example, he argued that "every member of that organization [the AOH] is, not only in a court of conscience, but in the eyes of the law, guilty of every murder as an accessory before the fact and liable to be convicted and hanged by the neck until he is dead."[78] In the Thomas trial, he informed the jury that "it has been reserved for you to be singled out to try not merely the question of the guilt of particular persons, but the far more transcendent issue of the guilt of the society itself which is now on trial for its life."[79] These were remarkable statements to make in a court of law.

One final, controversial allegation against the Ancient Order of Hibernians during the trials was that it was involved in extensive political corruption.[80]

75. Franklin B. Gowen, *Argument of Franklin B. Gowen in the Case of the Commonwealth v. Munley, 1877, for the Murder of Thomas Sanger* (Pottsville, 1876); RCK, "Argument of Franklin B. Gowen in the case of *Commonwealth v. Kehoe et al.*" Both arguments were widely publicized; the former was issued as a pamphlet and sold several thousand copies (Broehl, *The Molly Maguires,* 312).

76. Trench's work is discussed in chapter 1.

77. RCK, 176–81; see, also, 191, for the objections of the defense attorneys to Gowen's imputations of guilt by association.

78. *MJ,* May 17, 1876.

79. RCK, 176. The other prosecuting attorneys made similar, histrionic arguments throughout the trials. See, for example, RCK, 218, argument of George F. Kaercher; [Town], *Commonwealth v. Patrick Hester, Patrick Tully, and Peter McHugh, Argument of F. W. Hughes,* 17–18, 39.

80. *SH,* October 27, 1876; Leo Ward, "Political Tie Didn't Save Molly Necks," *Pottsville Republican,* February 5–6, 1994; Ward, "'Old Man in Harrisburg' Turned Back on Kehoe," *Pottsville Republican,* February 19, 1994.

In 1875, Cyrus L. Pershing had received the Democratic nomination for governor of Pennsylvania. Pershing was a popular choice in the heavily Democratic anthracite coal region, even to many Republicans. But in Schuylkill County, according to the informer John J. Slattery, the Molly Maguires (i.e., the AOH) had allegedly agreed to deliver the Irish vote to the Republican candidate George Hartranft, who eventually won the election. This story rapidly made its way into the myth and legend of the Molly Maguires. Dewees, for example, included the story in his early history, *The Molly Maguires* (1877), as did Munsell's *History of Schuylkill County* (1881), which claimed that the "Molly Maguires" held "the balance of power between opposing political parties" in the county. It was also claimed that the Republicans had paid the Mollys a lot of money to deliver the vote in 1876.[81]

The charge of corruption in 1875 had a peculiar relevance to the Molly Maguire trials. The defeated candidate, Cyrus L. Pershing, was the president judge of the Schuylkill County Court, and he presided over the great trials in Pottsville. His opponent, George Hartranft, was installed in the governor's mansion at Harrisburg, and it was he who would ultimately decide whether the condemned Molly Maguires should be pardoned or have their sentences commuted. Well aware of these political permutations, Gowen had introduced as evidence in the Thomas conspiracy case a conversation that Kehoe had allegedly had with the county jailer, George Byerle. According to Byerle's testimony, Kehoe had said to him: "If we don't get justice, I don't think the old man at Harrisburg will go back on us."[82] The obvious implication was that Hartranft would pardon any Molly Maguires who were convicted, in return for political favors rendered.

The defense had objected strenuously to the admission of this statement as evidence, but to no avail, and there the matter rested until John J. Slattery raised it again at the trial of John "Yellow Jack" Donahue three months later. Slattery testified that it had been arranged that "the entire 'Molly Maguire' vote was to be cast for Hartranft." Slattery himself claimed to have "fixed matters for Luzerne County," while a large sum of money was also sent to the AOH headquarters in Pittsburgh in return for the vote in that part of the state.[83] Add to this allegation the fact that a few members of the AOH, including John Kehoe and Patrick Hester, had been elected to local office, and yet another layer was added to the Molly Maguire conspiracy.[84]

81. Dewees, *The Molly Maguires,* 222; Munsell, *History of Schuylkill County,* 102; *Pottsville Evening Chronicle,* November 25, 1876.

82. RCK, 121.

83. See the report of the Donahue trial in *SH,* October 23, 1876; HML, A 1520, V 1744, stenographic reports of the Donahue trial; Dewees, *The Molly Maguires,* 225–26.

84. Kehoe was elected high constable of the mining village of Girardville in 1872. Hester was elected to the positions of school director and tax collector in the area of Northumberland Junction. Both men were active in Democratic politics, but neither had held a countywide political office.

The main problem with this conspiracy theory is that Pershing actually won Schuylkill County in 1875 by 1,338 votes, and the Democrats won all the other races in Schuylkill County as well. Even in northern Schuylkill County, the heavily Irish stronghold of the Molly Maguires, Pershing won a large proportion of the vote, in some cases a majority. In Shenandoah, for example, he won 56.7 percent of the vote, and in Gilberton 62.5 percent. It is true that in Girardville, the borough where John Kehoe lived, Pershing won only 175 votes (46.2 percent) compared to 203 (53.8 percent) for Hartranft. But if this was the extent of the great political conspiracy of 1875, then it was insignificant indeed.[85]

It is, nonetheless, quite likely that the Ancient Order of Hibernians was involved in political brokering of some sort. Deals between political candidates and ethnic or fraternal organizations were standard practice in nineteenth-century American politics. The Irish vote, in particular, was regularly "delivered" in this way, though more often to the Democrats than the Republicans. John Kehoe, who clearly had political ambitions of his own, may well have employed the AOH for deal-making of this sort after he became county delegate in August 1874. If so, he was engaging in an activity that was common throughout the United States at the time. Judge Pershing, as it turned out, was the man who sentenced John Kehoe to death in 1877. To assume that he did so to revenge his own frustrated ambitions two years earlier is to resort to yet another variety of conspiracy theory. Nonetheless, Pershing's involvement in Kehoe's trial clearly raised a conflict of interest, and the defense was surely entitled to ask him to remove himself from the trial.

Their failure to do so was one of several glaring errors and omissions on the part of the defense attorneys during the trials. Certainly, their attacks on the character and testimony of McParlan and Kerrigan were strenuous and sincere. And they insisted, albeit somewhat feebly at times, that mere membership in the AOH should not be considered an offense.[86] They pointed out that the AOH was a legal association, chartered by the state of Pennsylvania and entitled to just as much respect as the Masons or the Odd Fellows. The object of the AOH, as stated in its constitution, was "to promote friendship, unity, and true Christian charity among its members."[87] To reinforce this point, the constitution of the AOH was offered as evidence. Yet, on a series of other procedural points, the performance of the defense lawyers was deficient and highly questionable.

In the first two trials, for example, the defense had favored the selection of German-speaking jurors, apparently hoping that their lack of comprehension would lead them to acquit. If this was indeed the intention, the move backfired; thereafter, it was the prosecution that favored the selection of German-Americans. Given the deficiency of some of these jurors in English, why

85. These figures, from *SH,* November 5, 1875, appear in Aurand and Gudelunas, "The Mythical Qualities of Molly Maguire," 99–100.

86. See, for example, RCK, 138.

87. RCK, 139; see also, argument of James Ryon, 204.

did the defense not challenge their selection? Did they fail to impanel Irish Catholics because they feared the hostility of the "respectable" Irish to the Molly Maguires, or because they meekly acquiesced in the prosecution's strategy? Why did they not challenge the impanelment of those jurors in the trial of Alexander Campbell who admitted that they had already formed an opinion on his guilt? And why, despite their objection that the defendants should not be found guilty by association with the AOH, did they fail to make any coherent or convincing case for the innocence of their clients?[88]

Reading through the trial testimony, one has a strong sense that the defense attorneys were merely going through the motions of presenting a defense for their clients, while in reality being as convinced as all other contemporaries that the Molly Maguires were guilty and deserved to die. In professional terms, their involvement in the trials offered a welcome opportunity to work on a celebrated criminal case, with all the publicity adhering thereto. In ideological terms, it meant fulfilling the procedures and rituals whereby justice could be seen to be done, thereby maintaining the apparent universality and impartiality of the law and its legitimacy among the community at large.[89]

Excluded from that community, and hence from judicial impartiality, were the Molly Maguires. They had no apparent stake in the law. They were reputed to distrust and despise it, just as they had in Ireland. And their actions had long placed them firmly beyond the orbit of legality. Two forces were in fundamental conflict, the prosecuting attorneys repeatedly argued at the trials: rule by law and rule by criminality. The choice was between social order and social anarchy, and in the effort to ensure that the former prevailed, desperate measures were held to be quite justified. If the Molly Maguires were to continue to exist, prosecutor Francis W. Hughes insisted, "organized society must itself perish." The body politic was the "victim of a moral cancer as deadly as any physical one that ever struck the vitals of the human body." For civilized society to survive, the cancer must be cut out; otherwise, the whole body would perish. "It is better that five, ten, or five hundred Mollie Maguires should be suspended by ropes from the end of the gallows," Hughes concluded, "than that civilized society should disappear."[90]

88. Cf. Broehl, *The Molly Maguires,* 295, 308. As Morse pointed out in 1877 in his article, "The 'Molly Maguire' Trials," the defense attorneys in the trial of Kehoe et al. for conspiracy to murder "Bully Bill" Thomas had provided "no affirmative evidence of innocence . . . on behalf of any one of the arraigned band" (p. 249). Morse's point was not that the defense failed to prove the innocence of the defendants, which is not required in a jury system of criminal law, but that it made no apparent effort to rebut the case of the prosecution.

89. For two rather different versions of this argument on what Eugene D. Genovese calls the "hegemonic function of the law," see Genovese, *Roll, Jordan, Roll: The World the Slaves Made* (1972; New York, 1976), 25–27; E. P. Thompson, *Whigs and Hunters: The Origin of the Black Act* (New York, 1975), 259–63.

90. [Town], *Commonwealth v. Patrick Hester, Patrick Tully, and Peter McHugh, Argument of F. W. Hughes,* 112.

Time and again the prosecuting attorneys insisted that procedural irregularities were justified by the existence of an evil minority who embodied a serious threat to "civilized society" and an affront to the majesty of the law. This same defensive posture was evident in an article published in the *American Law Review,* endorsing the procedures of the prosecution at the trials. The author, John T. Morse, Jr., concluded that Franklin B. Gowen's extraordinary performance in the Thomas trial, which in effect put the AOH on trial and tainted all its members with guilt by association, had been justified by extraordinary circumstances. There could be no doubt, Morse insisted, that the AOH and the Molly Maguires were the same organization, and that this organization existed for the purpose of murder. Hence, Gowen's tactics were justified. In their separate but overlapping ways, the defense and prosecution attorneys upheld the legitimacy and ideological function of the law during the trials. As part of the same process, the Molly Maguires were excluded from the consensus of the law and placed firmly and permanently beyond the pale of respectable society.[91]

Not only were the Molly Maguires criticized and condemned by prosecuting attorneys, nativists, and the enemies of organized labor, they were also ostracized by two of the major institutions in their own immigrant, working-class community: the trade union movement and the Catholic church. They were pariahs not just in American society but in Irish-American society as well. This process of exclusion reached its peak during the trials of 1876 and 1877.

The leaders of the defeated WBA continued to voice their condemnation of the Molly Maguires as the trials proceeded. Only one, minor official of the WBA was ever implicated in a Molly Maguire crime. Cornelius T. McHugh, the erstwhile president of the WBA branch in Summit Hill, was accused of being involved in the assassination of Morgan Powell. He turned state's evidence in return for immunity from prosecution and on the basis of his testimony (along with that of several other informers) three men were sentenced to death. McHugh scarcely belonged to the upper echelons of the WBA; the head of a local branch of the union, he lived in an area where the AOH lodges were dominated by men from County Donegal, and his surname strongly suggests that he too came from that part of Ireland. Other than McHugh, no trade union leader was ever indicted for a Molly Maguire crime.[92]

At the end of the first Yost trial, John Siney took the opportunity to drive

91. Morse, "The 'Molly Maguire' Trials," 233–60. The article dealt with the Thomas conspiracy trial, but its findings are applicable to the trials in general. The defensive argument of the prosecuting attorneys that a desperate situation required desperate measures was perhaps most noticeable in the performance of Francis W. Hughes in the Hester case, but was evident in the speeches of the prosecutors throughout the trials.

92. Stenographic reports of the Campbell case, Pottsville Free Library; *SH,* especially December 15, 22, 29, 1876; Campbell, *A Molly Maguire Story,* 140–44.

home once again the essential differences between trade unionism and Molly Maguireism. On May 26 he published a letter in the *Philadelphia Times,* dissociating the miners' union, and the mass of ordinary Irish workers, from the Molly Maguires. The union, he pointed out, had always been "an open organization, without either signs, grip or password." Siney also insisted that most Catholic Irishmen obeyed the teachings of their Church regarding secret societies and shunned the Molly Maguires. "There are thousands of Irish men in this and other communities in this county who deplore any act of violence or lawlessness as much as it is possible for any man to do," Siney concluded.[93]

The procedures and publicity during the trials reinforced the notion that the Molly Maguires were a criminal conspiracy, opposed to the true interests of labor. As the *Philadelphia Inquirer* put it on May 20, 1876, "Siney's organization made the fight on capital, while the Mollie Maguires made war on labor." The *Pottsville Workingman* endorsed this position, insisting that "the best conservator of the peace that ever existed in the county, was the miners' Union." There was, of course, a small number of "bad and restless characters" in Schuylkill County, "but these men were mainly not Union men, not even in sympathy with labor or its trials."[94]

It might have been more accurate to say that these "bad and restless characters" were indeed in sympathy with the "trials" of labor, but favored more drastic measures of amelioration. The problem with dissociating the Molly Maguires entirely from labor activism was that it robbed them of any motive other than revenge or bloodlust. As a result, they could be portrayed as depraved sociopaths, indulging in evil for its own sake. But twelve of their sixteen victims were killed in attacks involving mine officials, most of whom were assassinated as part of a struggle to regulate conditions of life and labor in the mines, on an individual and local if not a collective and regional level. At the same time, the much-publicized attacks on Welshmen like Gomer James and "Bully Bill" Thomas were part of an ongoing interethnic dispute rooted in discrimination at the mines. But violence had always been taboo to the trade union leaders. In the wake of their own defeat, they condemned the Molly Maguires with understandable bitterness.

If the Molly Maguires were ostracized by respectable labor leaders, they were also shunned and condemned by the clergy and hierarchy of the Catholic church to which most of them belonged. The members of the AOH had been formally excommunicated after the incident at Wiggans Patch. During the trials of the following year, the Church played a remarkably zealous role in the ideological campaign against the Molly Maguires. On May 20, 1876, for example, the *Shenandoah Herald* published a letter from Fr. Daniel McDermott to the New York *Freeman's Journal,* in which the priest reiterated the condemnation of the Molly Maguires he and his fellow pastors had issued in October 1874. Lest

93. John Siney, letter to *Philadelphia Times,* May 26, 1876, quoted in Pinkowski, *John Siney,* 213–14.

94. *Pottsville Workingman,* May 27, 1876.

there be any lingering doubts on the matter, McDermott insisted that the AOH and the Molly Maguires were one and the same organization. McParlan's evidence, he announced, had finally proved what the "priests in Schuylkill county have long known the Ancient Order of Hibernians to be—*a diabolical secret society*, and that it is everywhere *the same society* in spirit and government."[95]

The Catholic church was active in other ways during the trials. The papers of Archbishop James Frederic Wood, for example, include a typed report from the Pinkertons listing the "outrages" in the lower anthracite region from October 31, 1874, to October 9, 1875, along with a copy of this report, apparently in Wood's handwriting. From other correspondence in the archive, it can be established that in April 1876 Wood sent this list to at least three other members of the Catholic hierarchy in Pennsylvania, Bishop Mullen of Erie, Bishop Tuigg of Pittsburgh, and Bishop Shanahan of Harrisburg.[96] Wood was also in regular correspondence with Franklin B. Gowen during the trials. In one letter, Gowen requested that the archbishop "urge the priests in the county to take advantage of the present opportunity to denounce the desperadoes and to save other innocent young men from joining it."[97] And he asked for Wood's assistance in forestalling perjury by defense witnesses in the remainder of the Yost trial. The witnesses in question were from Lansford and Storm Hill, in Carbon County. The best solution, Gowen thought, would be to have their parish priests come to court to monitor the proceedings. Wood evidently complied, as both priests, Fr. Brehoney and Fr. McEnroe, duly appeared in court on May 16.[98]

In a second letter, Gowen asked Wood for one more favor, and in doing so he unwittingly gave historians as clear a statement as they could wish for of the cooperation of the Catholic hierarchy with the railroad president in crushing the Molly Maguires. To prevent public opinion from swinging in favor of the Molly Maguires, it was crucial that the trials not appear as a nativist crusade against the Irish in general. "To do this effectively," Gowen informed the archbishop, ". . . I would like to have your permission to state publicly that you have been for some time cognizant of the means I had taken to break up the association of Molly Maguires and that you had most earnestly desired to destroy and disperse the organization."[99] Once again, Wood evidently complied, for in the trial of Thomas Munley a few months later, Gowen informed the jury: "I have the direct personal authority of Archbishop Wood himself to say that he denounces them all, and that he was firmly cognizant of and approved

95. *SH*, May 20, 1876; italics in original. On the position of the hierarchy and clergy during the trials, see Kenny, "The Molly Maguires and the Catholic Church," 360–65; Roohan, *American Catholics and the Social Question*, 169–74.

96. SCBS, Papers of Archbishop Wood. The outgoing correspondence has not survived, but see the letters to Wood from Tuigg (April 19), Shanahan (April 19), and Mullen (April 20), acknowledging receipt of the material on the AOH.

97. SCBS, Papers of Archbishop Wood, FBG to Wood, May 11, 1876.

98. SCBS, Papers of Archbishop Wood, FBG to Wood, May 14, 1876; Broehl, *The Molly Maguires*, 303.

99. SCBS, Papers of Archbishop Wood, FBG to Wood, May 14, 1876.

the means I took to bring them to justice.[100] On February 7, 1877, after considerable prevarication, Bishop William O'Hara of Scranton finally endorsed Wood's position in a much-publicized pastoral letter excommunicating the AOH in his diocese.[101] The Catholic church in Pennsylvania was now united in its opposition, and because of this the Molly Maguire trials never gave the impression of being a full-fledged nativist crusade.

But even if the prosecuting attorneys deliberately downplayed the extent to which immigrants were being scapegoated, nativism was still a consistent motif in their rhetoric. The most virulent form of this sentiment had been at the heart of Benjamin Bannan's antipathy to the Irish in the 1850s and 1860s. In the 1870s, especially at the time of the trials and executions, the Molly Maguires were systematically portrayed as alien and un-American, a depraved conspiracy that was a natural outgrowth of poverty-stricken, conflict-ridden Ireland, but a great anomaly amidst the liberty, equality, and opportunity of American life. As Francis W. Hughes announced in one trial, the Molly Maguires had no place in the United States, "where every man is equal before the law, where no man's rights are withheld him or denied him."[102] Harping on the familiar nativist theme of divided allegiance, Franklin B. Gowen pointed out that the AOH owed its ultimate loyalty not to any American authority but to "a society in a foreign land," "the so-called Board of Erin," consisting of delegates from Ireland, Scotland, and England.[103] The Molly Maguires were un-American. But, according to Catholic teaching, they were also un-Irish. They were, in short, outcasts from civilized society.

The centennial celebrations of 1876 provided the prosecuting attorneys with their central theme in this regard. Gowen had first raised the theme of the centennial at the legislative investigation of 1875, reminding the committee that, with the festivities only a year away, tens of thousands of Pennsylvanians were subject to unimaginable tyranny, "almost within the shadow of Independence Hall."[104] The *Miners' Journal* had made the same point in May 1876: "This is a pretty exhibition of culture and progress that Schuylkill makes to adorn the Centennial year of the nation."[105] Or, in the characteristically bombastic words of Charles Albright:

> We start the second centennial in our American history, a new century in the liberties of the American people, and what better time for the extermination of this society, that has grown into our social fabric. It is a putrefying and foul sore upon the body politic and it is an imperative duty that it should be removed.[106]

100. Gowen, *Argument in the Case of the Commonwealth v. Munley,* 86.

101. *SH,* February 13, 1877; *Catholic Standard* (Philadelphia), February 17, 1877.

102. [Town], *Commonwealth v. Patrick Hester, Patrick Tully, and Peter McHugh, Argument of F. W. Hughes,* 22.

103. RCK, 176.

104. FBG 1875, 79.

105. *MJ,* May 19, 1876.

106. Albright, *The Great Mollie Maguire Trials,* 46.

The centerpiece of the centennial celebrations in 1876 was the great exposition at Philadelphia. The exposition opened on May 10 and closed in mid-November, coinciding with the major Molly Maguire trials in Pottsville and Mauch Chunk. Almost 10 million people visited the various exhibits, with the huge Corliss Engine in Machinery Hall as the chief attraction. Designed to demonstrate to the world the superiority of American industrial civilization, the exposition abounded with ironies. It applauded the onset of mechanization in all walks of life, especially industry, but did so in the midst of massive poverty and unemployment. It celebrated the virtues of American industrial civilization, but took place at the height of the worst economic depression the United States had ever known, a depression caused in large part by the very railroads that symbolized the new mechanical age. And Pennsylvania, the state that had been the cradle of liberty in 1776, had become infamous a century later for the exploits of the Molly Maguires, whose trials were receiving national attention.[107]

The Philadelphia & Reading Railroad played a central role in the centennial celebrations. With a depot in the exposition grounds in Fairmount Park, the Reading carried more than 8 million passengers to the exhibition, from various points in Pennsylvania and along the city lines it controlled.[108] Among the visitors to the exposition were thousands of mine workers and their children from the lower anthracite region, who arrived in Philadelphia at the height of the Molly Maguire trials, on trips paid for by their employer, the Philadelphia & Reading Coal & Iron Company. On one such excursion, 1,170 employees of the PRCI and their wives and children arrived at the exposition in mid-July 1876. The men, being "practical," visited the Machinery Hall; the women, attracted instead to the "beautiful," congregated in the Art Gallery. All in all, the *Philadelphia Inquirer* found them to be "an intelligent and respectable looking set of people . . . orderly and decorous in their movements." At mid-day, they were treated by the company to a dinner of meat, vegetables, and ice cream, before taking the train home to the mining country that evening. The following day a thousand more visitors were shipped in from northern Schuylkill County, the heart of Molly Maguire territory.[109]

If excursions to the exposition were a way of demonstrating to the world that Pennsylvania's mine workers were orderly and respectable, they were also a way of reinforcing in the minds of these workers the benefits and virtues of

107. On the centennial, see Richard Slotkin, *Fatal Environment: The Myth of the Frontier in the Age of Industrialization, 1800–1890* (New York, 1994), 5–6; Robert W. Rydell, *All the World's a Fair: Visions of Empire at American International Expositions, 1876–1916* (Chicago, 1984), 2–10; [John Filmer], *The Illustrated Catalogue of the Centennial Exhibition, Philadelphia, 1876* (New York, 1876); [Leslie's Publishing House], *Frank Leslie's Illustrated Historical Register of the United States Centennial Exposition* (New York, 1877); James Dabney McCabe, *The Illustrated History of the Centennial Exposition* (Philadelphia, 1876).

108. McCabe, *The Illustrated History of the Centennial Exhibition,* 271. Many of these passengers would presumably have visited the exhibition more than once.

109. *Philadelphia Inquirer,* July 18, 1876, article on "Miners' Excursion."

mechanical, industrial civilization. Or so, at least, was the intention of those who organized the excursions. How the workers and their families behaved when liberated from the stultifying constraints of a company-sponsored day out was not reported in the mainstream press. But the ideological aims of these excursions were certainly made explicit, as for example in an article titled "Poor Man's Day at the Exhibition" in the *Philadelphia Inquirer* on September 8, 1876. Saturday was "cheap day" at the exposition, the day when ordinary working men and women congregated in Fairmount Park to enjoy the spectacle. According to the *Inquirer,* the women, true to prevailing conceptions of gender, once again headed with their children for the Art Gallery "or the other buildings designed to gratify mere curiosity." The men, on the other hand, gazed "with amazed interest" at the "wonder-working" machines in Machinery Hall. Contemplating these mechanical wonders, the worker came to realize that "unless he elevates himself above the low level of a thoughtless laborer for the bread of the passing day, he and his offspring must continually sink lower in the social scale, and perhaps perish in the end of starvation."[110]

Far from being the enemy of labor, mechanization was presented as "the friend of the workman who has brains enough to study and comprehend his own interest." The "cheap Saturdays" at the exposition, in short, were "a school of betterment" in which the worker could study the benefits of machinery. And if, in so doing, he failed to progress beyond "his own comparatively worthless life," he could at least ensure the prosperity of his children by heeding the onward march of progress.[111] Here, then, was the antithesis of the Molly Maguires: sober, industrious, respectable working men and women, edified by the sights at the exposition, laboring patiently to improve their own social standing and that of their children. As a solution to the ravages of the great depression of the 1870s this was scarcely realistic; but as an antidote to Molly Maguireism it was logical and convincing. In this emerging world of mechanical order and industrial efficiency there could be no place for the Molly Maguires. By February 1877 all the leading suspects in the alleged conspiracy had been convicted and fifteen men were on death row in Pottsville, Bloomsburg, and Mauch Chunk. In June, the executions began.

110. *Philadelphia Inquirer,* September 8, 1876, article entitled "Poor Man's Day at the Exhibition."

111. Ibid.

9

Black Thursday

The executions of the Molly Maguires consisted of powerful intimidatory rituals. The heyday of public executions had ended before the Molly Maguires were hanged, but the hangings were public spectacles nonetheless. The Pennsylvania legislature had abolished public executions in 1834 and required that capital punishment be inflicted within the walls or yard of the jail in the county where the criminal was convicted. But the new privacy did not mean that executions ceased to be occasions of ritual and spectacle. "In principle," as one historian has observed, "private executions were supposed to protect the sensibilities of all citizens, eliminate a scene of public chaos and confusion, and permit the prisoner to die quietly penitent." In practice, "they became a theatrical event for an assembly of elite men who attended the executions by invitation while the community at large was excluded."[1] This was certainly the case in the lower anthracite region of Pennsylvania, where a few hundred citizens were granted the privilege of attending the executions of the Molly Maguires, while thousands of their fellow-citizens congregated outside the prison walls. Armed troops and policemen kept guard and ostentatiously

1. Louis P. Masur, *Rites of Execution: Capital Punishment and the Transformation of American Culture, 1776–1865* (New York, 1989), 111. See, also, Michel Foucault, *Discipline and Punish: The Birth of the Prison* (1977; New York, 1979), 47–58.

paraded the streets of Pottsville and Mauch Chunk. Each of the participants in the rituals of execution had a carefully orchestrated role to play: the condemned men, the Catholic priests, the sheriff and the hangman, the jurors and the doctors, and the privileged observers. Once the hanging was done, the prison gates were thrown open and hundreds of men and women rushed in to inspect the gallows. Moreover, the privatization of hanging in the United States had coincided with the rise of an inexpensive popular press, so these ostensibly private events were portrayed in vivid colors for a wider audience than ever before. In the case of the Molly Maguires, the preparations, procedures, and aftermath of the executions were exhaustively reported in the press and in popular pamphlets and histories, not only in the anthracite region but throughout the United States. Most of this discourse was celebratory and some of it verged on the obscene.

In short, the executions of the Molly Maguires may have been formally private, but they were anything but secret. For those who witnessed them, the hangings were macabre theatrical spectacles. They also had a considerable impact on those who were not directly involved: the thousands of men and women who took the day off from work, joined the crowds milling about outside the prisons walls, observed the display of military force by the authorities, or at the very least, read about the executions in the newspapers and talked about them at home, at work, and in the taverns. To heighten the impact on the public, it was arranged for the first ten executions to take place on a single day, June 21, 1877, known locally as Black Thursday. The message was clear: As so many of the newspapers noted, the majesty of the law had been outraged and now it must be vindicated.[2] Together with the discourse that accompanied them, the rituals of execution sent a stern warning to the residents of the anthracite region, proclaiming the triumph of order over anarchy. They also consolidated the notion that the Molly Maguires were inherently depraved and had represented a conspiracy of enormous proportions. In this way, the myth of the Molly Maguires was refined and perfected.

After their convictions, several of the men appealed their cases to the Pennsylvania Supreme Court. But on March 13, 1877, the court rejected the appeals of Carroll, Boyle, McGehan, and Roarity, on March 26 it rejected Campbell's appeal, and on May 21 it rejected Duffy's. The court's ruling in the Campbell case was quite instructive on the legal issues involved in the Molly Maguire trials. Campbell's attorney pointed to four main reasons why the case should be

2. For the theme of the "vindication" of "the outraged majesty of the law" during the trials see, for example, *MJ*, February 3, July 3, 1876; and, during the executions, *SH*, June 21, 1877; *Pottsville Evening Chronicle*, June 21, 1877; *MJ*, June 22, 1877; *Philadelphia Press*, June 22, 1877; *Philadelphia Inquirer*, June 22, 1877; *Philadelphia Public Ledger*, June 21, 1877; *New York Sun*, June 22, 1877; *Chicago Tribune*, June 22, 1877.

dismissed: The jury was loaded, the accusations against the AOH were irrelevant, Kerrigan was an "infamous witness" whose testimony should be discounted, and McParlan had been an accessory before the fact in the Jones murder. The court rejected all four grounds for a dismissal, ruling on the fourth that "a detective who joins a criminal organization for the purpose of exposing it, and bringing criminals to punishment, and honestly carries out that design, is not an accessory before the fact, although he may have encouraged and counseled parties who were about to commit crime, if in so doing he intended that they should be discovered and punished." The testimony of a detective, therefore, was "not to be treated as that of an infamous witness."[3] Here, lest there be any lingering doubts, was a final exoneration of James McParlan from the charges leveled against him by the defense attorneys at the trials.

With the rejection of their appeals, the condemned men looked to alternative sources of mercy. A group of nine clergymen and three laymen wrote to Archbishop Wood from Ireland, vouching for the good character of Thomas Munley, apparently in the hope that Wood might intercede on his behalf. They could scarcely have known that he was not exactly the best man to turn to at this time. Alexander Campbell's lawyer, Daniel Kalbfus, went to see Governor Hartranft personally, to plead for mercy for his client. Campbell's wife accompanied Kalbfus on the trip to Harrisburg and presented Hartranft with a testimonial on his character signed by five prominent residents of his home town, Dungloe, in County Donegal.[4]

When the governor said he could do nothing, Kalbfus and lawyers for the other condemned men appealed the cases to the Pennsylvania Board of Pardons. District Attorney Siewers of Mauch Chunk, among others, demanded that the punishment be carried out as planned, while friends and relatives of the convicts sent letters pleading for mercy. Fr. Daniel McDermott, who was beginning to have second thoughts on the subject of the Molly Maguires, interceded on behalf of Michael J. Doyle and asked the board to commute his death sentence to life in prison. Doyle, he insisted, had been a mere pawn in the hands of ruthless leaders, and he could not have backed out of the Jones killing "without losing his own life."[5]

When the Pardon Board finally met on June 16, it upheld all ten convictions. The newspapers were exultant. The attitude of the *New York Herald,* always an outspoken opponent of the Molly Maguires, was typical:

> Only those who live in the coal regions, and have been forced to become familiar with the atrocious crimes committed by the infamous Molly Maguires, can adequately appreciate the feeling of satisfaction which prevails in this community at the recent action of the Board of Pardons.

3. Pennsylvania Supreme Court ruling, March 26, 1877, quoted in Shalloo, *Private Police,* 153.

4. SCBS, Molly Maguire Collection, undated letter from Michael Munnelly [sic] et al. to Archbishop Wood; Campbell, *A Molly Maguire Story,* 142.

5. Broehl, *The Molly Maguires,* 337.

All week long there had been worries that the Pardon Board would commute the sentences, "and the bare prospect of the gallows being cheated of its prey appeared to many like a public calamity." But now "these apprehensions have been dispelled and people breathe freer that it is certain that the majesty of offended law will be vindicated."[6]

With the last hope of the condemned men exhausted, the final preparations for the executions began. These preparations were both procedural and ideological. In part, it was a matter of drawing up a precise timetable for the hangings, and constructing and testing the gallows; in part a question of the psychological preparation of the condemned men, and of the residents of the anthracite region, for the events that unfolded on June 21. The people of Pottsville and Mauch Chunk had only to walk through the streets to see the extra policemen and the troops, or to pass by the prison yards in order to hear the sounds of the gallows being constructed. The newspapers were filled with maps of the prisons, sketches of the gallows, and detailed histories of the crimes of the Molly Maguires.[7]

The gallows were described in vivid and minute detail, and they deserved this treatment, for the "two Death Machines" were indeed quite ominous.[8] At Mauch Chunk, two cross-bars were added to the gallows, so that all four condemned men could be hanged at once. The scaffold was erected in a corridor within the prison itself, rather than in the yard. It was located just outside the cell of Alexander Campbell, who could hear every hammer-blow as the structure was being erected. The relatives of the condemned men had to pass the scaffold on their way in and out of the cells, and the *New York Herald* reported that when Mrs. Campbell first set eyes on "the awful machine which is to deprive her husband of his life she was thrown into hysterics, and her shrieks and groans were truly heartbreaking."[9]

The authorities at Pottsville went one better than those at Mauch Chunk, constructing a special gallows with three cross-beams, each capable of hanging two men. This elaborate structure, a contemporary pamphlet suggested, was designed so that the sheriff could "prevent a protraction of the horrible affair by hanging six murderers at once."[10] In other words, it was admirably designed to impress upon observers the power and majesty of the law. "The scaffold is in place and ready for its ghastly work," the *Miners' Journal* reported on June 21. "It was viewed yesterday afternoon by between 500 and 600 people. . . . Viewed

6. New York *Herald*, June 20, 1877.

7. Material on the executions can be found in *New York Herald*, June 17, 18, 19, 20, 21, 22, 1877; *NYT*, June 22, 1877; *New York Sun*, June 22, 1877; *MJ*, June 18, 21, 22, 23, 1877; *SH*, June 15, 16, 22, 23, 1877; *Philadelphia Inquirer*, June 21, 22, 1877; *Philadelphia Press*, June 21, 22, 1877; *Pottsville Evening Chronicle*, June 18, 19, 20, 21, 22, 1877; *Philadelphia Public Ledger*, June 20, 21, 1877; *Frank Leslie's Illustrated Newspaper*, June 16, 30, July 7, 1877; and Barclay, *Lives and Crimes*, 38–41.

8. The phrase is taken from Barclay, *Lives and Crimes*, 38–41.

9. *New York Herald*, June 20, 1877.

10. Barclay, *Lives and Crimes*, 38–39.

in the pale light of the moon last night and with the full knowledge of the work it is designed to do today, it was an object to chill the blood of the observer and to bring home to him a realization of what this day will bring forth."[11]

Alongside these descriptions of the "death machines," several newspapers reported that the Molly Maguires were planning an armed assault to free their comrades on the eve of their execution. Evidently alarmed by these rumors, the authorities in Mauch Chunk requested assistance from Harrisburg, and Governor Hartranft dispatched a military company, the Easton Grays. After parading through the city with open bayonets, applauded by a large crowd, the troops joined the Coal & Iron Police at the county prison. In Pottsville, the regular metropolitan police force was supplemented by special policemen appointed for the occasion, along with a detachment of the Coal & Iron Police under the command of Captain Robert J. Linden. "These latter," the *Miners' Journal* reported, "were armed with navy revolvers, Winchester rifles, and double-barreled shot guns loaded with buck shot." The *New York Times* reported that

> there were all sorts of rumors of impending disaster flying about, but one after another, on investigation, proved to be untrue. The detectives shadowed all suspicious persons. . . . Mounted police were sent out to assist the foot detail in patrolling the outskirts of the town, and sentinels were posted on the parapet of the jail.[12]

With both Pottsville and Mauch Chunk secured by armed force, the final preparations were made on the night of June 20. Undertakers arrived at the prisons to measure the men for their coffins, and the Reading Railroad arranged to have special trains to convey the bodies out of town and to transport the mourning relatives and friends. In Mauch Chunk, the condemned men bade their friends and families farewell on the night before their executions. In Pottsville the relatives were admitted early on the morning of the hangings. Thomas Munley's father, who had walked the fourteen miles from Girardville to Pottsville during the night, arrived at the prison gates at four o'clock. Thomas Duffy's father and brother, and Roarity's wife, brother, and two sisters were also admitted. Mrs. Roarity brought with her a letter to her husband from his father in Meencorvick, County Donegal.[13]

This poignant letter offers some insights into the consoling power of religion in times of extreme grief, as well as hinting at the fatalism of the Donegal Irish. "Dear Loving Son," Columbus Roarity wrote,

11. *MJ*, June 21, 1877. See also *New York Herald*, June 21, 1877, for a description of the scaffold; *Pottsville Evening Chronicle*, June 18, 19, 1877, for a sketch of the interior of Schuylkill County Prison, and interviews with the families of the condemned men.

12. *MJ*, June 21, 1877; *NYT*, June 22, 1877; *Philadelphia Inquirer*, June 21, 1877; *New York Herald*, June 20, 1877; *Philadelphia Public Ledger*, June 21, 1877.

13. *MJ*, June 21, 1877; *NYT*, June 22, 1877.

> I sit to write you the last letter I'll ever write again, and don't be afraid to meet your doom or your Judge. If you are going to suffer innocent I am sure God will spare your soul, and its far better to suffer in this world than in the world to come. No matter how long we suffer in this cursed world its nothing beside eternity.

After assuring his son that he believed in his innocence, Roarity's father told him not to be afraid, for he would shortly join him in heaven.[14] "Roarity was much affected by the reading of the letter, and like the rest of the men, was terribly shaken by the ordeal of parting," the *New York Times* reported.[15] His wife was the last to leave, at about half past eight. "Her cries at parting were horrible, resounding through and through the prison and making all within hearing nervous and uncomfortable. She went from the door moaning and sobbing most piteously."[16] Thomas Duffy's sister, who had come all the way from New York City to bid him farewell, arrived only at nine o'clock, and was refused permission to see her brother.[17] By that time, the final preparations for the hangings were well underway in both Pottsville and Mauch Chunk, and the priests were in the cells, helping the men to confront their impending death.

The four prisoners in Mauch Chunk were executed first. The condemned men had retired at about midnight and rose at four o'clock. Four Catholic priests arrived to hear their confessions and administer the sacrament of communion; the clergymen in attendance were Fr. Bunce of Mauch Chunk, Fr. McIlhone of Lawrytown, Fr. Heinan of East Mauch Chunk, and Fr. Wynne of Summit Hill. At daybreak, a crowd began to gather outside the prison walls. Trainloads of people arrived from other parts of the county. With the crowd growing, the Easton Grays took up position in front of the jail to preserve order. All those authorized to enter the jail as witnesses were directed to present themselves at the gates by half past nine. Just before ten they were admitted: twenty-four jurors, eighty deputies, perhaps fifty journalists, and seventy local citizens privileged with entry permits.[18]

On entering the corridor where the men were to be hanged, the first thing the witnesses saw was the scaffold. Ropes dangled from each of the four gallows, steel manacles for the feet and hands of each prisoner were placed in the four corners of the scaffold, and a white cap was laid beside each set of manacles.[19] Outside, a huge crowd continued to mill about. They were "excited," the

14. *SH*, June 22, 1877; Broehl, *The Molly Maguires*, 338–39.

15. *NYT*, June 22, 1877.

16. *MJ*, June 22, 1877.

17. Ibid.

18. *NYT*, June 22, 1877: "The executions took place in the presence of 150 people, a third of whom were representatives of the press."

19. *NYT*, June 22, 1877; *MJ*, June 23, 1877.

Philadelphia Inquirer reported, "not so much by the fact that four individual shedders of human blood were paying the penalty of their humanity, as by the knowledge that the most relentless combination of assassins that had been known in American history was meeting the fatal rebuke of offended law."[20]

On the scaffold, the condemned men and their clergy acted out a liturgy and a ritual that were at once doctrinal and ideological. At 10:26 A.M., Alexander Campbell emerged from his cell and walked toward the scaffold, attended by Sheriff Raudenbush and Fr. Wynne of Summit Hill. Like the other three condemned men, he was dressed in a black suit and carried a crucifix. Campbell took up position at the southwest corner of the scaffold and fixed his eyes on the crucifix. Asked if he had anything to say, he forgave his executioners and requested forgiveness in return. Attended by Fr. Bunce, Michael Doyle then took up position opposite Campbell, and spoke for about a minute, asking for forgiveness and blaming his plight on his failure to heed the teachings of the Catholic church on secret societies.[21]

While Doyle was speaking, John "Yellow Jack" Donahue was led up beside Campbell, accompanied by Fr. Heinan of East Mauch Chunk. "Campbell was now passionately kissing his crucifix, while his lips moved in prayer. Donahue and Doyle, holding their crucifixes and kissing them earnestly, were bowed forward and crossing themselves and beating their breasts."[22] Donahue declined to say anything, and Edward Kelly was then led onto the scaffold, attended by Fr. McIlhone of Lawrytown. He was placed beside Doyle and opposite Donahue. When asked if he had anything to say, Kelly was unable to remember the words he had prepared, and he was led through the speech by his priest.

> Speaking very distinctly Kelly said:
> "I have only to say that I forgive everybody, and if I had obeyed my bishops and priests I would not be here today."
> "And that you hope," suggested Father McIlhone.
> "And that I hope," repeated Kelly, "that God will forgive me."
> "And that you forgive every one," prompted the Reverend Father.
> "And that I forgive everyone that has injured me in any way."
> "And that in order that you may be forgiven," again prompted the Priest.
> "And that in order that I may be forgiven I hope."
> "That all whom you have injured."
> "That all whom I have injured."
> "Will forgive you."
> "Will forgive me."[23]

The priests were grim and sober but the Catholic church had finally been vindicated and the message was quite clear: Had the men obeyed the teachings of

20. *Philadelphia Inquirer*, June 22, 1877.

21. *MJ*, June 23, 1877; *NYT*, June 22, 1877; *Philadelphia Press*, June 22, 1877; Barclay, *Lives and Crimes*, 53.

22. *MJ*, June 23, 1877.

23. Ibid.

the Church they would never had found themselves in this position. In this respect, and in several others, the executions on Black Thursday reenacted a ritual that had been conducted countless times in Ireland; for example, the hanging of the "Molly Maguire" Patrick Hasty in County Roscommon in 1847 for the assassination of Major Denis Mahon.[24]

When the four men had taken their places, all present at the scaffold were directed to kneel and Fr. Bunce read the prayers for the dying. Placing their hands on the heads of the still kneeling men, the priests blessed and absolved them, shook their hands for the last time, and left the scaffold. The men continued to pray until they were ordered to rise. Their hands and feet were manacled, ropes were placed around their necks, and white hoods were placed over their heads.[25] "The prisoners were praying earnestly when at a quarter of eleven o'clock the drop was sprung and in an instant four figures were twisting and spinning around inside the four posts of the gibbet."[26]

All forms of capital punishment are cruel and unusual, but hanging is particularly barbaric. If the victim is lucky, his neck is broken and he loses consciousness rapidly or immediately; if he is especially lucky, he may even die of shock or heart failure at the moment the trap drops. But if he is unlucky (for example, if the noose turns and slips out of place on his neck), he is slowly strangled on the end of a rope. A rapid, efficient hanging requires considerable precision, and something clearly went wrong in the cases of Donahue and Kelly. While Doyle and Campbell had their necks cleanly broken and did not struggle, Donahue's neck "was not broken, and he struggled for about thirty seconds, rattling his manacles by the rapid motions of his hands and feet."[27] Immediately after the drop fell, "he drew up his legs and threw them forward four times in succession. Then, hanging quietly for an instant he drew up again, and quivering so that the rope was shaken he relapsed and hung quietly at full length."[28] Kelly, "drew his hands up on his left side, but not so much as Donahue. He also threw his feet forward slightly, but for the balance of the time hung quietly."[29] Within two minutes, "the men hung motionless, the four white caps appearing just above the place where the traps had rested."[30]

Though all four men may have been unconscious, they were not yet dead. Donahue's heart stopped beating six minutes after he was hanged, Kelly's after eleven minutes, Doyle's after thirteen, and Campbell's after fifteen. After the bodies were cut down, the sheriff invited the spectators to come onto the scaffold and look at them. Kelly's eyes bulged open, and his tongue protruded from his open mouth; Donahue's shirt-front was covered in blood; the faces of

24. Dublin *Freeman's Journal,* August 10, 1848; cf. chapter 1.
25. *NYT,* June 21, 1877; *MJ,* June 23, 1877; Barclay, *Lives and Crimes,* 53.
26. *MJ,* June 23, 1877.
27. *NYT,* June 22, 1877.
28. *MJ,* June 23, 1877.
29. Ibid.
30. *MJ,* June 22, 1877.

Campbell and Doyle, who had been luckier, were calm and composed. With the hanging done, the Easton Grays left Mauch Chunk, although detachments of the Coal & Iron Police were dispatched to the burial places of each of the executed men.[31] Thus ended the first executions in the history of Carbon County.[32]

In Pottsville, meanwhile, the six condemned men had also arisen at 4:00 A.M. After they had parted with their families, the priests arrived. An altar had been taken to the prison from St. Patrick's Church the previous night. At seven o'clock Fr. McDermott celebrated mass for Thomas Duffy, James Carroll, and James Roarity, and at half past seven Fr. Gately said mass for Hugh McGehan, James Boyle, and Thomas Munley. All six prisoners received communion, as did Duffy's brother, and sixteen-year-old Kate Boyle, the cousin of James Boyle who was serving a sentence for perjury committed on his behalf.[33] "The religious exercises were resumed and kept up without cessation until the arrival of the fatal moment."[34] By eight o'clock a vast crowd had formed outside the prison walls. The chief burgess of Pottsville had issued a proclamation asking the saloons to stay closed. According to the *New York Times,* the order was generally obeyed, and "as a consequence very little drunkenness was seen on the streets. As for symptoms of violence or even of excitement, they were entirely absent. The prevailing air, among men of all nationalities, was one of gravity and sadness."[35]

At the prison, the borough police and heavily armed Coal & Iron policemen kept order. At eight o'clock the officials, physicians, and the jurymen ("all of Pennsylvania Dutch descent") were allowed into the prison, and an hour later the reporters and others with official passes were admitted. These privileged observers were sworn in as temporary deputy sheriffs, empowered to use armed force to quell disorder if necessary. Fewer than two hundred people witnessed the executions directly; but, as the *Miners' Journal* reported, "The hills around the jail were full of those whose curiosity had led them thither." The mine workers of Schuylkill County evidently ignored an order by the Philadelphia & Reading Coal & Iron Company to stay at work that day, and hundreds of them arrived in Pottsville by train. According to the *New York Times,* "the neighboring hill-tops were soon covered with a heterogeneous but quiet and orderly assemblage of men, women, and children." Inside the prison yard, "the crowd gathered down to the thick rope that had been drawn across the green, 18 feet in front of the triple scaffold, and took up such positions as they considered most favorable for a good view."[36]

31. *MJ,* June 23, 1877; *New York Herald,* June 22, 1877; *NYT,* June 22, 1877.

32. There had been no executions in either Carbon County or Columbia County before the Molly Maguire hangings. In Schuylkill County there had been two: James Riggs, an African American convicted of murdering a white man, was hanged in 1847; and Joseph Brown was hanged in 1875 for murdering Daniel S. Kreamer and his wife. See *MJ,* March 29, 1878; June 14, 1878.

33. *NYT,* June 22, 1877.

34. Ibid.

35. Ibid.

36. *MJ,* June 22, 1877; *NYT,* June 22, 1877; Barclay, *Lives and Crimes,* 41.

Though a scaffold capable of hanging six men at once had been specially constructed, it was decided in the end to hang the men in pairs. The first to be executed were James Boyle and Hugh McGehan. At 10:57, a procession emerged from the cells, led by the sheriff and the warden of the prison. Boyle was accompanied by Fr. Beresford of Port Carbon and McGehan by Fr. Walsh of Heckscherville. The priests were dressed "in black cassocks, white surplices and black stoles bounded with white, with white crosses at either end," and they "prayed fervently."[37] McGehan wore "dark blue clothes, with a black necktie tucked under a long, turn-down collar over a white shirt front. In his bosom was stuck a bunch of red and white roses."[38] Boyle "wore a shirt of black cloth without collar or necktie, and carried in his hand a large red rose, which he smelled occasionally on his way to the gallows."[39] The priests carried large crucifixes, and each of the condemned men was given a crucifix to hold as the prayers for the dying were read. In their last words, Boyle and McGehan asked for forgiveness, and Boyle forgave those who were about to hang him. The priests held the crucifixes for the two men to kiss, and then stepped aside. At 11:10 the trap-door fell. The priests knelt and began praying, aloud at first, and then in more subdued tones.[40]

The next pair to be hanged were James Carroll and James Roarity. At 12:06 the second procession appeared, with Carroll accompanied by Fr. Gately of St. Patrick's Cathedral, and Roarity by Fr. Beresford. Roarity "wore dark striped trousers and waistcoat, black alpaca coat, and white shirt, without collar or tie. A bunch of roses was fastened on his breast." Carroll "was attired in a brown sack coat, black waistcoat, and trousers, white shirt and turn-down collar, with a black tie, and was without flower or ornament of any kind." According to the *New York Times,* Carroll "showed a quiet bravery, while Roarity was painfully nervous, heaving a profound sigh every few minutes during the prayers. Twice tears forced themselves from his eyes."[41]

Carroll was placed on the right trap and Roarity on the left. The day before he died, Carroll had dictated a final statement to Fr. Daniel McDermott, insisting that he was innocent of the murder of Benjamin Yost. Carroll, who had not been present at the scene of the crime, was convicted on the evidence of the informer Jimmy Kerrigan, and he insisted that Kerrigan was the man who had planned the murder. Fr. McDermott was now convinced that there had been a miscarriage of justice in the Yost case, and the day after the executions he announced, "I know, beyond all reasonable doubt, that Duffy was not a party to the murder of Policeman Yost, and I think the same remark will apply with almost equal force to Carroll."[42]

37. Barclay, *Lives and Crimes,* 45.
38. *NYT,* June 22, 1877.
39. Ibid.
40. Ibid.; Barclay, *Lives and Crimes,* 45.
41. All details from *NYT,* June 22, 1877.
42. *Philadelphia Times,* June 22, 1877 (quote); Barclay, *Lives and Crimes,* 51; *NYT,* June 22, 1877; *SH,* June 22, 1877.

After prayers had been said, Roarity and Carroll kissed the crucifixes and their priests, and they were allowed to make short speeches. Roarity had been convicted on the grounds that he had paid Jimmy Kerrigan to arrange the Yost murder, but he now strenuously denied Kerrigan's allegation and insisted that he was innocent. He also declared that Thomas Duffy had not been involved in the Yost case in any way. Carroll, having made his peace with his spiritual advisor, chose not to protest further on the scaffold. He simply said: "'I have nothing to say but that I am innocent of the charge'—he stopped and corrected himself—'of the crime I am charged with.'" Roarity reportedly interjected at this point: "That's what I forgot to mention. I am going to die an innocent man. The men that prosecuted me I forgive, and I hope God will forgive them and me too."[43] Without further ado, Carroll and Roarity were bound with leather straps, their nooses were fixed, and white hoods were placed over their heads. Then, at 12:21, as an anonymous pamphleteer put it, "two more of the thugs of Schuylkill County were hanged from the ends of dangling ropes."[44]

At 1:11 the third and final procession of the day approached the scaffold. Thomas Duffy was accompanied by Fr. McGovern of Minersville, and Thomas Munley by Fr. Depmar of Pottsville. Duffy "was attired in black clothing, with a velvet collar to his coat, a black, white, and red bow under his collar, a small white rose in his buttonhole, and a single stud in his shirt bosom." Munley "was dressed in a black broadcloth coat with a velvet collar, trousers and waistcoat of black ribbed cloth, white shirt and collar, and black necktie. He wore a jeweled cross in his bosom." Duffy stood on the left trap and Munley on the right. After the prayers, they were asked if they had anything to say. "There is no use," Duffy replied; and Munley answered, "It's too late now." The drop fell at 1:20.[45]

Of the ten men who were hanged on Black Thursday, the one whose conviction contemporary observers found most questionable was Thomas Duffy. The only evidence against him had been provided by the informer Jimmy Kerrigan, and it had come as a surprise even to the most hostile observers when he was convicted of first-degree murder the previous September.[46] It was widely rumored in Pottsville that he would win a reprieve at the last moment. "Inside the jail," the reporter for the *New York Times* wrote on the day of the executions, "rumors of a reprieve began to fill the air, Duffy's name, for some untraceable reason, being mentioned in connection with it."[47] The details are vague and incomplete, but according to several contemporary sources, Governor Hartranft had sent his private secretary, Chester N. Farr, to Pottsville with a reprieve for Duffy, to be used in the event that one or more of the other condemned men should declare Duffy innocent. Roarity did precisely that in his final words on the scaffold. But Farr apparently decided that this explicit

43. *NYT*, June 22, 1877.

44. Barclay, *Lives and Crimes*, 49.

45. All details from *NYT*, June 22, 1877.

46. *SH*, September 20, 1876; cf. the account of the Duffy trial in chapter 8.

47. *NYT*, June 22, 1877.

statement of Duffy's innocence was inadequate; the reprieve stayed in his pocket, and Duffy was duly executed.[48]

After the bodies had been removed, the prison gates were thrown open and the crowd was allowed in to inspect the scaffold. The *Miners' Journal* reported that three thousand people visited the prison yard that afternoon.[49] The bodies of the executed men were placed in ice boxes and transported to their places of burial. The Reading Railroad provided special trains to transport the bodies and to carry relatives and friends. Despite the protracted dispute between the Catholic church and the Molly Maguires, the executed men were not denied burial in consecrated ground. They had always been Catholics, even if their version of that religion had not conformed to the dictates of the hierarchy. All ten men were buried in local Catholic cemeteries, Campbell, Doyle, McGehan, and Boyle in coffins provided by their families and the other six men in coffins provided by the county.[50] In at least one case, that of Alexander Campbell, there was a protracted and boisterous wake, of precisely the type frowned upon by the Catholic church, conducted in the Irish language and featuring the distinctively Gaelic practice of "keening." According to the newspaper man who reported the wake, the participants switched to Irish as soon they noticed he was present. Here, once again, was some fleeting evidence of the closed, alien culture embodied by Molly Maguireism, from which outsiders were rigidly excluded. Here, also, was a cultural pattern that would need careful monitoring if the "wilder" Irish of west Ulster and Connacht were to be tamed. Black Thursday was a major step in that direction.[51] Not since "the hanging of twenty-six negroes in Charleston, on account of the Vesey plot," the *New York Sun* exulted, had "such a tribute been paid to the gallows in any state."[52]

A specific structure of meaning was formed around the Molly Maguires in the 1870s, especially at the time of the trials and executions. The historical evidence can be read as "a sort of battleground around the crime, its punishment and its memory," a particularly useful image for making sense of the Molly Maguires.[53] Representing the Molly Maguires was a matter of ideology in the nineteenth century, and it remains so today. There has always been considerable

48. *SH,* June 23, 1877; Barclay, *Lives and Crimes,* 44, 51.

49. *MJ,* June 22, 1877.

50. *MJ,* June 21, 1877; *NYT,* June 22, 1877; *SH,* June 29, 1877. Munley and Kelly were buried in Pottsville, Donahue and Duffy in Tamaqua, Doyle in Minersville, Carroll in Packerton (East Mauch Chunk), Roarity in Allentown, and Campbell, McGehan, and Boyle in Summit Hill.

51. On Campbell's wake, see *New York Sun,* June 23, 1877. "Keening" was a form of emotional expression, often unbridled, led by women and conducted in the Irish language. Cf. Connolly, *Priests and People,* chapter 4.

52. *New York Sun,* June 22, 1877. The Denmark Vesey slave conspiracy occurred in Charleston, South Carolina, in 1822.

53. Foucault, *Discipline and Punish,* 67–68; he was referring to eighteenth-century France.

disagreement on their nature and significance. But one specific narrative quickly became dominant in the 1870s: the Molly Maguires as a band of Irish cut-throats, engaging in violence for its own sake, for money, or for revenge, who terrorized the anthracite region for more than a decade before they were finally brought to justice by a heroic Pinkerton detective and his employer, the Reading Railroad. The story was told in several ways, but all had in common a number of basic rhetorical forms that belong to the realm of mythology.

The term *mythology* is used here to mean a process of conveying meaning that denies history and creates a static world, closed to the possibility of change; and related to this, a belief in essential, timeless categories of human nature, like goodness and badness. Mythology empties reality of history and fills it with nature; it denies that things are made rather than found; it claims that its concepts are applicable in all times and places, rather than seeing them as socially and historically contingent. It is a system of values masquerading as a system of facts. If the discourse on the Molly Maguires can be read as an ideological battle, the form of representation that emerged victorious was mythology. The victory was won, in rhetorical terms at least, by freezing time, by embalming history into static categories of good and evil.[54]

If a single theme dominated the myth of the Molly Maguires, it was the absence of any motivation for the crimes of which they stood accused. The crimes were explained in terms of a natural Irish propensity toward violence and savagery. The argument was ahistorical and perfectly circular: The Irish committed all these crimes because they were savage, and the proof of their savagery was that they had committed these crimes.[55] It was chiefly in terms of this dead, motionless world—this world of timeless, irremediable Irish barbarity—that the Molly Maguire myth was perfected in the 1870s. The Molly Maguire trials and the executions that followed, in short, were more than a question of enforcing a specific vision of justice. They also involved the construction of a specific kind of meaning, the myth of the Molly Maguires.

The makings of this myth were evident in the remarkable speeches of the prosecuting attorneys during the summer of 1876. In the Hester case, for example, Francis W. Hughes announced that the real "accessory before the fact" in all the crimes being considered was the Molly Maguires, also known as the Ancient Order of Hibernians, whose predecessors included the Persian *assassins* and the "Thugs of India."[56] All were of a type, a single evil strand running through history, and Hughes called upon the jury "to help exterminate this hellborn organization, and send it back to the Prince of Darkness whence it came."[57] George Kaercher referred to the Ancient Order of Hibernians as "one

54. Roland Barthes, *Mythologies* (1957; New York, 1990), passim, especially the final chapter, "Myth Today."

55. Ibid., 153. As in most myth-making, tautology replaced history.

56. [Town], *Commonwealth v. Patrick Hester, Patrick Tully, and Peter McHugh, Argument of F. W. Hughes,* 17–18.

57. Ibid., 31.

of the greatest criminal organizations of which mention can be found. . . . Never since the world began has there existed a more villainous society or more horrible organization than the one the leaders of which we have brought to this bar for trial."[58] Guy Farquhar described them as "a band of cut-throats and assassins, who have stopped at nothing for the purpose of carrying out their plans."[59]

Leading the condemnation throughout the mid-1870s was the *Miners' Journal.* Prior to their arrests, the newspaper claimed, the Molly Maguires had "dominated and terrorized the entire coal regions in this section of the commonwealth," robbing and beating all who stood in their way. "Their fiercest hostility was manifested toward the 'bosses,' who were shot down, in some instances in open daylight, as though they were so many rabid dogs, and as though their destroyers were clothed with power to trample upon all law, human and divine."[60] This excerpt from the *Miners' Journal* contains the three rhetorical forms that were central to the making of the Molly Maguire myth. First, hyperbole: The Mollys had "dominated and terrorized the entire coal regions." Second, the inherent depravity of the criminals: "bloodthirsty," "obdurate and fiendish," unfit for "freedom." And, third, a struggle between order and disorder, cast in manichaean terms: "law, human and divine," versus "turbulent, bloodthirsty lawlessness." These three rhetorical forms were to be found in one variety or another in nearly all the contemporary newspaper accounts and in the various pamphlets and contemporary histories published in the 1870s and 1880s.

The theme of a gigantic conspiracy, developed at considerable length by the prosecuting attorneys during the trials, continued to be elaborated in the newspapers at the time of the executions. For the *Philadelphia Inquirer,* the Molly Maguires were "the most relentless combination of assassins that had been known in American history." The *Philadelphia Public Ledger* lauded the mass executions of June 21, 1877, as "a day of deliverance from as awful a despotism of banded murderers as the world has ever seen in any age." According to the *Chicago Tribune,* "Modern history affords no more striking illustration of the terrible power for evil of a secret oath-bound organization controlled by murderers and assassins than the awful record of crime committed by the orders of the Mollie Maguires in the anthracite-coal region of Pennsylvania."[61]

Similar descriptions were found in contemporary pamphlets on the Molly Maguires. Barclay & Company's *The Lives and Crimes of the Mollie Maguires* (1877), for example, described in familiar detail how the Molly Maguires had terrorized eastern Pennsylvania for "fourteen years."[62] The anonymous author

58. RCK, 218.

59. RCK, 3.

60. *MJ,* June 22, 1877.

61. *Philadelphia Inquirer,* June 22, 1877; *Philadelphia Public Ledger,* June 21, 1877; *Chicago Tribune,* June 22, 1877.

62. Barclay, *Lives and Crimes,* 19.

of another popular pamphlet on the Molly Maguires set out to "get at the bottom of facts concerning an organization which for years has held high carnival in the Coal regions of Pennsylvania, and whose track has been marked with bloodshed, incendiarism, and robbery." The Molly Maguires, he announced, had perverted the good name of the Ancient Order of Hibernians in pursuit of "their own diabolical ends, and through the terrorism thus inspired . . . kept the entire community in a state of turmoil and distrust, unknown elsewhere in the civilized world during the interim." That such an association "could exist in a civilized community during the Nineteenth Century," the author found "almost incredible."[63]

The hyperbole of the trial lawyers, the newspapers, and the sensationalist pamphlets soon reappeared as historical "facts" in the early histories of Schuylkill County. Munsell's *History of Schuylkill County* (1881) concluded that "the history of this country does not record another instance in which, by the ordinary processes of law, so great, and so wide-spread and so dangerous an evil has been destroyed—so malignant a social cancer safely extirpated." Samuel T. Wiley's *Biographical and Portrait Cyclopedia of Schuylkill County* (1893) put the matter even more bluntly: "In the history of crime in the United States no criminal organization ever made as startling a record as the Mollie Maguires, who held the anthracite coal regions in a state of terror for many years."[64]

This general pattern of exaggeration was complemented by a second rhetorical form, which portrayed the Molly Maguires as inherently depraved and evil. The *Pottsville Evening Chronicle* applauded the execution of "a set of banded assassins, whose chief delight it seemed to be to redden their hands with the life-blood of their fellow-citizens." The *Philadelphia Public Ledger* agreed: "Their main purpose was 'terrorism' and revenge; and these were accompanied by brutal beatings, incendiary fires, and assassination." Hardened criminals, "they talked as glibly and sometimes as openly [of murder] as other men do of the most ordinary affairs." According to the *Chicago Tribune,* there was no evidence that the motive of the "Mollies" was anything "other than revenge, outrage and murder." The organization, the *Tribune* concluded, "was of abnormal growth. It is a monstrosity such as is seen but once in an age. We need not expect such another in a generation, if indeed ever again."[65]

This portrayal of the condemned men as subhuman sociopaths was perhaps the central element in the myth of the Molly Maguires. To depict the Mollys as intrinsically depraved was to dispense with any need for a historical explanation of how they originated and why they acted as they did. Instead, time was frozen and a depraved and unalterable human nature was presented as an explanation in itself. As the *Philadelphia Press* said of Alexander Campbell and John

63. [Eveland & Harris], *The Molly Maguires,* Preface.

64. Munsell, *History of Schuylkill County,* 106; Wiley, *Biographical and Portrait Cyclopedia of Schuylkill County,* 131.

65. *Pottsville Evening Chronicle,* June 21, 1877; *Philadelphia Public Ledger,* June 21, 1877; *Chicago Tribune,* June 22, 1877.

"Yellow Jack" Donahue, "Both were thoroughly vile, and had no more scruples about murdering a man than about a killing an ox." The *Philadelphia Public Ledger* agreed: "Killing their victims was to them a matter of common routine, and the superior assassins . . . ordered murder as butchers order the slaughter of cattle, and the tools . . . executed the order with as little compunction as they would have killed beeves or dogs."[66]

The most vivid and shocking individual portraits of this type were drawn by the reporter for the *New York Herald,* who went to observe the condemned men in Pottsville and Mauch Chunk prisons two days before their execution. He described Alexander Campbell as "cunning, unscrupulous, grasping and ambitious," and Thomas Fisher as "contemptible in figure, without a gleam of intellect in his countenance, sneaking, cowardly and cruel." "Yellow Jack" Donahue was "dark, sullen, cold, bloody, relentless—without love for his kind, pity for his victims or regret for his crimes"; and Edward Kelly "young, small, almost fragile and seemingly idiotic." Hugh McGehan was "uneducated, coarse and brutal . . . his appearance shows him a determined hater and ruthless in his hate, stopping at nothing to encompass revenge, and free from either remorse or shame." McGehan's associate, Boyle, "was young, careless, without ambition and without a thought beyond the whisky in Jimmy Kerrigan's bottle"; Thomas Duffy was "reckless and quarrelsome"; and James Roarity was "without any positive traits of character whatsoever."[67]

The most ominous description was reserved for John Kehoe, the alleged leader of the conspiracy. "His determination is very great, his selfishness supreme, his disregard of human life is inconceivable," the *Herald* declared.

> In fiction such a character would be regarded as not only unnatural but impossible. . . . A more terrible monster is not known in all the annals of crime, and it would require the pen of De Quincey to depict his murders in all their shocking, cold blooded and startling reality.

He was, the *Chicago Tribune* agreed, "a man who boasted that he had 'more power in Schuylkill County than God Almighty.'" Francis P. Dewees, the author of the first history the Molly Maguires, reached much the same verdict. Kehoe, he declared, was

> a man of great determination of character, of an intense selfishness, that permits neither friend nor foe, kindred, family, religion, or country, native or adopted, to stand in the way of his wishes or his safety. His disregard of human life is simply appalling and inconceivable.[68]

While these vivid descriptions were confined to the level of individual savagery, the mythology of the Molly Maguires achieved its full force only when that savagery was posited in collective terms. As one historian has recently

66. *Philadelphia Press,* June 21, 1877; *Philadelphia Public Ledger,* June 21, 1877.

67. *New York Herald,* June 19, 1877.

68. Ibid.; *Chicago Tribune,* June 22, 1877; Dewees, *The Molly Maguires,* 175.

demonstrated, the category of "savagery," borrowed from the Indian wars of the western frontier, was commonly employed in the 1870s to explain the social turmoil of industrial, urban society, especially the problems of vagrancy and labor violence. In this way, class conflict was racialized, entailing the eradication of the lawless, the turbulent, and the socially wayward. This "demonization" of labor was widespread throughout the late nineteenth century, and the description of the Molly Maguires in the mainstream press offers a fine example of the ideological process involved.[69]

Given that so many of the Molly Maguires in Pennsylvania appear to have been young, transient laborers, the equation of savagery with vagrancy and rootlessness is particularly significant. In an article called "Molly Maguires and Tramps," for example, the *New York Daily Tribune* of August 14, 1876, warned that the tramps of New Jersey were "threatening . . . to do dreadful deeds next Winter—to burn and rob and murder," and sternly advised them to take warning from the "coming retribution which the Molly Maguires are experiencing." The *New York Herald* of September 22, 1876, described the "Murderous Tramps" and "Rowdy Ruffians" of New England in language strikingly similar to that deployed against the Molly Maguires, claiming that they had imposed "a reign of terror" across the eastern portion of the United States.[70] This process of representation would reach its culmination the following summer, when the great railroad strike of July 1877 was blamed on "all the 'Unsettled Humors' of society . . . the hard customers, the bummers and tramps, the Mollie Maguires and the Communists, the hoodlums, the pickpockets."[71]

The theme of savagery assumed various forms. The equation of wildness with femininity, for example, was common in representations of labor violence. During the Long Strike; *Frank Leslie's Illustrated Newspaper* portrayed a scene from the coal region with the caption "A Marked Man," from an engraving by Joseph Becker. The man "marked" for vengeance was a company official passing on horseback by a group of mine workers. At the edge of this group stood a fierce young woman, dressed in black and brandishing her fist at the man on horseback, symbolizing the vengeance to be exacted by the Molly Maguires. Though graphic illustrations of this type were quite rare, most of the textual discourse on the Molly Maguires was constructed in terms of oppositions between chaos and order, wildness and civilization, irrationality and reason, terms that fit neatly with prevailing definitions of femininity and masculinity. The image of a "carnival of crime" that was so

69. Slotkin, *Fatal Environment,* especially chapters 15, 18, 19, 20; Eugene E. Leach, "Chaining the Tiger: The Mob Stigma and the Working Class, 1863–1894," *Labor History,* 35 (Spring 1994): 187–215. For similar descriptions of the Irish (and the AOH) in the wake of New York City's Orange Riots in 1870 and 1871, see Gordon, *The Orange Riots,* especially chapter 5.

70. *New York Daily Tribune,* August 14, 1876; *New York Herald,* September 22, 1876.

71. *New York Herald,* July 27, 1877.

frequently used to describe the Molly Maguires is highly suggestive in this respect.[72]

Even more frequent was the equation of the Molly Maguires with the "Thugs." The Thugs, or *thugee,* were a religious organization active in northern India, particularly in the early nineteenth century, who reportedly robbed and murdered in the service of Kali, the goddess of destruction. As early as 1863, the *New York Times* had compared the Molly Maguires to "Thugs" in its coverage of the assassination of George K. Smith. Allan Pinkerton made the same comparison in his letter calling for the formation of vigilante committees in Schuylkill County in 1875. The analogy was also used by the prosecuting attorneys at the trials; and it was frequently employed in the sensationalist pamphlets and the press at the time of the trials and executions.[73] At a time when the Irish throughout the United States were liable to be portrayed as savages and simians, it is particularly interesting to see the Molly Maguires in America being compared to another despised group within the British Empire. The linkage of Molly Maguireism with Thuggery in this way suggests a degree of cultural convergence between the American and British elites, complementing the transfer of British capital, entrepreneurs, and skilled laborers to the United States. In a world dominated by Anglo-American Protestants, the Molly Maguires were outcasts on both sides of the Atlantic.[74]

Against depravity of the sort represented by the Molly Maguires, it was but a short and logical step to positing its opposite, the triumph of good over evil, order over anarchy, civilization over savagery. For prosecuting attorney Francis W. Hughes, the existence of the Molly Maguires outside the law was a threat to the survival of "civilized society"; they were a moral cancer in the body politic and must be cut out if that body were to survive. As early as the first Yost trial, in May 1876, the *Philadelphia Inquirer* announced the emergence of "Order out

72. For the illustration from *Frank Leslie's Illustrated Newspaper,* April 10, 1875, see fig. 2. On the image of a "carnival of crime" and "disorder," see, for example, PBIS 1, 363; [Eveland & Harris], *The Molly Maguires,* Preface; Dewees, *The Molly Maguires,* 12; *Chicago Tribune,* June 22, 1877; *New York Herald,* June 27, 1877; *Philadelphia Inquirer,* May 20, 1876. On gender as a category of discursive analysis, see Scott, *Gender and the Politics of History,* chapters 1, 2; Baron, "Gender and Labor History," 1–46.

73. The *thugee* were suppressed between 1826 and 1835. For use of the term *thugs,* see *NYT,* November 7, 1863; LC, Pinkerton MS, Letterpress Copybook iv, letter of AP to George Bangs, August 29, 1875; [Town], *Commonwealth v. Patrick Hester, Patrick Tully, and Peter McHugh, Argument of F. W. Hughes,* 18; *New York World,* May 8, 1876; Barclay, *Lives and Crimes,* 49; argument of Franklin B. Gowen in the first Yost trial (Broehl, *The Molly Maguires,* 49).

74. I am grateful to Kerby Miller for this insight. Cf. Lewis Perry Curtis, *Apes and Angels: The Irishman in Victorian Caricature* (Washington, D.C., 1971). The historiography on the Irish in the United States has concentrated on their reception as racially inferior, along with their adoption of "whiteness" in the antebellum period. The manner in which the Molly Maguires were portrayed in the 1870s suggests a need to extend both types of analysis to the postbellum period. See Dale T. Knobel, *Paddy and the Republic: Ethnicity and Nationality in Antebellum America* (Middletown, Conn., 1986); Noel Ignatiev, *How the Irish Became White* (New York, 1995); Roediger, *The Wages of Whiteness,* especially chapter 7,

of Anarchy." In its heroic victory over the Molly Maguires, the law was portrayed not as benevolent but as angry and vengeful. A week before the executions began in June 1877, Thomas J. Foster exulted in the pages of the *Shenandoah Herald* that "whoso Sheddeth Man's Blood by Man Shall His Blood be Shed." The day before the executions, the *New York Herald* celebrated that "it is certain that the majesty of offended law will be vindicated." The day after the executions, the *Miners' Journal* echoed the *Shenandoah Herald:*

> In no spirit of exultation do we say it, but from a sincere conviction of what we owe to God and man, we declare that as long as the voice of this JOURNAL shall ring among the hills of Schuylkill, so long shall it be in support of the statute which ordains that, '*Whoso sheddeth a mans' blood, by man shall his blood be shed.*'

Here the mythology reaches its apogee, as the distinction between human and divine law is eradicated.[75]

The great theme in nearly all the newspapers over the following week was "the vindicated majesty of the law." The phrase appeared with monotonous regularity in the newspapers of the anthracite region, and in those of Philadelphia, New York, and Chicago. This sort of thinking also appeared in the pamphlets, one of which described the Irish residents of the remote mine patches as "despisers of all law and authority not set up by themselves; men who hold human life cheap, and are always prepared for any deed of bloodshed or violence."[76] Such was the myth of the Molly Maguires. That myth was perfected at the time of the trials and executions. It has exercised a peculiar hold over the minds of novelists and historians ever since.

While most contemporaries applauded the executions wholeheartedly, a small but consistent chorus of dissenting voices was distinctly audible, suggesting an alternative perspective on the Molly Maguires. The logical place to look for these voices would be the labor newspapers of the anthracite region. But, by the time of the executions, organized labor there was in disarray, and no sources have survived on what the union leaders thought about the executions.[77] Accordingly, the five dissenting voices examined here are drawn from a more general setting, from outside the coal region as well as within. The first two voices come from the world of labor in New York City; the third comes from the Irish immigrant press in Boston; and the other two come from more unlikely and ambivalent sources, the editors of the *New York Herald* and Fr. Daniel

75. [Town], *Commonwealth v. Patrick Hester, Patrick Tully, and Peter McHugh, Argument of F. W. Hughes,* 112; *Philadelphia Inquirer,* May 20, 1876; SH, June 16, 1877; *New York Herald,* June 20, 1877; *MJ,* June 22, 1877; italics in original.

76. Ernest W. Lucy, *The Mollie Maguires of Pennsylvania, or Ireland in America* (London, 1882), 2–3.

77. The successor of the Tamaqua *Anthracite Monitor,* the *Pottsville Workingman,* had moved to Wilkes-Barre in 1876 and soon went out of business.

McDermott, both of whom had previously gone on record as committed opponents of the Molly Maguires.

One of the most consistent opponents of the prevailing Molly Maguire myth was a socialist newspaper, the *New York Labor Standard,* edited by the Irish-born radical Joseph P. McDonnell.[78] The "legal murders . . . perpetrated on so-called Molly Maguires," the newspaper commented on June 23, 1877, "are . . . so deliberately planned that all good men recoil from their perpetrators with horror. Responsible for these murders are Bloodhound Gowen, his perjured agent McFarland [sic], and all the mining bosses of Pennsylvania."[79] That the executions were a form of murder distinguished only by their legality, the *Labor Standard* had no doubt. On July 7, 1877, it carried the following obituary notice: "Murdered according to the law on the 21st June 1877: Hugh McGehan, James Roarity, Thomas Duffy, James Carroll, James Boyle, Thomas Munley, M. J. Doyle, Edward Kelley, Alex Campbell, John Donahue, Andrew Lanaban."[80] This abhorrence of the death penalty was shared by another radical newspaper in New York City, the *Irish World,* which condemned "this slow torturing, barbarous mode of semi-crucifixion."[81]

The *Irish World* was edited by the Irish nationalist and labor reformer Patrick Ford, who jointly coordinated the newspaper's campaign in defense of the Molly Maguires with another Irish-born radical, Thomas Ainge Devyr.[82] Since the trials of the previous summer, the *Irish World* had consistently rejected the argument that the Mollys and the AOH were one and the same organization. Ford and Devyr dismissed this argument as a malicious attempt "to defame the Irish character in this republic." The entire allegation, they pointed out, was based on the evidence of the Pinkerton detective, James McParlan, "a consummate liar who proudly and ostentatiously boasts of his marvelous proficiency in that art."[83] On May 20, 1876, for example, the newspaper denounced its rival, the *New York Herald,* for "an Outrageous Calumny on the Ancient Order of Hibernians." When a massive explosion rocked the depot of the Delaware, Lackawanna & Western Railroad in Bergin Heights, New Jersey, the *Herald* first hinted that the local laborers had borrowed the methods of the Molly Maguires, and then claimed that the men responsible had actually organized their own branch of the Molly Maguires to carry out the conspiracy. The same issue

78. See, for example, the issues of September 9, 1876, and April 28, 1877. Cf. Herbert G. Gutman, "Joseph McDonnell and the Workers' Struggle in Paterson, New Jersey," in Gutman, *Power and Culture,* 93–116.

79. McParlan's name was spelled in various ways in the newspapers, including McParlan, McParland, McFarlan, and McFarland.

80. *New York Labor Standard,* July 7, 1877. The eleventh name, "Lanaban," is a misspelling of "Lanahan," an Irishman hanged for murder at Wilkes-Barre on the same day, whose crime was not connected to the Molly Maguire episode in the lower region.

81. *Irish World,* June 16, 1877.

82. On Devyr, see Henry Christman, *Tin Horns and Calico: A Decisive Episode in the Emergence of Democracy* (New York, 1945), 317.

83. *Irish World,* May 20, 1876.

of the *Herald* made the remarkable claim that one of its correspondents, on a twenty-four-hour visit to the anthracite district, "was forced to confront the victims of five murders and four crucifixions."[84] Such claims the *Irish World* dismissed as a dangerous form of hyperbole.

The erasure of any difference between the Ancient Order of Hibernians and the local phenomenon of Molly Maguireism meant that, wherever in the United States branches of the AOH had been organized, the Irish would be subject to all sorts of wild accusations. The events at Bergin Heights in May 1876 offered one example; another had been offered the previous month when an attack by "a band of masked ruffians" on the proprietor of a stove factory in Troy, New York, was also blamed on the ubiquitous Molly Maguires. The term *Molly Maguires* was continuing its career as a synonym for all forms of labor activism and popular crowd action, expanding from Pennsylvania to New Jersey and New York and throughout the Northeast. In the words of one historian of American labor, "The courts began to see a riot in every strike, and a Molly Maguire in every trade unionist."[85]

Virtually alone among contemporaries, the *Irish World* tried to present the Molly Maguires from the point of view of Irish immigrant labor rather than that of corporate capital or American middle-class society. The editors insisted that "as all the money, legal prestige and social influence are leagued together on one side," they would give the other side of the story. The real problem, Ford and Devyr claimed, was that the coal fields of Pennsylvania had gradually been absorbed by powerful railroad corporations. When there had been a variety of individual operators in competition, trade had been brisk and wages fair. But now a "combination" had taken control of the entire coal market—production as well as distribution—driving down the wages of labor in their relentless pursuit of profit. "It was the old, old story—Capital with iron hand oppressing and robbing Labor," and in this development, rather than in some pathological lust for blood, lay the origin of the labor violence in the anthracite region. "Some of the men thus left without support for themselves or their children grew maddened and desperate, and occasional deeds of violence were the natural result." Breakers were burned, mines were flooded, and "tyrannical bosses in some instances were shot and killed."[86]

The *Irish World* found this violence reprehensible, but also understandable. "Acts of violence were done by desperate men. We do not defend their methods, but we are satisfied that the number of such acts have been grossly exaggerated, while the provocation under which those men labored is a factor

84. Ibid.; *New York Herald,* May 8, 1876. It was subsequently determined that the blast in Bergin Heights had not been caused by foul play but by the combustion of redrock powder stored in a magazine.

85. Norman Ware, *The Labor Movement in the United States, 1860–1895* (New York, 1929), quoted in Henry J. Browne, *The Catholic Church and the Knights of Labor* (Washington, 1949), 45. The attack at Troy was reported in the *New York Daily Tribune,* April 27, 1876.

86. All quotes from *Irish World,* June 3, 1876. For similar sentiments, see *Boston Pilot,* June 30, 1877.

usually eliminated altogether from the discussion." Moreover, these scattered acts of violence were blown out of all proportion by the coal monopolists, eager to concoct a conspiracy in order to crush the struggle for labor rights once and for all. "After a while when any midnight deed was done, whether by isolated miner or special policeman, it was attributed to an organized band of conspirators who received the name of 'Mollie Maguires.'" The mine workers themselves, Ford and Devyr argued, may have helped "to color this belief, hoping thus to terrify the capitalists into a more equitable frame of mind." But they could find "no convincing evidence to show that any regular or extensive society, such as the 'Mollies' are alleged to be, ever existed in Pennsylvania!"[87]

How, then, did the theory originate? It originated, the *Irish World* insisted, in the efforts of Franklin B. Gowen to eliminate all labor associations and his willingness to employ Pinkerton spies, trained liars whose "main occupation ranks about midway between pimp and blackmailer." The affidavit of a man like McParlan was "hardly worth the toss of coin." There had, of course, been murders committed in the anthracite region, and some of them had been committed by Irishmen. But the leap from these facts to the notion of an immense conspiracy, threatening the very welfare and survival of the Commonwealth of Pennsylvania, made sense only in terms of the corporate desire to eliminate all attempts by workingmen to protest against their lot. The Molly Maguire conspiracy, the *Irish World* concluded, originated in "the greed and rapacity" of Franklin B. Gowen and his cronies; they, not labor, were the real "conspirators" against the general welfare of Pennsylvania. The *Boston Pilot* agreed with this analysis, arguing that corporate power had driven the miners into "Molly Maguireism and murder, and then virtuously hounded them to scaffold."[88]

In initially denying that there was any connection between the Ancient Order of Hibernians and the Molly Maguires, Ford and Devyr were overstating their case. In this respect, the position of the *Boston Pilot* was more convincing. The *Pilot* also believed that the Molly Maguires were "the direct outcome of the contest between labor and capital." But it made no attempt to deny the existence of "this red-handed organization." Molly Maguireism, the *Pilot* conceded, was more than a conspiracy theory; it was a real response to severe oppression. There can be no doubt that some of the lodges of the AOH in the Pennsylvania anthracite region were used for violent as well as fraternal purposes. Most of the members in some lodges, and a handful of the members in others, were "Molly Maguires" who occasionally met under the institutional cover provided by the AOH. Immigrants from the northwest quarter of Ireland, in particular, adapted their lodges to "Ribbonite" purposes. Within the leadership of the AOH in Schuylkill County there appears to have been a loosely organized inner circle of men who engaged in Molly Maguire activities. By the time of the mass executions in 1877, the *Irish World* was prepared to admit this,

87. All quotes from *Irish World*, June 3, 1876.

88. Ibid.; *Boston Pilot*, June 28, 1877. See also *Irish World*, September 16, 1876.

thereby rendering its critique of corporate capitalism all the more convincing. But, quite justifiably, it continued to insist, as did the *Pilot,* that there had been a miscarriage of justice and that the extent of the conspiracy had been grossly and deliberately exaggerated.[89]

Ford and Devyr stepped up their critique on the eve of the executions. On June 16, 1877, for example, the *Irish World* pointed to "the astounding fact that those men are condemned to this most horrible death on evidence that would not be entertained for a moment if they had been rich men with friends at their back." What the convicted men were really guilty of, the newspaper alleged, was resisting the designs of Franklin B. Gowen and attempting to combat "the inhuman reduction of their wages."[90] On June 30, 1877, in an editorial entitled "The Slaughter in Pennsylvania," the editors admitted that the Irish had been responsible for plenty of violence in the anthracite region. But, if the executed men were guilty of some of the crimes they had been convicted of, this simply begged the question of why they had been willing to resort to arson and murder in the first place. To the *Irish World*, the answer was clear: "The grinding tyranny of the coal ring!"[91]

Given that the *Irish World* and the *Labor Standard* devoted considerable space to attacking the position of the *New York Herald* on the Molly Maguires, it is all the more surprising that the *Herald* itself joined the small chorus of dissenting voices in June 1877. Up to this point the *Herald* had distinguished itself as a committed opponent of the Molly Maguires.[92] But, two days after the executions, it suddenly turned from scabrous descriptions of the condemned men to a rudimentary account of causation and social context. Evidently, the editors were shocked at the barbarity of the spectacle that had just occurred.

The *Herald* located the motivation for the Molly crimes in "the hardships to which the toilers in the mines have been subjected," and saw the Molly Maguires as a violent outgrowth of the labor union movement in the anthracite region. The union was justified in demanding fair wages and refusing to work for less, and if "outrages" were committed against "outsiders" who took the jobs of union men, this "was no more than is sometimes witnessed in the city of New York." But the miners were "a rough race," and when "the combination of capital against which they contended proved too powerful for them, some of the more reckless among them took a shorter and sharper method of redressing their supposed wrongs." Murder was resorted to, in the name of vengeance and in order to instill terror in the operators and recalcitrant workingmen. Out of these early, sporadic beginnings the Molly Maguires had emerged.[93]

Although the crimes of the Mollys were in no way justified, the *Herald*

89. Quotes from *Boston Pilot,* June 30, 1877.
90. *Irish World,* June 16, 1877.
91. Ibid., June 30, 1877.
92. Cf. *New York Herald,* June 19, 20, 1877.
93. Ibid., June 22, 1877.

concluded, the fact that those crimes were committed resulted from the tactics of the employers, and in particular the large corporations. "Capital, in the shape of monopolies and rich corporations, has stood between the producers and the consumer, refusing to yield one fraction of its own profits to the necessities of the times and the fluctuations of the market." Herein, for the *Herald,* lay the ultimate cause of the Molly Maguire tragedy: "From this oppressive mastership came the unions and the Molly Maguires, the secret assassination and the public butchery of yesterday." No amount of corporate profit justified such results, the editorial concluded. The Molly Maguires—"baffled, crushed, strangled"—had learned their lesson. Would the corporations learn theirs?[94]

This uncharacteristic piece of social analysis by the *New York Herald* was probably inspired by a lengthy article it ran the same day by Fr. Daniel McDermott. McDermott's trajectory on the Molly Maguires had been a tortuous one. The chief spokesman for the "Declaration of the Seven Pastors" in October 1874 and an outspoken critic of the Molly Maguires during the trials, he was increasingly convinced that there had been a miscarriage of justice. He was clearly outraged by the barbarity of the executions and by the general tendency to portray the condemned men as subhuman. In an article published the day after Black Thursday, McDermott went to some pains to point out that, far from being a case of violence for its own sake, the Molly Maguire episode had arisen from a deeply entrenched "antagonism of Capital and Labor." Even though McDermott did not question the guilt of the hanged men or the justness of their executions, he produced perhaps the most cogent piece of historical and sociological analysis of all the contemporary commentators.[95]

McDermott's analysis differed from the prevailing mythology precisely to the extent that it emphasized context, causation, and change over time. "There is no effect without a cause," McDermott began. "The murders in the coal region are not effects without causes, nor have they been perpetrated without some motive, however reprehensible it may be." History is so full of instances of the oppressed being driven in desperation to vengeance and revolt, he continued, that no society can remain healthy if too many of its members are oppressed. And it was in the oppression of the poor by the rich, of the employed by the employers, that the motivation of the Molly Maguires was rooted. "Nowhere in this country," McDermott insisted, "have capital and labor at so early a date been arrayed against each other as in the coal region. . . . No part of the world ever presented so favorable an opportunity as the

94. Ibid.; the *New York Tribune* of June 26, 1877, conceded that conditions of "utter stagnation and misery" provided the background against which the Molly Maguires had arisen, but also blamed the conspiracy on "a few hardened ruffians."

95. The article, coauthored with Fr. M. Sheridan, was also published in the June 30, 1877, editions of the *Freeman's Journal* (New York), the *Catholic Standard* (Philadelphia), and the *Pottsville Standard.* An editorial in the *Catholic Standard* commented that the Mollys had been driven by "desperation caused by previous oppression" to regard an unjustifiable cause as just.

coal regions for the rich to oppress the poor workingman."[96] The outcome of this oppression was the Molly Maguires. The assassinations they committed were "but injustice reacting upon the aggressor." A more acceptable expression of the general impulse to resist this oppression, McDermott observed, had been the miners' union, the Workingmen's Benevolent Association. In its heyday, he pointed out, there had been little or no violence, and workingmen had stood united "against the encroachments of capital." But the defeat of the WBA left the mine workers at the mercy of the operators, "until, in their rude way, they devised what they considered a remedy." That remedy was Molly Maguireism.[97]

Toward the end of the article, however, McDermott's argument doubled back upon itself. One has a sense that he was afraid he had gone too far toward justifying, rather than explaining, the Molly Maguires. The dictates of Catholic orthodoxy, no doubt, prevented him from carrying his analysis to its logical conclusion; his superior, after all, was James Frederic Wood of Philadelphia, an outspoken critic of the Molly Maguires and a good friend of Franklin B. Gowen. McDermott concluded, therefore, with a strident denunciation of the AOH, reverting to precisely the type of nonexplanation his article had been written to rebut: the Mollys as evil cutthroats, bent on committing acts of violence purely for the sake of violence. The AOH once more assumed the guise of an abominable organization: "Words can give no idea of this demoralizing, peace destroying, anti-Christian diabolical association, or of its soul destroying influences—an infernal serpent which can only be destroyed by crushing its head." It was, McDermott continued, "an association which not only plunged its dagger into the heart of the citizens, but by its innumerable perjuries struck at the life of society itself and what was even worse blasphemously insulted God." And so this association, "upon whose black heart rest the blood of men and the damnation of souls," had to be eradicated.[98]

Black Thursday was the climax of the campaign to eradicate the Molly Maguires, but there was to be a protracted denouement, including five more trials and ten more executions over the next two years. (For a chronology of the executions, see Table 9.1.) With the excitement of the summer over, a new Molly Maguire trial opened in Pottsville on November 17, 1877. Dennis "Bucky" Donnelly was charged with being an accessory before the fact in the murders of Sanger and Uren. Donnelly was the AOH bodymaster at Raven Run, where Sanger and Uren had been killed. James McParlan returned to the witness stand after an absence of almost a year; the other chief witnesses for the

96. All quotes from McDermott's article as it appeared in the *Catholic Standard,* June 30, 1877.
97. Ibid.
98. Ibid.

TABLE 9.1. The Executions

Name	Place and Date of Execution	Convicted of Killing
Alexander Campbell	Mauch Chunk, June 21, 1877	Morgan Powell John P. Jones
Michael J. Doyle	Mauch Chunk, June 21, 1877	John P. Jones
John Donahue	Mauch Chunk, June 21, 1877	Morgan Powell
Edward Kelly	Mauch Chunk, June 21, 1877	John P. Jones
James Boyle	Pottsville, June 21, 1877	Benjamin Yost
James Carroll	Pottsville, June 21, 1877	Benjamin Yost
Thomas Duffy	Pottsville, June 21, 1877	Benjamin Yost
Hugh McGehan	Pottsville, June 21, 1877	Benjamin Yost
Thomas Munley	Pottsville, June 21, 1877	Thomas Sanger William Uren
James Roarity	Pottsville, June 21, 1877	Benjamin Yost
Patrick Hester	Bloomsburg, March 25, 1878	Alexander Rea
Peter McHugh	Bloomsburg, March 25, 1878	Alexander Rea
Patrick Tully	Bloomsburg, March 25, 1878	Alexander Rea
Thomas Fisher	Mauch Chunk, March 28, 1878	Morgan Powell
Dennis Donnelly	Pottsville, June 13, 1878	Thomas Sanger William Uren
John Kehoe	Pottsville, December 18, 1878	Frank W. Langdon
James McDonnell	Mauch Chunk, January 14, 1879	George K. Smith
Charles Sharp	Mauch Chunk, January 14, 1879	George K. Smith
Martin Bergin	Pottsville, January 16, 1879	Patrick Burns
Peter McManus	Sunbury, October 9, 1879	Frederick Hesser

prosecution were the informers Patrick Butler and John J. Slattery, along with Dennis Canning, who had been convicted in the Thomas and Major conspiracy cases and now received an early pardon in return for his testimony.[99] Cross-examined by the defense, Butler admitted that he had been given immunity from prosecution when he turned informer, and had subsequently been employed by the Pinkertons as a detective in Philadelphia. The defense attorneys produced evidence that Butler himself had ordered the killing, along with an alibi for their client. But Donnelly was duly found guilty of first degree murder and sentenced to be hanged.[100]

After Donnelly's conviction the Pinkertons and the Coal & Iron Police continued their investigations into the killings of George K. Smith (1862), Patrick Burns (1870), and Frederick Hesser (1874). But the next major act in the drama came in Bloomsburg, Columbia County, on March 25, 1878, when Patrick Hester, Peter McHugh, and Patrick Tully were hanged for the murder of Alexander Rea. By all accounts, this triple execution was not only the most public of all

99. Broehl, *The Molly Maguires,* 341.

100. [Allen, Lane & Scott], *The Evidence in the Case of the Commonwealth v. Dennis Donnelly* (Philadelphia, 1877); Broehl, *The Molly Maguires,* 341.

the hangings, but a badly botched affair. These were the first executions in the history of Columbia County, and a huge crowd gathered in Bloomsburg to witness the event. Though the men were hanged on a scaffold inside the prison yard, hundreds of people viewed the event from outside, seated on walls and rooftops. According to some sources, Sheriff Hoffman, the man in charge of the executions, was so drunk that he could not walk straight. Before the hangings he placed three pine coffins in open view beside the scaffold, and the condemned men could see them as they approached the gallows.[101]

The immediate aftermath of the execution was the scene of considerable turmoil. "The drop had no sooner fallen than the crowd made a rush for the scaffold, some of the horribly curious ones almost brushing the swaying bodies in their eagerness to notice the death struggles," the *Miners' Journal* reported. Outside, the commotion was even worse. The roof of a shed crammed with observers collapsed, killing a thirteen-year-old girl named Sunny Williams. Joseph Engst, a farmer, fell to his death from the roof of the Exchange Hotel. On the scaffold, Hester's body "twitched continually" for six minutes after the drop fell. It took Hester nine minutes to die, Tully eleven minutes, and McHugh twelve. As for the guilt of these three men, there had always been considerable doubt in Hester's case, but shortly before his death Patrick Tully issued a widely publicized confession admitting his own guilt, implicating Hester, and claiming that the testimony of "Kelly the Bum" had been substantially true. Three days after the Bloomsburg executions, Thomas Fisher became the fourteenth Molly Maguire to die, when he was hanged at Mauch Chunk for the murder of Morgan Powell.[102]

Following the executions of March 1878, a new round of trials opened. In Mauch Chunk, James McDonnell and Charles Sharp faced trial for the murder of George K. Smith, while Martin Bergin was tried in Pottsville for the murder of Patrick Burns. McDonnell had fled the anthracite region during the showcase trials of 1876, but in December 1877 he was captured by the Pinkertons at Rock Island, Illinois, and returned to Mauch Chunk for trial.[103] Known as the "Hairy Man" because of his uncombed, shoulder-length hair and long whiskers, McDonnell was portrayed as the archetypal wild Irishman; his surname, like that of Sharp (Ó Geáráin) strongly suggests a west Ulster connection. The chief witnesses for the prosecution were two self-confessed murderers, the informers Jimmy Kerrigan and Charles Mulhearn. Both men claimed that McDonnell had told them that he had participated in Smith's murder, and a conviction of first-degree murder looked certain. At this point, McDonnell turned informer, in a desperate attempt to save his neck.

McDonnell continued to protest that he had no connection with the Smith killing, but now confessed that he had been involved in the killing of the mine foreman Patrick Burns at the Silver Creek Colliery, near Tuscarora, on April 15,

101. *MJ*, March 29, 1878; Campbell, *A Molly Maguire Story*, 181.
102. *MJ*, March 29, 1878; Campbell, *A Molly Maguire Story*, 181.
103. Schlegel, *Ruler of the Reading*, 146.

1870. According to McDonnell, the killing had emerged out of a conflict between Burns and an AOH member named John Kane, the outside boss at the mine. Kane had asked McDonnell to have Burns killed, in part because of a dispute over wages, and McDonnell had appointed Martin Bergin to do the job. Bergin had recently been arrested in Canada and brought back to the anthracite region. His trial began in Pottsville on April 22, with McDonnell as the chief witness for the prosecution. Five other men were charged in the crime: John Brennan, Thomas Stimson, John Reagan, Thomas O'Neil, and John Kane. Only Brennan and Bergin were in court, as the others were missing. Brennan turned informer to save himself; that left Martin Bergin, who was quickly convicted of first-degree murder and sentenced to death. But if the "Hairy Man" expected clemency in return for his cooperation, he was to be sorely disappointed. He, too, was found guilty of first-degree murder in the Smith case, along with Charles Sharp. All three men were sentenced to be hanged. Had McDonnell turned state's evidence a year or two earlier, things might have been rather different; but now the authorities had no further use for informers and the "Hairy Man" was dispensable.[104]

The newspapers were already losing interest in the Molly Maguires, and when Dennis Donnelly was hanged at Pottsville on June 13, 1878, the *Miner's Journal* reported the event under the headline "Hanging No Longer Attractive." "There was no more excitement perceptible yesterday than on the day before, or hundreds which preceded it," the *Journal* noted. "The execution of the fifteenth in the list of convicted Molly Maguires was not even attended by a single representative of a newspaper outside the region."[105] Much the same could be said of the final Molly Maguire trial, which opened at Sunbury, Northumberland County, early in August 1878. Peter McManus and John O'Neil were convicted of the first-degree murder of Frederick Hesser, on evidence provided by an informer, Dennis Canning. Both defendants were sentenced to be hanged, but the conviction of Molly Maguires was old news by now.[106]

The case of John Kehoe was a different matter, however, and the newspapers followed every twist and turn as he fought to save his life. Kehoe had been convicted of first-degree murder on January 16, 1877, and on April 16 he was sentenced to be hanged. The case went to the Supreme Court, which affirmed the decision of the lower court on October 1, 1877. An appeal was then made to the Pardon Board, the sole remaining option. When the plea for clemency was

104. HML, A 1520, V 1750 and 1751, stenographic reports of the trials of Sharp, McDonnell, and Bergin. Sharp and McDonnell were convicted chiefly on the testimony of the informers Jimmy Kerrigan, Daniel Kelly, and Charles Mulhearn. John J. Slattery joined Brennan and McDonnell in testifying against Bergin. Cf. Schlegel, *Ruler of the Reading,* 146–47. Reagan and O'Neill were named in a "List of Fugitive Mollie Maguires" circulated by the Pinkertons in 1879 (HSC, Molly Maguire Collection, Photo File). A similar list circulated in 1876 (HML 1520, B 1001, report of BF to FBG, June 5, 1876) included the name "Jerry" Kane, who may be the John Kane allegedly involved in Burns's killing.

105. *MJ,* June 14, 1878.

106. Schlegel, *Ruler of the Reading,* 147.

brought before the board in April 1878, Kehoe's lawyer presented sworn statements by John Campbell and Neil Dougherty admitting that they had taken part in the beating, but denying that Kehoe had played any role. In a deposition submitted to the board, Kehoe argued that "the combination of great corporations reaching into the County of Schuylkill and having large numbers of paid police and agents . . . made use of influence at their command to stimulate public sentiment against your petitioner and made it impossible for him to get a fair trial."[107]

In a private letter written from Pottsville prison, Kehoe went into further detail about the miscarriage of justice of which he claimed to have fallen victim: "By Bribery Perjury and Pregudise, I am under the sentence of Death. for a Crime I never Committed," Kehoe wrote. Neil Dougherty and John Campbell had already been convicted of the second-degree murder of Langdon, he continued, and Campbell had testified that the beating had been carried out by him and "Yellow Jack" Donahue alone. Donahue had since been hanged for the murder of Morgan Powell, but the day before his execution he had confessed "that he was the man that Beat Langdon . . . he said he Beat him with a swingletree and that no Person saw him do it But John Campbell that John Kehoe was not there or Knowd nothing About it. Kerrigan Slattery & others said the same."[108] Donahue's attorney, Martin L'Velle, also wrote to Kehoe's attorney confirming that his client had declared Kehoe innocent, and a number of Girardville residents signed a petition pleading for a commutation of Kehoe's death sentence to life imprisonment. In a further instance of the mounting ambivalence of Catholic clergymen on the subject of the Molly Maguires, the petition was organized by the local parish priest, Fr. Daniel O'Connor.[109]

The Pardon Board was to have decided Kehoe's fate in April 1878, but for reasons that are unclear, it failed to reach a decision at that time. According to a report in the *New York Times* the following December, the board had been unanimously in favor of commuting Kehoe's sentence to life imprisonment in April, but it was deemed inexpedient to announce the decision at that point, as it might have affected the outcome of the trials of McDonnell, Bergin, and Sharp, then underway in Pottsville and Mauch Chunk. By the time the board met again on September 4, one of its four members had been replaced by a new member, who believed Kehoe was guilty, and another member had changed his mind. The vote was split evenly, two for Kehoe and two against; by the rules of the appeal process, a tied vote meant that the case could not be reopened, and Kehoe's conviction was upheld. His only hope now was a pardon from Governor Hartranft, the man he had allegedly helped to elect in 1875.[110]

107. Quoted in Broehl, *The Molly Maguires,* 342.

108. HSC, John Kehoe File, M 170.18 MI, copy of undated letter from John Kehoe to W. R. Potts, probably written in March 1878; cf. Broehl, *The Molly Maguires,* 342.

109. See Broehl, *The Molly Maguires,* 343. Formerly the pastor at Mahanoy Plane, O'Connor had been transferred to Girardville in January 1877.

110. *NYT,* December 18, 1878; Broehl, *The Molly Maguires,* 341–44.

Despite the board's refusal to reopen the case, there had always been considerable doubt about Kehoe's guilt in the Langdon killing. In July the governor had announced:

> All agree that he deserves the same punishment as that administered to his numerous guilty companions; however, he should not be hung for a crime that he was not clearly proven guilty of merely because he has been implicated in other dark deeds that, according to the law, would consign him to the gallows.[111]

Among these "dark deeds" were the murders of Smith, Sanger, and Uren, for which Kehoe was also under indictment.[112] But, as Hartranft had pointed out, these indictments were irrelevant to the case at hand. The governor waited until the fall elections had passed before coming to a decision, and there may well have been an element of political expediency involved. Then, on November 21, he signed Kehoe's death warrant, and the execution was set for December 18. But Kehoe continued to protest his innocence. A new witness claimed that he had not been present at the Langdon beating. The members of the Pardon Board decided to meet one last time on December 17, but once again refused to reopen the case.[113]

The following morning John Kehoe was hanged in Pottsville prison yard, in front of about 150 people. Outside, a crowd of several hundred, "most of them by their appearance, miners and colliery laborers," stood and "gazed in blank curiosity at the walls."[114] On the scaffold Kehoe declared, "I am not guilty of the murder of Langdon; I never saw the crime committed; I know nothing of it."[115] At 10:27 the drop fell. After twelve minutes, "a convulsive movement of the body was noticeable, after which all was quiet." A few moments later the body was cut down. Death was pronounced by strangulation. "Upon an examination of the body the attendant physicians discovered that the pupil of the right eye had been slightly lacerated and a gash made as though with a blunt instrument, under the chin. The latter wound was attributed to the action of the rope, which slipped from its position in spite of the care exercised in its adjustment."[116] Kehoe's body was taken to his home at Girardville for a wake, before being buried in the Catholic cemetery at Tamaqua, alongside that of his sister-in-law, Ellen McAllister (neé O'Donnell), murdered at Wiggans Patch two years earlier.[117] The *Miners' Journal* could not refrain from drawing a moral, hailing Kehoe's demise as "the dawn of a new era. . . . Up to yesterday Mollie Maguireism in this region was

111. *SH*, July 10, 1878; Schlegel, *Ruler of the Reading*, 148; Broehl, *The Molly Maguires*, 343.

112. *Philadelphia Press*, December 19, 1878; *MJ*, January 15, 1879.

113. Schlegel, *Ruler of the Reading*, 148–49; Broehl, *The Molly Maguires*, 343–44.

114. *Philadelphia Press*, December 19, 1878.

115. *MJ*, December 20, 1878.

116. Ibid.

117. Ibid. Kehoe's wife, Mary Ann O'Donnell, died in 1885 at the age of thirty-seven and was buried beside her husband and sister.

but scotched. Yesterday it was killed."[118] There were to be four more executions, however, before the "new era" arrived.

James McDonnell and Charles Sharp, the convicted murderers of George K. Smith, were to have been executed on the same day as John Kehoe. But at the last moment they won a reprieve until January 14. Their lawyer, Mr. Longstreet, then tried to win a second reprieve, but when he arrived in Harrisburg on January 13 to see Hartranft, the governor was away on business in Washington. Hartranft returned late that night, but refused to consider the case until the following morning. Longstreet arrived at 8:00 A.M. the next day and waited until 10:00 A.M. for the governor to arrive. After half an hour, Hartranft agreed to grant a second reprieve, and a telegram was dispatched to Mauch Chunk. By the time the telegram arrived, Sharp and McDonnell had already said their last words, insisting on their innocence but blaming their demise on their failure to follow the teachings of the Catholic church.[119]

Just as the men were executed, a messenger arrived with the telegram, bearing the news that a reprieve had been granted until January 20. "The most intense excitement prevailed on this being known," the *Miners' Journal* reported. "A brother of McDonnell's, whose head was gray and whose brow seemed covered with sorrow, then lifted up his voice and said, 'These men are not his murderers; they are innocent. The murderers are the men around you.'"[120] Governor Hartranft claimed that he had not known that the execution would take place before 11:00 a.m. He also said that he had assumed Sheriff Raudenbush knew a reprieve had been asked for and would not proceed with the execution until the word came from Harrisburg.[121]

Even if they had won a temporary reprieve, McDonnell and Sharp would almost certainly have been executed eventually. The Pennsylvania Supreme Court was considering an appeal by a convicted Philadelphia wife-murderer, Alex B. Sayre, which challenged the constitutionality of a law whereby writs of error had to be taken out within twenty days after sentencing. In the unlikely event of Sayre winning his case, Longstreet had a slim hope of overturning the convictions of his two clients, or at least of winning a retrial. As the Sayre case might have some relevance to the cases of Sharp and McDonnell, Hartranft had finally agreed to grant a six-day reprieve, pending the result. The Supreme Court gave its ruling in the afternoon of January 14, a few hours after Sharp and McDonnell had been hanged. As expected, the court rejected Sayre's appeal. Whether the botched executions at Pottsville that morning had any influence on the justices is not known.[122]

But Hartranft's negligence, and the unseemly haste with which Raudenbush had dispatched the two men to their deaths, were widely condemned in

118. Ibid.

119. *MJ*, January 14, 15, 1879; *New York World*, January 15, 1879.

120. *MJ*, January 14, 1879.

121. *New York World*, January 15, 1879.

122. *MJ*, January 14, 1879; *New York World*, January 15, 1879.

the press. The *Miners' Journal* called it "an Awful Affair," and reported that Raudenbush had known of the appeal for a reprieve the night before the executions. Nonetheless, the *Journal* exonerated all the local officials, concluding innocuously that the reprieve had simply arrived "too late" and leaving the matter at that. The *New York World*, previously an outspoken critic of the Molly Maguires, issued an angry editorial, denouncing the double execution at Mauch Chunk as "a disgrace to public justice in the state of Pennsylvania." Hartranft could have looked into the matter long before, the *World* insisted, and he had opened himself to the charge of "trying to make political capital out of his function of pardoning." The official excuse, that the reprieve had simply arrived too late, was "no excuse at all," the editorial concluded.[123] The *World* extended its criticism of Hartranft's negligence in this specific case into a general criticism of how justice was being dispensed in the collective case of the Molly Maguires. Sharp and McDonnell were both "Molly Maguires" and they were both "disreputable persons," the newspaper conceded. But it was difficult to believe that they were guilty of the crimes they had been charged with. Instead, they had been condemned on the basis of "general principles" rather than their individual actions. "Hanging men on general principles in a time of excitement may be a wholesome remedy in desperate cases," the *World* concluded, "but it is apt to be worse in its results than the disease."[124]

Only two executions remained. Two days after McDonnell and Sharp were executed, Martin Bergin became the tenth and last Molly Maguire to be hanged at Pottsville prison. The executions of Peter McManus and John O'Neil were scheduled for October 9, 1879, at Sunbury, the capital of Northumberland County. McManus was duly executed on that day, but O'Neil's sentence was commuted to life imprisonment at the last moment, on the grounds that he was feeble-minded.[125] One cannot help feeling that John O'Neil's mental condition would not have helped him a year or two earlier. But by October 1879 the outraged majesty of the law had been thoroughly vindicated. The story of the Molly Maguires had run its course.

123. *MJ*, January 14, 1879; *New York World*, January 15, 1879.

124. *New York World*, January 15, 1879.

125. Schlegel, *Ruler of the Reading*, 149.

Epilogue

When the great railroad strike of July and August 1877 swept across the United States from the East Coast to the Midwest, Pennsylvania was one of the major sites of conflict. In Pittsburgh, the railroad yards were set on fire after troops brought in from Philadelphia killed twenty strikers. In Scranton, the heart of the upper anthracite region, local vigilantes formed a Citizens' Corps, which was soon deputized as the Mayor's Special Police Force. They met and trained at the office of the Lackawanna Coal & Iron Company, which provided two-thirds of the force's personnel and 90 percent of its weapons and ammunition. On August 1, the Citizens' Corps opened fire on a crowd of strikers in Scranton, killing six and wounding fifty-four. The city was then occupied by five thousand Pennsylvania National Guardsmen.[1]

Schuylkill County, hitherto the center of labor activism in the anthracite region, remained quiescent and played no part in the upheaval. When the wave of strikes began in July, neither the miners nor the railroad workers had a trade union. The mine workers employed by the Philadelphia & Reading Coal & Iron Company voted not to go on strike, even though their pay was cut by 30

1. Aurand, "The Anthracite Mine Workers, 1869–1897," 230–34; *New York Herald,* July 20–31, 1877.

percent. Some of the other mine workers protested, but when a crowd of two hundred demonstrators marched from Mahanoy City to Shenandoah on August 7, Captain Linden and the Coal & Iron Police arrested fifty of them, and the next day all the mines were in operation as usual. Strikes continued in Luzerne County until October, giving Schuylkill a temporary monopoly over the coal trade, reversing the pattern of labor disputes typical in the early 1870s.[2] When the strike had ended, a coroner's jury ruled that the victims of the Scranton riot had been murdered, and the members of the Citizens' Corps were arrested. Perhaps not surprisingly, their trial ended in acquittal. A committee of the Pennsylvania legislature endorsed the verdict, announcing that "too much praise cannot be awarded the mayor and citizens' special police force of Scranton for the admirable organization they created, and for the prompt and vigorous measures taken when the emergency arrived." Without the decision of the City Council to deputize the Citizens' Corps, the committee concluded,

> Scranton would, no doubt, have suffered as badly as did Pittsburgh; for nowhere in the State was there a harder set of men than at Scranton and vicinity, many of them Molly Maguires, driven out of Schuylkill County, having gathered in and about that city, besides the scores of other cases who had been there for years.[3]

Once the turmoil of the late 1870s had subsided, the Ancient Order of Hibernians succeeded in dissociating itself from the Molly Maguires and, in so doing, resolved its decades-old conflict with the Catholic church.[4] When the annual convention of the AOH had met in New York City in April 1876 at the time of the first Molly Maguire trials, resolutions were passed stating that "it is the most earnest desire of the AOH to think, judge and act in accordance with the government, teachings and practices of the Holy Catholic Church" and to "disown, denounce, protest against and ignore any connection with organizations, societies or bodies or individuals that hold, advance or do anything contrary to what their Church and Country demand of them."[5]

When the 1877 convention met in New York City the following April, the society's constitution was revised, "to remove every cause of an objectionable nature so as to make our rules in harmony with the teachings of our Holy Church."[6] The convention also issued an "Address to the People of the United States," insisting that "the Order does not recognize any connection" with "that terrible band of misguided men," the Molly Maguires. It was decided "to cut off from all connections with our organization the Schuylkill, Carbon, Northumberland and Columbia County lodges."[7] Not only were these lodges disavowed by the national organization, they were effectively written out of

2. Schlegel, *Ruler of the Reading,* 157–66.
3. Aurand, "The Anthracite Mine Workers, 1869–1897," 233–34.
4. Cf. Kenny, "The Molly Maguires and the Catholic Church."
5. *Boston Pilot,* April 15, 1876, quoted in Broehl, *The Molly Maguires,* 319.
6. *Irish World,* April 21, 1877.
7. Ibid.

history. While the AOH had been present in Schuylkill County since its foundation in 1836, the official history of the Pottsville division states that the first lodge in the county was "Division No. 1 of Pottsville, chartered in March, 1887."[8]

In May 1878, the AOH met in convention at Boston and amended its constitution once again, successfully meeting the remaining demands of the Catholic church. The resulting document transformed the AOH from a rather shadowy secret organization into a "Catholic society" of the type recommended and approved by Pope Pius IX. The new constitution pledged the order not only to confine its membership to Catholics in good standing but to require them to conform to their religious obligations. The order also declared its willingness to submit to ecclesiastical authority, and to present its rules and constitution to the hierarchy for approval.[9] A resolution was passed declaring "that if there is anything in the Order at present in opposition to the doctrines of the Church, we, as her obedient children, are willing to rectify it as soon as her decision is properly announced."[10] But the major bone of contention had always been the oath required of the members, and unless that issue could be resolved, the AOH would remain under condemnation. Accordingly, a new oath was introduced, one which omitted any mention of God, and made a significant concession to the Church. The prospective member promised to "keep inviolable all the secrets of this Society of Brethren from all but those whom I know to be members in good standing, *except the Roman Catholic clergy.*" He also promised not to join "secret societies with persons of *other denominations,* not meaning trades societies, sailors or soldiers."[11]

A final possible objection to the Order was that its purpose was "antisocial," that is, politically radical or revolutionary. To allay any suspicions in this respect, a resolution was adopted stating "that our respect for civil law and our admiration of the free institutions of this free country are as steadfast and as undying as our devotion to the Church, whose traditions and teachings we much revere."[12] When the AOH met in convention at Cincinnati in 1879, Archbishop Purcell offered a high mass for the delegates at the cathedral and declared his confidence that, despite the aberrant events in Pennsylvania a few years earlier, the AOH was a good, law-abiding, Catholic society. This approbation was not universal; in Cleveland, for example, Bishop Gilmour continued to criticize the AOH. And in Pennsylvania, where old suspicions died hard, the bishops of Philadelphia, Pittsburgh, Erie, and Scranton continued to enforce the excommunications they had issued at the time of the trials and executions. Archbishop Wood refused to follow Purcell's precedent in Cincinnati, denying the

8. Broehl, *The Molly Maguires,* 345.

9. Fergus Macdonald, *The Catholic Church and the Secret Societies in the United States* (New York, 1946), 86.

10. Quoted in ibid, 87.

11. Quoted in ibid., 88; italics added.

12. Quoted in ibid., 87.

AOH delegates a mass when their annual convention met in Philadelphia in 1880. Nonetheless, the AOH had by that time become thoroughly respectable, and its relationship with the Catholic church was soon as amicable in Pennsylvania as elsewhere.[13]

With both the trade union and the Molly Maguires removed from the scene, the men and women of the anthracite region searched for alternative ways to improve the conditions in which they lived and worked. John Siney had always favored third-party politics, and he continued to pursue this route in the late 1870s. In March 1875 he had attended the convention at Cleveland where the Independent (or "Greenback") party was formed, and he was made a member of its executive committee. Siney also served as chairman of an "anti-monopoly" convention that met in Cincinnati the following September, and was instrumental in uniting the Greenback and antimonopoly forces. Greenback clubs were formed in Siney's home town, St. Clair, and in various other parts of the anthracite region. The "Greenback-Labor" ticket won 10 percent of the vote in the anthracite region in the state elections of 1877. The following year they elected several candidates to the state legislature, among them John F. Welsh, the last president of the WBA.[14]

The search for alternatives was also manifested in the growth of Irish nationalism in the anthracite region. Nationalist activities had been common elsewhere in the United States for decades, but they did not gain momentum in the anthracite region until the late 1870s. The collapse of the WBA and the Molly Maguires left a significant vacuum, and it was perhaps not by coincidence that the hard-line Irish republican organization, Clan-na-Gael, made its first appearance in the anthracite region in 1876. A successor of the Fenian Brotherhood, Clan-na-Gael was dedicated to the use of armed force to achieve a republic in Ireland, and it represented the extreme wing of Irish-American nationalism. Because of its extremism, its secrecy, and the association of its members elsewhere in the United States with the AOH, Clan-na-Gael was quickly identified with Molly Maguireism.[15]

A more popular alternative to the single-minded republicanism of Clan-na-Gael was the Land League of the early 1880s. Through the influence of Patrick Ford, the Land League joined nationalism with labor radicalism, rather than seeing them as incompatible. Ford had been deeply concerned with the fate of the anthracite mine workers in the mid-1870s and the region became an important center of support for the Land League in the early 1880s. The northern counties, in particular, sent impressive contributions to the League, via Ford's newspaper, the *Irish World and Industrial Liberator.* That Irish nationalism, and

13. Ibid., 9.

14. Killeen, "John Siney," 365–69. On third-party labor politics elsewhere in the United States, see Montgomery, *Beyond Equality,* especially chapter 11.

15. Broehl, *The Molly Maguires,* 323; James P. Rodechko, "Irish-American Society in the Pennsylvania Anthracite Region: 1870–1880," in John E. Bodnar, ed., *The Ethnic Experience in Pennsylvania* (Lewisburg, 1973), 29.

even its hard-line republican variant, could serve as a complement to the labor movement was strikingly illustrated by Terence Powderly, the head of the Knights of Labor, who also served as vice president of the Land League Council and as finance chairman of Clan-na-Gael. He spent a great deal of his time fending off accusations that these organizations were merely a cover for the Molly Maguires.[16]

The Knights of Labor, in particular, were widely accused of being the Molly Maguires under a new name, partly because of the secrecy that surrounded their organization, and partly because of their rapid expansion in the anthracite region after the collapse of the miners' union in 1875.[17] After the violence in the upper anthracite region in 1877, and Powderly's unprecedented election as mayor of Scranton in 1878, accusations of a link between the Knights and the Molly Maguires intensified. Allan Pinkerton openly accused the Knights of being "an amalgamation of the Molly Maguires and the Commune." These accusations were particularly frequent in the old Molly Maguire stronghold of northern Schuylkill County.[18]

While the Knights of Labor filled the vacuum left by the WBA to some extent, the mine workers never regarded it as a satisfactory substitute. In the late 1870s, the idea of a revived industrial union of mine workers became increasingly popular, and the Miners' and Laborers' Amalgamated Association (M&LAA) was organized, with the old WBA as its model. Shortly after the M&LAA was formed, John Siney succumbed to the "miners' consumption" he had contracted when working underground. His old trade union colleagues raised a few hundred dollars to send him to a sanitorium, but when the money ran out he returned to his home in St. Clair, where he died on April 16, 1880. In November 1888 the M&LAA unveiled a granite shaft in the local cemetery, dedicated to Siney, "In Memory of His Devotion to the Cause of Labor." At this time, the new trade union was still expanding and, like Siney's WBA, the southern and middle anthracite fields were the chief centers of activity. But the expansion of the M&LAA, and the eventual emergence of the United Mine Workers of America, are part of a different story.[19]

16. Eric Foner, "The Land League and Irish America," in Foner, *Politics and Ideology in the Age of the Civil War* (New York, 1980), especially 170–74.

17. The Knights of Labor was founded in Philadelphia in 1869. Powderly, born of Irish parents in Carbondale, in the upper anthracite region, dated his conversion to the cause of labor to the speech he heard John Siney give in Avondale, after the great mining disaster of 1869. Whether he was actually present in Avondale that day is another matter. Harry J. Carman, Henry David, and Paul N. Guthrie, eds., *The Path I Trod: The Autobiography of Terence V. Powderly* (New York, 1940), 23–35; cf. Richard Oestreicher, "Terence V. Powderly, the Knights of Labor, and Artisanal Republicanism," in Melvyn Dubovsky and Warren Van Tine, eds., *Labor Leaders in America* (Urbana, 1987), 30–61, especially 41.

18. Allan Pinkerton, *Strikers, Communists, Tramps, and Detectives* (1878; New York, 1969), 88; Browne, *The Catholic Church and the Knights of Labor*, 52; *Scranton Republican*, February 15, March 4, 1879.

19. Killeen, "John Siney," 369–78.

As for the Reading Railroad, significant victories had been won in the 1870s but, like most operators in the lower region over the previous forty years, the railroad ultimately failed to turn a profit from mining anthracite. The geological problems in the lower region were still formidable, and they were not really overcome until the advent of mechanical diggers and strip mining in the twentieth century. Moreover, the Reading had gone heavily into debt to finance its massive purchase of coal lands in the first half of the 1870s. Ironically, the railroad had prospered during the depression of the mid-1870s but went into decline as the depression ended. Dividend payments were stopped in July 1876, and short-term debt climbed to over $8 million by early 1877. Finally, in 1880, the Reading Railroad went into receivership and, the following year, Gowen was ousted from the presidency. Though he quickly regained the position of president, the railroad went into receivership again in 1883 and was taken over by J. P. Morgan. This time, Gowen was removed from the presidency permanently. The same year, he lost a good friend with the death of Archbishop James Frederic Wood of Philadelphia.[20]

Gowen returned to private law practice, but was evidently a disillusioned man. On Friday, December 13, 1889, he purchased a pistol, returned to his hotel room in Washington, D.C., and shot himself through the head. Though most newspapers eventually conceded that Gowen had committed suicide, rumors flew that the Molly Maguires had finally taken their revenge. The *New York Star* reported allegations that the man who had actually bought the pistol was a Molly Maguire selected for the job because of his uncanny resemblance to Gowen. The *New York Herald* also expressed the view that it may have been a case of murder rather than suicide. But the *New York World* said that "it was undoubtedly a case of suicide" and the *Philadelphia Evening Telegraph* agreed with this verdict, as did Captain Robert J. Linden, who dismissed the conspiracy theory as "utterly ridiculous."[21] Though there were rumors of Molly Maguire revivals at sporadic intervals throughout the 1880s, the idea that the Mollys had murdered Gowen was too farfetched to receive much credence, and within a few weeks of his death nothing more was heard of this accusation.[22]

James McParlan survived Gowen's death by thirty years, working his way up through the ranks of Pinkerton's National Detective Agency to the position of superintendent of the agency's office in Denver, Colorado. It was in the West that he met his match, in the person of Clarence Darrow. The Western

20. Broehl, *The Molly Maguires,* 347–48; Schlegel, *Ruler of the Reading,* 186–272.

21. *New York Star,* December 29, 1889; *New York Herald,* December 24, 1889; *New York World,* December 15, 1889; *NYT,* December 15, 1889; *Philadelphia Evening Telegraph,* December 23, 1889. The theme of physical resemblance between murderer and victim was the central plot device in Conan Doyle's *The Valley of Fear.*

22. Rumors circulated throughout the late 1870s and 1880s that the Mollys were resurfacing. See, for example, *Scranton Republican,* February 15, March 4, 1879; *Hazleton Plain Speaker,* August 19, 1885; *New York Herald,* November 27, 1888. Cf. Browne, *The Catholic Church and the Knights of Labor,* 52.

Federation of Miners was suspected of having played a role in the dynamite assassination of Frank Steunenberg, the former governor of Idaho, and as an expert on labor violence, McParlan was asked to carry out an investigation. He concentrated his attention on Harry Orchard, the man who was accused of carrying out the assassination. McParlan apparently persuaded Orchard to confess and turn state's evidence, possibly by telling him about the Molly Maguire informers of the 1870s. Just before the trial, Orchard issued a widely publicized statement, in which he claimed to have committed no less than eighteen major "outrages," including the assassination of Steunenberg and several other bombing missions, killing scores of people. In a striking parallel with the Molly Maguire case, Orchard claimed to have acted under orders from an "inner circle" of WFM leaders. This inner circle, he announced, was composed of three men, Charles Moyer, George Pettibone, and William "Big Bill" Haywood, who were promptly arrested for conspiracy to murder.[23]

"Big Bill" Haywood was brought to trial in Boise, Idaho, in June 1907, in what proved to be a sensational case. Senator William E. Borah of Idaho led the prosecution, Clarence Darrow the defense. In Darrow, McParlan faced an attorney of an entirely different caliber from the defense team at the Molly Maguire trials three decades earlier. By exposing McParlan's underhand tactics in his treatment of both the Molly Maguires and Harry Orchard, Darrow won the case and secured Haywood's freedom. The argument for the prosecution was built almost entirely around Orchard's evidence, and Darrow undermined this testimony quite easily, in part because Orchard had accused himself of several murders that turned out to have been accidental deaths. He also compelled Orchard to tell the court about the role that McParlan had played in the whole affair, and he lambasted McParlan and his employers in his final argument, contemptuously referring to him as a professional liar.[24] Harry Orchard's testimony was shown to be inconsistent and incredible, and Haywood was acquitted on July 27, 1907. Moyer and Pettibone also subsequently went free. Orchard was tried in May 1908 and sentenced to be hanged, a sentence later commuted to life imprisonment. As for McParlan, he died peacefully in Denver in 1919.

A generation later, J. Walter Coleman became one of the first historians to debunk the Molly Maguire myth, basing much of his "final judgment" of McParlan on the Orchard affair. Subsequent interpretations of the subject, however, did not generally take up the challenge posed by Coleman's work, and morality tales of heroic detectives and evil terrorists have remained the standard fare.[25] One indication of how the history of the Molly Maguires might be rewritten came in the 1970s, when a movement was organized in Schuylkill County to obtain a posthumous pardon for John Kehoe. Among those agitating

23. Broehl, *The Molly Maguires,* 354–57; Coleman, *The Molly Maguire Riots,* 169–72; Melvyn Dubovsky, *We Shall Be All: A History of the Industrial Workers of the World* (Chicago, 1969), 96–105.

24. Broehl, *The Molly Maguires,* 354–57; Coleman, *The Molly Maguire Riots,* 169–72; Dubovsky, *We Shall Be All,* 96–105.

25. Broehl, *The Molly Maguires,* 357; Coleman, *The Molly Maguire Riots,* 169–72.

on his behalf were his granddaughter, Mrs. Alice Wayne, his great grandson, Joseph Wayne (the proprietor of the Wayne Hotel, at 21 Beech Street, Girardville, where John Kehoe's tavern, the Hibernia House, had been located), and several members of the Pennsylvania Labor History Society. On September 6, 1978, Pennsylvania Governor Milton J. Shapp issued a statement joining the latter group in paying tribute to the Molly Maguires. "In an era of shortened work weeks and paid vacations," Shapp wrote, "it is impossible for us to imagine the plight of the 19th Century miners in Pennsylvania's anthracite region." It was John Kehoe's popularity among the workingmen, Shapp argued, that led Franklin B. Gowen "to fear, despise and ultimately destroy" him. Gowen saw Kehoe as the leader of a secret miners' union known as the Molly Maguires, and his "fervent desire to wipe out any signs of resistance in the coal fields" led to the controversial trials which sent twenty men to the gallows. The whole affair had been a dreadful miscarriage of justice, the governor concluded, "but we can be proud of the men known as the Molly Maguires because they defiantly faced allegations which attempted to make trade unionism a criminal conspiracy." All Pennsylvanians, Shapp wrote, "join with the members of the Pennsylvania Labor History Society in paying tribute to these martyred men of labor."[26]

Joseph Wayne continued to agitate on behalf of his great grandfather and on January 11, 1979, the Pennsylvania Board of Pardons recommended a posthumous pardon for John Kehoe, which Governor Shapp signed the following day. On June 21, 1980, exactly 103 years after Black Thursday, a plaque was dedicated at Schuylkill County Prison. Sponsored by the Pennsylvania Labor History Society and the Schuylkill County Commissioners, the plaque was unveiled by Alice and Joseph Wayne. If you visit Pottsville today and walk up to the county prison on the outskirts of the city, you can see the plaque on the wall just to the left of the main entrance. It reads:

> Here in this Schuylkill County prison yard on June 21, 1877, the largest mass execution in Pennsylvania took place with the hanging of six alleged "Molly Maguire" leaders. That same day, four other alleged "Mollies" were hanged at Mauch Chunk in Carbon County. Between 1877 and 1879, twenty alleged "Mollies" were hanged in Bloomsburg, Columbia County, Mauch Chunk, Carbon County, and Pottsville, Schuylkill County. One hundred and one years following the hanging execution of Jack Kehoe, December 18, 1878, in this Schuylkill County Prison, the Commonwealth of Pennsylvania granted posthumous pardon to Kehoe, reflecting the judgment of many historians that the trials and executions were part of a repression directed against the fledgling mineworkers' union of that historic period.

26. HSC, Molly Maguire Collection, John Kehoe File, M 170.18 MI, letter of Governor Milton J. Shapp, September 6, 1978.

Conclusion

The Pennsylvania anthracite region was a remarkably violent place in the 1860s and 1870s, and the Irish were responsible for much of the violence. Certain immigrant workers, particularly those from north-central and northwestern Ireland, used their lodges of the Ancient Order of Hibernians for classic "Ribbonite" purposes, adapting to local conditions in Pennsylvania a strategy of violent protest that had its origins in the Irish countryside. The lodges of the AOH controlled by this distinctive minority of Irish immigrants were the institutional reality corresponding to the nativist and antilabor polemics of Benjamin Bannan and Franklin B. Gowen. To this extent, the Molly Maguires did indeed exist as an organized conspiracy, even if the conspiracy was nowhere near as vast and as ominous as contemporaries claimed.

There was always a considerable disparity between what the Molly Maguires did and how contemporaries described and interpreted it. The term *Molly Maguires* referred to a sustained but sporadic pattern of Irish collective violence that unquestionably existed. But it also became a ubiquitous shorthand explanation for the wide variety of social, economic, and political ills besetting the anthracite region in the mid nineteenth century. Above all, "Molly Maguireism" offered a convenient explanation for an ongoing contradiction at the heart of the free labor ideology espoused by men like Benjamin Bannan and Henry C. Carey. The Irish, so many of whom were unable to move upward through the social scale, and some of whom turned to violence as a result, were a living refutation of the tenets of that ideology: social mobility; a dignified, independent work force reaping the benefits of its own labor; and a general harmony of interests between labor and capital. As the case of the Irish unequivocally demonstrated, the social advancement of some was predicated in large part on the social degradation of others. This contradiction became even more pronounced with the advent of widespread wage labor and corporate control in the 1860s and 1870s. In an effort to resolve the dilemma, or at least to explain it away, the term *Molly Maguires* was expanded from a shorthand term for Irish laziness, violence, and depravity, to a general label covering all forms of labor activism. The demonization of the Irish that had begun in the early 1850s was extended over the next two decades to a demonization of organized labor in general, as the trade union movement and the alleged secret society were identified as one and the same.

None of this is meant to deny that the Molly Maguires existed as a group of Irish immigrants who assassinated their enemies. It is simply to point out that their existence was put to all sorts of ideological uses, transcending the limited matter of Irish collective violence and raising fundamental questions about the nature of American and Irish-American society. The principal parties to this debate were small mine owners, corporate capitalists, anti-Irish nativists, the Commonwealth of Pennsylvania, the Workingmen's Benevolent Association, and the Molly Maguires.

Though there was undoubtedly a small overlap in personnel, the trade union and the Molly Maguires were clearly very different modes of labor organization. The Mollys differed sharply from the trade union in their cultural origins, their inchoate organization, and their strategy of direct violent action. They fought for justice on the individual and local level and did not apparently see their struggle as part of a wider regional or national conflict between social classes. Some of them wanted to settle strictly personal grievances, but most were engaged in a sporadic battle to defend a specific vision of what was fair and just in social relations.

The Workingmen's Benevolent Association, by contrast, had a coherent organizational structure, a collective social vision, and a well-developed theory of labor relations. It ran its own newspaper, lobbied for legislation on safety and work hours, provided social welfare to its members, tried to open cooperative mines, and participated in third-party politics. It self-consciously represented the members of one social class in their dealings with another, thereby gaining recognition for labor as the fundamental constituent of industrial society. Despite a protracted battle with the employers from 1868 onward, the union leaders believed in the ultimate compatibility of labor and capital, but only if the growing power of corporations could be checked. Never wavering from their denunciation of violence, they condemned Molly Maguireism as a misguided and self-destructive deviation from the proper goals of the labor movement. The contrast between the Molly Maguires and the trade union could not be starker. Yet they were systematically identified as one and the same by their detractors, and this deliberate conflation paved the way for the destruction of both.

Thus ended the first phase in the violent history of the Pennsylvania anthracite region. Its subsequent history would be violent too, but Molly Maguireism had been eradicated and would not be revived. Labor relations in the United States as a whole were to be remarkably turbulent in the late nineteenth century, especially in mining areas. Yet, even more than in the 1860s and 1870s, the bulk of the violence came from capital rather than labor, in the form of private police forces, undercover agents, vigilante groups, and military intervention by the state. Labor, too, had recourse to violence, mainly in the form of intimidation, beatings, and industrial sabotage. But a particular Irish tradition of retributive justice had died on the scaffold with the Molly Maguires. Trade unionism would soon reemerge in the mining country. The Workingmen's Benevolent Association was the precursor of the United Mine Workers of America. But the Molly Maguires were the last of their line.

Appendix 1

Biographical Data on the Molly Maguires

Asterisks indicate the twenty men who were executed.

*Bergin, Martin. Hanged at Pottsville on January 16, 1879, for the murder of Patrick Burns.

Boyle, Barney. Convicted of committing perjury in the Yost trial while testifying on behalf of James Boyle. Sentenced to three years in prison.

*Boyle, James. AOH member, Storm Hill, Lansford, Carbon County. Born in Schuylkill County about 1852 of immigrant parents from Donegal. Worked at the No. 5 Colliery in the Panther Creek Valley, for the Lehigh & Wilkes-Barre Coal Company. Hanged at Pottsville on June 21, 1877, for the murder of Benjamin Yost.

Boyle, Kate. Sixteen-year-old girl convicted of committing perjury in the Yost trial while testifying on behalf of James Boyle. Sentenced to two and a half years in prison.

Butler, Patrick. AOH bodymaster, Lost Creek, Schuylkill County. Informer. Turned state's evidence when on trial for conspiracy to reward Thomas Hurley for killing Gomer James. Sentenced to two years in prison.

*Campbell, Alexander. AOH treasurer, Storm Hill, Lansford, Carbon County. Born in Dungloe, County Donegal, in 1833. Came to the United States in 1868. Worked in the mines for a year and a half, then opened a hotel, the

Columbia House, in Tamaqua. Moved to Summit Hill, where he opened another tavern. Hanged at Mauch Chunk on June 21, 1877, for the murders of Morgan Powell and John P. Jones.

Campbell, John. Miner. Convicted of the second-degree murder of F. W. Langdon and sentenced to five years in prison.

Canning, Dennis. AOH bodymaster, Locust Gap, Northumberland County. Convicted in the Thomas and Major conspiracy cases, and sentenced to seven years in prison on each count. Later turned state's evidence, testifying for the prosecution in the trials of Dennis Donnelly and Peter McManus. Died in prison while serving a fourteen-year sentence for participation in the murder of Frederick Hesser.

*Carroll, James. AOH secretary, Tamaqua, Schuylkill County. Born about 1837 near Wilkes-Barre in Luzerne County, of parents who had emigrated from Ireland. Married a niece of Margaret O'Donnell, matriarch of the extended Donegal-born family of Wiggans Patch. Moved in 1872 to Tamaqua, Schuylkill County, where he opened a hotel, the Washington House. Took over Alexander Campbell's saloon in Tamaqua, when Campbell moved to Summit Hill. The assassination of Benjamin F. Yost was allegedly planned in Carroll's saloon. Hanged at Pottsville on June 21, 1877, for his role in the Yost case.

Cull (or Coll), Manus. See Daniel Kelly.

Dolan, Barney. AOH member, Big Mine Run, Schuylkill County. County delegate for Schuylkill County prior to John Kehoe.

Dolan, Patrick, Sr. AOH bodymaster at Big Mine Run, Schuylkill County. Convicted of conspiracy to reward Thomas Hurley for the murder of Gomer James and sentenced to eighteen months in prison.

*Donahue, John "Yellow Jack." AOH bodymaster, Tuscarora, Schuylkill County. Convicted in the Thomas, Major, and James conspiracy cases. Hanged at Mauch Chunk on June 21, 1877, for his role in the murder of Morgan Powell.

Donnelly, Christopher. AOH treasurer for Schuylkill County. Convicted in the Thomas, Major, and James conspiracy trials. Sentenced to two seven-year prison terms in the first two cases, and a two-year term in the third.

*Donnelly, Dennis "Bucky." AOH bodymaster, Raven Run, Schuylkill County. Hanged at Pottsville on June 11, 1878, for the murders of Thomas Sanger and William Uren.

Dormer, Pat. AOH member, St. Clair, Schuylkill County. Proprietor of the Sheridan House, a Pottsville tavern, where McParlan went on his arrival in the coal fields.

Dougherty, Daniel. AOH member, Mahanoy City, Schuylkill County. Acquitted of murdering George Major.

Dougherty, Neil. Convicted of the second-degree murder of F. W. Langdon and sentenced to nine years in prison.

Doyle, Michael ("Mike"). AOH member, Shenandoah, Schuylkill County. An alleged participant in the shooting of William "Bully Bill" Thomas and the murders of Thomas Sanger and William Uren. Fled the anthracite region and was never captured.

*Doyle, Michael J. AOH member, Mount Laffee, Schuylkill County. Born in Mount Laffee of Irish parents. Worked at the No. 5 Colliery in the Panther Creek Valley, for the Lehigh & Wilkes-Barre Coal Company. Hanged at Mauch Chunk on June 21, 1877, for the murder of John P. Jones.

Duffy, James. Convicted of committing perjury in the Yost trial while testifying on behalf of Thomas Duffy. Presumably a relative of the latter, hence with some connection to Donegal. Sentenced to two and a half years in prison.

*Duffy, Thomas. AOH member, Tamaqua, Schuylkill County. Born about 1852 in County Donegal. Came to the United States with his parents as a child. Lived at Buckville, two miles from Tamaqua, Schuylkill County. Worked as an engineer at the Buckville Colliery, owned by the PRCI. Hanged at Pottsville on June 21, 1877, for his role in the murder of John P. Jones.

*Fisher, Thomas. AOH delegate for Carbon County. Born in County Donegal in 1837. Came to the United States in 1849. Worked in the mines at Summit Hill, Carbon County, before opening the Rising Sun Hotel there in 1872. Active in Democratic politics, he served as AOH county delegate for Carbon County. Hanged at Mauch Chunk on March 28, 1878, for the murder of Morgan Powell.

Gibbons, John. AOH member, Shenandoah, Schuylkill County. Sentenced to seven years in prison for conspiring to murder William "Bully Bill" Thomas.

*Hester, Patrick. AOH bodymaster, Junction, Northumberland County. Born in County Roscommon in 1825. Emigrated to the United States in 1846, settling at Minersville, Schuylkill County. Moved to Locust Gap Junction, Northumberland County, where he opened a hotel and tavern, the Junction House. Active in local Democratic politics, he served in the positions of school director and tax collector in Northumberland County, and was the county's most prominent AOH leader. Executed at Bloomsburg, Columbia County, on March 25, 1878, for the murder of Alexander Rea.

Hurley, Thomas. AOH member, Shenandoah. Alleged to have killed Gomer James and to have participated in the attempted murder of "Bully Bill" Thomas and James Johns as well as the plans to assassinate Sanger and Uren. Fled the anthracite district and was never captured. Michael O'Brien, Christopher Donnelly, John "Yellow Jack" Donahue, James Roarity, and Patrick Dolan, Sr., were jailed for conspiring to reward Hurley for killing Gomer James.

Hyland, Bridget. Convicted of committing perjury in the Munley trial. Sentenced to two and a half years in prison.

Kane, Jeremiah. AOH bodymaster, Mount Laffee, Schuylkill County. Alleged participant in the conspiracy to reward Thomas Hurley for the murder of Gomer James. Fled the anthracite region and was never captured.

★Kehoe, John (Jack). AOH delegate for Schuylkill County. Tavern-keeper at Girardville, Schuylkill County, and the alleged "King of the Molly Maguires." Born in County Wicklow, Ireland, in 1837. Came to Schuylkill County with his family in 1850. Married Mary Ann O'Donnell, a native of Gweedore, County Donegal, in 1866. Worked first as a miner and went into the tavern-keeping business in 1870. Served two terms as high constable of the borough of Girardville, where he ran the Hibernia House tavern. Related by marriage to the O'Donnell family of Wiggans Patch. Convicted and jailed in the Thomas and Major conspiracy trials. Hanged at Pottsville on December 18, 1878, for the murder of F. W. Langdon.

Kehoe, Mrs. Mary Ann (née O'Donnell). Born in Gweedore, County Donegal, in 1848. Wife of John Kehoe and sister of James "Friday" O'Donnell, Charles O'Donnell, and Ellen McAllister, the victims of the vigilante attack at Wiggans Patch, December 10, 1875. Died in 1885.

Kelly, Daniel (a.k.a. Manus Cull and "Kelly the Bum"). Informer. Born in County Donegal in 1842. Came to the United States in 1865. Self-confessed murderer of Alexander Rea, turned state's evidence and served as the chief witness for the prosecution in the trials of Patrick Hester, Peter McHugh, and Patrick Tully for the murder of Alexander Rea, and the trial of Charles Sharp for the murder of George K. Smith. Was never tried for his own part in the Rea case.

★Kelly, Edward. AOH member, Mount Laffee, Schuylkill County. Born in Mount Laffee, Schuylkill County, of Irish parents. Hanged at Mauch Chunk on June 21, 1877, for the murder of Benjamin Yost.

Kerrigan, James "Powder Keg." Informer. AOH bodymaster in Tamaqua, Schuylkill County. Born near Tuscarora, Schuylkill County, about 1845. Served in the Union army during the Civil War. Worked at the Alaska collieries, Tamaqua. Self-confessed participant in the assassinations of Benjamin Yost and John P. Jones. Appeared as a chief witness for the prosecution in the trials of James Carroll et al., Alexander Campbell, John Kehoe et al., John "Yellow Jack" Donahue, James McDonnell, and Charles Sharp. Was never tried for his own part in the killings of Yost and Jones. Lived after the trials in exile in Richmond, Pennsylvania, under the name of his wife's family. Died in Manchester, Virginia, on October 1, 1898.

Lawler, Michael ("Muff"). Informer. AOH member, Shenandoah, Schuylkill County. Saloon-keeper. Implicated in the killings of Sanger and Uren, he turned state's evidence and testified for the prosecution. Convicted as an accessory after the fact in the Sanger-Uren case and sent to prison.

Malloy, John. AOH member, acquitted in the Morgan Powell case.

McAllister, Charles. Suspect in the Sanger-Uren killings. Escaped from Wiggans Patch when vigilantes attacked his home on December 10, 1875, killing his wife, Ellen (née O'Donnell), a sister of John Kehoe's wife. Mistakenly arrested instead of his brother James for the Sanger-Uren murders, but released when his case came to trial in September 1876. Imprisoned for the attempted murder of James Riles.

McAllister, Ellen (née O'Donnell). Wife of Charles McAllister, and sister-in-law of John Kehoe. Killed by vigilantes at Wiggans Patch, December 10, 1875.

McAllister, James. Alleged participant in the Sanger-Uren killings. A target of the vigilante attack at Wiggans Patch on December 10, 1875, he fled the anthracite region and was never captured.

*McDonnell, James. Hanged at Mauch Chunk on January 14, 1879, for the killing of George K. Smith. Testified for the prosecution in the 1878 trial of Martin Bergin for the murder of Patrick Burns, but if he expected a commutation of his sentence in return, none was forthcoming.

McGee, Columbus. AOH bodymaster, Centralia, Columbia County. Accused of killing F. W. Langdon, along with his brother Michael. A native of west Donegal.

McGee, Michael. AOH member, Centralia, Columbia County. Acquitted of killing F. W. Langdon, along with his brother Columbus. A native of west Donegal.

*McGehan, Hugh. AOH member, Summit Hill, Carbon County. Kept a saloon at Summit Hill. Born about 1852 in Carrickfin, County Donegal. Emigrated to the United States with his family as a child. Worked for the mine superintendent John P. Jones, who blacklisted him. The prosecution alleged that he had participated in the Yost killing in the understanding that the favor would be returned by the murder of Jones. Hanged at Pottsville on June 21, 1877, for the murder of Benjamin Yost.

McHugh, Cornelius. AOH bodymaster and president of the Summit Hill chapter of the WBA. Informer. Tried in 1876 for the killing of Morgan Powell, he turned state's evidence and helped convict Alexander Campbell of the crime.

McHugh, Frank. AOH secretary, Mahanoy City. Informer. Born in Tamaqua in 1856 or 1857. Worked as a mine laborer in Mahanoy City. Charged with conspiracy to murder William "Bully Bill" Thomas, he turned state's evidence and testified against his codefendants. Convicted in the Thomas case with a recommendation of mercy from the jury, he was later released.

*McHugh, Peter. AOH county delegate, Northumberland County. Born in Ireland (probably Donegal) in 1834, moved to England as a child, and came to the United States in 1864. Settled in Nothumberland County, where he lived until his arrest, except for an eight-month stay in Rhode Island in 1872. Hanged at Bloomsburg on March 25, 1878, for the murder of Alexander Rea.

McKenna, Patrick. AOH member, convicted of the second-degree murder of Morgan Powell and sentenced to nine years in prison.

*McManus, Peter. AOH bodymaster, Coal Run, Northumberland County. Hanged at Sunbury, Northumberland County, on October 9, 1879, for the murder of Frederick Hesser. The twentieth and last Molly Maguire to be executed.

Monaghan, Ned. AOH member and policeman, Shenandoah, Schuylkill County. Sentenced to seven years in prison in the Thomas conspiracy case.

Morris, John. AOH member, Shenandoah, Schuylkill County. Born in Pittston in November 1855, the first American-born child of parents who had recently emigrated from County Mayo. Sentenced to seven years in prison for conspiring to murder William "Bully Bill" Thomas.

Mulhearn, Charles. AOH member, Tamaqua, Schuylkill County. Informer. Convicted in 1876 in the Major conspiracy case, but had his sentence postponed when he turned state's evidence. Admitted his part in the killing of Morgan Powell in 1871 and implicated Alexander Campbell, John "Yellow Jack" Donahue, and Thomas Fisher, against whom he testified in court.

*Munley, Thomas. AOH member, Gilberton, Schuylkill County. Born in Tallaughn, parish of Kilcommon, County Mayo, in 1845. Came to the United States in 1864. Went first to Stockbridge, Massachusetts, where members of his father's family lived at the time. Moved to Gilberton, Schuylkill County, where he lived until the time of his arrest. Worked at the Draper Colliery, but was unemployed when arrested. Hanged at Pottsville on June 21, 1877, for the murders of Sanger and Uren.

O'Brien, Michael. AOH bodymaster, Mahanoy City, Schuylkill County. Convicted in the Thomas, Major, and James conspiracy trials, and sentenced to seven years in prison in the first case, five years in the second, and two years in the third.

O'Donnell, Charles. Alleged participant in the Sanger-Uren killings. Killed by vigilantes at Wiggans Patch, December 10, 1875, along with his sister, Ellen, wife of Charles McAllister. A brother of James "Friday" O'Donnell and Mary Ann O'Donnell (John Kehoe's wife), Charles O'Donnell was part of an extended emigrant family from Gweedore, County Donegal.

O'Donnell, James "Friday." Alleged participant in the Sanger-Uren killings. Member of the O'Donnell family from Gweedore, County Donegal. Brother of Ellen McAllister (née O'Donnell) and Charles O'Donnell, both of whom were killed by vigilantes at Wiggans Patch on December 10, 1875, and of Mary Ann Kehoe (née O'Donnell). James O'Donnell fled the anthracite region after the Wiggans Patch incident and was never captured.

O'Donnell, Patrick. AOH member, convicted of the second-degree murder of Morgan Powell and sentenced to five years in prison. (Another Patrick O'Donnell, a cousin of the family living in Wiggans Patch, spent some time in the anthracite region in the late 1870s, before returning to Ireland and killing James Carey, the informer in the sensational Phoenix Park assassinations of May 1882).

O'Neil, Francis. AOH bodymaster, St. Clair, Schuylkill County, sentenced to two years in prison for conspiring to reward Thomas Hurley for the murder of Gomer James.

O'Neil, John. Sentenced to death for the killing of Frederick Hesser, his sentence was commuted to life in prison on the grounds that he was feeble-minded.

*Roarity, James. AOH bodymaster, Coaldale, Schuylkill County. Born near Dungloe, County Donegal, in 1845. Worked for five years as a stonemason's helper in Scotland. Emigrated to the United States in 1869. Settled first at Allentown, Pennsylvania, then moved to Coaldale in June 1869. Worked there as a laborer in the No. 10 Colliery of the Lehigh and Wilkes-Barre Coal Company. Convicted in the Thomas, Major, and James conspiracy trials. Hanged at Pottsville on June 21, 1877, for his role in the murder of Benjamin Yost.

*Sharp[e], Charles. Hanged at Mauch Chunk on January 14, 1879, for the murder of George K. Smith. His origins are unknown, but his surname may be an anglicization of Ó Geáráin (*geár* meaning Sharp), a name peculiar to Donegal.

Slattery, John J. AOH member. Informer. Convicted in the Major conspiracy case but turned informer during the trial, so his sentence was postponed. Testified for the prosecution in the trial of "Yellow Jack" Donahue for the killing of Morgan Powell. Implicated John Kehoe in extensive political corruption. Also testified against Martin Bergin in 1878, when Bergin stood trial for the murder of Patrick Burns.

Stanton, John. Tried and acquitted in the Thomas and Major conspiracy cases.

*Tully, Patrick. Born in the parish of Drughn, County Cavan, on December 17, 1830. Emigrated to Scotland in 1844, and came to the United States in 1854 or 1863 (or possibly both). Lived in turn in Reading, Berks County; Glen Carbon, Schuylkill County; and Centralia, Columbia County, settling in the latter in 1865. Hanged at Bloomsburg on March 25, 1878, for the murder of Alexander Rea.

SOURCES

ABBREVIATIONS USED BELOW

HML Hagley Museum and Library, Wilmington, Delaware

HSP Historical Society of Pennsylvania

MJ *Miners' Journal*

RCK *Report of the Case of the Commonwealth v. Kehoe et al.*

SH *Shenandoah Herald*

James Boyle: *SH*, June 16, 1877, Barclay, *Lives and Crimes,* 37, interview with Patrick Campbell, October 6, 1992; Alexander Campbell: Campbell, A *Molly*

Maguire Story, 1, Barclay, *Lives and Crimes,* 37; James Carroll: *SH,* June 16, 1877, *Philadelphia Press,* June 21, 1877, Barclay, *Lives and Crimes,* 36; Michael J. Doyle: *Pottsville Evening Chronicle,* June 19, 1877, Barclay, *Lives and Crimes,* 37; Thomas Duffy: Barclay, *Lives and Crimes,* 36–37; Thomas Fisher: *MJ,* March 29, 1878; Patrick Hester: *MJ,* March 29, 1878; John Kehoe: McCarthy, *The Great Molly Maguire Hoax,* 90, 101–3; Daniel Kelly: HML, A 1520, B 979, F, "Statements and Depositions," statement of Manus Cull; Edward Kelly: *Pottsville Evening Chronicle,* June 19, 1877, Barclay, *Lives and Crimes,* 37; James Kerrigan: Barclay, *Lives and Crimes,* 35; Columbus and Michael McGee: interview with Patrick Campbell, October 6, 1992; Hugh McGehan: Campbell, *A Molly Maguire Story,* 155, Barclay, *Lives and Crimes,* 36, interview with Patrick Campbell, October 6, 1992; Frank McHugh: RCK, 111–15; Peter McHugh: *MJ,* March 29, 1878, interview with Paddy McHugh, Dungloe, June 23, 1993; John Morris: interview with Nancy Morris, December 15, 1994; Thomas Munley: Barclay, *Lives and Crimes,* 37, HSP, papers of Owen Hunt; the O'Donnell family: interview with Patrick Campbell, October 26, 1992, McCarthy, *The Great Molly Maguire Hoax,* 101, information provided by Máirín Seoighe; James Roarity: Barclay, *Lives and Crimes,* 36; Patrick Tully: *MJ,* March 29, 1878.

Appendix 2

Geographical Analysis of the Surnames of the Molly Maguires

With the exception of clearly documented cases, the only way to determine where in Ireland the Molly Maguires came from is the admittedly problematic technique of surname analysis. In light of the debate among historians on the usefulness of this technique, a note is in order on the aims, scope, and method of the analysis used here.[1]

The names of the leading individuals in the Molly Maguire episode in Pennsylvania were selected for analysis. Most of the men and women selected were either executed or tried for a crime; the remainder were either related by family to an accused Molly Maguire or acted as informers during the trials. All were implicated in one way or another in the Molly Maguire episode, and most were members of the Ancient Order of Hibernians. Fifty-one surnames were analyzed. Where two or more family members were involved, a single entry was made for the entire family (i.e., the Boyle, Duffy, McAllister, McGee, and O'Donnell families). In cases where unrelated individuals bore the same surname, a separate entry was made for each individual (i.e., Dolan, Donnelly, Dougherty, Doyle, Kelly, McHugh). Documented evidence on the nativity of

1. See, in particular, Thomas Purvis, Donald Akenson, Forrest McDonald, and Ellen McDonald, "The Population of the United States, 1790: A Symposium," *William and Mary Quarterly,* 41 (January 1984): 85–135.

fourteen of the fifty-one individuals is available from contemporary sources, mainly newspapers, as listed in Appendix 1. For the remaining thirty-seven, the standard source on Irish names and their locations is Edward MacLysaght's *The Surnames of Ireland.*

Certain surnames are so common throughout Ireland that they cannot be traced to a single region. Others are more typical of certain regions, including some that are most typically found in north-central and northwest Ireland. Thirteen of the fourteen documented cases definitely came from this part of the country, and the goal of the surname analysis was to see if a similar pattern was evident in the surname location of thirty-seven undocumented cases. Six of these thirty-seven names (Carroll, Donahue, Doyle [2], Kelly, O'Brien) are so common that they cannot be traced to specific locations. Twenty-four (77.5 percent) bore names most commonly found in north-central and northwestern Ireland: Campbell (John), Canning, Dolan (2), Donnelly (2), Dougherty (2), Gibbons, Kane, Kerrigan, McDonnell, McHugh (3), McKenna, McManus, Monaghan, Mulhearn, O'Donnell (Patrick), O'Neil (2), Sharp[e], and Stanton. Only seven (22.5 percent) bore names most commonly found elsewhere in Ireland (i.e., east Ulster, north Connacht, Leinster, and Munster): Bergin, Butler, Hurley, Lawler, Malloy, McAllister, Slattery. Clearly, the results of this analysis are by no means conclusive; but, viewed in tandem with the documented evidence that has survived, they are suggestive of a general pattern.

The single county of Donegal stands out as exceptional. Eight of the fourteen documented individuals were born in Donegal, and a ninth was the offspring of immigrants from that county. Moreover, six of the twenty-four surnames found typically in north-central and northwestern Ireland were more commonly found in County Donegal than elsewhere: Campbell, Dougherty, McDonnell, Mulhearn, O'Donnell, and Sharp[e] (Ó Geáráin). In other words, fifteen (one-third) of the forty-five American Molly Maguires whose names can be analyzed were associated with Donegal.

Moreover, the nativity of ten of the twenty Molly Maguires executed in Pennsylvania (Boyle, Campbell, Duffy, Fisher, Hester, Kehoe, McGehan, Munley, Roarity, Tully) is known, and only one of them, John Kehoe, was born outside northwest and north-central Ireland. And Kehoe, of course, had intimate connections with Donegal, having married into the O'Donnell family of Wiggans Patch. Five of the executed men were born in Donegal (Campbell, Duffy, Fisher, McGehan, and Roarity) and one (Boyle) was born in Schuylkill County to a family from Donegal. One came from Leinster (Kehoe), one from Ulster (Tully), and two from Connacht (Hester and Munley). In the other ten cases, where definite information on nativity is lacking, five names (Donnelly, McDonnell, McHugh, McManus, and Sharp[e]) were most commonly found in west Ulster, especially Donegal; four (Carroll, Donahue, Doyle, and Kelly) were too common to be used in a surname analysis; and only one (Bergin) had a Leinster name. Combining the documented cases with the surname analysis, the results are striking: fourteen of the sixteen executed Molly Maguires whose names could be analyzed (87.5 percent) came from north-central and northwestern Ireland, and eleven (68.75 percent) were from Donegal.

Given the limited and tentative nature of this analysis, it is clear that most of Donald Akenson's strictures on the technique of surname analysis do not apply, particularly because no projections, extrapolations, or comparisons are made from these figures. It is true, as Akenson points out, that figures on surname frequency from one century (in this case MacLysaght's model) cannot provide a scientific basis for the analysis of names drawn from another century (in this case west Donegal and the Pennsylvania anthracite region in the nineteenth century). But, as Purvis and the McDonalds have pointed out, this objection is the least convincing of Akenson's otherwise cogent criticisms, as (i) the pattern of naming is likely to change drastically over time only in areas of in-migration, not areas of out-migration (like the northwest quarter of Ireland); and (ii) given Akenson's point about internal migrations within individual countries, distinctive regional names (such as O'Donnell, Boyle, Coll [or Cull], and McGehan in west Donegal) are likely to have been more typical of their region, and less common in the country as a whole, the further one goes back in time. On these grounds, it is reasonable to conclude that the surname analysis offered here confirms a general pattern already evident in the documented sources.

GUIDE TO SYMBOLS

+ indicates that there is documented evidence of origin in County Donegal, west Ulster

* indicates that there is documented evidence of origin in other parts of west and south Ulster or north and east Connacht

** indicates a surname most common in west and south Ulster or north and east Connacht

NAMES

Bergin (Martin). A surname most commonly found in counties Laois and Offaly (Leinster).

+ Boyle family (Barney, James, and Kate). The Boyles were born in Schuylkill County of Irish parents who had emigrated from west Donegal (west Ulster).

Butler (Patrick). A surname of Norman derivation, common throughout Ireland, especially in counties Kilkenny (Leinster) and Tipperary (Munster).

+ Campbell (Alexander). Born in Dungloe, County Donegal (west Ulster), in 1833; came to the United States in 1868.

** Campbell (John). A surname most commonly found in counties Donegal and Tyrone (west Ulster).

** Canning (Dennis). A surname of English origin most commonly found in County Derry (mid-west Ulster).

Carroll (James). Born near Wilkes-Barre, Luzerne County, of Irish parents. The surname is common throughout Ireland.

** Dolan (Barney). A surname commonly found in counties Galway and Roscommon (mid-north Connacht); also found in counties Leitrim (north Connacht), Cavan (south Ulster), and Fermanagh (south-west Ulster).

** Dolan (Patrick, Sr.). See Dolan, Barney.

Donahue (John). A surname common throughout Ireland.

** Donnelly (Christopher). A surname most commonly found in County Tyrone (west Ulster).

** Donnelly (Dennis). See Donnelly, Christopher.

** Dougherty (Daniel). A surname found throughout Ireland but most commonly found in west Ulster, especially in County Donegal.

** Dougherty (Neil). See Dougherty, Daniel.

Doyle (Michael). A surname common throughout Ireland, especially in Leinster.

Doyle (Michael J.). Born in Mount Laffee, Schuylkill County of Irish parents. See Doyle, Michael.

+ Duffy (James and Thomas). Thomas Duffy was born in County Donegal (west Ulster) and came to the United States as a child. The surname is especially common in counties Monaghan (south Ulster), Roscommon (mid-north Connacht), and Donegal (west Ulster). James Duffy, who was convicted of perjury on Thomas's behalf, was presumably a relative.

+ Fisher (Thomas). Born in County Donegal (west Ulster) in 1837; came to the United States in 1849.

** Gibbons (John). A surname most commonly found in north Connacht, especially County Mayo.

* Hester (Patrick). Born in County Roscommon (mid-north Connacht) in 1825; came to the United States in 1846.

Hurley (Thomas). A surname most commonly found in counties Clare, Cork, and Limerick (Munster).

** Kane (Jeremiah). A surname most commonly found in counties Derry and Tyrone (west Ulster).

Kehoe (John). Born in County Wicklow (east Leinster) in 1837; came to the United States in 1850.

+ Kelly (Daniel "the Bum"). Also known as Manus Cull. Cull, or Coll, is one of the most common surnames in west Donegal. Daniel Kelly was born in County Donegal (west Ulster) in 1842 and came to the United States in 1865.

Kelly (Edward). Born in Mount Laffee, Schuylkill County, of Irish parents. The surname is the second most numerous in Ireland, after Murphy.

** Kerrigan (James). A surname most commonly found in County Mayo (north Connacht). Born in Tuscarora, Schuylkill County, ca. 1853.

Lawler (Michael). A surname most commonly found in Leinster.

Malloy (John). A surname most commonly found in Leinster.

McAllister (family). A surname common throughout Ulster, especially in County Antrim (East Ulster).

** McDonnell (James). A surname most commonly found in west Ulster, but also in County Antrim (east Ulster).

\+ McGee (Columbus and Michael). Both born in the Rosses, County Donegal. A common Donegal name, found throughout west Ulster, also in County Antrim (east Ulster).

\+ McGehan (Hugh). Born in County Donegal (west Ulster).

** McHugh (Cornelius). A surname most commonly found in north Connacht and west Ulster.

** McHugh (Frank). See McHugh, Cornelius.

** McHugh (Peter). See McHugh, Cornelius. Peter McHugh was born in Ireland in 1834, probably in the Rosses, west Donegal.

** McKenna (Patrick). A surname most commonly found in north Connacht and west Ulster.

** McManus (Peter). A surname most commonly found in counties Roscommon (east Connacht) and Fermanagh (west Ulster).

** Monaghan (Ned). A surname most commonly found in counties Roscommon (east Connacht) and Fermanagh (southwest Ulster).

* Morris (John). A surname most commonly found in counties Galway and Mayo (south Connacht). John Morris was born in Pittston in 1855, the first American-born child of parents who had recently emigrated from County Mayo.

** Mulhearn (Charles). A surname most commonly found in Ulster, especially County Donegal.

* Munley (Thomas). Born in County Mayo (north Connacht) in 1845; came to the United States in 1864. The surname is typical of Mayo.

O'Brien (Michael). The fifth most numerous surname in Ireland.

\+ O'Donnell (family). Manus, Margaret, and their children, Charles, James, Mary Ann (wife of John Kehoe), and Ellen (wife of Charles McAllister) came from Gweedore, County Donegal (west Ulster) and settled at Wiggans Patch, Schuylkill County.

** O'Donnell (Patrick). The classic west Donegal surname. Found also in counties Galway (south Connacht) and Clare (Munster).

** O'Neil (Francis). A surname found throughout Ireland, but most common in County Tyrone (west Ulster).

** O'Neil (John). See O'Neil, Francis.

\+ Roarity (James). Born near Dungloe, County Donegal (west Ulster), in 1845; came to the United States in 1869. The surname is peculiar to Donegal.

** Sharp[e] (Charles). The name Sharp[e] is probably an anglicized version of Ó Geáráin (from *geár,* sharp), peculiar to County Donegal (west Ulster).

Slattery (John J.). A surname most commonly found in County Clare and adjacent counties in Munster.

** Stanton (John). A surname of English origin, commonly found in County Mayo (north Connacht).

* Tully (Patrick). Born in County Cavan (south Ulster) in 1830; came to the United States in 1854 or 1863.

Appendix 3

The Donegal and North-central Irish in the Anthracite Region

In the mid-1870s the Pinkertons drew up a list of known members of the AOH in the anthracite region. ("List of members of the A.O.H. Schuylkill, Luzerne, Carbon, Columbia, and Northumberland Counties, Pennsylvania," HML, A 1520, B 979, F, "Memoranda and Papers.") Of the 347 names on the list, 158 (45.5 percent) were more common in north-central and northwestern Ireland than elsewhere, according to the same methodology and sources used in Appendix 2. That this figure is substantially lower than the figure yielded by the initial analysis of Molly Maguire surnames (82.25 percent) is not at all surprising. The list included all known members of the AOH in the region; but, despite the arguments of the prosecution and other conspiracy theorists, many (perhaps most) of these men would not have been involved with the Molly Maguires. Instead, they were members of a fraternal organization, in which only some lodges (and perhaps some inner circles within individual lodges) engaged in violence.

The names on the Pinkerton list were arranged under eighty-two headings, each corresponding to a local lodge of the AOH. In several lodges, roughly half the members listed bore names more common in north-central and northwestern Ireland than elsewhere: Big Mine Run, five of eight (Gavin, McHugh, Sweeny, Dolan, Dolan), Buck Mountain, six of eleven (Boyle, Gallagher, McCahill, McCahill, McGinity, McColl), Mahanoy City, nine of twenty-three (Boyle, Dougherty, Dugan, McGinity, McDonell, McHugh, Sheridan, Dugan,

Dugan), Shenandoah, nineteen of thirty-four (Boylan, Boyle, Burke, Burns, Burns, Cooney, Donnelly, Drumm, Dyer, McAndrew, McAnnulty, McGrail, McHugh, McKanna, Monahan, Monahan, Monahan, Monahan, Morris).

Seven other lodges had members whose names were drawn entirely (or almost entirely) from west Ulster, and in particular west Donegal. All four members of the Coal Dale lodge fit into this category (Bonner, Gallagher, Gallagher, Roarty [sic]), nine of eleven at Hazleton (Boyle, Boyle, Cull, Duffy, Duffy, McCarron, McGinn, O'Donnell, Sweeny), five of six at Junction, Northumberland County (Campbell, Campbell, Campbell, Campbell, Cannon; the sixth member, and the leader of the lodge, was Pat Hester, the executed Molly Maguire who hailed from Roscommon), all three members at Mauch Chunk (McGinely, McGinely, Mulhearn), twelve of thirteen at Storm Hill (Boyle, Boyle, Boyle, Campbell, Campbell, Maguire, Maguire, McKanna, McKanna, McKanna, McNellis, McNellis), all thirteen members at Summit Hill (Boyle, Boyle, Fisher, Fisher, Gallagher, McGinity, McGehan, Mullhearn, Mullhearn, O'Donnell, O'Donnell, Sweeny, Sweeny), and five of six at Wiggans Patch (Huston, McCallister [sic], O'Donnell, O'Donnell, Rodgers). These lodges were located in the heart of Molly Maguire territory.

One of the obvious questions raised by this second surname analysis is what proportion of the Irish residents of the lower anthracite region as a whole came from the northwest quarter of Ireland. This question could be answered, if at all, only by a large team of researchers. Given the absence of evidence in the census on counties of birth, the method would be to examine the original census returns (which are incomplete and sometimes illegible) and analyze the geographical origin of the names of each head of household along with guests and boarders. This study would not yield results worth the effort, as surname analysis, on its own, cannot produce scientifically reliable data. Once again, it is of use only if it can supplement a pattern verified elsewhere, for instance in the press, as in the case of some of the Molly Maguires.

GUIDE TO SYMBOLS

The six names marked with an * indicate executed Molly Maguires on whom there is documented evidence of origin in this part of the country: Roarty [sic] (Donegal), Munley (Mayo), Hester (Roscommon), Campbell (Donegal), Fisher (Donegal), McGehan (Donegal). The other executed man on the list, Dennis Donnelly, is marked with **, as there is no documented evidence on his place of birth, though his name is typical of west Ulster (Donegal and Tyrone).

LOCALITIES

Beaver Dale: McCool
Big Mine Run: Dolan (2), Gavin, McHugh, Sweeny
Buck Mountain: Boyle, Gallagher, McCahill (2), McGinity, McColl
Cass Township: McHale

Coal Dale: Bonner, Gallagher (2), *Roarty [sic]
Connor's Patch: McLaughlin, Padden
Ebervale: Gallagher
Eckley: Conahan
Fish Back: Durkin
Forestville: Keenan
Frackville: Harkins (2)
Gilberton: *Munley
Girardville: Crean, McDonough (2), McKanna
Hazleton: Boyle (2), Cull, Duffy (2), McCarron, McGinn, O'Donnell, Sweeny
Houtzdale: McKenna
Junction, Northumberland County: Campbell (4), Cannon, *Hester (Patrick)
Locust Gap: Cannon, Dougherty
Loss Creek: Demleavy, Dunleavy, Munley (2)
Mahanoy City: Boyle, Dougherty, Dugan, McGinty, McDonell, McHugh, Sheridan, Dugan (2)
Mahanoy Plane: McDonell, McGettigan
Mauch Chunk: McGinely (2), Mulhearn
Mount Laffee: Donnelly, Kane, Moran
Number Three: Monaghan
Ohio: McGowen
Palo Alto: Breslin, McAloon
Parson Station: Moran
Pittsburgh: Gallagher (head of Pennsylvania AOH)
Plainville: Monahan
Plank Road: Laughlin
Pottsville: Durkin, Farley, Rogers, Shovelin
Rappahannock: Monaghan (2), Munley
Raven Run: **Donnelly (Dennis)
Reeves Dale: Duffy
Saint Clair: O'Neill, Ward
Saint Nicholas: Gormerly
Schuylkill Falls: Devitt
Scranton: Kilcullen
Shamokin: McGann
Shenandoah: Boylan, Boyle, Burke, Burns (2), Cooney, Donnelly, Drumm, Dyer, McAndrew, McAnnulty, McGrail, McHugh, McKanna, Monahan (4), Morris
Silver Brook: Burns
Silver Creek: Kane
Shoemaker's Patch: Flannagan, McDonnell
Storm Hill: Boyle (3), Campbell (2, including *Alexander Campbell), Maguire (2), McKanna (3), McNellis (2)
Sugar Notch: Gibbons

Summit Hill: Boyle (2), Fisher (2, including *Thomas Fisher), Gallagher, McGinity, *McGehan (Hugh), Mulhearn (2), O'Donnell (2), Sweeny (2)
Tamaqua: Gallagher, McNellis, Mundy
The Run: McDonell, Mulhearn, Mundy, O'Donell [sic]
Weigans Patch [sic]: Huston, McCallister, O'Donell (2), Rodgers
Wilkes-Barre: Gallagher (2), Jennings, McGroarty

Appendix 4

Coffin Notices

Notices A through K were presented by Franklin B. Gowen at the end of his argument before the Pennsylvania Legislature in 1875 (FBG 1875, Appendix). They were allegedly posted in Schuylkill County during the "Long Strike" of that year and were published as an appendix to FBG 1875. Notice L is from *SH*, April 14, 1876, and notice M from *SH*, June 1, 1876.

A

Mr. John Taylor.—Please leave Glen Carbon or if you dont you will suffer, by the order of the B.S.H. WE will give you one week to go but if you are alive on next Saturday you will die. Remember and leave. [no signature]

B

[The following message came with a drawing of a pistol instead of a signature:]

Now men I have warented ye before and I willnt warind you no more—but I will gurrintee yo will be the report of the revolver.

C

[This one came with a drawing of a pistol, and below it a coffin:]

Notice is here given to you men the first and last notice that you will get for no man will go down this slope. After to night if you Do you Can Bring your Coffion Along With you for by the internal Crist We Mean What this notice says you Drift man stop at home and Cut no more Coal let him go and Get Coal himself I Dont mean Engineer Or forearms let them mine there one work now men the Next Notice you will get I Dont mean to Do it With my Pen I will Do it with that there Rolver I Dont want no more Black legs at this Collary. [no signature]

D

[With pistols and coffin; inside the drawing of the coffin was written "Tis is your hous":]

Notice you have Caried this as far as you can By cheating thy men you three Bosses Be Carefull if the Above dont Be your home in a short time.
From a Stranger he nowes you.

E

Take notice Avery Black Leg that will Take Aney Eunnion man plac you will have A hard Road to travel you will Rot in this shape if you wish to Escape this home. [Picture of coffin]

By a stranger.

F

If Thomas Martin Dont Stop we will burn down his breaker. [no signature]

G

NOTICE

Any blackleg that takes a Union Mans job while He is standing for His Rights will have a hard Road to travel and if he dont he will have to suffer the consequences. [Picture of a coffin with a body inside]

H

Any man starting to work in the rail road now going to begin under the basis will have to stand the consequences. So black legs to notice. [Picture of pistol]

M.M.N.

[and picture of pistol:]
Black Legs Take Notice—
that you are in dang er of your Life by working in the mines without the Consent of the union men of Swatara Branch 14 Dis at Middle Creek Mines. [no signature]

I

[Notice found posted at Locust Summit, May 31, 1875:]

Black legs if you dont leave in 2 days time you meet your doom their will Bee an open war immeatley. [no signature]

J

[Notice found in yard of D. Patchen, engineer, Cressona:]
from the gap Daniel Patch
remember you will be running in this coal ragion at night you took on nother mans engin we will give you fair warning in time and some more. VL.
—M.M. H.S.T., [pistol and coffin]

K

We hear notify you to leave the Road for you took a nother man chop take a warning to save your life

to Yost.

L

On Monday evening the following notice was received through the post by the gentlemen to whom it is addressed:

CENTRALIA, April 8, 1876

> To Harry and Tom Jasper: You are nothing but mean skunks and you do no nothing but ____ Mr.Baldwin for work. you have got all your boys working while their is poor men in the patch that can't get a job to do, and if you don't give up your work and quit the Tunel you will die like ____ with a ball in your heart.

So take warning by this, the rong man was attacked last monday but we will go four you Sons of Biches and Mr. Baldwin will share the same fate if he don't look out. we will give you one week notice so quit the place; an sure you are nothing but a set of English Sons of Bitches and shot you will be. You can send this to the Erald the skunk of a paper.

M

[To a Mr. Charles Dress, Night Watchman at Heckscher's Colliery:]

May 27, 1876

CD

you are wach man at Heckschers you S ___ B ___ you Hav Ten Days Time To leve if you donT DoWn Gose your sHandy By orDer you FinD OUT

Appendix 5

Two "Molly Maguire" Ballads

The first ballad is from Pinkerton, *The Molly Maguires and the Detectives* (pp. 77-78) and was allegedly sung by McParlan at Pat Dormer's saloon, just after he arrived in Pottsville in October 1873. The second is from a collection of songs, *Irish Nights* (No.6) [Dublin, ca. 1903]. Mr. Bell, the Protestant magistrate mentioned in both songs, was a justice of the peace murdered in County Cavan in 1845.

(i)
Pat Dolan, it's my Christian name,
    Yes, an' my surname too, sir;
An' oft you've listened to me sthrane,
    I'll tell you somethin' new, sir!
In Cavan-town, where we sat down,
    Our Irish hearts to inspire,
There's bould recruits an' undaunted yout's,
    And they'r led by Mollie Maguire!

[Chorus]
With my riggadum du, an' to h—l wid the crew
    Wouldn't help to free our nation;
When I look back, I count 'em slack,
    Wouldn't join our combination!

Said Mollie to her darlin' sons,
"What tyrant shall we tumble?
That filthy tribe we can't abide,
They rob both meek and humble;
There is one Bell, a child of h—l,
An' a Magistrate in station,
Let lots be drew an' see which av you
Will tumble him to damnation!"

[Chorus]
The lot's now cast, the sentence passed,
I scorn to tell a lie, sir!
I got my chance, it wur no blank;
I wur glad to win the prize, sir!
To swate Bill Cooney's I did repair,
To meet the parson, Bell, sir!
At his brain I took me aim,
Sayin' "Come down, ye fin' o' h—l, sir!"

[Chorus]
Those Orangemen, they gathered then,
An' swore they'd kill us all, sir!
For their frien' Bell, who lately fell,
An' got a terrible fall, sir!
But Mollie's sons, wid swords an' guns,
Wid pikes—pitchforks—glancin',
Those bould recruits an' undaunted yout's,
Stepped into the field just prancin'.

[Chorus]
Those Orangemen, they all stood then,
To fight they thought it a folly;
They'd rather run an' save their lives,
An' leave the field to Mollie!
Altho' I'm in a foreign land,
From the cause I'll ne'er retire,
May heaven smile on every chil',
That belongs to Mollie Maguire!

[Chorus]
One night as I lay upon me bed,
I heard a terrible rattle,
Who wor it but Bell, come back from h—l,
To fight another battle!
Then at his brain I took me aim—
He vanished off in fire—
And as he went the air he rent
Sayin', "I'm conquered by Mollie Maguire!"

[Chorus]
Now I'm in America,
An' that's a free nation!
I generally sit an' take my sip
Far from a police station!
Four dollars a day—its not bad pay—
An' the boss he likes me well, sir!
But little he knows that I'm the man
That shot that fin' o' h—l, sir!

[Chorus]
With my riggadum du, an' to h—l wid the crew
Wouldn't help to free our nation;
When I look back, I count 'em slack,
Wouldn't join our combination!

(ii)
Pat Dolan, it's my Christian name, likewise my surname
too, sir;
An' if ye listen to me a while I'll sing ye something
new, sir,
To sweet Miltown I did go down, against tyrants to
conspire,
Where I saw youth and bold recruits well headed by
Molly Maguire.

[Chorus]
With my rigadum-doo! to hell with the crew
Wouldn't come to aid the nation;
When I look back, I count 'em slack—
Wouldn't join our combination.

Says Mollie to her darling sons, "those tyrants we must
tumble
Such filthy tribe we can't abide—we'll rule them meek
and humble.
There is one Bell, an imp from hell, a land agent by
station—
Lots must be drew to see which of you will tumble him
to damnation!"

[Chorus]
So let the toast go merrily round,
Each Irish heart conspire;
Those tyrant hounds will be crushed down
By matchless Molly Maguire!

It's lots were drew, and cuts went through—I scorn to
tell a lie, sir;

But as for me, ye may plainly see, I own I won the
prize, sir.
It's to Crossdooney I did go to meet big Andrew Bell,
sir;
It was at his brains I took fair aim—"Come down, ye
imp of hell, sir!"

[Chorus]
With my swaggering bob, wasn't that a good job
To tumble him out of his phaeton,
An' Molly's sons with swords and guns
To keep us from bein' taken.

Then I was on my banishment, wanderin' up and down,
sir.
For to catch poor Pat was all their chat, an' they
offered five hundred poun', sir.
The polis, too, that traitor crew, oft ran my trace
breath high, sir;
But when they would see poor Pat's pistols cocked,
they'd sooner pass him by, sir!

[Chorus]
So let the toast go merrily round,
Each Irish heart conspire;
Those tyrant hounds will be crushed down
By matchless Molly Maguire!

One night as I lay in a shed I heard a terrible rattle
The ghost of Bell came back from hell to fight another
battle
Then at his brains I took good aim—he vanished off in fire,
And in the sulphur flames he thus exclaims, "I'm conquered
by Molly Maguire!"

[Chorus]
So let the toast go merrily round,
Each Irish heart conspire;
Those Brunswick hounds will be crushed down
By matchless Molly Maguire!

Bibliography

PRIMARY SOURCES

Manuscript Collections

Historical Society of Schuylkill County, Pottsville, Pennsylvania

Miners' pay books.
Molly Maguire Collection.
Papers of Francis P. Dewees.
Papers of Jay Oliver Roads.
Papers of C. W. Unger.
Papers of Thomas J. Walker.
Stenographic reports of the trials of John Kehoe, Thomas Duffy, James Roarity, and Neil Dougherty.

Free Library, Pottsville, Pennsylvania

Stenographic reports of the trials of Alexander Campbell, Michael J. Doyle, Thomas P. Fisher, Patrick McKenna, Edward Kelly, and James McDonnell.

Historical Society of Pennsylvania, Philadelphia, Pennsylvania

Molly Maguire Papers.
Papers of Owen Hunt.

United States Census Office. Seventh, Eighth, and Ninth Censuses on Population, 1850, 1860, and 1870, for Schuylkill County, Pennsylvania. Original unpublished returns.

St. Charles of Borromeo Seminary, Overbrook, Pennsylvania

Molly Maguire Collection.
Papers of Archbishop James Frederic Wood.
Scrapbook on Catholic Archdiocese of Philadelphia, 1864–79.

Hagley Museum and Library, Wilmington, Delaware

Philadelphia & Reading Railroad Collection.
Historical Information. Molly Maguire Papers.
Stenographic reports of the trials of John Donahue, Patrick Hester et al., Martin Bergin, James McDonnell, and Charles Sharp.
Papers of Glenn E. Thompson.

Pinkerton Investigations and Security Services, Inc., Van Nuys, California

Molly Maguire Collection.

Library of Congress, Washington, D.C.

Pinkerton's National Detective Agency, Manuscript Collection.

New York Public Library, Manuscript Division, New York City

Moses Taylor Collection, Papers of Charles A. Heckscher Company.

Beinecke Rare Book and Manuscript Library, Yale University

Dime novel collection.

Butler Library, Rare Book and Manuscript Division, Columbia University

Papers of Charlemagne Tower.

Published Trial Records

Albright, Charles. *The Great Mollie Maguire Trials. Commonwealth v. James Carroll et al., 1876. Arguments of General Charles Albright and F. W. Hughes for the Commonwealth.* Pottsville: Chronicle Book and Job Rooms, 1876.
[Allen, Lane & Scott]. *The Evidence in the Case of the Commonwealth v. Dennis Donnelly, 1877.* Philadelphia: Allen, Lane & Scott, 1877.
Gowen, Franklin B. *Argument of Franklin B. Gowen in the Case of the Commonwealth v. Munley, 1877, for the Murder of Thomas Sanger.* Pottsville: Chronicle Book and Job Rooms, 1876.

———. "Argument of Franklin B. Gowen in the case of *Commonwealth v. Kehoe et al.*," in R. A. West, *Report of the Case of the Commonwealth v. John Kehoe et al.* Pottsville: Miners' Journal Book and Job Rooms, 1876.

[Supreme Court, Pennsylvania]. *Dennis Donnelly v. the Commonwealth of Pennsylvania, 1878.* Pottsville: "Emerald Vindicator" Print, 1878.

[Town, G.V.]. *Commonwealth v. Patrick Hester, Patrick Tully, and Peter McHugh, 1877, Tried and Convicted of the Murder of Alexander W. Rea. Argument of Hon. F. W. Hughes, for Commonwealth.* Philadelphia: G.V. Town & Son, Printers, 1877.

[West, R. A.]. *Report of the Case of the Commonwealth v. John Kehoe et al. . . . for an Aggravated Assault and Battery with Intent to Kill William M. Thomas . . . , August 8, 1876 . . . Stenographically reported by R.A. West.* Pottsville: Miners' Journal Book and Job Rooms, 1876.

[York, E. D.]. *Report of the Case of the Commonwealth v. John Kehoe, January 9, 1877.* n.p.: E. D. York, Official Stenographer, 1877.

Unpublished Stenographic Trial Records

Hagley Museum and Library

A 1520, V 1744–51. Proceedings in the cases of *Commonwealth v. John Donahoe et al.*, October 1876, at Mauch Chunk, Carbon County; *Commonwealth v. Patrick Hester et al.*, February 1877, at Bloomsburg, Columbia County; *Commonwealth v. Martin Bergin et al.*, April 1878, at Pottsville, Schuylkill County; *Commonwealth v. James McDonnell*, April 1878, at Mauch Chunk, Carbon County; *Commonwealth v. Charles Sharp*, April 1878, at Mauch Chunk, Carbon County; statements and depositions by Patrick Butler, Dennis J. Canning, Thomas Munley, and Manus Cull.

Historical Society of Schuylkill County

Reports of the trials of John Kehoe, Thomas Duffy, James Roarity, and Neil Dougherty.

Pottsville Free Library, Schuylkill County

Reports of the trials of Alexander Campbell, Michael J. Doyle, Thomas Fisher, Patrick McKenna, Edward Kelly, and James McDonnell.

Contemporary Accounts of the Molly Maguires

Aiken, Albert. "The Molly Maguires; or the Black Diamond of Hazelton [sic]. A Story of the Great Strike in the Coal Region." In *Fireside Companion*, no. 436 to no. 449 (March 6, 1876, to June 5, 1876).

[Barclay & Co.]. *The Lives and Crimes of the Mollie Maguires. A Full Account.* Philadelphia: Barclay & Co., 1877.

Dewees, Francis P. *The Molly Maguires: The Origins, Growth, and Character of the Organization.* Philadelphia: J. B. Lippincott & Co., 1877.

Doyle, Daniel. "Molly Maguire, The Terror of the Coal Fields." In *New York Weekly Story-teller*, 31, no. 17 to no. 33 (March 13, 1876, to July 3, 1876).

[Eveland & Harris]. *The Molly Maguires: A Thrilling Narrative of the Rise, Progress, and Fall of the Most Noted Band of Cut-Throats of Modern Times.* Tamaqua: Eveland & Harris, n.d., ca. 1876.

Foster, Thomas Campbell. *Letters on the Condition of the People in Ireland.* London: Chapman & Hall, 1846.

Foster, Thomas J. "The Molly Maguires." Unpublished manuscript, ca. 1940, Pinkerton Corporate Archives, Van Nuys, California.

Gowen, Franklin B. *Argument of Franklin B. Gowen Before the Joint Committee of the Legislature of Pennsylvania, Appointed to Inquire into the Affairs of the Philadelphia and Reading Coal and Iron Company, and the Reading Railroad, July 29th and 30th, 1875.* Philadelphia: Press of Helfenstein, Lewis and Greene, 1875.

Lucy, Ernest W. *The Mollie Maguires of Pennsylvania, or Ireland in America.* London: George Bell & Sons, 1882.

McCabe, James Dabney [Edward Winslow Martin pseud.]. *The History of the Great Riots, Being a Full and Authentic Account of the Strikes and Riots on the Various Railroads of the United States and in the Mining Region . . . Together With a Full History of the Molly Maguires.* Philadelphia: National Publishing Company, 1877.

McMahon, Patrick Justin. *Philip, or the Mollie's Secret.* Philadelphia: H. L. Kilner & Co., 1891.

[*Miners' Journal*]. *Among the Assassins! The Molly Maguires and Their Victims. Full Report of the Evidence of Detective McParlan, Jimmy Kerrigan, and Others, at the Celebrated Molly Maguire Trials, at Pottsville.* Pottsville: The Miners' Journal Print, 1876.

Moffett, Cleveland. "The Overthrow of the Molly Maguires." *McClure's Magazine,* 4 (December 1894 to May 1895): 90–100. New York: McClure's, 1895.

Morse, John T., Jr. "The 'Molly Maguire' Trials." *American Law Review* (January 1877): 233–60.

O'Donnell, Sergeant. *Coal-Mine Tom; or, Fighting the Molly Maguires.* The Five Cent Wide Awake Library, no. 620 (July 23, 1884).

Pastor, Tony. "Down in a Coal Mine; or, The Mystery of the Fire Damp." In *Fireside Companion,* no. 302 ff. (August 11, 1873, ff.). Reprinted under the same title with "Old Sleuth" as author, Old Sleuth Library, no. 48 (March 29, 1890); and under the title *Foiled by Love; or, the Molly Maguires' Last Stand,* in *Old Sleuth Weekly,* no. 44 (1909).

Pinkerton, Allan. *The Molly Maguires and the Detectives.* 1877; New York: Dillingham, 1905.

Trench, W. Steuart. *Realities of Irish Life.* 1868; London: MacGibbon & Kee, 1966.

"A U.S. Detective." *The Molly Maguire Detective; or, A Vidocq's Adventures Among the Miners.* New York Detective Library, no. 179 (May 8, 1886).

British, Irish, and American Government Reports and Publications

Parliament [U.K.]. *House of Commons: Reports of the Committees. Report from the Select Committee on Destitution (Gweedore and Cloughaneely).* London: House of Commons, 1858.

———. *Report of the Commissioners of Inquiry into the State of the Law and Practice in Respect of the Occupation of Land in Ireland* (Devon Commission). 4 vols. Dublin: Alexander Thom, 1845.

———. *Evidence Taken Before Her Majesty's Commissioners of Inquiry into the State of the Law and Practice in Respect to Occupation of the Land* (Devon Commission Digest). 2 vols. Dublin: Alexander Thom, 1845.

———. *The Parliamentary Gazetteer of Ireland, 1844–45.* Dublin, London, and Edinburgh: 1845.

Pennsylvania Bureau of Industrial Statistics. *Annual Reports, Number 1 (1872–1873).* Harrisburg: State Printer, B. Singerly, 1873.

———. *Annual Reports, Number 2 (1873–1874)*. Harrisburg: State Printer, B. Singerly, 1874.

Pennsylvania, Commonwealth of. *Annual Report of the Secretary of Internal Affairs for the Commonwealth of Pennsylvania, 1875–76. Industrial Statistics.* Harrisburg: State Printer, B.F. Meyers, n.d.

Pennsylvania General Assembly. Senate. *Committee on the Judiciary. Report of the Committee on the Judiciary, General, of the Senate of Pennsylvania, in Relation to the Anthracite Coal Difficulties, with the Accompanying Testimony*. Harrisburg: State Printer, B. Singerly, 1871.

Pennsylvania Inspectors of Mines. *Annual Reports of the Inspectors of Coal Mines of the Anthracite Regions of Pennsylvania, 1870–1887*. Harrisburg: State Printer, B. Singerly, 1870–87.

United States Census Office. *The Seventh Census. Report of the Superintendent of the Census for December 1, 1852.* Washington: Robert Armstrong, Public Printer, 1853.

———. *Census of the United States: 1850.* Washington: Robert Armstrong, Public Printer, 1853.

———. *Population of the United States in 1860; Compiled from the Original Returns of the Eighth Census.* Washington: Government Printing Office, 1864.

———. *Manufactures of the United States in 1860; Compiled from the Original Returns of the Eighth Census.* Washington: Government Printing Office, 1865.

———. *Statistics of the United States in 1860 (Including Mortality, Property, &c.,); Compiled from the Original Returns of the Eighth Census.* Washington: Government Printing Office, 1866.

———. *Ninth Census.* Vol. 1. *The Statistics of the Population of the United States.* Washington: Government Printing Office, 1872.

———. *Ninth Census.* Vol. 3. *The Statistics of the Wealth and Industry of the United States.* Washington: Government Printing Office, 1872.

———. *A Compendium of the Ninth Census of the United States, 1870.* n.p., n.d.

United States Government. *Report of the Committee on the Conduct of the War at the Second Session of the Thirty-eighth Congress.* Vol. 1. *Battle of Petersburg.* Washington: U.S. Government Printing Office, 1865.

United States House of Representatives. *The Reports of the Committees of the House of Representatives for the Second Session of the Fiftieth Congress, 1888–89.* Report no. 4147, *Labor Troubles in the Anthracite Regions of Pennsylvania, 1887–1888.* Washington: U.S. Government Printing Office, 1889.

United States War Department. *War of the Rebellion: A Compilation of the Official Records of the Union and Confederate Armies.* Washington: U.S. Government Printing Office, 1889–1901.

Newspapers

Ballyshannon Herald (County Donegal, Ireland); *Pilot* (Boston); *Tribune* (Chicago, Illinois); *Derry Journal* (Derry City, Ireland); *Harrisburg Patriot* (Harrisburg, Pennsylvania); *Freeman's Journal* (Dublin, Ireland); *Times* (London, England); *Mauch Chunk Democrat* (Mauch Chunk, Carbon County, Pennsylvania); *Daily News, Daily Worker, Evening Post, Frank Leslie's Illustrated Newspaper, Freeman's Journal & Catholic Register, Herald, Irish World, Labor Standard, Star, Sun, Times, Tribune, World* (New York City); *Catholic Standard, Evening Bulletin, Evening Telegraph, Inquirer, Press, Public Ledger, Record, Times* (Philadelphia); *Emerald Vindicator, Evening Chronicle, Miners' Journal, Republican, Standard* (Pottsville, Schuylkill County); *Eagle* (Reading, Pennsylvania);

Republican (Scranton, Pennsylvania); *Herald* (Shenandoah, Schuylkill County); *Anthracite Monitor, Herald* (Tamaqua, Schuylkill County).

Other Published Writings by Nineteenth-century Observers

[Beers & Co.]. *County Atlas of Schuylkill, Pennsylvania.* New York: F.W. Beers & Co., 1875.

Carey, Henry C. *Principles of Political Economy.* 3 vols. Philadelphia: Carey, Lea & Blanchard, 1837.

Carman, Harry J., Henry David, and Paul N. Guthrie, eds. *The Path I Trod: The Autobiography of Terence V. Powderly.* New York: Columbia University Press, 1940.

Doyle, James Warren. *The Pastoral Address of the Right Rev. Dr. Doyle, R.C. Bishop of Kildare and Leighlin, Against the Illegal Associations of Ribbonmen.* Dublin: J. J. Dolan, 1822.

Evans, Chris. *History of the United Mine Workers of America from the Year 1860 to 1890.* 2 vols. Indianapolis, n.p., n.d.

[Filmer, John]. *The Illustrated Catalogue of the Centennial Exhibition, Philadelphia, 1876.* New York: John Filmer, 1876.

Heywood, E. H. *The Great Strike: Its Relations to Labor, Property, and Government, Suggested by the Memorable Events Which, Originating in the Tyrannous Extortion of Railway Masters, and the Execution of Eleven Labor Reformers Called 'Mollie Maguires,' June 21, 1877, Culminated in Burning the Corporation Property in Pittsburg* [*sic*], *July 22 Following.* Princeton [Mass.]: Cooperative Publishing Co., 1878.

Hill, Lord George. *Facts From Gweedore.* 5th ed., 1887; reprt., Belfast: Institute of Irish Studies, 1971.

[Leslie's Publishing House]. *Frank Leslie's Illustrated Historical Register of the United States Centennial Exposition.* New York: Frank Leslie's Publishing House, 1877.

Lewis, George Cornewall. *On the Local Disturbances in Ireland.* London: B. Fellowes, 1836.

Lewis, Samuel. *A Topographical Dictionary of Ireland.* 2 vols. London: S. Lewis & Co., 1837.

McCabe, James Dabney. *The Illustrated History of the Centennial Exposition.* Philadelphia: The National Publishing Company, 1876.

McClure, Alexander K. *Old Time Notes of Pennsylvania.* 2 vols. Philadelphia: The John C. Winston Co., 1905.

———. *Lincoln and Men of War Times.* 1892; Philadelphia: Rolley and Reynolds, 1961.

McGrath, T. F. *History of the Ancient Order of Hibernians from the Earliest Period to the Joint National Convention at Trenton, New Jersey, June 27, 1898.* Cleveland: T. F. McGrath, 1898.

[Munsell & Co.]. *History of Schuylkill County, Pa., with Illustrations and Biographical Sketches of Some of its Prominent Men and Pioneers.* New York: W. W. Munsell & Co., 1881.

Patterson, Joseph F. "Reminiscences of John Maguire After Fifty Years of Mining." Pottsville: Publications of the Historical Society of Schuylkill County, 4, 1914.

———. "Old W.B.A. Days." Pottsville: Publications of the Historical Society of Schuylkill County, 2, 1909.

Philadelphia & Reading Railroad. *Reports of the President and Managers to the Stockholders, 1846–86.* Philadelphia: various publishers, 1846–86.

Pinkerton, Allan. *Strikers, Communists, Tramps, and Detectives.* 1878; New York: Arno Press, 1969.

Pinkerton's National Detective Agency. *General Principles of Pinkerton's National Detective Agency.* Chicago: Fergus Printing Company, 1873.

Roy, Andrew. *A History of the Coal Miners of the United States.* 1905; Westport, Conn.: Greenwood Press, 1970.

———. *The Coal Mines.* Cleveland: Robison, Savage & Co., Printers and Stationers, 1876.

Schlack, Adolph W., and D. C. Henning, eds., *History of Schuylkill County, Pennsylvania.* 2 vols. n.p.: Pennsylvania State Historical Association, 1907.

Thomas, B. B. *The Coal Monopoly: Correspondence Between B. B. Thomas and F. B. Gowen.* New York: Coal Trade Circular Print, 1873.

Tuke, James Hack. *Irish Distress and its Remedies: The Land Question: A Visit to Donegal and Connaught in the Spring of 1880.* London: Ridgway, 1880.

Virtue, G. O. "The Anthracite Mine Laborers." *Bulletin of the Department of Labor,* 13 (November 1897): 728–74.

Wallace, Francis B. *A Memorial of the Patriotism of Schuylkill County.* Pottsville: Benjamin Bannan, 1865.

Wiley, Samuel T. *Biographical and Portrait Cyclopedia of Schuylkill County, Pennsylvania.* Philadelphia: Rush, West & Co., 1893.

SECONDARY SOURCES

Amsden, Jon, and Stephen Brier. "Coal Miners on Strike: The Transformation of Strike Demands and the Formation of a National Union." *The Journal of Interdisciplinary History,* 7 (Spring 1977): 583–616.

Anbinder, Tyler. *Nativism and Slavery: The Northern Know Nothings and the Politics of the 1850s.* New York: Oxford University Press, 1992.

Appleby, Joyce, Lynn Hunt, and Margaret Jacobs. *Telling the Truth About History.* New York: Norton, 1994.

Archbald, Hugh. *The Four Hour Day in Coal.* New York: The H. W. Wilson Company, 1922.

Aurand, Harold D. "The Anthracite Mine Workers, 1869–1897: A Functional Approach to Labor History." Unpublished Ph.D. diss., Pennsylvania State University, 1969.

———. "The Anthracite Miner: An Occupational Analysis." *Pennsylvania Magazine of History and Biography,* 104 (October 1980): 462–73.

Aurand, Harold D., and William A. Gudelunas, Jr. "The Mythical Qualities of Molly Maguire." *Pennsylvania History,* 49 (April 1982): 91–103.

Avrich, Paul. *The Haymarket Tragedy.* Princeton: Princeton University Press, 1984.

Baird, W. David. "Violence Along the Chesapeake Canal: 1839." *Maryland Historical Magazine,* 66 (Summer 1971): 121–34.

Baron, Ava. "Gender and Labor History: Learning from the Past, Looking to the Future." In Baron, ed., *Work Engendered: Toward a New History of American Labor.* Ithaca: Cornell University Press, 1991.

Barthes, Roland. *Mythologies.* 1957; New York: The Noonday Press, 1990. Trans. Annette Lavers.

Beames, Michael R. *Peasants and Power: The Whiteboy Movements and Their Control in Pre-famine Ireland.* New York: St. Martin's Press, 1983.

———. "The Ribbon Societies: Lower-Class Nationalism in Pre-Famine Ireland," and "Rural Conflict in Pre-famine Ireland: Peasant Assassination in Tipperary, 1837–47." In C. H. E. Philpin, ed., *Nationalism and Popular Protest in Ireland.* Cambridge and New York: Cambridge University Press, 1987.

Bergin, James J. *History of the Ancient Order of Hibernians.* Dublin: Ancient Order of Hibernians, 1910.

Berlanstein, Lenard, ed. *Rethinking Labor History: Essays on Discourse and Class Analysis.* Urbana: University of Illinois Press, 1993.

Bernstein, Iver. *The New York City Draft Riots: Their Significance for American Society and Politics in the Age of the Civil War.* New York: Oxford University Press, 1990.

Bew, Paul. *Land and the National Question in Ireland, 1858–82.* Atlantic Highlands, N.J.: Humanities Press, 1979.

Bimba, Anthony. *The Molly Maguires.* 1932; New York: International Publishers, 1950.

Blatz, Perry K. *Democratic Miners: Work and Labor Relations in the Anthracite Coal Industry, 1875–1925.* Albany: State University of New York Press, 1994.

———. "Ever-Shifting Ground: Work and Labor Relations in the Anthracite Coal Industry, 1868–1903." Unpublished Ph.D. diss., Princeton University, 1987.

Blessing, Patrick. "Culture, Religion, and the Activities of the Committee of Vigilance, San Francisco, 1858." Working paper, Series 8, no. 3 (1980), Charles and Margaret Hall Cushwa Center for the Study of American Catholicism, University of Notre Dame.

Bodnar, John, ed. *The Ethnic Experience in Pennsylvania.* Lewisburg, Penn.: Bucknell University Press, 1973.

Borgeson, Richard D. "Irish Canal Laborers in America: 1817–1846." M.A. thesis, Pennsylvania State University, 1964.

Bradshaw, Brendan. "Nationalism and Historical Scholarship in Modern Ireland." *Irish Historical Studies,* 26 (November 1989): 329–51.

Broehl, Wayne G., Jr. *The Molly Maguires.* 1964; New York: Chelsea House, 1983.

Brown, Joshua. "*Frank Leslie's Illustrated Newspaper*: The Pictorial Press and the Representations of America, 1855–1889." Unpublished Ph.D. diss., Columbia University, 1993.

Browne, Henry J. *The Catholic Church and the Knights of Labor.* Washington: Catholic University of America Press, 1949.

Bulik, Mark. "Mummers and Mollies: The Political Semantic of Irish Folk Drama and Its Uses in Rebel Symbolism." Unpublished paper delivered at "Irish Literature: Old and New Worlds" conference, Hofstra University, July 17–20, 1996.

Campbell, Patrick. *A Molly Maguire Story.* Jersey City, N.J.: Templecrone Press, 1992.

Campbell, Stephen J. *The Great Irish Famine: Words and Images from the Famine Museum, Strokestown Park, County Roscommon.* Strokestown, Ireland: Famine Museum, 1994.

Catton, Bruce. *The Civil War.* 1971; New York: American Heritage Press, 1980.

Chandler, Alfred D., Jr. "Anthracite Coal and the Beginnings of the Industrial Revolution in the United States." *Business History Review,* 46 (Summer 1972): 141–81.

Christman, Henry. *Tin Horns and Calico: A Decisive Episode in the Emergence of Democracy.* New York: Henry Holt & Co., 1945.

Clark, Samuel J., and James S. Donnelly, Jr., eds. *Irish Peasants: Violence and Political Unrest, 1780–1914.* Madison: University of Wisconsin Press, 1983.

Coleman, James Walter. *The Molly Maguire Riots: Industrial Conflict in the Pennsylvania Coal Region.* Richmond: Garrett & Massie, 1936.

Collins, Brenda. "Proto-industrialization and Pre-famine Emigration." *Social History,* 7 (1982): 127–46.

Commons, John R., et al. *History of Labour in the United States.* 4 vols. 1935–36; New York: Augustus M. Kelley, 1966.

Connolly, S. J. *Priests and People in Pre-famine Ireland, 1780–1845.* New York: Gill & Macmillan, 1982.

Conway, Alan, ed. *The Welsh in America: Letters from Immigrants.* Minneapolis: University of Minnesota Press, 1961.

Cook, Adrian. *The Armies of the Streets: The New York City Draft Riots of 1863.* Lexington: University Press of Kentucky, 1974.

Cousens, S. H. "The Regional Pattern of Emigration During the Great Irish Famine, 1846–51." *Transactions of the Institute of British Geographers,* 28 (1960): 119–33.

———. "Emigration and Demographic Change in Ireland, 1851–1861." *The Economic History Review,* 14 (December 1961): 275–88.
———. "The Regional Variations in Population Changes in Ireland, 1861–1881." *The Economic History Review,* 17 (December 1964): 301–21.
Crawford, W. H. *The Handloom Weavers and the Ulster Linen Industry*. 1972; Belfast: The Ulster Historical Foundation, 1994.
———. "The Rise of the Linen Industry." In L. M. Cullen, ed., *The Formation of the Irish Economy*. 1968; Cork: Mercier Press, 1976.
———. "The Evolution of the Linen Trade of Ulster before Industrialization." *Irish Economic and Social History,* 15 (1988): 32–53.
Cullen, L. M. *An Economic History of Ireland Since 1660*. London: B. T. Batsford, 1972.
———, ed. *The Formation of the Irish Economy.* 1968; Cork: The Mercier Press, 1976.
Curtis, Lewis Perry. *Apes and Angels: The Irishman in Victorian Caricature*. Washington, D.C.: Smithsonian Institution Press, 1971.
Davies, Edward J. *The Anthracite Aristocracy: Leadership and Social Change in the Hard Coal Regions of Northeastern Pennsylvania, 1820–1930*. DeKalb: Northern Illinois University Press, 1985.
Davis, Natalie Zemon. *Society and Culture in Early Modern France*. Stanford: Stanford University Press, 1975.
Delaney, John J. *Dictionary of American Catholic Biography*. Garden City, N.Y.: Doubleday, 1984.
Denning, Michael. *Mechanic Accents: Dime Novels and Working-Class Culture in America.* New York: Verso, 1987.
Diner, Hasia R. *Erin's Daughters in America: Irish Immigrant Women in the Nineteenth Century*. Baltimore: Johns Hopkins University Press, 1983.
Dolan, Liam. *Land War and Eviction in Derryveagh, 1840–1865*. Dundalk, Ireland: Annaverna Press, 1980.
Donnelly, James S., Jr., "The Whiteboy Movement, 1761–65." *Irish Historical Studies,* 21 (March 1978): 20–54.
———. "Irish Agrarian Rebellion: The Whiteboys of 1769–76." *Proceedings of the Royal Irish Academy,* C, 83 (1983): 293–331.
———. "The Rightboy Movement, 1785–88." *Studia Hibernica,* 17 & 18 (1977–78): 120–202.
———. "The Terry Alt Movement." *History Ireland,* 2 (Winter 1994): 30–35.
Douglas, J. N. H. "Emigration and Irish Peasant Life." *Ulster Folklife,* 9 (1963): 9–19.
Doyle, Sir Arthur Conan. *The Valley of Fear.* 1915; Oxford: Oxford University Press, 1994. Edited with an Introduction by Owen Dudley Edwards.
Doyle, David Noel, and Owen Dudley Edwards, eds., *America and Ireland, 1776–1976: The American Identity and the Irish Connection*. Westport, Conn.: Greenwood Press, 1980.
Dubovsky, Melvyn. *We Shall Be All: A History of the Industrial Workers of the World.* Chicago: Quadrangle Books, 1969.
Eagleton, Terry. *Ideology: An Introduction*. New York: Verso, 1991.
Fields, Barbara Jeanne. "The Nineteenth-Century American South: History and Theory." *Plantation Society,* 2 (April 1983): 7–27.
Foner, Eric. *Free Soil, Free Labor, Free Men: The Ideology of the Republican Party Before the Civil War*. New York: Oxford University Press, 1970.
———. *Reconstruction: America's Unfinished Revolution*. New York: Harper & Row, 1988.
———. "The Land League in Irish America." In Foner, *Politics and Ideology in the Age of the Civil War*. New York: Oxford University Press, 1980.

Foster, R. F. *Modern Ireland, 1600–1972*. London: Allen Lane, Penguin Press, 1988.

———. "History and the Irish Question." *Royal Historical Society Transactions,* 5th ser., 32 (1983): 169–92.

Foucault, Michel. *Discipline and Punish: The Birth of the Prison*. 1977; New York: Vintage Books, 1979. Trans. Alan Sheridan.

Garvin, Tom. "Defenders, Ribbonmen, and Others: Underground Political Networks in Pre-famine Ireland." In C. H. E. Philpin, ed., *Nationalism and Popular Protest in Ireland*. Cambridge and New York: Cambridge University Press, 1987.

Genovese, Eugene D. *Roll, Jordan, Roll: The World the Slaves Made*. 1972; New York: Vintage Books, 1976.

Gienapp, William E. *The Origins of the Republican Party, 1852–56*. New York: Oxford University Press, 1987.

Gill, Conrad. *The Rise of the Irish Linen Industry*. Oxford: The Clarendon Press, 1925.

Ginger, Ray. "Company-sponsored Welfare Plans in the Anthracite Industry before 1900." *Bulletin of the Business Historical Society,* 27 (June 1953): 112–120.

Gordon, Michael. *The Orange Riots: Irish Political Violence in New York City, 1870 and 1871*. Ithaca, N.Y.: Cornell University Press, 1993.

Gudelunas, William A., Jr., and William G. Shade. *Before the Molly Maguires: The Emergence of the Ethno-Religious Factor in the Politics of the Lower Anthracite Region, 1844–1872*. New York: Arno Press, 1976.

Guha, Ranajit. *Elementary Aspects of Peasant Insurgency in Colonial India*. Delhi: Oxford University Press, 1983.

Guha, Ranajit, and Gayatri Chakravorty Spivak, eds. *Selected Subaltern Studies*. New York: Oxford University Press, 1988.

Gutman, Herbert G. *Work, Culture and Society in Industrializing America*. New York: Vintage Books, 1977.

———. *Power and Culture: Essays on the American Working Class*. Ed. Ira Berlin. New York: The New Press, 1987.

Handley, James Edmund. *The Irish in Scotland*. Cork: Cork University Press, 1945.

Hay, Douglas, ed. *Albion's Fatal Tree: Crime and Society in Eighteenth-Century England*. New York: Pantheon Books, 1975.

Hobsbawm, Eric. *Primitive Rebels: Studies in Archaic Forms of Social Movement in the Nineteenth and Twentieth Centuries*. New York: Norton, 1965.

———. *Workers: Worlds of Labor*. New York: Pantheon, 1984.

Hobsbawm, Eric, and George Rudé. *Captain Swing*. New York: Random House, 1968.

Horan, James, and Howard Swiggett. *The Pinkerton Story*. New York: G. P. Putnam's Sons, 1951.

[Hudson Coal Company]. *The Story of Anthracite*. New York: Hudson Coal Company, 1932.

Hunt, Lynn, ed. *The New Cultural History*. Berkeley: University of California Press, 1989.

Huston, James L. "The Demise of the Pennsylvania American Party, 1854–58." *Pennsylvania Magazine of History and Biography,* 109 (October 1985): 473–97.

Ignatiev, Noel. *How the Irish Became White*. New York: Routledge, 1995.

ILWCH Roundtable. "What Next for Labor History?" *International Journal of Labor and Working-Class History,* 46 (Fall 1994): 7–92.

Itter, William. "Early Labor Troubles in the Schuylkill Anthracite District." *Pennsylvania History,* 1 (January 1934): 28–37.

Jackson, John Archer. *The Irish in Britain*. London: Routledge and Kegan Paul, 1983.

Jameson, Fredric. *The Political Unconscious: Narrative as a Socially Symbolic Act*. Ithaca, N.Y.: Cornell University Press, 1981.

Johnson, J. H. "Harvest Migration from Nineteenth-Century Ireland." *Transactions of the Institute of British Geographers,* 20 (1965): 97–112.

Jones, David J.V. *Rebecca's Children: A Study of Rural Society, Crime and Protest.* New York: Oxford University Press, 1989.

Katznelson, Ira. "Working Class Formation: Constructing Cases and Comparisons." In Ira Katznelson and Aristide Zolberg, eds., *Working-Class Formation: Nineteenth-Century Patterns in Western Europe and the United States.* Princeton: Princeton University Press, 1986.

Kennedy, Robert E., Jr. *The Irish: Emigration, Marriage, and Fertility.* Berkeley: University of California Press, 1973.

Kenny, Kevin. "Making Sense of the Molly Maguires." Unpublished Ph.D. diss., Columbia University, 1994.

———. "Nativism, Labor, and Slavery: The Political Odyssey of Benjamin Bannan, 1850–1860." *The Pennsylvania Magazine of History and Biography,* 118 (October 1994): 325–61.

———. "The Molly Maguires in Popular Culture." *Journal of American Ethnic History,* 14 (Summer 1995): 27–46.

———. "The Molly Maguires and the Catholic Church." *Labor History,* 36 (Summer 1995): 345–76.

Killeen, Charles Edward. "John Siney: The Pioneer in American Industrial Unionism and Industrial Government." Unpublished Ph.D. diss., University of Wisconsin, 1942.

Knobel, Dale T. *Paddy and the Republic: Ethnicity and Nationality in Antebellum America.* Middletown, Conn.: Wesleyan University Press, 1986.

Knott, John William. "Land, Kinship and Identity: The Cultural Roots of Agrarian Agitation in Eighteenth- and Nineteenth-Century Ireland." *Journal of Peasant Studies,* 12 (October 1984): 93–108.

Korson, George G. *Minstrels of the Mine Patch: Songs and Stories of the Anthracite Industry.* Philadelphia: University of Pennsylvania Press, 1938.

Krause, Paul. *The Battle for Homestead, 1880–1892: Politics, Culture, Steel.* Pittsburgh: University of Pittsburgh Press, 1992.

Larkin, Emmet. "The Devotional Revolution in Ireland, 1850–75." *American Historical Review,* 77 (June 1972): 625–52.

Leach, Eugene E. "Chaining the Tiger: The Mob Stigma and the Working Class, 1863–1894." *Labor History,* 35 (Spring 1994): 187–215.

Lee, Joseph. "The Ribbonmen." In T. Desmond Williams, ed., *Secret Societies in Ireland.* Dublin: Gill and Macmillan, 1973.

Lens, Sidney. *The Labor Wars: From the Molly Maguires to the Sitdowns.* Garden City, N.Y.: Doubleday, 1973.

Lewis, Arthur H. *Lament for the Molly Maguires.* 1964; New York: Pocket Books, 1969.

Long, Priscilla. *Where the Sun Never Shines: A History of America's Bloody Coal Industry.* New York: Paragon, 1989.

McCarthy, Charles A. *The Great Molly Maguire Hoax.* Wyoming, Penn.: Cro Woods, 1969.

Macdonald, Fergus. *The Catholic Church and the Secret Societies in the United States.* New York: Catholic Historical Society, 1946.

MacLysaght, Edward. *The Surnames of Ireland.* 1957; Dublin: Irish Academic Press Ltd., 1991.

Masur, Louis P. *Rites of Execution: Capital Punishment and the Transformation of American Culture, 1776–1865.* New York: Oxford University Press, 1989.

Merriman, John. *1830 in France.* New York: New Viewpoints, 1975.

Miller, David W. "Irish Catholicism and the Great Famine." *Journal of Social History*, 9 (Fall 1975): 81–98.

Miller, Kerby A. *Emigrants and Exiles: Ireland and the Irish Exodus to North America*. New York: Oxford University Press, 1985.

———. "Class, Culture, and Immigrant Group Identity in the United States: The Case of Irish-American Ethnicity." In Virginia Yans-McLaughlin, ed., *Immigration Reconsidered: History, Sociology, and Politics*. New York: Oxford University Press, 1990.

Montgomery, David. *Beyond Equality: Labor and the Radical Republicans, 1862–1872*. New York: Knopf, 1967.

———. "Labor and the Republic in Industrial America: 1860–1920." *Le Mouvement Social*, 110 (1980): 250–56.

———. "The Irish and the American Labor Movement." In David Noel Doyle and Owen Dudley Edwards, eds., *America and Ireland, 1776–1976: The American Identity and the Irish Connection*. Westport, Conn.: Greenwood Press, 1980.

Morn, Frank. *The Eye That Never Sleeps: A History of the Pinkerton National Detective Agency*. Bloomington: Indiana University Press, 1982.

Nolan, William. *Fassidinin: Land, Settlement and Society in Southeast Ireland, 1600–1850*. Dublin: Geography Publications, 1979.

O'Dea, John. *History of the Ancient Order of Hibernians and Ladies' Auxiliary*. 3 vols. Philadelphia: Keystone Printing Co., 1923.

Oestreicher, Richard. "Terence V. Powderly, the Knights of Labor, and Artisanal Republicanism." In Melvyn Dubovsky and Warren Van Tine, eds., *Labor Leaders in America*. Urbana: University of Illinois Press, 1987.

Ó Gallchobhair, Proinnsias. *The History of Landlordism in Donegal*. 1962; Ballyshannon, Ireland: Donegal *Democrat*, 1975.

Ó Gráda, Cormac. "Seasonal Migration and Post-famine Adjustment in the West of Ireland." *Studia Hibernica*, 13 (1973): 48–76.

Palladino, Grace. *Another Civil War: Labor, Capital, and the State in the Anthracite Regions of Pennsylvania, 1840–68*. Urbana: University of Illinois Press, 1990.

Palmer, Bryan D. *Descent Into Discourse: The Reification of Language and the Writing of Social History*. Philadelphia: Temple University Press, 1990.

Philpin, C. H. E., ed. *Nationalism and Popular Protest in Ireland*. Cambridge and New York: Cambridge University Press, 1987.

Pinkowski, Edward. *John Siney, The Miners' Martyr*. Philadelphia: Sunshine Press, 1963.

Póirtéir, Cathal, ed., *The Great Irish Famine*. Cork: Mercier Press, 1995.

Potter, David M. *The Impending Crisis, 1848–1861*. New York: Harper Torchbooks, 1976.

Potter, George W. *To the Golden Door: The Story of the Irish in Ireland and America*. Boston: Little, Brown and Company, 1960.

Purvis, Thomas, Donald Akenson, Forrest McDonald, and Ellen McDonald. "The Population of the United States, 1790: A Symposium." *William and Mary Quarterly*, 41 (January 1984): 85–135.

Rhodes, James Ford. *History of the United States, 1850–1896*. Vol. 8. 1919; New York: The Macmillan Company, 1928.

———. "The Molly Maguires in the Anthracite Region of Pennsylvania." *American Historical Review*, 15 (April 1910): 547–61.

Roberts, Peter. *The Anthracite Coal Industry*. New York: The Macmillan Company, 1901.

Rodechko, James P. "Irish-American Society in the Pennsylvania Anthracite Region: 1870–1880." In John E. Bodnar, ed., *The Ethnic Experience in Pennsylvania*. Lewisburg, Penn.: Bucknell University Press, 1973.

Rodgers, Daniel T. "Republicanism: the Career of a Concept." *Journal of American History,* 79 (June 1992): 11–38.

Roediger, David. *The Wages of Whiteness: Race and the Making of the American Working Class.* New York: Verso, 1991.

Roohan, James Edmund. *American Catholics and the Social Question, 1865–1900.* New York: Arno Press, 1976.

Rudé, George. *The Crowd in the French Revolution.* New York: Oxford University Press, 1972.

Rydell, Robert W. *All the World's a Fair: Visions of Empire at American International Expositions, 1876–1916.* Chicago: The University of Chicago Press, 1984.

Scally, Robert James. *The End of Hidden Ireland: Rebellion, Famine, and Emigration.* New York: Oxford University Press, 1995.

Schlegel, Marvin W. *Ruler of the Reading: The Life of Franklin B. Gowen.* Harrisburg: Archives Publishing Co. of Pennsylvania, Inc., 1947.

———. "The Workingmen's Benevolent Association: First Union of Anthracite Miners." *Pennsylvania History,* 10 (October 1943): 243–67.

Scott, James C. *The Moral Economy of the Peasant: Rebellion and Subsistence in Southeast Asia.* New Haven: Yale University Press, 1976.

———. "Protest and Profanation: Agrarian Revolt and the Little Tradition." *Theory and Society,* 4 (Spring and Summer 1977): 1–38, 211–46.

———. "Hegemony and the Peasantry." *Politics and Society,* 7 (1977): 267–96.

Scott, Joan Wallach. *Gender and the Politics of History.* New York: Columbia University Press, 1988.

Shalloo, Jeremiah P. *Private Police: With Special Reference to Pennsylvania.* Philadelphia: American Academy of Social and Political Science, 1933.

Shankman, Arnold M. *The Pennsylvania Anti-War Movement, 1861–1865.* Rutherford, N.J.: Fairleigh Dickinson University Press, 1980.

———. "Draft Resistance in Civil War Pennsylvania." *Pennsylvania Magazine of History and Biography,* 101 (April 1977): 190–204.

Sheehan, Thomas. *All Those Folks from St. Patrick's.* Limited private edition, 1994.

Slotkin, Richard. *Fatal Environment: The Myth of the Frontier in the Age of Industrialization, 1800–1890.* New York: Harper Perennial, 1994.

Smyth, W. J. "Locational Patterns and Trends Within the Pre-famine Linen Industry." *Irish Geography,* 8 (1975): 97–110.

Solar, Peter M. "The Irish Linen Trade, 1820–1852." *Textile History,* 21 (Spring 1990): 57–85.

Thompson, E. P. *The Making of the English Working Class.* 1963; Harmondsworth, England: Penguin, 1968.

———. *Whigs and Hunters: The Origins of the Black Act.* New York: Pantheon, 1975.

———. "The Moral Economy of the English Crowd in the Eighteenth Century." *Past and Present,* 50 (February 1971): 76–136.

———. "The Crime of Anonymity." In Douglas Hay, ed., *Albion's Fatal Tree: Crime and Society in Eighteenth-Century England.* New York: Pantheon Books, 1975.

Trachtenberg, Alexander. *A History of Legislation for the Protection of Coal Miners in Pennsylvania, 1824–1915.* New York: International Publishers, 1942.

Vaughan, W. E. *Sin, Sheep and Scotsmen. John George Adair and the Derryveagh Evictions, 1861.* Belfast: Appletree Press, 1983.

Vaughan, W. E., and A. J. Fitzpatrick, eds. *Irish Historical Statistics: Population, 1821–1971.* Dublin: Royal Irish Academy, 1978.

Wall, Maureen. "The Whiteboys." In T. Desmond Williams, ed., *Secret Societies in Ireland.* Dublin: Gill and Macmillan, 1973.

Wallace, Anthony F. C. *St. Clair: A Nineteenth-Century Coal Town's Experience With a Disaster-Prone Industry*. New York: Knopf, 1987.

Walsh, Brendan M. "A Perspective on Irish Population Patterns." *Éire-Ireland: A Journal of Irish Studies,* 4 (Autumn 1969): 3–21.

———. "Marriage Rates and Population Pressure: Ireland, 1871 and 1911." *The Economic History Review,* 23 (April 1970): 148–62.

Ward, Leo. "Political Tie Didn't Save Molly Necks," and "'Old Man in Harrisburg' Turned Back on Kehoe." In *Pottsville Republican,* February 5–6 and 19, 1994.

Ware, Norman. *The Labor Movement in the United States, 1860–1895; A Study in Democracy*. New York and London: D. Appleton, 1929.

Way, Peter. *Common Labour: Workers and the Digging of North American Canals, 1780–1860*. New York: Cambridge University Press, 1993.

———. "Evil Humors and Ardent Spirits: The Rough Culture of Canal Construction Laborers." *Journal of American History,* 79 (March 1993): 1,397–1,428.

———. "Shovel and Shamrock: Irish Workers and Labor Violence in the Digging of the Chesapeake and Ohio Canal." *Labor History,* 30 (Fall 1989): 489–517.

Weber, Max. *The Protestant Ethic and the Spirit of Capitalism*. 1904–05; New York: Scribner's, 1958.

Wheeler, Richard. *On Fields of Fury. From the Wilderness to the Crater: An Eyewitness History.* New York: Harper Collins, 1991.

Whelan, Kevin. "Pre- and Post-famine Landscape Change." In Cathal Póirtéir, ed., *The Great Irish Famine*. Cork: Mercier Press, 1995.

Wilentz, Sean. *Chants Democratic: New York City and the Rise of the American Working Class, 1788–1850*. New York: Oxford University Press, 1984.

———. "Against Exceptionalism: Class Consciousness and the American Labor Movement, 1790–1920." *International Labor and Working Class History,* 26 (Fall 1984): 1–24.

———. "Artisan Republican Festivals and the Rise of Class Conflict in New York City, 1788–1837." In Michael H. Frisch and Daniel J. Walkowitz, eds., *Working-Class America: Essays on Labor, Community, and American Society.* Urbana: University of Illinois Press, 1983.

Williams, David. *The Rebecca Riots: A Study in Agrarian Discontent*. Cardiff: University of Wales Press, 1955.

Williams, Raymond. *Culture and Society, 1780–1950*. 1958; New York: Columbia University Press, 1983.

———. *The Country and the City.* New York: Oxford University Press, 1973.

Williams, T. Desmond, ed. *Secret Societies in Ireland*. Dublin: Gill and Macmillan, 1973.

Woodham-Smith, Cecil. *The Great Hunger*. London: Hamish Hamilton, 1962.

Yans-McLaughlin, Virginia. *Immigration Reconsidered: History, Sociology and Politics*. New York: Oxford University Press, 1990.

Yearley, Clifton K., Jr. *Enterprise and Anthracite: Economics and Democracy in Schuylkill County, 1820–1875*. Baltimore: Johns Hopkins University Press, 1961.

Index

Note: Entries for most newspapers refer only to explicit references to the Molly Maguires